God Bless !

Lamentations 3:22-23

Veda Boyd
Jn

ONE CAME TO STAY

"If I have learned anything
from reading about writing,
it is this:
There is a better chance
of becoming the victim of a terrorist's bomb
than author of tomorrow's novel."

- Veda M. Boyd, Author

---

by Veda M. Boyd

ONE CAME TO STAY

Copyright © 2001

Library of Congress Control Number: 2001-130257

International Standard Book Number: 1-930353-28-6

Published 2001 by
Masthof Press
219 Mill Road
Morgantown, PA 19543-9701

Dedicated
to my children
Kim
Henry Lee
Cory
Andrew
And my grandchildren
Grace Ellen
Luke

. . . it would be a profound mistake to confuse the organized disasters of even the greatest writer of tragedy with the complex circumstances and factors which attend the sufferings of real life.

One tiny slice of real life, observed at first hand, provides better grounds for our conclusions than the whole fairy world of fiction.

The Manipulation of Providence
Your God Is Too Small by J.P. Phillips

One Came To Stay

Dedicated To Veda

Within
The deepest
Parts
Of our
Secret selves
Is love. . . .

Every moment
A continual momentum
Of
Light filled emotions
Flowing
From each-to-each. . . .

A youthful spring
Openly expressed
Creates us all
Into a
Divine mosaic
Called the
Great human heart. . . .

Each beat pounds
A knock
On our soul's door
Every act

Or action
In our lives
Is a wisdom
To be learned
And usher'd
Through our days
Not to be
Withheld
But shared
As a blessed
Insight
Gifted from
Above. . . .

Peace be within
You
Peace surround you,
Allow the
Vital
Spirit of God
To pulse
Into the essence
Of your
Human core. . . .
Forever you shall never be alone.

- D. Long

Prologue

From the beginning (and beginnings are strange because you don't always know exactly where they start) Jean Marlow, a well-known hat designer; Mrs. Edward Blair of Blairsouth Estate; David DuLaney, the Blairs' charming French chauffeur; and Mimmie, the Blairs' maidservant, each played a very important part in my life.

My name is Leta. While I hadn't yet been born when these significant others began to shape my future, nevertheless, through endless stories relayed by family members, diaries, anonymous revealers, and from the very lips of Mimmie, the Blairs' maidservant herself; a picture began to take form . . . just as I did, some years later.

In 1998, I stood in awe as I viewed masterpieces from the Van Gogh Museum in Amsterdam, on exhibit at the National Gallery of Art in Washington, D.C., a long time after 1935 . . . the year my life began.

As I meandered through each room of the exhibit, every painting revealed a little more of the famous artist's life. There was one painting in particular called to our attention by the curator of the Museum . . . it was a group of older women, no doubt during the 1800s, sitting around an old kitchen table peeling potatoes. The curator said, "If you stand and look at the painting long enough, you will smell the potatoes cooking on the stove." I thought to myself, *Sure I will.*

Following my skepticism, however, the aroma of boiling potatoes slowly began to fill my nostrils. I was astonished at how a picture could come to life like that!

But I had another thought: What if I used the pages of a book as my canvas, a pen as my paintbrush, and words as the colors to tell the story of my life . . . would readers be able to taste the salt of my tears, feel the pain of my wretchedness, or derive joy from the "sun" in my life, just as I had smelled the boiling potatoes on the stove in the Van Gogh painting that day?

The exhibit is open. Enter here.

. . . ONE . . .

Rainbow-glazed puddles lined the cobblestone courtyard of Blairsouth Estate. There was a fine mist, encore of a former rain, falling on the tender grass and flowers that surrounded the magnificent property that sat on a hill overlooking Lancaster County, Pennsylvania.

Jean Marlow, a passenger in the limousine driven by David DuLaney, had traveled to Blairsouth Estate on many occasions, behind glass, separating chauffeur and milliner.

More than glass separated the classes of people in January 1935. Strict etiquette, character, race, nationality, and societal recognition were worn as badges of entry into the best that life had to offer.

Mimmie, the Blairs' maidservant, was aware that day of the approaching limousine and its occupants. Mrs. Blair was attending to last minute details for their annual dinner gala, hoping they would produce unending accolades long after the last dinner guests had left the Blairsouth mansion.

The perfect attire was an integral part of the Blairs' successful dinner parties, and that is where Miss Marlow's expertise had come in. Presenting credentials in millinery and fabric design, Miss Marlow was generally the first person summoned to the Blair mansion during such gala festivities, events reported in the following day's newspaper headlines and social columns.

David DuLaney held the large umbrella high in order not to disturb the beautiful before-six hat that Miss Marlow chose to wear to her appointment with Mrs. Blair, one of her preferred millinery clients.

He had observed Jean Marlow's lovely face, auburn hair, and penetrating eyes through the rearview mirror of the limousine many times, while escorting her to the Blair mansion. Occasionally, he would make small talk with her, and once he spoke to her about his life and how he had come to be behind the wheel of the limousine that now carried her.

He had come to the United States from France, he had told her, in order to find better employment, and met the Blair family when he responded to a newspaper advertisement for a limousine driver. He had a passion for fast cars, but hadn't had the money to fuel the passion. Chauffeuring had helped pay his bills and provided a roof over his head to keep him dry, unless, he teased, he was escorting Jean Marlow to the door of the magnificent Blairsouth mansion on a rainy day. She had listened intently as he shared bits and pieces of his journey. She in turn had chosen not to talk about her past. She knew very little about her ancestry, and her background was as much a mystery to her as was her growing interest in his words and responses.

She took David's arm as she stepped out of the limousine, and together they walked to the front door of the Blair mansion. For the first time, something inside her stirred, as if awakened by an alarm, indicating she had overslept.

Mimmie met them at the door and hurried Miss Marlow inside, dismissing David as if he were a fly on her nose. Jean's attention, however, was still on the cobblestone steps, with David's hand protectively around her arm. *What is wrong with me?* she asked herself. *I'm acting like a schoolgirl.* Mentally shaking herself, she extended her hand, and Mrs. Blair took it, warmly.

Since becoming Mr. Blair's wife, Mrs. Blair had become well known for her exquisite apparel, and Jean Marlow had received all the credit. Mimmie stood there thinking how fortunate she was to be employed by the Blairs, especially during one of their gala events. Today, Miss Marlow would critique Mrs. Blair's choice of dinner gown and then proceed to design an evening hat that would complement the color and fabric of the gown. Jean's millinery creations repeatedly assured Mrs. Blair that, when the guests arrived, she would be guaranteed a room full of admiring glances.

Meeting deadlines and complying with the demands of the privileged classes were not considered at all troublesome to Jean; to the contrary, it aroused in Jean a desire for her own degree of social status, apart from being just a milliner. But with several failed relationships and a child to support, it was highly unlikely that she would ever be afforded that kind of luxury. She was a single mother, and she worked hard to just pay the bills and provide a good home for her daughter and herself.

She tried to concentrate on the reason she had come to Blairsouth Estate, and this meant getting on with the business of completing her appointment with Mrs. Blair. Before she left, she promised to return later that day for the final fitting. Mrs. Blair would be the best-dressed woman among all the guests that evening.

Jean took the arm of David DuLaney. Only this time, she caught herself leaning just a little too hard on him as they made their way to the limousine.

Mimmie watched them leave. She had been trained to withhold her personal commentaries, and in the presence of Mr. and Mrs. Blair, she had always done so. Nevertheless, she had quite frequently fantasized about David and Jean.

On the ride from Blairsouth to her flat in the nearby city of Yorktown, Jean was unable to focus on anything except the soft radio music and David's reticence. Neither spoke for the entire length of the drive. But she studied him. He had removed his chauffeur's hat, revealing a thick head of dark hair that matched his well-groomed mustache. How handsome he was, she thought. The distinctive bone structure of his face was so typically French, so touchable.

It seemed like a long time before the car finally came to a stop. The next thing she knew, the door opened and his hand was waiting. She put her hand in his. His hands were ungloved and warm. She wanted to hold on to his hand forever. She thanked him, and agreed to be picked up at six o'clock that evening for the final fitting of Mrs. Blair's after-six hat.

The climb to her second-floor flat seemed longer than usual. Jean was glad Bassie, her daughter, was not at home. Bassie was fifteen years old and already quite independent for her age. She was also the daughter of John McFarland.

John McFarland had been Jean's lover for many years, until she became pregnant. She had loved John very much. She never imagined he would abandon her after Bassie was born. There were still things between them that she held dear; one was his name, which she gave to their daughter . . . another was Bassie herself. It had been impossible not to think of John every time she looked at Bassie. But that was a long time ago. Looking at Bassie now, she saw a beautiful young lady, and not the remains of a broken heart.

She changed her clothes and then made her way to the sewing room. Now and then, she allowed her mind to drift back to David. Selecting rare feathers and the finest black velvet, she went to work on Mrs. Blair's hat, stopping only once for a cup of hot tea.

Bassie returned home, somewhere between cutting and sewing, and announced that she planned on going to the home of a friend that evening for a sleep-over, if her mother had no objection. Jean knew Bassie's friend's family well; they had been good for Bassie. Their home was like her second home, so she had not objected.

Feeling the velvet as it passed through her fingers, Jean found herself re-visiting the gentleness of David's hand, and his dark eyes, the eyes that, for some reason, always seemed fixed on hers. She shivered. She would never allow herself to be caught in love like some unsuspecting fish again, only to be abandoned later in a deep sea of loneliness. She had Bassie to remind her of that.

It was five o'clock in the evening. One hour separated chauffeur and milliner. Taking an apple from a fruit bowl, Jean made her way into the bedroom. She had grown weary from the diminutive stitches and invading thoughts. She sat down on the duvet, fell backwards, and closed her eyes. Some time later, startled by the sound of a passing vehicle, she realized she had fallen asleep with the half-eaten apple beside her. Reaching for her watch which was engraved with the words, "Forever yours, John," that she still wore around her neck, a gift from Bassie's father, she realized that in thirty minutes she would hear the door chimes, and David would be there to escort her back to Blairsouth Estate.

With little time to refresh or redress, she quickly ran a brush through her medium-length auburn hair, now flattened from her unintended afternoon nap. Her simple black skirt and white blouse would have to suffice, although she would feel naked without a hat on her head. A final glance in the mirror assured her that she was still young, attractive . . . and vulnerable. She only wished she had known better how to guard her heart.

Moments before David arrived, she reflected on how she and Bassie had survived over the years. Bassie had meant the world to her, but her little girl was growing up fast. It was hard for her to accept the fact that Bassie no longer needed her, but even harder for her to admit was that she herself needed more than Bassie. Perhaps she had counted too much on Bassie for affection over the years, but understandably so, considering her situation. Or, had she designed all this retrospection to justify some kind of a response to David, if need be.

She returned to the sewing room, placed the beautifully designed hat into a box, and waited for the door chimes to announce David's arrival.

The chimes were deafening, intruding into her private thoughts. Putting on her well-worn fur coat, a hand-me-down from Mrs. Blair, she picked up the hatbox and opened the door. The night air was cold and she pulled the fur collar closer to her face. David was standing by the door of the limousine awaiting her entry.

"Hello again," was all that she could think to say. For a moment, she thought he was about to say something. She hesitated; but when no words came, she got into the car.

It was approximately a forty-five-minute drive from Yorktown to Blairsouth Estate. She had forgotten the book she usually kept in her handbag and generally had read during her trips to Lancaster; so instead, she focused her attention elsewhere. She gazed directly into David's eyes looking at her in the rearview mirror. Fearing he might lose control of the car and run off the road, she quickly lowered her eyes.

The silence between them was harsh and unwelcome. David spoke first.

"Miss Marlow . . . any objection to me calling you Jean?"

"No, of course not," she replied.

A discernable tension existed between the two of them, and having become quite skeptical, and less trusting regarding men, she began to query herself about David's persistent attempts to engage her in conversation.

Arriving at Blairsouth Estate, David assured her that he would keep the coach warm while she completed her engagement with Mrs. Blair.

Mimmie met her at the door, dressed in a starched black and white dress in preparation for the evening's gala event. She also had a mischievous smile on her face.

Repeat visits to Blairsouth Estate had provided ample time for the two of them to become well acquainted. Mimmie's life seemed more parallel to hers than did the lives of most of her friends and acquaintances. Mimmie seemed to know everything that was going on. She suspected Mimmie even knew what she was thinking . . . at times.

As Jean juggled the hatbox in one hand and tried removing her coat with the other, she wondered what had been behind Mimmie's grin. But her mind was somewhere outside the Blair mansion that day . . . and those thoughts were put aside when Mrs. Blair arrived on the scene.

Mrs. Blair carefully removed the hat from the box. In a show of approval and appreciation, she rewarded Jean with a hug . . . and a sizable check. Mimmie, on the other hand, boasted of feeling like she was in a theatre with a front row seat. She shared in the pleasure Jean received when pleasing Mrs. Blair. She also suspected that Jean had taken a liking to the Blairs' chauffeur.

David was waiting to usher Jean into the back seat of the limousine.

Again, David took the initiative and spoke first as he pulled out of the now-dry courtyard of Blairsouth Estate.

"I take it Mrs. Blair was pleased?"

"Yes, very," she replied.

When he spoke again, it was in the form of an invitation.

"Jean, would you consider having dinner with me tonight?"

"Do you really think that's a good idea, David?" she asked, then quickly added a postscript: "It is just that you are an employee of the Blair family, and I am not sure that would be the proper thing to do."

David steered the large black car off the road and into a wide grassy knoll meant for summertime picnickers.

"I'm not going to crawl into the back seat, if that's what you're thinking, Jean, but I am finding it increasingly difficult to drive safely," he said.

He switched on the dim interior light, revealing their faces.

"I would very much like to be with you, Jean, without a glass partition between us. I'd like to get to know you better. Please say that you will accompany me to dinner this evening. I do have my own automobile, and it isn't long and black."

His eyes were imploring hers to say yes.

"I will come to your flat about nine o'clock tonight. I know this little place, French of course, unless you have something against the French?"

"No, but I have always believed that the French had something against us," she teased.

"Then we'll call a truce for tonight, yes?"

Feeling victorious, he drove the limousine back onto the road and turned off the interior light. Jean smiled to herself.

She couldn't describe precisely how she was feeling at that moment. She had always been adventurous and easily smitten . . . the reason for her single motherhood. She had managed to maintain her dignity in the community, due primarily to her association with the Blair family, her good looks, charm, and gift for millinery design, and she had every intention of keeping it that way.

Had Bassie planned on being home that evening, she would have had a very good excuse not to accept his invitation.

Her stomach churned as the limousine came to a stop at the steps of her flat.

"I'll walk you to the door, Jean, and I'll look forward to seeing you about nine o'clock then?"

He was different now, she thought. No longer the chauffeur. He was David, the handsome Frenchman who had shown a surprising interest in her. A gentleman with a few rough edges, she guessed, but that was the part she wanted to know.

Trying hard not to appear eager, she replied, "Thank you, David. I'll see you about nine. Just ring and I'll come down."

She entered her flat. She felt like a stringed marionette, her legs dangling loosely beneath her.

She was forty-some years old; and although she hadn't felt her age, the fact that David appeared to be considerably younger than herself was reason enough to make her question her own judgement regarding their prospective dinner date.

There seemed to be little purpose for changing clothing for her evening with David. However, she reconsidered and elected to replace her skirt with a pair of casual wool tweed pants, her "rebel outfit," as she referred to it. A dash of fragrance and a quick brush through her hair, and she considered herself ready to meet David.

She thought about Blairsouth Estate and wondered what Mimmie and Mrs. Blair would have thought had they known that, in just a few minutes, she would be in David's company, in his personal car, going to a French café. Mimmie would probably have cheered her on, she supposed, except for the wool tweed pants. Mrs. Blair, on the other hand, would probably have lectured her on the meaning of propriety. Jean had known

Mrs. Blair and Mimmie for many years, and she hadn't kept many secrets about her life from them. She cared very much about what they thought.

At nine-fifteen, she heard the chimes announcing David's arrival. Grabbing her coat, she descended the stairs.

He held out his arm and she slipped her arm in his. She got into the front seat of his car, a strange experience for her. It was a beautiful car, and just as he had said, it was neither long nor black. She immediately removed her coat from around her shoulders.

"Are you too warm?" he asked.

"Yes . . . and no," she replied.

He looked at her and smiled. She returned the smile. She felt as though the entire heat of summer had just settled on her. But it was nine o'clock on a winter's night, and there was no sun.

"You must know how very pleased I am that you accepted my invitation tonight, Jean."

"I'm still not certain that I did, really," she replied.

He laughed out loud.

Oh, he's pretty confident of himself, she thought.

She had been in David's company so many times before and they talked, not always comfortably; but he wasn't a total stranger either, she reminded herself. But this time was different. It was personal.

"Have you ever been to Jacques, east of town?" he inquired.

"As a matter of fact, David, I always chuckle when someone mentions that place. I can picture the women having their buttocks pinched every time they turn around, just like I've heard it's done in France."

"Then I take it you have never had your buttocks pinched?"

"No, indeed," she assured him. And just to make sure he knew she hadn't taken him seriously, she forced one of her chuckles.

He reached over and patted her hand. "The French are such romantics, I admit, and it does get them into a lot of trouble. But, I can assure you, you are in no immediate danger, my dear." She thanked him for his reassurance. But the word "immediate" sparked some minor trepidation; and she couldn't stop herself from thinking about the "thereafter."

To break the moment of awkward silence, she introduced the Blair family into their conversation, but he very quickly interrupted her. "The Blair family, and most certainly Mimmie, are out of bounds for tonight."

"I'm sorry, David, but you must know I'm feeling a bit awkward."

"Jean, you needn't feel anything, or, you can feel everything. Relax and enjoy yourself. You will love the café. A few glasses of wine and your needless trepidation will vanish."

It crossed her mind that he could have just as easily invited himself to her flat; at least he had been a gentleman and had invited her out for the evening. That would be a plus for him, she thought. Each time he spoke, she turned to look at him, repeatedly astonished at how handsome he was; the depth and color of his eyes were incredibly hypnotic; his profile unquestionably French; and he had just about the most perfect mouth you could possibly fix beneath a mustache! She was smitten.

They entered the parking area of Jacques Place. She glanced at him, and he smiled back at her, as if to reassure her that everything was going to be just fine. If the truth had been known, she really wanted him to take her in his arms and just hold her.

As she stood beside him, she was suddenly aware of his height; he was much taller than she had remembered. They hurried into the warmth of the café. Once inside, he took her coat, and then removed his own. Causal wool black slacks and a brown suede shirt as soft as fine velvet, she observed. She took his arm and walked to the table that had been reserved just for them. David being escorted to the table seemed out of character somehow; but both of them had stepped out of character that night.

The bottle of wine was already on the candle-lit table. He held the chair for her, and she sat down. As though reading from a cue card, he removed the bottle from the bucket of ice and poured two glasses of wine. *Oh*, she thought, *he's been here before*. She was getting the distinct impression that she hadn't been the only one who had sat in that chair, at the very same table, and looked into the same deep brown eyes.

As they raised their glasses, he said, "Here's to the end of the war between the French and the Americans."

That made her laugh.

"Tonight we will draft an accord that will unite us forever."

"And how is that, David?"

"The only glass between us from now on will be these," he said as he caressed his wine glass.

She laughed again. Their eyes met, and before she could look away, he spoke.

"Jean, you know I have been attracted to you from the first moment I took your hand and helped you into the limousine. French men usually don't procrastinate when it comes to women, but with you it's different."

The waiter handed them the menus. David suggested a French dish and ordered for both of them. A second bottle of wine was delivered to the table. Just as she had begun to relax, he reached across the table and took her hand as she placed her glass of wine on the table. He curled her hand inside his, then brought her hand to his face and kissed it.

"Your hands are beautiful, Jean. I envy every stitch you guide into place with those delicate fingers."

"David, you are making me blush."

After some time had passed, the waiter arrived with the food. She looked at her plate and then at David.

"And what do they call this in France?" she asked him.

"Meat and potatoes."

They were not just any potatoes, of course. They were French fried potatoes, along with the prettiest steak she had ever seen. By the look on David's face, he was enjoying Jean's reaction to what had been put in front of her.

"I wanted you to know that all Frenchmen are not alike. A real Frenchman eats French fried potatoes *and* quiche."

If he intended to humor her, he had. She was finally enjoying herself.

They ate, drank, and laughed.

Those were moments she would always remember, she thought to herself.

When they had finished eating, they spent a considerable amount of time over the last glass of wine. She was impressed with David's inherent politeness and sincerity. She would begin making a conscious effort to trust him.

Nearly everyone had left the café. David moved his chair closer to hers. As accordions played in the background, she felt like she was in France, in a real French café, in full view of the Eiffel Tower, with a light coating of snow covering the ground. She imagined men with their *beau monde* ladies strolling down a Parisian boulevard, leaving their footprints in the snow. Oh, how she had wanted to have a shop of her own in Paris one day. She was certain that Blairsouth Estate was as far as she would go on that flight of fancy.

She felt his warm hand somewhere between her throat and face. She leaned into his hand. He brought her mouth to meet his. Lightly touching her lips, he continued, until his lips were brushing her cheek, then touching her ear, and then moving ever so slowly down her throat. She took the hand that had guided her face to his and kissed his fingers. His mouth slowly urged her lips apart, and then he kissed her, passionately.

. . . TWO . . .

Leaving a trail of dust, another black car with the words "Lancaster County Children's Bureau" painted on its side approached the modest farmhouse belonging to the Carpenters. When the dust settled and the car came to a stop, Grace Carpenter let the screen door close quietly behind her and hurried to meet Mrs. Grant, the principal supervisor of the Children's Bureau.

Grace Carpenter had loved James Carpenter from the moment she laid eyes on him, which, strangely enough, was through a knothole in the covered bridge where he and his friends went to swim in the nude (referred to as skinny-dipping). That particular creek ran conveniently through Grace's parents' property.

Grace was as shy as she was slim. She wore a white mesh hair covering (which some affectionately referred to as a "soup strainer") along with a dress cape that matched the handmade conservative flowered dress customarily worn by women of the Mennonite religious sect that flourished in Lancaster County, Pennsylvania. It was a plain sect that followed strict rules and regulations in their dress and in their worship of God, in an attempt to appear set apart for God to keep them from looking like the rest of the world. More than disciplines derived from the Holy Scriptures, they closely followed the traditions of their earthly fathers, who, in turn, felt they were following the ways of God.

James Carpenter was short in stature, strong in temperament, and impervious in his opinions. He was a handsome man, quick-witted, and could easily captivate an audience with his jokes. And in the next minute, he could display a temper that would turn his face red and send you running. He and Grace attended the same Mennonite church.

Many months later, James asked Grace to marry him, forever blaming the hole in the wall of that covered bridge.

*   *   *   *   *

Not more than two dozen homes made up the rural community of Reading Junction, the place Grace and James Carpenter chose to set up housekeeping.

Rich farmland and robust crops rendered an abundant yearly harvest. During the summer, trees rich with apples, cherries, pears, and paw-paw fruits dominated the landscape. The garden produced an unending variety of fresh vegetables. Pulling carrots and turnips out of the ground, then quickly hand-pumping enough well water over them to remove some of the dirt before devouring them was a common practice on the farm. It helped prove the farmer's claim that one had to eat about a pound of dirt a year to remain healthy.

The Reading Railroad ran through the Junction, providing the owner of a local potato warehouse the means with which to ship his crop to distant customers. Mr. Peter Casset employed both young and old in his business. Available jobs consisted of grading and bagging potatoes, to the eventual hard work of loading the "over the road" eighteen-wheel trailers whose cabs were driven by well paid, strong, and generally handsome young men.

The Reading Railroad employed several men from the Junction. One of those men was James Carpenter. Along with light farm work, caring for the crops, feeding the pigs, and collecting honey from the hives that hung beneath the eaves of the barn, was his most important job, that of Railroad Maintenance Crew Supervisor. He was a very robust muscular man and usually had a heavy tan in the summer months as a result of working outdoors on the railroad. In the winter, he would be out all night during heavy snowstorms clearing his lane, then calling out the rest of his crew to clear the tracks for the train, providing safe passage through Reading Junction and beyond.

Grace and James lived long enough to see covered bridges become nearly extinct. They were also the first couple in Reading Junction to purchase a television set. They kept the sinful forbidden box hidden beneath a hand-quilted coverlet, hoping to disguise it as a piece of furniture being protected from dust, particularly before the Mennonite bishop and the elders came to pay their monthly visit. Grace also successfully disguised herself by using a colorful head scarf over her mesh covering to attend the Mt. Pines outdoor theatre, which was located about eight miles from where she and James lived.

Never forsaking the Mennonite Church, Grace wore her white head covering and black bonnet and faithfully attended church until she died. James Carpenter himself had been an elder in the Mennonite Church. But at one point, the stringent rules and regulations of the church and James Carpenter parted ways. He used that period of time to engage in activities contrary to his religious ancestry. The apparent introduction to alcohol and the game of golf, by a worldly brother working for the government, set him on a different course. He eventually abandoned his rebellious

behavior, but he never renounced his contentious disposition . . . that
continued until he died.

* * * * *

  Grace and James Carpenter loved children, but for some reason,
they had never been blessed with children of their own.

* * * * *

  With two other children trailing behind her, Grace welcomed the
newest member into the Carpenter family as she greeted Mrs. Grant from
the foster child placement service. Particular care was given in handing
over six-week-old Leta, whose small face was hidden deep within the
confines of a white cuddly blanket.
  Two rocking chairs sat alone on the darkest shade of green grass
beneath a large oak tree, the larger one for James Carpenter, and the smaller
one for his wife. The camera was readied as they took their places on the
chairs for a family portrait.
  Leta had been the youngest child they had ever received through
foster care. Careful instructions accompanied the small bundle that day,
just short of the traditional "can be hand washed in cold water and laid flat
to dry."

* * * * *

  The earliest memories I had were the sounds of clicking cameras
and assorted faces hovering over me.
  Mother and Daddy took good care of me when I was small. I
always had clean clothing and polished shoes, and a bow in my hair. There
was not much hair on top of my head until I was about three and a half,
and those were barely visible. My hair was as white as sugar and matched
the long white stockings that I loathed from the time I could call them by
name. I recognized other colors, but never on my legs. Checks, plaids, and
stripes, with a few polka dots thrown in, made up my wardrobe, and sometimes I wore them all at the same time. When the feed mill, which was
located not far from the Carpenter farm, got a new load of feed, we hurried to claim the flowered feed sacks, which my mother then quickly turned
into dresses. No one paid attention to my clothes, but the color of my hair
was another matter. I recall my mother saying, "We must always wash
your hair in rainwater and rinse it with lemon juice to keep it white." Long
after I could wash my own hair, I continued to use that magic concoction.

When the newness of my arrival had worn off and the fuss subsided, I took my place as just another Carpenter.

There were no plastic baby bottles back then, or at least my mother didn't have any, and so I would venture outside on the front porch with my glass milk bottle and satisfying rubber nipple every chance I got. On one such occasion, my mother and sisters came running when they heard breaking glass and a chorus of continuous screams. I had fallen off the porch! The bottle ended up broken on the cement walk, with me on top of it. A large piece of glass embedded itself in my right arm. I recall Mother picking me up and issuing orders to my sisters to go next door and call the doctor. We did not have a telephone. Next thing I knew, I had a rag tied around my small arm and was being carried across the lawn to another house where a car was waiting to rush me to the doctor's office. Many stitches later, I proudly displayed a "boo-boo" the length and width of a string bean. Nearly everything, except that scar, changed after that accident.

Mother was an excellent cook, and Daddy was a good provider. My size evidenced those qualities as I began to put on extra "baby fat," something I was told I would lose as I grew older.

*   *   *   *   *

When I was about five years old, another black car with writing on the side, resembling the one that had delivered me to the Carpenter home, drove in our lane leaving a similar trail of dust and another baby. That baby was larger than I was when I came to the Carpenters. Her name was Sally, and she looked to be about two years old. Sally immediately became my parents' favorite daughter. All eyes were on her, and I didn't like it one bit! While I had snow-white hair, Sally had beautiful brown curly locks and large captivating eyes, which she used to capture the hearts of everyone. She was cute, I had to admit, but I was no longer the favorite. It hurt me a lot, but I didn't let anyone know how I had felt about Sally.

I resented my older sisters as well. They established, by edict, every rule in the house, and Mother seemed helpless to intervene. My sister Hannah seemed to enjoy giving orders and would have made a great drill sergeant in the Army. I always thought Mother had been a little afraid of her and well she may have been, but Mother was so passive that she wouldn't have raised her voice, let alone her hand, to Hannah. Rose, on the other hand, was nice, but the warmest response from her came while she held me on her lap for photographs, repeatedly saying, "Smile, Leta, smile." Truthfully, she probably deserved a lot more credit than I gave her, because that smile managed to get me many substantial television commercial contracts some thirty years later.

Sally and her curls continued to attract attention, especially the photographer's, who accompanied the newspaperman to our house to interview Mother and Daddy. The photographer would just pat me on the head and call me "towhead." I really didn't understand what had been going on at five years of age; however, several days later I recall Mother and Daddy showing us our picture in the newspaper. I had wondered at the time why our pictures appeared on the front page of the newspaper. The picture included my mother, Rose, Sally, and me. I later learned that providing a home for up to fourteen unwanted children by that time had been something to write about.

*   *   *   *   *

Early on, a neighborhood girl named Dolly and I made a childhood covenant of friendship. Although we were both Caucasians, Dolly's skin color was very dark. When we stood side by side, she looked like night, and I looked like day. We loved each other, night and day. The two of us spent more time together than we spent with our own sisters. Time not spent with Dolly was usually spent with Sally, the one with the curly hair. It wasn't long before she became my favorite sister, in spite of how cute she was. I had decided that befriending her was far better than playing alone.

Mrs. Grant, the lady in the black car with the writing on its side, made regular trips to our house. She and my mother would sit and talk about all of us. I recall having heard them talking about expenses and how too much money was being spent on dental and medical bills. That was good news to me. It meant fewer trips to both. Sometimes Mrs. Grant brought total strangers along with her and they would look at us as though they were trying to decide which one of us to buy.

*   *   *   *   *

Several years later, the black car with those letters written on its side appeared in the lane once again. After parking the black car, the lady I easily recognized as Mrs. Grant came around to the passenger's side of the car and opened the door. A woman I did not recognize stepped out of the car and walked up to our front porch where Sally and I were playing. My mother, wiping her hands on her apron, politely greeted them. It was summer, and the flies also gathered for the occasion.

I noticed that my mother appeared to be a bit somber that day, but I didn't realize why until I heard her say, "Sally, your mother has come to take you home."

What? I asked myself. *What does she mean by "your mother has come to take you home"? Isn't this Sally's home? Isn't my mother and daddy her mother and daddy, too?* I looked at Sally and she began to cry. Soon I was crying, too. How could some woman whom we had never seen before come to our house and take Sally away? But it was apparent that Mother had been prepared for the stranger's visit. She instructed Rose and Hannah to "fetch" Sally's bag. I looked at the bag sitting beside the car, but I couldn't look at Sally.

"Will we be able to visit Sally, Mother?" I asked, hiding my face in her apron.

"Yes, of course. She won't be far away and we'll go to see her sometime."

Mother and Daddy never stopped talking about Sally's curls. I wondered how a mother could give her little girl away. Sally's new mother had handed her a beautiful doll, and I thought I saw Sally smile, but I cried.

When the car was out of sight, I ran to my friend Dolly for comfort. I suppose I feared she would be next to leave, and she was the only real friend I had left. How could I ever explain to her where Sally had gone? But I didn't have to. She put her arm around me and she gave me a hug, and that made everything all right. Dolly and I became inseparable.

We visited Sally twice.

Dolly's family soon became my family, too, in spite of the cruelty her youngest brother inflicted upon me when he persisted in calling me "Whitehead." Bonding between Dolly and me took place at an early age. I claimed her mother, father, three brothers, and two sisters for my very own, especially on grocery night. Grocery night meant fresh bologna sandwiches with mayonnaise, and ice cream for dessert. I rarely missed it.

Fifty-five years later, Dolly's youngest brother confessed that he thought I had been the prettiest girl in school. "Whitehead" had just been his way of saying he liked me.

Dolly and I were playing outside when the black car with the writing on its side darkened our lane once more.

Earlier that day my mother suggested that I try to stay clean because we were getting special company. Of course, that excited Dolly and me, but I still ended up with smudges on my face and a tear in my dress. When Mother heard the car coming down the lane, she quickly retrieved me from the dust, washed my face and hands, and we were off to meet Mrs. Grant.

Mrs. Grant introduced the visitors to my mother. Dolly ran home. The first things I noticed at five years old in a flowered feedbag dress were the nice clothes the visitors had on. The taller one had on a large hat to match her beautiful dress. It shaded almost half her face. I recall having to do deep knee bends just so I could get a peek at her face. The shorter visitor stood quietly by the taller one's side, and she kept looking at me. After Mother had served homemade root beer and cookies, the taller one dug into her satchel and produced several packages and handed them to me. I didn't recall it being my birthday or any other holiday for that matter, but, being a child, presents were considered good anytime, and so I joyfully removed the wrappings. A doll with a soft body and porcelain head emerged from the box; it also included a beautiful hat to put on the doll's blonde curls. I was thrilled. The other box revealed delicious-looking candy, which thrilled me even more. After several minutes and a thank you, I was off to find Dolly.

She and I sat beneath an old shade tree in our front lawn. She played with my doll, and I ate the candy. I still prefer candy to dolls.

At the sound of my mother's voice, I returned to the house.

"Who were those people?" I asked her.

"Oh, just some visitors," she said.

"Well, why did they bring me presents?"

"They like you, that's why."

I accepted that explanation, but the thing was, why hadn't they liked Rose and Hannah enough to bring them presents too? I wondered.

I would usually be expected to pose for pictures with the two visitors before they left, and often times, only the three of us would be in the picture; Mother had stood aside.

Every month for the next seven years, those same two visitors came with presents just for me.

The black car carrying Mrs. Grant came to our house just about as often as did the two visitors. Mrs. Grant would bring other strangers with her, and they would take another one of my sisters away. I had sisters coming and going. As soon as I would become attached to one, Mother and Daddy would let the strangers take another one away.

I began to hide the moment the infamous black car entered our lane. If for some reason they wanted a "whitehead," I didn't plan to be around!

It wasn't long before I began feeling much like a "leftover." Maybe I wasn't pretty enough or good enough to be picked. Some of my sisters were actually delighted with their new parents, and I suspect that is when my feeling of rejection began. Although I didn't really want to be taken away, I couldn't help feeling "left behind."

Because of the lovely clothing gifts that were given to me by the two visitors, Mother began dressing me in much finer outfits. My coats and hats matched and they were store bought, but I never did seem to outgrow the long white stockings that matched my hair.

There was little indecision when it came time to entertain myself. Anything that required strength, endurance, and getting dirty got my vote. Touch football was my favorite, and mostly because it meant playing with the boys.

It occurred to me one day that Mother never told me she loved me, nor had I ever recalled being a recipient of hugs and kisses. Good food and a roof over my head somehow hadn't made up for the missing affection, but touch football did.

There were a number of things I hated. I hated the outhouse. It was the one place I could find blindfolded! Especially revolting were the corncobs and Sears Catalogue pages provided for its occupants. I recall feeling embarrassed as I viewed the undergarment pages while passing time in that little house with a cutout half-moon on the side. I think the whole experience was meant as a teaching tool, since Mother would have been much too shy to share personal things such as undergarments with any of us girls.

Second to the outhouse was my hatred for the chamber-bucket. Many nights, in my sleep, I mistook the laundry basket for the chamber-bucket and received a soft reprimand from Mother in the morning. Thirdly, but not necessarily less annoying, were the once a week basin baths. There was no indoor plumbing. After closing the blinds, I would stand naked on a Saturday morning, and with a wash cloth and basin of hot water, I would soap and scrub myself. I was not familiar with rinsing. We just towel-dried ourselves and that was our bath for the week.

To make matters worse, the upstairs was unheated, except for a lone coal oil stove that served to lessen the chill. Its fumes permeated the room and my nostrils. I was never quite able to decide which was the most repugnant: the chicken houses on the farm, the outhouse, or the fumes from the coal oil stove. I deliberately did not include the pigpen, because quite frankly, not only did I have a fondness for the pigs, but I loved to "slop" the pigs (our word for feeding) and was even known to have tasted their feed mix on occasion. I suppose you could say there was some correlation between the pigs and the feedbag dresses I wore. Hurrah for the pigs!

My informative years included some horrific experiences.

When I was still small enough to fit into a large bail-handle bucket, my daddy would make me get into it in preparation for my descent into the abyss of the rainwater well. He would tie a heavy rope to the handle of the bucket and lower me slowly into the well to retrieve dead furry animals that had accidentally found their way into the deep well, and to their eventual death. A day's catch would consist mostly of dead rats and rabbits. Because I was considered braver than most, I would feign courage and do as I was told. But the moment I entered that dark, damp musty well, with walls that closed in after me, I began to shiver and shake. Sometimes I hadn't been able to hold back the tears as I was lowered into the smelly water.

Then there was the attack rooster named Petee. For some reason, Daddy would get a great deal of satisfaction by releasing the feathered beast upon request and send me off running, with Petee taking chase. I wasn't always successful at outrunning Petee and I would end up getting "flopped" by the sharp-like spurs on the end of his wings, leaving a pattern of bloody streaks down my legs, evidence that Petee had won and I had lost. I have never figured out how anyone could have gotten pleasure out of such a bloody display.

Like every child needs a pet, my daddy thought every child needed to see a steer get shot between the eyes. My turn eventually came. I had already learned to put the head of a chicken between two nails on a tree stump and chop off its head. I had learned to skin rabbits and pluck chickens. But the most horrendous memory was seeing that poor steer stand there helpless as the bullet entered the space between his eyes. I screamed and cried.

Not to excuse my actions, but some years later, I showed no remorse as I took the heads and tails of baby mice and literally pulled them apart in the corn bin on the second floor of our barn. But Daddy got his "come-uppins" when a rat the size of a cat ran up his pant leg and sent him screaming and jumping for his life!

*   *   *   *   *

There were good times, too, particularly the after-hunting banquets that were held around a large wooden farm table. As was the custom, the ladies served the men in the family first, and then the ladies took their turn at the table. But they served themselves. The children had their own table. The men were generally found in the living room resting and exchanging hunting stories. There was no political living room conversation as you might find today; as a matter of fact, most Mennonites at that time had never even voted for a political candidate in their life. The ladies talked mostly about food. Fried rabbit happened to be one of my favorites. After skinning the poor things, you would have thought I wouldn't have even been able to eat them! "One's heart and mind becomes hardened after a time," I once heard a Mennonite preacher say. That may have been the reason I could eat rabbit and enjoy it.

Speaking of Mennonite preachers, from day one, I faithfully attended the plain brick church where the middle aisle separated a sea of black bonnets and men in black suits. A tuning device substituted for the customary church piano and organ. I didn't much like it, but the crackers inside Mother's purse placated me for that agonizing hour and a half. I would look across the parted sea at my daddy singing, the part of church he enjoyed most. But the open Bible on my mother's lap left a much deeper impression in my memory.

I learned about Jesus during those early years, but something deep within my bones caused me to abandon the Mennonite way of life at an early age. I wanted nothing to do with wearing a covering and black bonnet, nor did I want a cape over my dress and sit separated from the men in my life. Instead, many years later, as a teenager, accepting the invitation from a neighbor girl to attend another denomination, I made a personal commitment to Jesus Christ and began attending her church. That decision is particularly relevant to my story.

*   *   *   *   *

In lieu of the many horseback rides on my daddy's back, there was the occasional ride on a real horse, borrowed from one of our neighbors. There was a feeling of dominance when riding high on that saddle, and perhaps in retrospect, the beginning of my hunger for recognition and significance.

I truly believe my dad had a heart for children and a talent for entertaining them. He expressed it in the many jokes he told and in his innate ability to juggle a half dozen oranges in the air at one time. I would watch in absolute amazement as they passed from hand to hand. He loved to sing, as I said, and he had hundreds of lyrics memorized. He taught us songs like "Freckles," "A Frog He Went a Wooing Go," and "Chicory Chic, Challock Chula," and some I can no longer recall. His legacy, however, and something that has been passed down from generation to generation, was his response when someone doubted his word. He would quickly respond to the doubter with a question:

Do you have the nerve to doubt my word, to insinuate that I prevaricate? If so, your phynoxious disposition is far beyond my recompensibility, why you're too copperas for my dominion of apprehension, why it's quite embarrassing!

He should have been in vaudeville, but instead, he performed for anyone who would listen to his endless jokes, watch his tricks, and believe his stories. We were a captive audience. He once claimed to know the answers to every question, and the ones he didn't know he said his brother knew, and between the two of them they claimed to know everything. We believed him.

*   *   *   *   *

I started kindergarten when I was five years old. Sadly though, our house was about two miles from the one-room schoolhouse I attended. Sad because it meant that when we had a huge snowstorm in the winter, my mother would invite the teacher to stay overnight at our house instead of returning to her own home some ten miles away. The only happy part was dinner, which Mother took great pains to prepare while Mrs. Lochner was staying with us. I guess Mother thought it would help win brownie points for me, which I needed badly. I attended that one-room, same-teacher school for eight years. The two-seater outhouse stood obtrusively on the playground. Its walls were filled with naughty words and phone numbers . . . and that was the girls' outhouse.

Airy Dale School, as it was known, was where I learned to read, write, and hate arithmetic. I did very well in recess and excelled in boys! Given a choice, I would have picked a boyfriend over a girlfriend any day, or weekend, for that matter. Girls seemed so fickle. Boys, on the other hand, and something I learned quite early, could keep a secret, and if they liked you, they would defend you with their lives.

When teams were drawn for recess games, I was not usually picked. Dolly's brother would say, "No one wants a whitehead on their team." But it was always the other boys who came to my rescue. It was not unusual for me to end up being the only girl on an all boys' team. Subsequently, I learned to guard my body and heart in those tender years.

While most girls my age majored in dolls, I majored in touch football, baseball, wrestling, and tree climbing. But beneath the dirt there was a touch of sugar and spice.

The excessive wear on my shoes from walking to and from school every day created more than a rattle for my mother and daddy. They said I would have to go barefoot more often, because Mrs. Grant threatened not to replace them as frequently because of how hard I was on my shoes. In time, I was able to run barefoot as fast on stones as I was able to run on grass. I was well on my way to becoming a tough little girl. Unfortunately, not tough enough.

After a day of torment by Dolly's brother in the schoolyard and a couple of tackles that left me black and blue, I walked home. When I was alone and out of sight of the other kids, tears rolled down my cheeks. Just as the crackers in Mother's handbag soothed me in church, the ice cream she had waiting for me at home eased the pain of rejection I was experiencing. Food became a marvelous healer.

Along with hating the color of my hair, I hated the color of my stockings. I couldn't have appeared more anemic if I had fallen into a bucket of white paint. I was beginning to think it was the color of my hair that kept the visitors from choosing me over my sisters, but it did save me from having to tell them that I was already spoken for. Some things really did work out for the best.

The "forebay" (the definition and spelling of which I have been unable to find in Webster's Dictionary) was located between the garage and barn. It was a cozy protected area I claimed as my "secret garden." It was there, in the privacy of that forebay, where I began to act out my interpretation of a happy family, a caring doctor, and a movie actress. I spent hours cooking imaginary meals, caring for imaginary patients, and performing imaginary three-act plays. Jimmy John, my neighbor, was my best imaginary patient. He was a willing participant in my make-believe world. It was there that I avenged others and gave myself rewards. It was referred to as "playing house." The forebay became my shelter and comforter in times of pain and disappointment; portend of things to come.

I watched sisters come and sisters go, in the black car with the letters printed on the side. For some reason, I remained behind. Surely it had to be because Mother had explained to Mrs. Grant that I belonged to them. That presumption, however, hadn't eased my feeling of rejection. I became increasingly insecure and, just for insurance, took cover in the forebay (that never-heard-of-before place) at the slightest hint of a black car in our lane. The exception was the visitors who brought gifts just for me. I began to look forward to their visits.

It was a household of changes. Nothing seemed quite as permanent as my white hair and stockings. The unrivaled change was yet to come.

*   *   *   *   *

I had just eaten my last piece of toasted bread dunked in home-made hot chocolate and, forgetting to brush my teeth, grabbed a sweater and headed up the road to Airy Dale School, a typical move for an almost-teenage youngster.

During afternoon recess, I overheard one of my girlfriends saying to another girl, "My mother said that Mr. and Mrs. Carpenter aren't Leta's real parents." I retreated from my intended path and walked around the side of the outhouse and listened as the conversation continued. "Mom and Dad were talking the other night and they said Leta doesn't even know it, but her mom gave her away."

The playground blurred as I looked back through my tears to see if anyone had followed me as I raced toward home. Halfway there, feeling exhausted, confused, angry, and betrayed, I sat down by the side of the road and sobbed uncontrollably. I don't know exactly how long I sat there, but long enough to conjure up enough anger to confront my mother.

*   *   *   *   *

She was sitting at the table over a mound of shell peas. She looked surprised as she glanced at the clock. I didn't give her a chance. My right foot landed right below her knee. At the same time, I heard myself saying, "I hate you!" She looked shocked, absolutely bewildered, and immensely wounded.

"For goodness sake, Leta, what in the world is going on here? Why are you home from school, and why did you kick me?"

I saw pain in her eyes.

I prepared to inflict another blow to her lower body when she grabbed my foot and I fell backwards onto the floor.

"Leta, you will not kick your mother one more time, do you hear me?"

"You aren't my mother and Daddy isn't my daddy either!" I cried.

"Where in the world did you get that idea?" she asked.

My face burned from salty tears as I squeaked out the words. "I heard the girls talking about it at school. They said their parents told them I wasn't your daughter. I hate you!"

By that time I was so emotionally exhausted that my small body fell into a heap on the cool linoleum floor. I felt her arm around me for the first time since I had been a baby.

"Here," she said, as she handed me a glass of water.

I couldn't bring myself to look at her.

"It is true, Leta," she began to explain, "we aren't your real parents. I suppose it's time you knew the truth. We are your foster parents, Leta. You came to us when you were six weeks old, and we have cared for you like you were our own little girl. It is cruel that you had to find out the way you did, but I want to try and explain it to you."

I had no noteworthy thoughts at that moment.

"You know, sometimes things don't work out for people," she tried explaining, "and they must make some very difficult choices. You are too young, of course, to understand that, and I can't say I really understand it myself, but your mother could not take care of you. She gave you to us so that you would have someone to care for you. Haven't we taken care of you, your daddy and I?"

I had no reply.

"We have done the best we could to make a good home for you and for the rest of the girls."

I interrupted. "So why do the other girls get to live with their parents, and not me?"

"It is not always a parent that comes for the girls, Leta; sometimes they are just relatives who want to care for them. Most of them do not have parents at all. Some of their parents have died and gone to Heaven," she explained.

That wasn't the first time I wondered how a mother and daddy could give their baby away to someone else. It was the question I asked myself every time strangers snatched away one of my sisters, especially when they had taken Sally from us.

As Mother continued her attempt to make me understand, I was already formulating a plan in my mind, but I knew I wouldn't be able to carry it out just then. The big question was still begging to be asked. It was on the tip of my tongue, and too late to swallow.

"So who are my real parents?"

She sat quietly for a moment and was visibly bracing herself for my reaction. "You know the visitors who have been bringing you gifts?"

"You mean the woman in the hat and the girl who always comes with her?"

"Yes, Leta, the woman in the hat is your mother, and the young woman who comes with her is your half-sister."

My mind was turning large somersaults. *I had a mother and daddy. Now I don't have a mother and daddy. I do have a mother. I had sisters, then I had no sisters. Now I have a half-sister, and not even a whole sister.* There didn't seem to be an end to the maze of deception.

Even at my young age, I could see Mother struggling to explain. She lowered her eyes and laid her folded hands in her lap, then sat watching them as she spoke. She never embellished anything; her explanations were simple and plain, just like her.

"Your . . . last . . . name isn't Carpenter."

Suddenly the thought came to me that I had always written my name, Leta Marlow. I had never been taught to use the name Carpenter. But I had never questioned why.

"Your name is Leta . . . Marguerite . . . Marlow. Isn't that a pretty name?"

"I hate that name and I hate you and Daddy, too!" With that, I picked myself off the floor and ran upstairs into my bedroom. *How am I ever going to tell Dolly and her family that I am not who they think I am; I'm not even who I thought I was.*

Mother didn't follow me. She either knew I needed to be alone, or she was afraid of being kicked again.

It wasn't unusual for a young girl to want to be with the people who were her rightful parents, but it hadn't yet occurred to me that I hadn't heard the name of my father mentioned.

I began making plans to run away from Reading Junction and the Carpenters' home. I would find out where my mother lived and I would go and live with her. She hadn't been all that bad, really. She and my half-sister always brought me nice things, and they always wanted their picture taken with me. Yes, that's what I would do.

It was settled.

. . . THREE . . .

It was a quiet birthday for me that year. We really never had extravagant parties. Chocolate cupcakes and ice cream for birthdays, and oranges and nuts for Christmas . . . and if we were really good, maybe a new pair of pajamas to go with the fruit and nuts.

Having learned something of the truth concerning my identity, another year older also meant growing closer to my plans to run away. I thought I was being careful in concealing my plans. Only a thirteen-year-old would think she was getting away with something.

My foster parents had already predicted my running away. But after a considerable amount of time had passed, they thought they had been wrong in their suspicions.

Carefully folding some clothing, which I packed into a tattered drawstring feedbag, I looked at my small "forty-five" record player and some of my favorite records and decided that I could not live without them, so I stuffed those items into the bag with my clothes. I could barely throw the bag over my shoulder, but I didn't want to surrender anything of importance.

The following day, as Mother was picking vegetables in the garden, I walked away from home. I chose the daylight hours because I was somewhat fearful of the dark. Although, by that time I had spent many dark nights alone in the farmhouse while my mother and dad visited relatives. Some of those times I had my foster sisters as company, while they still lived there, of course, but there were many nights I did not.

The direction I chose to go was a familiar road leading away from Airy Dale School heading south. I walked past the Casset Potato Warehouse. They had already begun to grade potatoes for the day, and large trucks were backed up to the platform waiting to be loaded. I hoped no one had taken notice of me. I rounded the bend at the end of the road, and after some time, lost sight of the Carpenter farm.

I walked for what seemed like a long time. At dusk, I entered unfamiliar territory. I did not know where I was, and I didn't care. I began feeling a strange sensation in my chest; it burned and moved into my throat. Fighting back tears, I kept on walking. Each step grew more difficult to take. My feet hurt and it was getting dark. I was thirsty and frightened. I sat down on the bank beside the road.

By that time my foster parents had already been in touch with the police regarding my disappearance and had discussed and settled on at least one possible solution to their dilemma, with regards to my behavior.

Headlights appeared on the deserted road where I stopped for a rest. As they came closer I could see it was a patrol car. I pressed my body against the bank, hoping I wouldn't be seen. Was there a chance it might pass by and the person inside wouldn't see me? Soon the car came to a stop. A tall uniformed State Policeman walked over to me and asked me where I was going. Having been taught that you do not lie to a policeman, I admitted to him that I was running away.

"Who are you running away from?" he asked.

"The people I thought were my parents," I answered. "They lied to me and pretended they were my real parents, and I hate them and I never want to go back!"

"Where are you going, if you are running away?" he asked.

"To find my real mother."

"Do you know where she lives?"

"No, but I will find her somehow."

"Well, I will make a deal with you. If you come with me, I will help you find your mother. What do you think about that idea?"

I thought that was a good idea, but he had to be more convincing before I would get into the patrol car. Then he added an unwelcome postscript.

"First," he said, "we will have to go back to your parents' house and find out where your real mother lives."

"O.K, if I don't have to stay there," I pleaded.

The handsome uniformed policeman provided a certain degree of protection. I felt secure as I sat on the seat beside him. He said he really *was* going to help me find my mother. I believed him. I listened as he talked to someone on the police radio about locating the MP (missing person). He was telling them to contact the Carpenters and tell them that we were on our way.

Returning to the Carpenter farm was something that I had not counted on.

The policeman, who told me his name was Philip, steered the marked car into our lane. My mother and daddy were nowhere in sight. After much coaxing, I walked with my police escort into the farmhouse.

Mother and Daddy were sitting at the kitchen table. The policeman pulled a chair out for me to sit on, and then he sat down beside me. He explained to me that arrangements had been made for me to go and live with my real mother, and he was going to be the one to accompany me to Yorktown.

There was no sendoff kiss from my dad or mother.

A suitcase, a half-step up from my tattered feedbag, was waiting for me at the door. I said good-bye and was once again in the front seat of the patrol car. I knew then that Grace and James Carpenter had been much wiser than I thought. They had known exactly what I was going to do and exactly what they were going to do about it.

My own grief kept me from recognizing the hurt in their eyes. I hadn't realized that they really did think of me as their own daughter. But how was I to know they loved me when they never told me so? Now, I was really going home. Finally, I would have a real mother and dad, just like some of my foster sisters had. Not only hadn't I considered my mother and dad's feelings at the time, I had also left Dolly, my best friend, without so much as a word. That realization caught me by surprise. *Well, I can't think about that now,* I decided. I was on my way home.

* * * * *

It was a considerable drive to Yorktown. The policeman asked me several questions as we put the Carpenter farm behind us.

"What do you suppose you will do if you find out you don't like living with your mother?" he asked.

"I will like it," I quickly retorted. "It will be much better than the Carpenter farm."

"Well," he continued, "you know, you can always go home again if you find you are not happy there."

I was thinking, *Why wouldn't I be happy? I'm going to be with my real mother.* I wondered why he kept reminding me that I could go back to the Carpenters.

We talked occasionally, the policeman and I, but I was preoccupied with thoughts of my real mother. I was apprehensive about my new home and totally ignorant of what I would find there, and I began to fidget in my seat. The policeman noticed my uneasiness and reached across the seat and patted my folded hands. That made me feel better. There was something in his touch that made me feel safe.

We stopped along the way to have a sandwich and a soda. Perhaps it was the uniform; perhaps it was the man, I don't know, but I sure liked being with him. His presence left an ineradicable mark on my life which became significantly clearer to me three years later.

It wasn't long before I saw a sign that read: Welcome to Yorktown. The town appeared very different from rural Reading Junction. There were so many buildings and people. I sensed it wouldn't be very long before we arrived at my mother's house.

You cannot imagine my disappointment when, instead, we pulled into a large parking lot in front of a tall building in the middle of town. On the marquee I read, YWCA. I had no idea what that meant, but it sure didn't look like a house. It wasn't long before the policeman spoke.

"We will be meeting your mother and half-sister in the lobby of this building."

"Why aren't we going to their house?" I asked.

Before he could answer, I had the door of the car open and he quickly came around the other side of the police car to meet me.

When we entered the lobby of the large building, I saw the visitors (as I had come to know them) sitting on a large sofa. Jean Marlow, who I now knew to be my mother, greeted the policeman first.

"Thank you for delivering Leta."

I felt like a sack of feed dropped off at the mill in Reading Junction.

Philip (he told me I could call him by his first name) turned to me and gently said, "I will be leaving you with your mother now, Leta; I hope you will be very happy with her."

For some reason I didn't want him to go, and I noticed reluctance on his part as well. However, he had done his job, and I would probably never see his face again, the person in whom I had found such comfort. I watched him until the door of the YWCA closed and his car was no longer in sight.

My mother turned to me and said, "Leta, this is Bassie, your sister, and my name is Jean."

I knew their names; but why hadn't she said, "I'm your mother," I wondered.

Bassie seemed much too old to be my sister and I knew I wasn't going to like her right away. She had been living with "our" mother, while I had been farmed out to the Carpenters. Furthermore, we certainly wouldn't be able to play together, she's too old, I thought. I already missed my friend Dolly.

Another woman entered the lobby, apologizing to my mother for being late.

"That's fine," my mother said. "We are ready to go up and show Leta her room."

What did she mean, my room? I asked myself. I wasn't going to stay there; I was going home to their house. But instead, we took three flights of steps to where "my room" was located.

"Leta, this is Mrs. Shapp, and she will be taking care of you while you are here," she explained. "I work all day and am very busy, and Bassie has a job as well. She works for the Yorktown Theatre, and I design hats. I do not want you to be alone in our small apartment, so we thought this would be the best place for you. You will be well taken care of. We'll come and get you for most of your evening meals. Mrs. Shapp will make sure you have everything you need. But first, we must get you settled in, then we will show you where your school is located. It's just down the street, not very far at all."

The same discomfort in my chest and the burning sensation in my throat that I experienced when I was alone and running away from the Carpenters returned. I opened my mouth to object, but closed it again. It was late at night, and my mother wanted to show me where I would be going to school. Why couldn't we just go home . . . school didn't start until September, and it was only early August. Nothing made sense to me.

In my room there was the usual bed, desk, chair, and a bathroom. A bathroom! I would get to take my first real bath in a bathtub! I stared at that tub for what seemed like fifteen minutes.

Bassie's words jolted me out of my trance. "Come on, Leta, Mother wants to go and show you your school."

I took Jean's hand (I hadn't yet called her Mother, at least not out loud). Just as she had said, the school I was scheduled to attend was a short distance from the YWCA. Except for the security lights outside the building, strategically placed over the entrance illuminating the words, YORKTOWN MIDDLE SCHOOL, I would not have recognized it as a school. It looked just like all the rest of the buildings to me. It definitely was not a one-room, one-teacher, same-seat country schoolhouse.

I admit I was fascinated with the town. It was very impressive to a thirteen-year-old. It was fun walking around the busy streets of an intriguing new place.

All of that ended abruptly when we returned to the YWCA.

Jean and Bassie left me in the care of Mrs. Shapp. No hugs or kisses, no words of reassurance, no display of affection whatsoever. Mrs. Shapp had an adjoining room to mine. She told me she had lived there for a long time. It was inexpensive and she was able to find odd jobs close by without having to drive; I suppose I was one of her "odd jobs."

It was Mrs. Shapp, not my mother, who shared the next day's plans with me. After a bath and breakfast in the morning, my mother and sister would pick me up in a taxicab and take me with them to a large house to visit some very good friends. That hadn't sounded like much fun to me. With Mrs. Shapp's door to her room slightly ajar, I crawled into bed and pretended to be asleep.

I couldn't wait for my first bath in the morning, in a real bathtub.

Quietly closing the bathroom door, not to disturb the still-sleeping Mrs. Shapp, I began the morning experimenting with the faucets. That resulted in a burnt hand from inadvertently placing it under an inappropriately marked cold water faucet! My reaction aroused Mrs. Shapp. Her less than gingerly entrance into the room made me feel guilty. She checked to see if I was O.K, murmured something under her breath, and went back to her room.

I had spent too much time in the bathtub (according to Mrs. Shapp) and she urged me to towel dry and dress for breakfast.

In her room she had a little stove and a table and chairs. She prepared a simple, but ample, breakfast. The summer sun was shining through a solitary window in Mrs. Shapp's small room. The sun felt warm. I again wondered why my mother had insisted on me seeing the school I was going to attend. She probably thought that seeing the school would discourage me and that I would ask to return to Reading Junction.

It was about ten-thirty that morning when Jean and Bassie walked into the lobby. It had been my turn to sit on the couch and wait. When they finally arrived, their greetings were disingenuous. *But at least we are getting out of this place!* I said to myself.

Forty-five minutes seemed like an eternity sitting in the taxicab between Jean and Bassie on our way to a place that they called Blairsouth Estate.

As the taxicab entered the courtyard in front of the very large mansion, my mouth fell open. *This is probably where Jean and Bassie live,* I thought. Jean talked to the taxicab driver, while Bassie and I started toward the large house. Before we could ring the doorbell, a woman in a black and white uniform greeted us.

"What a wonderful surprise!" she exclaimed as she gave Bassie a hug . . . but she was addressing her comment to me. I had never met this person, and yet she was glad to see me. She leaned over and gave me a big hug, and for some reason, I wanted to hug her back.

Jean had now joined us.

"Where is Mrs. Blair?" my mother asked the woman who answered the door.

"Oh, she'll be here in a minute," the woman in black and white replied. "Mr. Blair is not feeling well and he was calling for her."

"Leta, this is Mimmie. She's a very good friend of mine. We've known each other for a very long time."

We followed Mimmie into a large sitting room filled with big comfortable-looking chairs, and there were large beautiful paintings hanging on the walls. Large lamps, which I now know were priceless Tiffanies, stood on beautiful shiny wood-grained tables (everything was large). The large chair I sat on wrapped itself around me. I rubbed my hands over the velour that covered the arms of the chair. I had never felt anything like it before. This was where I wanted to stay, and I hoped it would be my new home.

"Well, well, let me take a look at you," exclaimed the lady who entered the room and who seemed to get everyone's attention. She looked directly at me and said, "If you aren't the pretty one, such beautiful white hair!"

If I could have hidden my hair at that moment, I would have. I didn't want to be known for my white hair . . . or my white stockings.

"Leta, this is Mrs. Blair," my mother said. "She is a very dear friend and a client of mine."

My mother motioned for me to acknowledge the introduction. But I wasn't adept at etiquette and formalities, so I just smiled and said hello. She did seem like a nice person, but I liked the woman who met us at the door better. Everyone seemed to be talking at once, except me. It was easy going unnoticed in such a grand room. My refuge was in the arms of the overstuffed chair.

Mimmie, the woman who had met us at the door, announced that lunch was being served on the veranda. I wondered what kind of table that was. Bassie took my hand, and together we walked into another beautiful room.

A large bouquet of fresh flowers filled a basket sitting on a fresh white linen tablecloth in the middle of the table. Sparkles of light from the afternoon sun bounced off the flower-design silverware. A tall glass of lemonade caught my eye. Everything was fresh: the flowers, the table-cloth, and the lemonade. It was like playing house beneath the forebay at my old house in Reading Junction. My eyes surveyed the grounds. It was beautiful. The food looked more like a picture in a book. I fell in love with the place, and I decided I was going to live there forever.

After our veranda lunch, we moved to the lawn where white high-back chairs, covered in large floral pillows, beckoned us to recline. Mimmie arrived with a small expensive-looking dish of after-lunch mints and passed them to each of us. I took a handful, my usual response to c-a-n-d-y! Mimmie slipped me a couple of extra candies.

The sun felt good under the cool examining eyes of our hostess. Mimmie, on the other hand, invited me to tour Blairsouth Estate with her. Leaving the rest of the party behind, Mimmie took my hand, and we began, as I called it, an adventure in wonderland. However, there was something miss-ing on the tour that day. Although I stood in awe at what I had seen, I felt betrayed. The prospect of hearing Mimmie say, "This is your room, Leta," never materialized. The tour ended and we rejoined the lawn party.

"Leta, you must come and visit us again sometime. It has been so nice meeting you. We have been waiting for this moment for a long time. I presume your mother told you that she designs hats for me and she comes here quite often. I know that she is delighted that you came to stay with Bassie and her." I wanted to correct her presumption and assure her that that was not the case, but I said nothing. I was sure Mrs. Blair didn't know that I was living at the YWCA.

I had come a long way to find my mother, only to be farmed out again. Without angering my mother, there was no way to communicate the truth to Mrs. Blair.

The remainder of the afternoon was spent in conversation that didn't seem to include me, although I did catch Mimmie and Mrs. Blair staring at me now and then, but that was not the same as being included.

After a long day of visiting, Mother was first to thank Mrs. Blair for her kind hospitality. Mrs. Blair handed me a beautifully wrapped package as we were leaving. It revealed two lace handkerchiefs. In the corner of each handkerchief were my initials, embroidered in gold. The lacey squares smelled of perfume.

The fairy tale afternoon ended with a taxicab ride back to the YWCA. I had fallen asleep for most of the return trip; it was a sleep from which I didn't want to awaken. My room was completely devoid of the glamour and opulent surroundings of Blairsouth mansion.

My mother gave me a half-hearted good-bye, but it was Bassie who walked me up the steps to Mrs. Shapp's room. I looked into the mirror when I entered my little room, and the reflection of one singular emotion glared back at me: disappointment. I thought about the baby mice that I had so cruelly pulled apart to their death in the corn bin on the second floor of the barn in Reading Junction, and I was sorry.

With that picture in my mind, I told Mrs. Shapp that I wanted to skip my evening meal and take a bath instead . . . which she allowed me to do.

Shortly thereafter, I developed an acute case of homesickness and cried myself to sleep.

*   *   *   *   *

Sometime during the middle of the night, Grace Carpenter shook her husband to arouse him from his sleep and said, "James, I really miss Leta. I wonder how she is doing."

"You will know soon enough."

She thought about what he said. Did he really think Leta would come home again, or was he simply implying that a report would be forthcoming. She wasn't sure.

She hadn't cried very often in her life. She was taught not to put her emotions out where everyone could see them. But since she was alone, in bed with her husband, she allowed herself to cry.

James Carpenter came from the same conservative upbringing, but he had no problem expressing himself, in less than congruous ways, most of the time. That night, he simply told his wife to go back to sleep and not to worry about Leta.

*   *   *   *   *

Jean Marlow did not go to bed. She sat alone on the small balcony of her flat above the street below. The events of the last few days had her mind reeling. She sat with her hands clenched, as if trying to keep a secret from getting away. *What am I to do?* she asked herself. If anyone, especially her friends, found out about Leta, she and her reputation would be doomed. She had to think of something. She began to cry. Her sobbing sounds aroused Bassie, who came to her mother's side.

"Don't worry; things will work out," she said, as she put her arm around her mother.

"I just don't know what to do. What if she [meaning me] decides to stay here?"

Trying her best to reassure her mother, Bassie replied, "Maybe we just need to wait and see what she does. I don't think she is happy here. I got the impression she was quite discouraged when she saw the school, just as you had predicted, and she can't possibly be happy living at the YWCA. Just give it some time, Mother."

"How could I have let this happen? Why did we ever go to visit her?" she said, blaming herself.

*   *   *   *   *

Meanwhile, exhausted from my bout of homesickness, I fell asleep, in my bed, in my little room, at the YWCA.

*   *   *   *   *

The smell of bacon was better than an alarm clock. Jolted out of bed by the sounds of pots and pans coming from the kitchen next door, I rubbed my swollen eyes, wet my parched lips with my tongue, and sat up in bed. I began to cry like a child lost in a department store after she's been found. I reached for my little purse on the only table in the room and rummaged through its contents. Clear lipstick; a picture of Dolly and me together; two bobby pins; a used Kleenex; several pennies; and finally, the treasure I was digging for—a small piece of paper with a largely written telephone number on it.

. . . FOUR . . .

A phone rang in Reading Junction.

James Carpenter was already on the scene of a derailed Reading freight train some distance from his home.

Grace Carpenter had just sat down to have her first cup of coffee for the day when she was interrupted by a knock on the door.

It was Anna, Grace's neighbor, and one of the few people in Reading Junction to own a telephone. She told Grace that there was someone on the telephone who wanted to talk to her, and she was fairly certain it was her daughter calling from Yorktown.

*   *   *   *   *

At the sound of my mother's voice, I began to sob.

My voice quivered as I asked, "May I come home?"

Mother's voice was full of compassion; but she wasn't a pushover! "Your daddy was called out on an emergency," she said coolly, yet without condemnation. "When he returns, we will come and get you."

After hanging up, I wondered if she and Daddy had known that I was living at the YWCA since I left their home. I expected they did. And I expected them to say, "I told you so." But that wasn't something my foster mother would say. She was too kind, and not the least bit vindictive. I was realizing about then just how good she had been to me. I wondered if she would be as glad to see me as I was going to be to see her.

Mrs. Shapp had taken pity on me by allowing me to call my foster mother, but it wasn't long before she thought it best that we inform my real mother about what had taken place.

She rang for the operator, and soon Jean's voice came on over the line. Mrs. Shapp motioned for me to take the receiver. I suppose she thought it only fair that I should be the one to tell my mother about the phone call, but I had about as hard a time doing that as I did liking my white hair.

"This is Leta," I said. "You don't have to come for me today."

I hesitated. When she didn't respond, I announced cautiously, "I—will—be—going home today."

I didn't detect any deep sigh of relief, but the news did not seem to surprise her either. I hadn't expected her to beg me to stay, but I did expect her to say she hated to see me go, even if only to make me feel good. I knew she was glad I was leaving, and she didn't lead me to believe otherwise.

"Well, we actually weren't planning to come for you today, Leta. Bassie and I had other plans, so this worked out just fine. You know how much we have enjoyed having you with us, but you probably would never have been happy here. You will have to come and visit us sometime, or we could still visit you at Reading Junction, if you'd like."

"You never wanted me here in the first place," I blurted out, "and you never even asked me to call you Mother, so visiting me in Reading Junction isn't going to change anything. You never wanted me, ever; that's why you gave me away and kept Bassie. I don't ever want to see you again. It's all my fault. I shouldn't have wanted to live with you in the first place."

At thirteen, I had already established a pattern of self-blame.

Mrs. Shapp was in my corner, with a clean handkerchief and a pair of comforting arms. Tough little girls cry . . . and I did.

The two of us took a walk outside. We stopped by a little bakery and bought two sticky buns. I drank a glass of milk, ate the two sticky buns, and probably would have eaten a third had Mrs. Shapp not intervened. She said she was afraid I would get a stomachache.

God told a grieving man in the Bible to get up and eat, after he had wallowed in his sorrows for a long period of time. But I'm sure God didn't intend food as the prescription of choice to make me feel better about myself . . . a lesson I learned some years later.

Time passed slowly as I sat in the lobby of the YWCA, waiting to be reunited with my foster parents.

When my mother walked through the door of that cold and impersonal building, I felt so ashamed. I blamed myself for the hurt I must surely have caused them. She took my hand, thanked Mrs. Shapp for taking care of me, and we turned to walk outside where my dad was waiting in the car.

My foster parents displayed no hard feelings, at least that I could detect. We spoke very little on the ride home. But somewhere between Yorktown and Reading Junction, Daddy suggested that we stop for an ice cream cone. It was the start of more ice cream, more candy, and more of everything that would turn me into a fat teenager.

We arrived in Reading Junction about dusk. I felt very lucky to be home again.

*   *   *   *   *

A mixture of pain and passion filled the next two years.

Because of my love for acting, which I had done regularly beneath the forebay, Daddy decided to build a real stage on our lawn, close to the barn. I suppose he hated to see me return to that world of make-believe.

The stage that Daddy built stood obtrusively on our lawn, and I spent most of my time playacting on it.

By age fourteen, I was writing short plays and eating longer meals. The plays consisted of more comedy than tragedy; the food—more ice cream than vegetables. I starred in every play and grew fatter and fatter.

Then we had an idea! We would make my acting, and Daddy's jokes and juggling, a profitable adventure.

First, we worked on developing our show. Daddy would tell a series of jokes and then juggle his oranges. Dolly and her two sisters, Peggy and Nancy (or Toot, as we affectionately called her), were eventually invited to join our vaudeville act. They had harmonizing voices and could even hold a tune. They became famous in Reading Junction for their rendition of the song, "The Three Little Sisters" (which they were). I performed mini-skits, convincingly playing all parts, and worthy, I thought, of the freewill offering we "charged" for each performance. Not to be outdone by Broadway, we even had a makeshift curtain that we pulled back and forth in front of the stage, concealing our presence, until the time of the performance.

We sold potato chips, pretzels, candy, and sodas. We attracted a crowd from Reading Junction, along with neighboring families and friends from nearby villages. The productions continued for several years, with enthusiasm, and without making any money.

Those were some of my happiest days on the farm.

*   *   *   *   *

When I was fifteen, a boy came to our house. He came the same way I did, in a black car, with Mrs. Grant . . . only he was much older . . . about sixteen at the time. His name was Ted. He was the first and last boy the Carpenters ever fostered. It was my first close encounter with a boy. And it took place on the floor of the kitchen.

Mother and Daddy had gone away, expecting to return home early that evening.

For the life of me, I can't remember how it all began, but the ending is as vivid as chartreuse.

Ted and I exchanged a few words; from there, it grew into a heated discussion. Challenging my response, he wrestled me to the floor. He was strong, and he held me down in a way that inhibited my breathing. In the same way I used words to inflict pain on my real mother the day I left

Yorktown, I used my hand to create a persuasive-looking fist, and let Ted have it, right between the eyes. The blood spurted out like a fountain, and he cried out in pain.

"Do you give up?" I yelled.

At the same time I was reloading my weapon for a second go at him, Mother and Daddy drove in the lane.

At first glance, the scene did not appear morally convincing; and as Mother shared with me years later, had that been the case, Daddy would have beaten us both and I would not have lived to tell this story. I must add that if Ted were telling this story today, instead of me, he would most assuredly claim victory in that battle.

*   *   *   *   *

Ted came and went, just like everyone else did at the farm.

*   *   *   *   *

Many years later, when Ted and I were both adults, I opened a local newspaper one day and read that a veteran by the name of Ted Watson would be leading a Veterans Day Parade and performing some sort of exhibition in the city of Lancaster. It was the same name as my foster brother with whom I had lived in Reading Junction. But, could it possibly be the same person? I wondered.

After a little research, I was able to acquire his phone number through the newspaper where I had read the announcement. Much to my surprise, it was indeed the same Ted Watson. I learned that Ted was a decorated Vietnam War hero; and as a result of that war, and his valiant stand against the enemy, he had lost both legs. Tough and determined, he had gone on to be one of those people who break cement blocks with their bare hands, an exhibit I wasn't sure I wanted to see.

It was a reunion of another kind for us; not particularly oozing with fond memories. As expected, we disagreed on the outcome of our kitchen floor battle; and yet, we were glad to have found each other, if just for a few brief moments. We had both come a long way from Reading Junction, and I doubt that our tussle on the floor had in any way prepared him for the real war.

*   *   *   *   *

Bill Casset, the potato warehouse owner's son, provided another close encounter during my freshman year in high school. He was a year or two older than I was. Aided by an old pair of binoculars that I kept hidden in my bedroom, I was able to see his house at the other end of a large field directly across from our house. His bedroom was in the front of the house, facing my bedroom. I would take my binoculars and follow him in the door of his house, then into his bedroom. I had a distinct advantage. The warehouse where he spent most of his time was only a garden's length away from our house. His comings and goings were easily observed. The warm feeling I got when I zoomed in on him lasted only a short time. His bedroom curtain was drawn shortly after he entered his room. It was impossible not to notice his masculine physique every time I watched him working at the warehouse. I liked Bill Casset very much.

Schoolgirl crushes can last for years . . . and mine did.

One Saturday morning I walked to the potato warehouse, hoping that I just might run into Bill. That day, I noticed that his car was parked near the rear loading dock. Not wanting to appear presumptuous, I walked around to the front of the building and tried opening the door. It was unlocked. I walked in and called out, "Yoo-hoo, anybody there?" No one answered. I ventured a little further and repeated the call. "Yoo-hoo, anybody there?" Then I heard his voice. I went limp.

"What are you doing here?" he said, as he climbed part way up the basement steps.

"Oh, I just thought I would come and say hello to your dad," I lied. But it wasn't too far from the truth. I often went to the warehouse to visit Mr. Casset. He was a kind man. He had said more than once that, in a year or two, I could go to work for him as his secretary. I thought he was joking, of course, but when I took a job several years later helping out in the office, I realized then that he had been serious.

"Well, don't make me come all the way up the steps, Leta. I'm doing some work down here, so come on down."

He had been stacking hundred-pound bags filled with potatoes. His shirt was off and the perspiration gathered on the small of his back. I crawled up on a pile of boxes that were stacked nearby, and I watched every move he made. We talked about school . . . mostly about sports. He was on the football team, and I soon learned, by reading between the lines, that he also had his eyes on one of the cheerleaders. My heart sank. After some time had passed, he asked me if I wanted to join him in something to drink. I said, "Sure." He disappeared for a few minutes and returned holding two drinks in his hand. As he handed me a bottle of soda pop, his hand brushed my hand, causing me to fidget on the stack of boxes that I had made my private bleacher, and it nearly caused me to lose my balance. But he caught me. We stood together for a few minutes, and then he stepped backwards. He looked directly into my eyes, as I stood motionless before him.

"Leta, I could really take advantage of you right now, but I know it wouldn't be right. You are very pretty, and I'm only human. I don't think it's a good idea for you to be here alone with me."

I hadn't thought of myself as pretty; I had been putting on quite a bit of weight lately. And we disagreed even more on the part about my being alone with him; I thought it was a very good idea.

He did not know how much I cared for him. I thought, in fact, that I loved him. But more than that, I wanted to be loved by him. It was a biting case of puppy love. But I took his advice and left the warehouse shortly thereafter, disappointed, but still hopeful.

*   *   *   *   *

There was a game we played in Reading Junction. It was called, "OFFS." The game consisted of two teams, and it was played at night. Members of one team would hide, individually, while the capturing team would try and find them. Both teams would split up in order to succeed in the more sophisticated version of Hide and Go Seek. The capturing team required a verbal signal as a clue to his opponent's hiding place. Carefully choosing your response, not to give away your location, you would then try and escape, without detection, until the signal was called for again, or you would be captured, whichever came first. We planned the timing of the game when we knew everyone would have a free night. The best times, of course, were full to three-quarter moonlit nights. There were no qualifying factors for entering the game of OFFS, but it did help if you were over fourteen and not afraid of the dark. The game even drew participants from Bucherville, some three miles from the Junction.

Getting down and dirty in the game of OFFS meant inadvertently climbing into a barrel of rotten potatoes at Cassets' Warehouse, or a pile of doggie-do on the train tracks beneath a stationary railroad car, while at the same time, gloating over your apparently undetectable hiding place.

OFFS had special meaning for me. There was always the possibility Bill Casset, who rarely missed a game, would capture me. Those were some of my most memorable times in Reading Junction . . . a far cry from the Dungeons, Dragons, and Drugs that came later.

I'd like to think it was the hand of God, although that claim might appear irreverent or even sacrilegious, but on a cool moonlit Friday night in September, at eight o'clock, a game of OFFS was scheduled to take place. That particular game involved friends, ages fifteen through eighteen. The game had become advanced, particularly in the length we would go to hide and seek; anyone younger stood in danger of getting hurt. So, along the way, the rules, relative to age, had changed.

The two teams met at Cassets' Potato Warehouse. They were divided equally to include the same number of guys and girls on each team. Bill Casset did not go unnoticed. Guided by the stars, I concluded, I was chosen for the opposite team. That meant that Bill would be one of the seekers. I was already writing the script for the end of the game: Bill would find me in a still lush green pasture, and with the moon bright above us, he would take me in his arms and promise to love me forever. My hallucinatory vignette ended when Betty, a girl in Bill's class in school, landed in a deep barrel of rotten potatoes. Unable to disengage herself from her odorous confines, the game was called off, and everyone rushed to help extricate her. Smelling like five-day-old roadkill in the middle of summer, and the dead rats I had fished from the deep, dark well, Betty made her way to my house, where she washed and changed into some of my clothes, and then we were OFFS again.

Because of Betty's misfortune, we were granted another turn to hide. This time, I chose a spot in the middle of a wheat field, about a quarter of a mile away from home base. My body left a distinguishing imprint in the tall brownish-yellow grass as I lay in quiet contemplation of the galaxy above. The silence was eerie as I waited for one of the capturing team to call for a signal. With my hands beneath my head and my eyes turned upward, I wished upon a star.

Twenty minutes into the game, still maintaining my cover, I heard Bill's voice in the distance; he was calling for a signal. Following the rules, I responded by impersonating a hoot owl. Unlike other times, I elected to hold up right where I was, waiting breathlessly for his approaching footsteps. It wasn't long before I could smell his presence. My heart was pounding so loud that I was sure it would give me away.

"Give me a signal," I heard his hand-cupped voice repeat.

By the sound of his voice, he couldn't have been more than twenty-five yards away from me. I tried croaking like a frog. Something happened, and I started to cough uncontrollably. His sneakers were the first things I saw. He stood towering over me and I had no choice but to surrender. He appeared out of breath from another chase.

"Boy," he said, "I have had some tough ones! I've had two captures; you're my third . . . and easiest."

He sat down beside me. Tearing off a handful of wheat, he offered me half, and we began chewing on the golden pieces of grass. He made some remark, and I laughed. I leaned over and touched his leg, in a display of approval and affection. He reached down and took my hand. We fell backwards on the bed of wheat, and it was there, still holding hands, that I remember falling in love for the first time.

Our second abbreviated encounter left me wallowing in self-pity and rejection. And his obvious infatuation with the cheerleader, whom I had seen him with several times, left me heartbroken.

The third encounter, which provided enough evidence to convince me not to give up on Bill, took place shortly before I left the Airy Dale one-room schoolhouse to attend Bucherville High School.

I was asked by my mother to deliver a package to Bill's mother. As I walked across the field to their house, it occurred to me that I had seen Bill's car leaving the warehouse sometime earlier. As soon as I reached the middle of the wheat field, I could see the top of his car. I knocked on the door.

Bill answered the door.

"Hi!" I said, sounding much too jovial. "Mother sent this package over for your mother."

"Thanks, are you coming in?"

I accepted the invitation. We went into the living room where he deposited the package on a table. He then said he wanted to show me something he had made and to follow him upstairs. Obediently, I followed.

By that time I realized we were alone. As we entered his bedroom, the first thing I noticed was the window that faced my bedroom across the field. *If only he knew how many times I invade his privacy,* I thought, *our friendly dialogue would vanish as quickly as our fleeting rendezvous.* He turned and faced me, then he walked toward me and took me in his arms. I did not resist. His lips teased, but never touched mine. We did not go where forbidden love goes. He honored his promise to never take advantage of me. My reputation remained untarnished. The hope I had of being with him forever died, but not before one final encounter.

*   *   *   *   *

The prospect of leaving the archaic environment of Airy Dale School and Reading Junction by matriculation into Bucherville High School stimulated my enthusiasm. It "temporarily" alleviated some of the painful insecurities and despondent residue from my visit to Yorktown, and the deception by my foster parents . . . and the kiss that never came.

Food had already become a soothing salve in my life. I stuffed into my mouth everything that was not glued down. If it hadn't been for my long, pale blonde hair and sense of humor, I may very well have gone completely unnoticed by the opposite sex. But I had learned very quickly how to use tools of persuasion, flirtation, and personality to captivate teachers, win friends, and influence enemies. Any diplomatic corps would have been remiss not to sign me up on Career Day. I thought I would have made an excellent FBI or CIA agent, and it was all I dreamed of doing some day. But the spell of rejection had been cast, and it would take more than illustrious ideas and dreams to exorcise it from my life.

My freshman year in high school was a culture shock. Spending eight years in a same-teacher, one-room schoolhouse hadn't adequately equipped me scholastically, or mentally, for the change. Fortunately, Dolly and her sisters were there for moral support, and together we waded through the marsh of advanced studies and social adaptation. Due to our different career goals, we were separated fairly soon. Just as quickly, I was able to make new friends.

At the end of the day, on the bumpy road home to Reading Junction, in the gold-colored school bus, we turned into "country bumpkins" once again.

During that time of transformation, I was invited by a friend to attend a revival service at a Protestant church in Bucherville. Refusing to become a member of the Mennonite sect, against the wishes of the Mennonite preacher at the church where I attended, I welcomed any change that didn't require me to wear a white mesh cap and sit on the opposite side of the church from the boys. It was there, in the Evangelical United Brethren Church, under the preaching of Reverend Tobias, that I underwent my second transformation.

After an extensive explanation from the Bible on how I could be assured of eternal life in Heaven with God, including repenting of my sins, I made a decision to trust Jesus as my Savior and ask Him to come into my heart and life and save me. After making that decision, and acknowledging it by walking to the front of the church, along with many others, I became a new person. I began attending an intensive Bible Study and couldn't get enough of God's Word. It was as though I had been spiritually dehydrated, and now I was being offered an abundance of fresh drinking water. No bolt of lightning or thundering herd of buffalo struck me . . . but it was every bit as powerful! I wanted everyone to feel as I did. It was a no-strings-attached faith, just plain simple truth. I didn't even have to do anything to earn it; it was a free gift. I just had to believe and accept it.

I began as a very bold Christian. I carried my Bible to school with me; and on weekends, I visited local bars and stood on street corners handing out pamphlets explaining how you can know for sure you are going to Heaven. Sometimes I got no further than the front steps of a barroom, but on many occasions, I sat on a barstool next to a drunken man and shared God's Word. My early teenage years were filled with joy and significance. God's Word assured me that "if my mother and father would forsake me, God would never leave or forsake me." That made all the difference in the world to me.

The tattered bag that had once held my meager belongings and forty-five-rpm record player also had enough blame, self-pity, and rejection in it for a trip around the world. When I could no longer carry that bag of sorrow, God took it from me and filled it to overflowing with joy.

Memories of days spent with Jean Marlow and Bassie in that small bedroom at the YWCA; the recollection of that damp, dark well; and the bullet hole between the steer's eyes slowly diminished. When I did recall them, it was not with the same repugnance. However, the consequences from those childhood experiences, just like the consequences of my years of disobedience, were burned in my memory and visited upon the second and third generations of my family, as the following chapters will reveal.

*   *   *   *   *

By my sophomore year in high school, I was BIG. I weighed 180 pounds; and I had never had a date. It was a most miserable time. The reality of my condition was exposed during tryouts for cheerleading, baton twirling, and center-half position for the girls' field hockey team. I could yell with the best of them and throw my baton as high as anyone else, but I had a big problem chasing a hockey puck. In my particular case, the coaches, instead of the players, huddled and decided I should become a pompom girl. That meant waving a stick with a school-colored fuzzy ball on the end of it in the Halloween Parade, and any other sundry reasons for a parade, with all the other fat girls.

The feeling of rejection returned. I knew I had the talent to do all the things the other girls did, but I did not have the figure. I soon began another journey on the road to self-pity. Temporarily appeased by my role as pompom girl, I got to ride on the band bus to "away" games and parades, and I shook my fuzzy ball like nobody's business. As I said, it was a most miserable time.

I no longer attracted anyone's attention . . . with the exception of Mr. Casey, a teacher who gathered swoons from every female student, including me. He was immensely handsome, and I was immediately drawn to him. We talked endlessly about what I planned to do when I graduated from school, moving quickly to subjects involving government intelligence and my interest in becoming an FBI or CIA agent. He encouraged me to enroll in a school in Washington, D.C. The thought intrigued me.

You can imagine my disappointment when a substitute teacher replaced Mr. Casey. I inquired into his whereabouts and was told that he had taken a job elsewhere. I was not satisfied with that explanation. After further inquiries, I discovered he himself had joined the Federal Bureau of Investigation. For a very long time I seriously considered following in his footsteps. I began to fantasize about joining him some day in the fight against crime, helping to capture saboteurs, spies, and the world's ten most wanted criminals. I took inventory of the possibilities. They were laden with discouragement and hopelessness. *Who would want a fat partner who couldn't run?* I asked myself.

The motivation to change the way I looked began with my dream to become an FBI agent.

. . . FIVE . . .

The basic seven-course Pennsylvania Dutch meal of meat, potatoes, corn, chow-chow, homemade bread, whole milk, and dessert was set before me, but I had set my sights on a different "course."

In spite of the assorted aromas coming from the kitchen table, I chose instead to feast on hard-boiled eggs and water. I was very unhappy with my appearance, and my long, pale blonde hair, my only redeeming feature that I could see, began to lose its power as a "drawing card" to attract the opposite sex.

The abundance of hard-boiled eggs and water I consumed began to take its toll on me. I simply did not smell very good. I consumed enough water to serve as a holding tank for the Bucherville Reservoir; and much to the objections of my foster parents and friends, little else passed through my mouth. Fainting spells soon became my gymnastic class routine, a performance I repeated on every parade route. Some of my friends tried to convince me that I was headed for trouble and that I was bound to get sick if I continued on my "no food" course. But I had only one goal in mind: 127 pounds. It was a long way from 180-some pounds, but I felt I could go the distance. And I did.

In a little less than four months, I had lost almost fifty pounds. Somewhere between fat and slim, my social life began to change. Several of the most popular guys in school began asking me out on dates. Two of them even gave their class rings back to their steady girls and asked me if I would go steady with them. I nearly had one of my fainting spells when I unintentionally made two dates in one night, and both of them showed up at my door at the same time. "First come, first serve," I said, laughing. And that was exactly how I decided which one I was going to go out with that night.

Balancing my new social life with my new spiritual life became increasingly more difficult.

*   *   *   *   *

The teasing all but ceased when I carried my Bible to school. And even though I continued to be involved in a Bible study class, I didn't allow it to interfere with my active social schedule.

School dances were my favorite. I loved to dance . . . and still do.

Known for my investigative prowess and fearless character, I was asked by the school principal to circulate during regular school dances and proms, in search of students who may have been drinking alcohol, or suppliers of those who were, and report them to the chaperones. Cutting in on girls and their dates was not favorably looked upon; and the danger I faced came mostly from their deadly stares. Thankfully, my popularity didn't wane as a result.

By my junior year in high school, I had already donned my second class ring—a distinctive honor among classmates. Wearing a boy's class ring, with a ton of string around it to keep it on, read as a "hands-off, this-one-belongs-to-me" manifesto!

The school newspaper held a popularity contest twice a year. The whole school voted on their choice for most talented, most intelligent, best sports figure, best personality, prettiest hair, the most humorous, and best dresser (and kids think there's peer pressure today!). Without fail, I always won first place in the prettiest hair category, and Dolly came in first for the friendliest personality. It was not uncommon for people to ask to touch my hair when sitting behind me on a bleacher at some sports event. Very quickly, the nickname "Whitehead" lost its negative power over me.

*　　*　　*　　*　　*

A clique, consisting of about eight female classmates including myself, occupied an entire row of seats in the local movie theatre on Friday nights and reigned supreme at just as many pajama parties that usually followed a night out at the movies. It was like having our own private club. Dating was generally reserved for Wednesday and Saturday nights. Most of us had a special boy in our lives, but that didn't negate an occasional chance rendezvous with someone else . . . a subject causing much controversy at the next Friday night pajama party. To this day . . . and at this writing, most of us still meet six times a year in an attempt to keep the past alive . . . or as a reminder that we're not yet dead!

During my last few years in high school, I had the honor of writing several high school plays that were performed on stage at Bucherville High School. I was also given leading parts in many more plays written and produced by others. Acting came naturally to me, and I loved making people laugh. Memories of the forebay in Reading Junction, where I claimed to have gotten my first break in theatre, returned to me with each performance. Not only did acting provide an outlet for my feelings of insecurity, but it was also a way to achieve recognition. But I wanted more.

*   *   *   *   *

If I had wished on a star for popularity in the wheat field that night in Reading Junction, and not for Bill Casset's attention, my wish would have come true. I had more friends than I could have ever wished for. That attention, however, was temporarily diverted as I began working harder to maintain good grades in school; but Bill Casset kept jaywalking across my mind. I could not stop thinking about him. We still lived across the field from each other, but he was soon to graduate from Bucherville High School, and then he planned to go off to college. He was just one of the many boys I liked . . . but he was the first one I ever loved. As I watched his relationship with the cheerleader become more obvious, I became more and more discouraged. One Saturday night during a "ladies choice" dance at school, I asked Bill to dance with me. I felt like Cinderella. He occupied the largest room in my life for many years, but I don't think he was ever aware that he had taken up residence there. First love has squatter's rights to your heart, I have found.

*   *   *   *   *

Sixteen years old meant one thing: a driver's license! But first, there was the dreaded driver's education class with Mr. Savitz, a very patient driving instructor; a temporary permit; some practical driving experience; a driving test at the State Police building; A SECOND DRIVER'S TEST at the State Police building; and finally, the license.

"You will have to wait a while, Leta," my dad said. "We aren't going to allow you to drive just yet. You can ride the motorbike around the farm until you get used to steering."

After I had my driver's license, and for some time to come, the family car remained off-limits to me, but I circled Cassets' Potato Warehouse on my motorbike, until I got dizzy.

My dad's decision not to allow me to drive the family Pontiac left me totally dependent on either my foster parents or friends to jockey me back and forth from school, and from one social event to another. There was the weekend movie, the school dances, and all the sports events that took place weekly. How was I ever going to convince my dad that those things were imperative to my popularity!

*   *   *   *   *

It was a Saturday night, and Mother and Daddy had gone away. By then, the last foster child had left the Carpenter home. I was the only one remaining, and home had taken on a new perspective. I did not think about my real mother and half-sister very much anymore; I blocked them out of my mind, wishing that I had been as successful with respect to Bill Casset.

I found myself stranded in Reading Junction, while all my friends were planning to attend a "stag dance" at school. "Stag" meant that everyone went without a date, giving them the opportunity to dance with just about anyone they had courage enough to ask. It was my favorite kind of dance. But there I sat, stuck at home, without transportation. Then I got an idea. I would call Bill on our new telephone and ask him if he was going to the dance, and if he would mind giving me a ride into town. I was a bit nervous as I dialed his number. He answered the phone.

"Bill, this is Leta," I said, suddenly out of breath, hearing his voice. "Are you going to the dance tonight at school?"

"No, but I'm going to town. Did you need a ride?" he asked.

Of course, I thought, *he's going to his girlfriend's house.* My options were limited, so I humbly accepted his offer of a ride into town.

You would have thought I was going on a first date with Bill, for all the fuss I made getting ready for that night. I had to remind myself that Bill was only my transportation to Bucherville, not an evening in Paris.

We rode in silence; then I popped the question.

"May I also come home with you tonight?"

"Yeah, of course you can. Where and what time do you want me to pick you up?"

"Oh, I don't know, what time will you be leaving to come home?"

"Well, I guess around 11:30. Is that all right with you?"

"Sure, I will meet you at Dolly's house, if that's O.K."

"That will be fine," he said.

Dolly and her family had moved from Reading Junction to Main Street in Bucherville. I missed the easy access to her family and their food. However, food didn't hold the same attraction for me anymore, and so I can honestly say their friendship meant more to me than anything else, except my friendship with Bill Casset. I spent a good portion of my time at Dolly Witman's house. The friendship between Dolly and me, which began in the single digits, continued long into our teen years and beyond.

On our way to town, Bill and I exchanged opinions on the movies we had seen and high school sporting events. I had finally made the field hockey team and enjoyed sprint racing as a member of the track team. Bill was an all-around sports figure, excelling in everything he did. There was little doubt that Bill would become a very good coach some day, a career he had chosen long before graduation.

We arrived at the school . . . much too soon, as far as I was concerned. He left me standing on the sidewalk as he drove off to be with the cheerleader. My heart ached, even though I no longer held out any hope of becoming anything but a friend to him.

Sometime during the dance, there was talk of an eclipse that night. As Dolly and I walked home from the dance, there was something unfamiliar and strange happening in the sky. We reached Dolly's house about eleven o'clock. My stomach had already begun to churn in anticipation of my ride home with Bill.

Like clockwork, I heard the light touch of his automobile horn in front of Dolly's house. Waving good-bye to Dolly, who was standing on the porch, I opened the door and climbed into the front seat of Bill's car.

As we approached the cemetery that sat on a hill outside of Bucherville on the way home to Reading Junction, there was a strange phenomenon in the sky. I told Bill about the eclipse that my friends had been talking about at the dance.

He quickly detoured into the cemetery.

He parked the car and we got out and looked up into the heavens. It was a very eerie feeling. After viewing the night sky for some time, we climbed back into the car. But he didn't start the car. Instead, he just sat and looked at me. I looked back, not knowing what to expect. He drew me close to him, not eagerly expectant, but gently, like he was protecting me from the darkened sky. I fit perfectly in his arms. He placed his hand beneath my chin and raised my eyes to his. With that, he said, "This is long overdue." It was my first ever kiss.

Knowing Bill, as I do today, I am sure his greatest regret, other than wishing he had kept his promise to not take advantage of me, was betraying his girlfriend. That kiss, no matter how wonderful it was . . . was only a kiss; and instead of it beginning a relationship between us, it ended whatever chance I had of winning Bill Casset's heart. It was our final rendezvous.

Bill married the cheerleader. Our encounters, no matter how miniscule in meaning or brief in duration, left a visible scar on my sleeve . . . the place I wore my heart.

Forty-five years later, he is still married to the cheerleader . . . the mother of his children. We have remained friends. I correspond with him and his wife. They are very happily married.

Time changes all things.

. . . SIX . . .

With no misgivings regarding winning the heart of Bill Casset, I fixed my mind, once again, on school studies.

I won more than my share of attention from the boys in our school since having lost weight, and it was time to concentrate on my education. The commercial skills required to prepare me for the job of private secretary, versus academic requirements for college, came easy to me. During shorthand and typing tests, I performed less than ethical maneuvers when I completed shorthand and typing assignments, not only for myself, but for some of the boys in my class who were less commercially disposed, in order for them to receive passing grades. It was called cheating. I was unaware that, even in the act of doing someone else's work for them, it was just another way of winning acceptance. Having felt rejected and unloved for so long, I thought, and wrongly so, that the fruits of that anomaly would produce even more popularity.

*   *   *   *   *

The older I became, and in spite of our differences, Grace and James Carpenter became more like real parents to me. They were making sacrifices for me, quite similar to those of real parents for their birth children. My heart, however, still felt completely devoid of "belonging." Often times I experienced repeated dreams of being thrown from a train and left on the side of the tracks for some "bum" to find me. Popularity, I believe, sheltered me for a time from making a personal debacle of my life, plus, there was no denying the presence of a living Spirit within me, talking to me, and chiding me along the way.

*   *   *   *   *

Another "stag dance" was held at Bucherville High School. Sometime during that evening, Ken, a friend and classmate, asked Dolly and me if we wanted to join him and his friend in taking his friend's new Cadillac for a ride. Well, that sounded like fun to us, so we agreed to leave the dance and meet them outside. We both knew Ken's friend Rich, and although he was older and had already graduated from high school, the invitation hadn't implied anything inappropriate.

When Rich drove up to the steps of the high school, we couldn't help exclaim over his new Cadillac. Dolly and I climbed into the back seat. We left Bucherville and headed for country roads, where the traffic was lighter on a Saturday night. After we had been driving for some time, Rich pulled the car off the road and suggested that Ken drive his new car. Ken emphatically insisted that he didn't want to drive the car. He said that he was not comfortable driving such a large car, because he was accustomed to driving a very small sports car. But after some coaxing by Rich, Ken took his place behind the steering wheel of the Cadillac. Ken said to me, "Come on and sit in front with me, Leta. It's really pretty impressive." When I moved in front with Ken, Dolly was left with a seating choice disadvantage. Rich, the owner of the Cadillac, climbed into the back seat next to her. Rich instructed Ken to take a rural route north of Bucherville. Ken knew that the road Rich suggested was better known as the "roller-coaster." The road was composed of exaggerated humps; and when you went over them at a high rate of speed, they generated a "roller-coaster" thrill sensation in your stomach.

We went over the humps at a reasonable speed, at first. It nevertheless took my breath away. The unanimous utterances from the back seat of the car consummated the thrill.

Rich was not satisfied with the speed Ken was traveling when he approached the largest hump. First he claimed, his new car "could go a lot faster over the hump and still hold the road!" Secondly, Rich guaranteed that we would experience an even greater "roller-coaster" high if we repeated the act going at a higher rate of speed. It was better known as "joy-riding."

Following Rich's suggestion, yet not wanting to drive faster, Ken turned the car around and approached the hump for the second time. Ken raised his voice from the back seat, "Floor it, Ken! It can hold the road, go ahead, floor it!"

The last thing I recall was Ken putting his foot on the accelerator, then feeling the car go airborne, and I thought, *We're never going to make it!* If anything further was said, I didn't hear it. The car slammed into a huge tree on the right side of the road, followed by a number of somersaults, until it came to rest, right side up, on the opposite side of the road some distance from the impact.

I had no way of knowing how long I remained unconscious, but somewhere in the distance, like a muffled echo, I heard my name being called. I was disoriented and unable to move. Soon I heard cries and moans coming from the back seat. But it still sounded like it was coming from somewhere far away. My name grew louder and louder. I tried to open my eyes, but only one seemed to function. Ken was calling my name from somewhere outside the car. I tried to move, but I could not. My body was wedged between the steering wheel and the front window of what was left of the car. The steering wheel was broken and had embedded itself in the palm of my right hand. I used my other hand to feel my face; all I felt were pieces of glass protruding from my forehead and eye. The moans from the back seat aroused me. At the same time, I could hear Ken asking me over and over again, in hopeful desperation, "Are you all right, Leta? Are you O.K.? Please be O.K., please."

I remember replying, "Yes—but—I'm really hurt, I think. What happened?" I asked. "Are Dolly and Rich all right?"

"I don't know," Ken said, obviously more frightened than hurt. "I think Dolly is hurt badly, but I can't get Rich to answer."

I called out to them from my very painful position, and Dolly answered.

"I think I'm hurt, but I can't get Rich off me. He isn't moving and there is blood everywhere! I can't feel my front teeth; I think they're broken."

With Ken and God's help, we managed to pull the broken steering wheel out of my right hand. Most of my clothing had been torn away and there was a huge hole in my knee and head. Particles of glass were embedded in my torso. The pain finally registered, and I quickly reached for the piece of glass that had been stuck in my right eye, and pulled it free. We were covered in blood. Ken and I put our pain aside as we made our way to the back seat of the car.

We both called out to Dolly. We finally had to extricate her from beneath Ken's body. But how we did it, I'll never know. Considering our injuries, the only plausible explanation was that we were in a state of shock. Rich, however, did not respond to our calls; but a low, painful whimper and moan came from his mouth. It was a sound we wouldn't forget for a very long time.

I prayed aloud on the highway that night for God to send someone to help us. Soon a car came by, and we tried everything to get them to stop, but they did not. Instead, they drove past the mangled vehicle and ignored our call for help. I prayed some more. And God sent another car. This one stopped. It happened to be someone we knew, and while visibly shocked at what he saw, the passerby had the presence of mind to go for help.

Before long, a State Police car pulled up, with its sirens blaring. The officer immediately displayed a great deal of concern for each of us and assured us that an ambulance was on the way. The same comfort I received when Philip the policeman had rescued me when I had run away from home comforted me then. He took complete control of the accident scene, and in reply to our pleas regarding Rich's injuries, he remained coolly noncommittal. At one point he took a blanket and covered my torso, which I had totally forgotten was exposed. He expressed amazement at the degree of injuries we had suffered and that we were able to assist at all.

We heard the sirens; and shortly thereafter, an ambulance arrived on the scene. The State Policeman directed the ambulance crew toward us first. Dolly and I were helped into the front of the ambulance. To this day, I don't recall where Ken was or how he got to the hospital; his physical injuries were minor in comparison to the rest of us, but he had to be going through mental agony, having been the driver of the car. The fact that I was thrown over the steering wheel on impact no doubt served to cushion Ken from more serious injury.

I was aware of the stretcher being placed in the back of the ambulance. Dolly and I continued to inquire about Rich's condition, without success. I began to cry and demand that someone inform us if Rich was still alive. But my outburst went unheeded and they just kept saying that we would know more when we got to the hospital.

Just as we pulled into the emergency area of the hospital, I began to feel the extreme pain of my injuries. Dolly was taken into one room, and I was taken into another. The few pieces of clothing that still remained on my body were removed, and a sheet was placed over my body as the nurses worked at removing the large pieces of glass from various areas of my body. They picked numerous pieces from my back and face. Stitches were placed in my head, hand, and knee, closing the deep holes and gashes in my flesh. They must have given me something for the pain, because I don't recall the extraction of additional pieces of glass from my eye, but later realized that my eye had been patched.

The hospital was full that night, and I had to be moved to a sunroom on the upper floor of the hospital. As they were preparing to move me, I got a hazy glimpse of the room where Rich was lying. A sheet covered his large body. I screamed, "He's dead, isn't he? He's dead!"

*   *   *   *   *

My worst suspicion was confirmed when the State Policeman, pen and pad in hand, walked into the sunroom. He pulled up a chair and sat down by my bed. He asked me if I wanted him to hand me the glass of water sitting on the table next to my bed. After an affirmative nod of my head, which hurt with every move, he held the glass for me as I sipped the cool water from a straw. Then I waited. But he said nothing about Rich.

The questions began. But his first assumption that alcohol had been the cause of the accident was met with impassioned denial. I knew that none of us, especially Dolly, Ken, and myself, did not drink alcoholic beverages and had not done so that night. If Rich had consumed any alcohol, well, it didn't much matter; he hadn't been the one driving. I thought it rather presumptuous on the part of the officer to accuse us of drinking. If, on the other hand, it was an investigative maneuver to extract information from me, he was sorely disappointed. The reason for the accident was rather obvious as far as I was concerned. But I was less confident that we hadn't done something tremendously wrong. He said I had to answer his questions as required by the police. I assumed he had asked each of us involved in the accident the same questions.

As the policeman sat writing my answers on his little wire-bound pad, I had an opportunity to observe him more closely. His broad-rimmed trooper hat was resting at the foot of my bed. His legs were crossed. His shiny knee-high black uniform boots and riding-type pants were visibly imposing. He was every bit as gentle and kind as Philip had been, the only other State Policeman I had ever met. My eye (the one without a bandage over it) focused on his nametag. It said: Sgt. Michael Banks.

I soon found myself providing all the details of that evening, preceding the accident, and everything that I had remembered at the time of the accident, which was very little. I again assured him that none of us had been drinking. I knew he didn't believe me. When he came to the end of the questioning, he drew his chair closer to my bed.

"Leta . . . did I pronounce your name correctly?"

"Yes," I replied.

"Your friend Rich died in the emergency room tonight, Leta," he announced, "but everyone else is going to be fine."

He sounded sympathetic enough, sentiments he no doubt had to express many times before to family and friends of victims, I was sure.

Even though I somehow knew that Rich had died, I broke down and cried. I cried until falling into a deep sedated sleep that lasted until the next morning.

The sun arrived early on my bed in my unconventional hospital room. That morning, visitors and mobile patients would find the sunroom off limits for reading newspapers and drinking coffee, because I had taken up residence there instead. The first thing that came to my mind that morning was why my parents hadn't yet come to see me. Hadn't they heard? I wondered. Surely they would have been notified by this time. Didn't they wonder where I was and why I hadn't come home last night? As I was thinking about my parents, Michael Banks walked into the sunroom.

"G-o-o-d morning," he said, stretching the "good."

"Hello," I said, less enthusiastically.

"Your mother will be coming in to see you today; that should make you feel better this morning."

"When did she find out about the accident?" I asked.

"Well, to tell you the truth, she wanted to come in last night, but she had no one to bring her to the hospital. Your dad apparently couldn't be located anytime during the night."

Of course not, I said to myself, quite sarcastically, *he was the one drinking alcohol last night, not me.* Mother was probably alone all night, not knowing the whereabouts of my dad. His problem just seemed to get worse. She must have been devastated to find out that I had been in a fatal accident and she had no way to get to the hospital. I imagined her staying up all night not knowing what to do. She would never have awakened a neighbor in the middle of the night; she would have considered that an imposition.

Michael Banks pulled out a morning newspaper from under his arm and asked me if I wanted to see the article about the accident. I said, "No, not right now."

"You should know that the headline in the paper states that you were killed in the accident along with your friend Rich. The newspaper is rescinding the report and printing a correction in tonight's newspaper. Are you sure you don't want to read it?"

The fact that I had been listed as dead piqued my interest. What I saw was not a pretty sight. The big Cadillac was ripped to pieces, particular the passenger side of the vehicle where I had been sitting. It was literally pushed into the middle of the car from the impact. Looking at it made me sick to the stomach. It was a strange feeling seeing my name in the headlines as one of two people who had lost their lives in the reported "Joy Ride" accident. I had a lot to be thankful for. God had spared my life.

Michael Banks took the breakfast tray from the morning hospital aide and put it on my bedside table. I wondered why he was being so accommodating, and why he had come to visit me for the second time. He sat beside my bed, just as he had done the night before. The attention he gave me was very touching.

"Leta, there is something you need to know," he began.

"What else? Hasn't there been enough?" I pleaded.

"I must tell you that Ken is being charged with manslaughter and you will undoubtedly be required to testify in court regarding the accident."

"But Ken didn't do anything wrong!" I protested, although I wasn't sure that was the truth. "He only did what Rich told him to do. He didn't want to go over that hump that fast. You can't charge him with a crime. He is a nice person, and he wouldn't hurt anyone intentionally, ever!"

I knew that Michael Banks, being a State Policeman, had a job to do. I was also taught to respect officers of the law, or my response may have been quite different. Informing me of the charges against Ken could not have been an easy thing for him to do. But I had all the confidence in the world that Ken would be exonerated.

Prosecuting attorneys for the state hadn't shared my layman's opinion, and it appeared we would be in for a long trial.

*   *   *   *   *

Mother had come and gone after a short visit, apologizing for not being there for me the night of the accident, and for Daddy's reluctance to come in to see me. He remained in the car. Daddy hated hospitals. He believed that if you were ever admitted to a hospital, you would never come out again. He would not only refuse to ever be admitted to one, but went one step further and avoided even visiting people in the hospital. I was not the exception.

Mother was relieved to know that the newspaper had made a mistake and that I was still alive, as Officer Banks had assured her the night of the accident. My job then was to attempt to convince her that we had not been drinking, as the paper and police had reported. She believed me.

*   *   *   *   *

On my fifth day in the hospital, Michael Banks and a doctor came into the sunroom, trailed by the mail person and a cart filled with fresh flower arrangements. As the doctor and Officer Banks stood talking, I opened a couple get-well cards. Then I saw a letter with Jean Marlow's name on it. I anxiously opened the letter. After reading a few lines, I broke down and cried uncontrollably. The doctor asked me if he could see the letter, and I responded by nodding my head. Michael Banks, who was looking over the doctor's shoulder, appeared shocked and saddened by what he read. The letter turned out to be a seething disclaimer from my birth mother, accusing me of drunkenness, wild living, and behavior not befitting a daughter of hers. She made it undeniably clear that she wanted nothing to do with me. She said she was ashamed to call me her daughter and didn't want to ever see me again. And although we had not developed a close relationship, her out-and-out rejection of me was devastating.

Many months later, I discovered the real reason my mother disowned me for life. My name, which appeared in the paper as a result of the accident, somehow had been linked with hers as far as Yorktown, embarrassing her, and revealing to her friends that she had another daughter.

When I realized that, I actually felt sympathy for her. I blamed myself again for causing someone else's pain. I was more convinced than ever that I should never have been born.

*   *   *   *   *

At long last, I was discharged from Lancaster General Hospital. Seeing Dolly and Ken again was difficult, yet somehow comforting. So much had happened since leaving the dance floor that eventful night. We hugged one another and knew that we would be drawn together even more because of the impending trial.

There were no facts to get straight, no rehearsed lines, and no legal coaching required. There was only the naked truth of that night. Ken, however, was going to need all the support he could get, and a very good lawyer.

The trial date was set; the character witnesses and offers of support were pouring in. Even Rich's parents and siblings came to Ken's defense. We were told that the victim's parents and family would not take the side of the prosecutors. It was the most heart-rending endorsement for Ken's flawless character and innocence that we could have ever hoped for.

The trial began.

*   *   *   *   *

The courtroom was filled to capacity. The first day of the trial was the hardest. And although we knew the prosecutors could not prove alcohol as the cause of the accident, they certainly had enough evidence for a "joy-riding" case. What ramifications, if any, that was going to hold for Ken, or for us, remained to be seen.

Fifteen minutes before the judge's hammer called for silence in the courtroom, my eyes surveyed the room. The prosecutor's table sat front and left of the judge's bench. Michael Banks sat beside the state's attorney, in his pressed uniform . . . his boots still shining, and his hat resting on the table. I had visions of our first encounter in the hospital room.

Ken looked small and defenseless, beside his attorney on the opposite side of the room.

Dolly and I occupied the front row bench, where we waited to take our turn on the witness stand. Behind us were benches occupied by those who planned to testify on Ken's behalf. Practically the whole school had shown up. From the corner of my nearly healed but still red eye, I saw Rich's family. His mother, father, and siblings occupied another bench directly across from the many friends and classmates who had come to show their support. It was an emotional display. My heart ached for both Rich and Ken's families. The trial reminded me of two teams gearing up for a traditional game of Tug of War.

As the bold-faced clock on the courtroom wall registered twelve o'clock noon, and after an extensive morning inquisition, the judge got hungry and recessed until two o'clock that afternoon.

My parents were sitting in the back of the courtroom. Up until then, little reference had been made by them concerning the trial, and I wasn't quite sure why. All I knew was that I was beginning to feel more and more like a criminal. But as I made my way between the rows of benches to the exit door during the recess, Mother reached for my hand and squeezed it. I knew she was praying for me.

I left the eerie tomb-like courtroom structure, hoping to be alone. The experience was very traumatic for me, but when I thought of what Ken must be going through, I thought less about how I was feeling. There just wasn't a way to put the whole thing behind us without first going through the trial, the road grief usually travels.

I walked down the hall outside the courtroom. The sound my steps made on the shiny gray marble tiles forbid any secrecy regarding my whereabouts.

Wishing to appear mature and more responsible, contrary to my usual tomboy haberdashery, I had chosen to wear a borrowed pastel-flowered dress and black Mary Jane style shoes for the first day of our trial. My shoulder-length, pale blonde hair covered my face as I rested my head on my hands on a railing near a window at the end of the majestic hall. I prayed for Ken. I felt the presence of God, a vital sign that my faith was still alive. The tears ran down my cheeks.

I heard approaching footsteps. As I looked up, I saw Sgt. Michael Banks, the State Policeman, coming towards me. He leaned on the railing beside me . . . and after a moment or two, he spoke.

"Are you all right?" he asked.

"No," I answered, "I'm afraid for Ken."

"Well, you just tell the truth about what happened that night and it'll be all right. But I do think it's time to admit that Ken was drinking the night of the accident."

I turned to face him; and with deserving hostility, I vehemently replied, "There was no alcohol, and you know it! You are trying to put Ken in jail, and that is the only way you can do it, by proving we were drinking. Well, we weren't, so I hate to disappoint you." I turned to leave, but not before the officer took hold of my arm.

"Leta, I'm sorry," he said with obvious sincerity, "but I had to try one last time to get a confession from one of you, and I thought you would tell me the truth. I truly am sorry, but it is part of my job, you know. I guess you really are telling the truth."

"Well, I don't care if you believe me or not," I said. "I thought you were very nice in the hospital, but now I know you were only trying to gain my confidence so I would give you something to convict Ken. I am sorry, too, but it didn't work, did it?"

"Leta, please," he said, almost imploring me to pay attention to what he was about to say. "Ever since that night on the highway, I have felt sorry for all of you. I know this is probably the most inappropriate time to say this to you, but I am going to say it anyway. I am much older than you are, twelve years older as a matter of fact, but I think you are a very special girl, and I care about what happens to you. I really sympathize with you, particularly after reading that letter from your mother. When this whole thing is over, I would like to keep in touch with you. May I?"

I was totally stunned by his unexpected request.

"I don't know. It's not something I want to talk about right now," I said. Hey, I didn't even like him anymore after what he had just done to me.

We were due back in the courtroom. Michael walked ahead of me, presumably to avoid any misinterpretation of our meeting. I was a bit dazed as I reentered the courtroom. I found it very difficult digesting the line I had just been fed.

The trial resumed.

*   *   *   *   *

I found it difficult to watch Michael Banks testify concerning the specifics of the accident, but as one of the victims, I was forced to participate. I raised my eyes, and for the first time, I really looked at Michael Banks. I rewound his words in my mind and listened again to his disclosure of a personal interest in me. I would soon be seventeen and a senior in high school. He was twenty-eight. There was a savory element to my musing; I had to admit to myself, the idea of having a policeman for a friend fascinated me.

Michael Banks sat tall on the padded chair beside the judge as he gave testimony to what he determined happened that horrible night. Using information we had given him, and his own account of what had happened, and without the confession he so desired to inculpate Ken, his sworn testimony finally came to an end.

Dolly, Ken, and myself gave our versions of what happened the night of the accident. And as hard as the prosecution tried, they were unable to produce the necessary evidence to convict Ken of voluntary manslaughter.

The day ended without a verdict.

*   *   *   *   *

As we sat at the dinner table that evening, Daddy suggested that he drive me to the garage where the Cadillac had been towed after the accident. Since I had my driver's license by that time, he thought it would be a good idea, as he put it, "to get back on the horse." He knew I wasn't riding the horse, so to speak, but he was sure that the inevitable aftershock might inhibit me from ever wanting to drive again. In retrospect, that probably wasn't a bad idea. Seeing the car, and where I had been sitting when the accident occurred, impacted my life more than the injuries I sustained. Looking at what was left of the Cadillac reminded me again of how my life had been miraculously spared.

*   *   *   *   *

Day two of the trial began with another rap of the hammer and a call to order in the courtroom. Unlike day one, more summation than condemnation was the order of the day. Believing the worst part was behind us, I began to relax a little. But then the unexpected happened. I heard my name being called once more.

"Leta Marlow, please take the witness stand," the judge announced.

How could they do this? I thought. I had already testified to all I knew about the accident.

Over and over again, the same questions were hurled at me. If indeed the truth sets you free, I said to myself, then I had no reason to fear the badgering attempts to confuse and frighten me into the lie the prosecution wanted to hear.

Finally satisfied at my determination to stick to my story (the truth) and my persistence in affirming the testimonies of the others, the prosecution rested its case.

Again, we retreated to the marble-paved hallway and hard wooden benches that made up the courtroom hallway, where we waited for the announcement of our fate.

There were several possible verdicts: voluntary manslaughter or involuntary manslaughter . . . the latter carrying with it a much lighter sentence. Dolly and I had already been guaranteed by our attorney that we would not be implicated in any way since we were simply passengers in the automobile that night; nevertheless, Ken's fate was our fate. We had suffered along with Ken throughout the trial, and the verdict would be ours, if not physically, most certainly emotionally.

Those were the moments when I wished I had learned to drink coffee. Everyone seemed to have a Styrofoam cup of the steaming black substance, and the satisfaction it seemed to invoke convinced me that I was missing something extremely pleasurable.

Friends began assuring us that the jury would never dare to put Ken behind bars after all the character witnesses that had stood up for him, and in particular, the testimony of our dead friend's family. How we hoped they were right.

After several hours in that venerable hall of justice, we were summoned back into the courtroom.

The judge, no doubt returning from his own cup of coffee, took his seat, and we followed suit.

The stoic-faced jurors returned one at a time to the jury box. The judge asked the chairman of the jury if they had reached a verdict. He replied that they had.

It was over. Ken was now at the mercy of the court.

The chairman was asked to read the verdict.

As Ken stood to receive the adjudication, time also stood . . . still. There was a deafening silence as the chairman began to read the words from the piece of paper he held in his hand: "In the case of voluntary manslaughter—we the jury, find the defendant—NOT GUILTY." Cheers were heard throughout the courtroom.

Involuntary manslaughter meant some serious inconveniences for Ken, but at least he wasn't going to go to prison. To maintain some dignity and respect for our dead friend's family, we suppressed a good portion of our elation.

As the courtroom emptied, I could see Michael Banks speaking to the prosecuting attorney. Wanting to get out of there, like everyone else, I headed for the back of the courtroom, but he managed to catch up with me.

"I am still not convinced, you know," he said, with an accusing tone.

"I know you aren't, and that's really too bad; it just shows what a poor judge you would make!" I replied sarcastically.

With that, he smiled and walked away, but not before taking one last look over his shoulder as he left the room.

. . . SEVEN . . .

I had just begun my senior year in high school when a FOR SALE sign was erected in the middle of the front yard at our home in Reading Junction, beckoning interested parties to inquire within. The decision to move to Bucherville had been an agonizing one for Mother and Daddy.

There were only the three of us now: Mother, Daddy, and me; the remaining foster children had been "placed" in other homes; "a good time to sell the farm," my dad said to my mother. What followed was some serious talk about building a small modest house somewhere in the town of Bucherville; and so the search for a building lot began.

Meanwhile, knowing my parents were not financially well-off, I decided it was time for me to look for a job; that meant a visit to Peter Casset's potato warehouse; after all, he had said I could work for him one day.

After a short interview with Mr. Casset the following week, at which time I proudly produced my typing, shorthand, and bookkeeping grades, he hired me for a clerical position in his office, just as he had promised.

Having been reprimanded by Mrs. Grant from the Children's Bureau for having spent too much money on my care, Mother and Daddy had long since stopped taking me to the dentist for regular visits. As a result, my teeth appeared extrinsically healthy . . . but intrinsically, they were full of decay. I determined that my first paycheck would go toward some badly needed dental work. Thankfully, however, I now wore shoes on my feet instead of going barefoot most of the time, and I no longer wore long white cotton stockings. I celebrated the day when my legs no longer matched the color of my hair.

I began working at the potato warehouse on Saturday mornings. Along with generating paychecks for Mr. Casset's employees, I was also expected to check the records of the drivers of the tractor and trailer rigs that transported potatoes to surrounding states, just to make sure the mileage was correct, and that Mr. Casset wasn't being overcharged. I was particularly aware of a handsome blond-haired truck driver who could have doubled as Richard Widmark, the movie star. No more than a lingering smile or two had passed between us; that is, until my mother decided to send me on a late night errand.

Mother had an enlarged heart; not literally, of course . . . just when it came to our resident railroad hobos. She always made sure there was extra food left over from our evening meal to satisfy their hungry stomachs, in the event they happened to come knocking at our door . . . and they always did. When the hobos didn't show up as expected, she always seemed to find someone who needed a warm meal.

It was a moonlit night, and Mother's heart rose to the occasion once more. She told me to take a dish of food up to the "poor truck driver" who had to sleep in the cab of his truck all night. Because we lived next to the potato warehouse, Mother was as familiar with the truckers' routine as I was of Bill Casset's comings and goings. The truckers would arrive late, after the warehouse had closed, and would sleep in the cabs of their trucks until the warehouse opened in the morning and their trucks could be loaded for the long trips to potato chip factories in various states.

Mother received no resistance from me as she handed me the covered dish; I always looked forward to seeing the pleasure on the truckers' faces after they ate one of her hearty meals.

"Wait," I heard her call as I was going out the door. "Here is a piece of apple pie for his dessert."

"Forbid that anyone should ever miss dessert," I said, under my breath.

I hesitated just long enough to retrieve the pie from her hands, and then I was out the door and on my way to fulfilling my mother's good deed.

The moon was very bright that night. It was a perfect OFFS night, but there were no more of those. I found myself thinking about those nights as I made my way to the warehouse. I also thought about Michael Banks, the State Policeman, who for some reason, I didn't think I had heard the last of; but emotions that did not conform to my conservative upbringing manifested themselves every time I thought of Bill Casset, my first ever love.

God's presence in my life had kept me on the straight and narrow track thus far, along with Bill Casset's reluctance to indulge my appetite for love. The also-rans were the teachings of the Mennonite and Methodist Churches on purity and sin, where apparently some seeds had fallen on good soil; all of which helped me, to some degree, determine the boundaries I had set for myself. But had my foster mother known me better, she never would have chosen to send her daughter into the arms of a handsome truck driver on a moonlit night.

*   *   *   *   *

Balancing a plate of food in one hand, while knocking on the door of the mile-high cab with the other, I finally succeeded in making my presence known.

Ignoring Wilm Devon's good looks was next to impossible; his smile and his cellophane-blue eyes captivated me every time I saw him at the warehouse. You can imagine my surprise when I discovered that it was he who would be the recipient of my mother's generosity that night.

Of all the times I had delivered care packages from my mother to the truckers at Casset's warehouse, this was the first time I had ever been invited to join one of them in the cab of his truck while he ate, and I decided to accept the invitation.

As we talked, I guessed that the "Richard Widmark" look-alike was about twenty-seven years old. To a seventeen-year-old, that was pretty old. He appeared to be about the same age as Sgt. Michael Banks.

By the time the handsome truck driver finished his hobo plate of food, we were on a first-name basis. He put the dishes aside and asked me to stay and visit with him for a while. He and I were not total strangers, but sitting alone with him in the cab of an eighteen-wheeler, apart from the customary noisy atmosphere of the potato warehouse, was an unfamiliar and dangerous place for me to be.

"Have you ever ridden on a motorcycle?" he asked.

"Well, I have a motorbike, but I guess you wouldn't call that a real motorcycle," I replied.

"Would you like to go for a ride with me sometime on my motorcycle?" he asked.

"You have a motorcycle? Sure, I'd love that! But I'd have to ask my parents first."

"Do you think they would mind?" he inquired, appearing hopeful.

"I don't think so, but it would be best to get their permission anyway," I explained.

He shared a few Harley Davidson motorcycle stories with me, the intentions of which were to convince me that he was a very accomplished rider. He told me how he had grown up in Lancaster County, the son of Mennonite parents. It was obvious from the way my mother dressed, in her white bonnet and plain dress, that I, too, had been reared in a Mennonite home, something he said we had in common. I really liked him and I felt very comfortable talking to him. However, I was thinking that my mother would now be wondering where I was, since I hadn't returned after delivering the meal, but I wasn't persuaded to act on my thoughts. Eventually, I decided that I had better go home. As I reached for the door handle, Wilm's hand reached out for me. I stopped and turned to look at him.

It was love at first kiss.

*   *   *   *   *

A stolen kiss between a girl and boy (particularly with an age difference of ten or twelve years) was considered a serious transgression in those days. But to me, a kiss at any age was a most gratifying experience, next to holding hands and chocolate candy. I derived abundant pleasure in the little things of love; so unquenchable was my thirst for affection.

*   *   *   *   *

The wind was against our faces and my arms were wrapped tightly around Wilm Devon's waist, as we rode with Harley Davidson abandon into the night.

*   *   *   *   *

What started out as a motorcycle ride on the country roads of Lancaster County ended with plans to walk down the aisle of a church in Bucherville. Wanting to belong to someone was a harmless enough longing; but the motives behind wanting it, as a quick fix for my feelings of rejection, were not as benign.

After many such motorcycle rides, and shortly after an introduction to Wilm's family, our engagement appeared in the local paper. I proudly displayed my left ring finger to the world. I was so happy! But I still had my senior year of school ahead of me.

Three weeks after our engagement, Wilm was drafted into the Army. I vividly recall the night he broke the news that he would be leaving to serve his country. For the first few minutes, I showed astonishing calm, followed by a torrent of tears and accusations. The United States government had intruded into our private lives, and I decided right then and there, I would get even; I was never going to vote! Of course, I had those words for lunch years later when I became a political activist and thought that non-voters deserved a jail sentence.

*   *   *   *   *

At seventeen years of age, I was already credited with the attention of three older men, numerous male classmates my own age, two "going steady" rings, and one engagement ring. That was not an extraordinary feat in those days. As a matter of fact . . . if you didn't have at least one engagement ring by the time you graduated from high school . . . you were considered a reject. But I would have felt right at home with that title as well.

*   *   *   *   *

Wilm left for the Army as I was beginning my senior year in high school. I held on to him as though he was about to become the first POW. We had very little time together before he was sent to Germany. I was sure I would miss him terribly. Soon after arriving in Germany, he sent me a fine handcrafted German clock. His letters were warm, newsy, and frequent. That's how it was in the beginning.

*   *   *   *   *

The sale of our farm came shortly after Wilm's departure for overseas. It kept me occupied for weeks. Moving into a new house, with a bathroom, and much closer to my school, was very exciting! Our new home was a modest two-bedroom wood frame house on Fulton Street, at the west end of Bucherville. It looked like a dollhouse compared to our large farm home in Reading Junction. It also stood second from the end in a row of five or six dollhouses. Long before the plaster dried, I had taken my second bubble bath, and another new admirer.

I considered myself "grown up" after becoming engaged, and I entertained the idea of moving into an apartment of my own. I had taken an after-school job as a waitress at a local restaurant, and with the generous tips and minimal salary, I began formulating a plan to make the move. Somewhere between that idea and the actual move, I became familiar with a certain senior. He was very handsome and considered a "catch" by just about every girl in school.

One day, while I was closing my locker door and getting ready to walk home after school, "the catch" was waiting at the exit door. He was not particularly athletic or even big in stature; but he was large in artistic talent and good looks. There was also something mysterious about him. Maybe it was his dark puppy-dog eyes or his slight slouch and defined facial features, I'm not really sure; he was just quietly impressive, but I never once entertained the slightest notion to win his attention. His steady date was one of the prettiest and most intellectual girls in the class. Evan (that was his name) simply got in step beside me that day as I walked out the schoolroom door. Just like you would mark a AAA map before you start out on a summer vacation, he began highlighting the direction he intended to go with me.

"Well, when are we going to go out together?"

I suppose I was a little surprised by his question; otherwise, my reply might have been more rehearsed. "I beg your pardon, are you talking to me?" I asked.

He laughed. "Nah . . . just to myself. Of course I'm talking to you. I'd like to go out with you sometime; and don't worry, I'm not dating Carol anymore. We broke up."

He obviously hadn't heard that I was engaged. I was sure that once I reminded him of that fact, he would withdraw his invitation. But his response to my announcement was completely unexpected.

"We can take care of that problem," he assured me.

He took my left hand and turned my diamond engagement ring toward the inside of my hand.

"There, that should take care of everything," he said, as he looked endearingly into my eyes.

*   *   *   *   *

I could offer a dozen reasons why I began dating Evan, but only one would be true: Wilm was thousands of miles away and Evan was close by, and I needed to have a special man in my life. It was that simple.

Since my very first date with Evan, I felt guilty and was unable to continue writing endearing letters to my fiancé. It wasn't long before I received a phone call from a long-distance operator from Frankfurt, Germany. She said she had a call for me from a Wilm Devon. At that moment, I felt tremendous guilt for what I had done. Evan and I did not have a physical relationship, but even I knew that just one kiss betrayed my engagement to Wilm. His voice sounded so far away, which it was. That fact presented its own consolation: at least he wasn't able to reach out and touch. Instead of the expected outburst, I heard only the sound of my own conscience. For some reason, I thought Wilm had heard about Evan and me. I didn't know exactly how he would have found out, but that is how deep the guilt had gone. Instead, he was calling to give me good news. He was coming home! I gulped. I had written to him earlier about moving out on my own, and now he was encouraging me to move faster in my search for an apartment, promising to help pay the rent. I hadn't read between the phone lines, but his reason for wanting me in my own apartment was entirely different than mine, as I soon discovered. We talked a while longer, then we were disconnected.

*   *   *   *   *

I broke the news to my mother and dad that I had found an apartment close to Bucherville High School, thinking that explanation would soften the blow. With my engagement, I am sure they considered it just a move closer to marriage. They were aware that Wilm was coming home from Germany and, as always, did not question his intentions or mine.

It was a dark and dingy second-floor apartment, with only a hotplate to warm up food, and a small toy-like refrigerator that sat lonely and cold in one corner of the room. It was to be my first attempt at housekeeping.

Evan was completely understanding of my situation. After all, he wasn't exactly an innocent bystander in the whole scheme of things. He agreed to "wait on the shore," he said, "until the coast was clear."

*   *   *   *   *

A new electric fan supplied the "tropical breeze" in my one-room apartment. It was a Friday night and a few minutes shy of Wilm's arrival at my apartment. I sat on one of the old rockers on the front porch below my rented room. I occupied one side; the landlady occupied the other. She was an eighty-year-old lady; deaf, but not dumb. I had a premonition that she knew just about everything that was going on. Perhaps by smell, keen eyesight (and I had good reason to doubt that), or just from her eighty-year stockpile of wisdom. But seldom did I have the porch to myself. I was thankful the door to my room had a lock on it. We rocked in opposite directions . . . out of sync . . . and it annoyed me. As I looked at her frown-lined face, nearly hidden by her large black bonnet, I wondered if she had ever waited to meet the love of her life. But we seldom spoke, and I doubted that she would ever share one thread of her personal life with me.

I had no doubt whatsoever that he had been faithful to me. He couldn't stop kissing me. His kisses were as I remembered them. I eventually called a truce and suggested that we try talking. The tropical breeze began to feel like the noonday sun. He was overly aggressive, and he apologized, saying how much he had missed me. I believe he really did love me. Unfortunately, he found it difficult to contain himself emotionally, and before long, he began making unwanted advances again, saying how much he needed me. When I objected, his face reddened and he stood looking at me in utter disbelief.

"What do you expect me to do, Leta?" he shouted, "stand on my head and stack nickels? I have been away for so long, and all I've thought about was you, and now you won't even let me touch you!"

"We aren't married yet," I exclaimed emphatically.

He didn't take my explanation lightly. He was very angry with me. The way I figured it, he had come all the way from Germany to be with me, and I was resisting. In a way, I felt sorry for him, but I refused to go against my promise to God to remain pure until after I was married. I wanted to be a very special gift to my future husband; and I thought that person was going to be Wilm.

The strange thing was, I hadn't thought of Evan. Seeing Wilm again renewed the feelings I once had for him. But now, the double guilt I felt, having refused Wilm's advances after coming all the way from Germany to see me and having betrayed him by dating Evan behind his back was something I couldn't deal with. Instead of telling him the truth, and perhaps salvaging our engagement, I removed the ring from my finger and handed it to him. To make matters worse, he handed the ring back to me and said, "I bought this diamond just for you; it will never belong to anyone else. You keep it. Do anything you want with it. Even change your mind about wearing it again if you want, but it's yours."

As I began to cry, he walked out the door and was gone.

*   *   *   *   *

I have never entirely succeeded in forgetting the look on Wilm's face that evening: the rejection, the disappointment, and the pain. *Another consequential scar lives on, buried deep in my mind; I shan't go "anywhere" without it.*

*   *   *   *   *

Many months later, unable to wear my engagement ring, or even look at it, I packaged it and mailed it to Wilm Devon's home. He had already returned to Germany.

Evan and my relationship dissolved as quickly as it had jelled.

I moved back to Fulton Street to the home of my foster parents.

*   *   *   *   *

There is one sure thing: You never know what, or who, is just around the corner.

. . . EIGHT . . .

As a high school senior, I worked hard to get my name placed on a list of "elite" students most likely to obtain employment consideration with a large corporation, upon graduation. I was relatively certain I would get that consideration due to my excellent typing and shorthand skills, but I didn't want to take any chances. However, there was one distraction in the plan to keep my nose in the books, and less consolation in the fact that more than fifteen other female students were distracted as well. Our distraction was a good-looking and, yes, hard-of-hearing emotional fifties recording artist who shed genuine tears when he sang his biggest hit: "Cry." His name was Johnnie Ray. We all responded coequally to his emotional performance, which literally took him to his knees and brought us to our feet in tearful responding screams. But that is not the end of the story.

Johnnie Ray was scheduled to appear in concert at a local high school auditorium about ten miles from Bucherville. A group of us (and perhaps this is where the word "groupie" got its origin) decided to play hooky and spend the day at the concert. We piled as many as possible into two cars, and off we went for a day with Johnnie Ray; "and what a day it was, it really was!" (to quote words from one of his songs). We were all star-struck, right down to our bobby socks. A day later, however, we were all sentenced to solitary confinement in a classroom and forced to listen to eight hours of Johnnie Ray's "Cry." We were required to write the lyrics repeatedly until our confinement ended. It is still the topic of conversation between those of us who are alive and remember it . . . forty-five years later.

Twelve years later, when Tom Jones took the stage, I repeated that "idle" worship.

*   *   *   *   *

A request to write several plays for production at my school took up the rest of my time. The only view of the world I got while writing was when it peeped through my window. There was a tremendous feeling of personal satisfaction and achievement when the curtains opened and the program read: "A three-act play, written by Leta Marguerite Marlow." Not only did I enjoy writing plays, but I also loved to perform in them. There was definitely theatrical blood in my veins. I recall Jean Marlow telling me that Bassie had been active in the Yorktown Theatre. No coincidence, I suppose.

*   *   *   *   *

On a warm Saturday afternoon, after completing a dozen revolutions in the sun as part of my "enviable tan" maintenance program, I gathered my beach towel and headed for the back door of the house. At the same time, my attention was drawn to a State Police patrol car maneuvering to fit between two parked cars in front of our house. Since it was of no particular interest to me, I continued into the house. Before I got to my bedroom, where I planned to cover myself with Noxzema (an old remedy for burnt flesh), I caught a glimpse of a tall figure standing at the front door. *Oh my goodness,* I thought, *it's him! It's Michael Banks!* There I stood, in a bathing suit, my skin burnt to a crisp, eyes all puffy from the sun, and still covered in baby oil. I was the only one home, so I wrapped a towel tightly around me and went to the door.

"Hello there," he said, as I opened the screen door.

My first thought was that his visit must have had something to do with the accident.

"What are you doing here?" I asked. "Is something wrong?"

"Remember when I told you that I wanted to keep in touch with you?" he reminded me.

"Yes, but I had forgotten all about that," I replied. I still didn't know whether or not I liked him after what he had put me through at the trial.

He continued to explain, as he removed his wide-brim hat and laid it on a table next to the only reading chair in our living room. His good looks hadn't diminished, and he was undeniably imposing in his dark gray uniform, just as I remembered him on the witness stand and sitting beside my bed in the hospital.

"I just wanted to know how you were doing," he said. "I'm patrolling your area this week, so I thought I'd stop and say hello. I'll be on duty all night, so I'll keep check on your place."

"Why would you do that? Am I in some kind of danger?"

"No, it's just something I want to do. I also want to take you out to dinner some time, if your parents will let you go."

Little chance that my parents will say anything at all, I thought. There hadn't been any notable discipline since the time I hid from them in the basement of our Junction home late at night, scaring them half to death when they opened the cellar door to investigate my whereabouts. The incident had gotten me a good swift kick in the pants. I had always felt they didn't love me enough to care about what I did or didn't do, or even what might happen to me. I never had a curfew, or even a set of rules to follow. Mother just lived an exemplary life, and I think she expected me to mirror her behavior and not need disciplinary guidelines. So when Michael Banks, a man twelve years older than myself, asked to take me out to dinner, I hardly thought my parents would object, especially since the invitation had come from a policeman. I wondered how he knew that we had moved from Reading Junction to Bucherville. Had he really been keeping tabs on me all that time, or was it routine police work that brought him to our door?

I assured him that my parents would have no problem with me going out to dinner with him; but I said it somewhat sarcastically.

"Well then, I'll take that as a yes. Next week I will have day patrol so I'll give you a call just to make sure it's all right."

As I was asking myself, *Why are you doing this, Leta,* he picked up his hat and walked out the door, but not before taking one last look over his shoulder. *Déja vu.*

I mentioned Michael's visit to Mother and Daddy, and as expected, there was no show of disapproval.

*   *   *   *   *

One week later, I received a phone call from Michael Banks, at which time I accepted his invitation to dinner.

A two-toned brown and tan car arrived just when he said it would. I felt as though butterflies had gathered for a family reunion in my stomach. I had a few misgivings about seeing Michael; and the difference in our ages created a very particular disturbance, in light of what had transpired between Wilm and me.

Michael Banks looked very attractive in his starched brown and white checked shirt and khaki pants. The neighbors, their curiosity getting the best of them, peeked through the curtains as we walked to his car. My going out with a Pennsylvania State Policeman was probably the most exciting thing that ever happened in our neighborhood. You would have thought he was the Prince of Monaco.

Michael was a gentleman, opening doors, pulling my seat out for me to sit down at the restaurant, and promising to protect me with his life. It was an irresistible combination. I hadn't stopped to analyze why I found such comfort in a man twelve years older than myself, but what I did know was that my interest in police work extended far beyond job description; in this case (no pun intended), it was the person in the uniform. I was thoroughly enamoured by both. I had not objected when he suggested that we see each other again.

*   *   *   *   *

Everyone was frantically preparing for Graduation Day. Until then, even my closest friends did not know about my friendship with Michael Banks. I had pretty much kept it a secret from everyone, except my neighbors. It was going to be bad enough when they did find out, when they would most certainly accuse him of robbing the cradle.

While rehearsing for Graduation Day, I learned that I would indeed be the recipient of a commercial-honors award. I was also told that Armstrong Cork Company, one of the largest floor covering and extended services companies, with an impressive reputation and comparable facilities, was interested in employing me immediately after graduation. I had been asked to get in touch with their Human Resource department and set up an appointment for an interview. It was a great beginning for my secretarial career.

As a 1950s schoolgirl, becoming a nurse, secretary, or schoolteacher seemed to be the only career choices available, and no one ever took the time, at least not with me, to point out the monetary differences in salaries, or the opportunities that a college education would afford us. I realized later that I probably hadn't made the right choice. My dream of becoming an FBI agent haunted me; but when I was selected for an interview at Armstrong Cork Company, the thought of immediate employment took precedence over becoming an agent. *I have always regretted not chasing my dream.*

The auditorium was filled to capacity for graduation. I sat among the honor students waiting to be called on stage to receive my commercial achievement award. I finally heard my name announced. I proudly took my place on stage and received my honorary piece of paper. After receiving the customary applause, I looked out over the sea of faces, and only one stood out . . . Michael's. He was obviously on duty that night and was standing in the middle of the aisle at the rear of the auditorium. There was no way he would go unnoticed at the end of the ceremony. Suddenly, I was nervous, even among my friends and classmates. How was I going to explain his presence to my friends? I only hoped he would not stay around for the post-ceremony activities.

The diploma presentations ended. I lingered longer than usual, but it did not keep Michael from walking down the aisle towards me. Feeling cornered, I introduced Michael to my friends. It was quite apparent that some of them recognized him immediately and showed surprise that the man who had tried to indict our friend after that fatal night had the nerve to show up on the night of our graduation. Immediately, I picked up on one girl in particular who was doing her best to get his attention. Michael remained completely focused on me. I, on the other hand, displayed annoyance with my flirtatious friend. So gracious was Michael, and quite probably because he was on duty, he didn't try to coerce me from joining my friends that night at The Chatterbox, a popular gathering place for young people. With the exception of a couple of beers, which made their way into the popular night spot in the pockets of several of our more insurgent classmates, it turned out to be a rather uneventful evening.

The following day, Michael called and said he would stop by the house that night since he would be patrolling our area. It was a routine I had become accustomed to. I always looked forward to seeing him in his uniform. In the end, I considered his presence at my graduation something very special. I had no one else there to cheer me on, except for my foster parents.

By that time, Mother and Daddy had come to know and like Michael, but for some reason, and one I couldn't put my finger on, they seemed to be somewhat reluctant regarding our relationship; something that later proved rather consequential.

*   *   *   *   *

It was a Friday afternoon when I arrived for my interview and battery of tests for the private secretary position at Armstrong Cork Company. A neighbor man who was employed by the same company kindly drove me to my interview and graciously offered to take me home again. His position with the company afforded him some extra perks, which included not having to punch a time clock. The interview was more frightening to me than the "dive-bombing bat" that entered our home in Reading Junction one night, forcing me to take cover under the sheets in my parents' bed. As I sat with my legs crossed, pencil and shorthand pad in hand, in front of the executive with whom I had the interview, he began dictating three consecutive letters. He talked so fast that I was forced to memorize some of the words and go on to the next ones. Every time he took a breath or said "ah," I quickly wrote the word above the shorthand symbol, in the event I couldn't read my writing later on. I was definitely intimidated. When he completed dictating the letters, I was directed to a room where a manual typewriter sat on a table. There was just enough paper and envelopes to complete the assignment and not one piece more.

There was no correction tape. A bottle of "whiteout" stood alone like a miniature snowman in a black top hat on the desk beside me. I began to translate.

After completing the assignment, I proudly took the documents to Mr. Thatcher, the executive, for his approval. I waited as he read what I had typed. He stopped and, with a semi-frown on his face, looked straight at me.

"You have done a very nice job, Leta; however, you forgot one of the most important things in any correspondence. Would you like to look at these letters and tell me what you think is missing?"

He handed me the letters, and after reading all three letters twice, I couldn't come up with the "most important missing things." As I handed them back to him, I admitted that I was unable to determine what was missing; he obliged me.

"The date, the date, the very important date!" He almost sang his response.

"Oh, I am so sorry, Mr. Thatcher. I will type those in right now."

"No, Leta, that's fine. You did an amazing translation. I talked much faster than I normally do, and I didn't expect perfection, this time. I am well pleased with the interview. Can you begin work next week?"

With a great deal of excitement, I replied, "Yes, of course I can."

"Good. I will have Helen, my secretary, whose shoes you will be filling, show you around today, if you have some extra time?"

"Yes, I'd like that," I assured him.

How impressive, I thought, as I was shown around the most private executive offices. Everyone was very friendly. I was even going to be assigned my own private office next to Mr. Thatcher's office. All of a sudden, I couldn't wait to have my teeth fixed, buy some nice clothes, and talk Mother and Daddy into buying me a car. Surely, I would have to have a car to get to work.

After the tour ended, I contacted the office where my neighbor worked, and we arranged to meet in the parking lot for the trip home. I couldn't wait to get home and announce to my parents and my friends that I had gotten the job.

It became clear that evening that I wouldn't be getting a car. The neighbor who had graciously offered to take me for my job interview had also made arrangements for me to travel with him to work each day, as long as I would help pay for the gas, saving my parents the expense of buying me a car.

I couldn't wait to share my good news with Michael.

*   *   *   *   *

Michael and I had decided to go to a special place for dinner that weekend. It was a beautiful castle overlooking a city some forty miles from Bucherville. Apart from the food, it was also known for its "lookout areas" that surrounded the castle. The large towering stone structure sat on top of a high hill (a trifle short of a mountain) and provided a spectacular view of the city below. It was so high that, at night, the city lights looked like fields covered with fireflies. There were convertibles and sedan cars parked in just about every space that provided a view of that magnificent sight; and each car contained a single occupant . . . or at least that's how it appeared. However, that turned out to be an aberration. The backdrop of tall trees, starlit skies, and the firefly-studded abyss below brought two people so close together it created a single silhouette.

After a wonderful dinner, Michael drove his car into the only available lookout space left. He turned off the motor, and we became a single silhouette. We remained there until the castle lights dimmed, and the lanterns that lined the road to the castle made their last flickering effort to illuminate the way home.

Michael and I had a wonderful relationship. I looked to him as my protector, and he evidently loved taking care of me. He never expected me to betray my covenant of purity with God . . . but neither was he devoid of passion. Temptation would rear its head quite often, but we always managed to refrain from any indecorous behavior. I adored and respected him, and I never doubted for one minute how he felt about me. With him, I felt safe and secure.

Michael hadn't shared my enthusiasm about going to work for Armstrong Cork Company. The company employed a fair number of sales trainees from all over the country. They were handsome upcoming businessmen, trained in domestic and international sales, and that aspect of my employment concerned Michael. The trainees occupied a very large mansion, with all the trimmings, on the outskirts of the city where the company was located. It was common knowledge that a baby grand piano stood in the middle of the great room and was the centerpiece for many weekend sing-along parties. It was large enough to accommodate a line of dancers doing the "Bunny-Hop," with plenty of space left over. If you got invited to their "private club," you were considered part of the in-crowd. I had a hard time convincing Michael that he had nothing to worry about, after I had told him about the trainees and the mansion. As it turned out, I was the one who should have been concerned, and it had nothing to do with my job or the trainees at Armstrong Cork Company.

*   *   *   *   *

I began my job with that prestigious company as Mr. Thatcher's private secretary. I purchased several professional looking outfits and the high-heeled shoes to go with them. In the department where I worked, everyone was well dressed. The job that I had acquired was an enviable one, particularly since it became mine fresh out of high school. It was immensely rewarding to be able to use all the secretarial skills I had excelled in. I could hardly wait until I received my first paycheck. I determined to use some of it to begin work on my teeth, and to purchase a car. Of course, they were grandiose plans, for soon after I opened the envelope and had my first check in my hand, it looked like someone else had made a withdrawal from it first, and of course, they had. I couldn't believe what I had earned, but more unbelievable was the amount left over. Well, I thought, no way was I going to be afford a car or dental work. I would just have to save money for a while and hope that eventually my plans would come to fruition.

One evening, after returning home from a very long day at work, and looking forward to sharing some of my day's accomplishments with Michael, I walked into a room that smelled of death. I saw the same pain on the face of my mother that I remembered seeing the day she had to tell me I was someone else's child.

Daddy had already left for who knows where, leaving Mother to explain the reason for the morbid fog that hung over our house. She asked me to sit down. Then she said she had something to tell me. That alone was a definite indication to me that some major catastrophe had taken place. I found myself holding my breath. I also found myself pitying her. She always seemed to be left alone to deal with the unpleasant situations in our home.

"I—really don't know how to tell you this—Leta—but I must tell you, for your own good. We—found out today that—Michael—is married."

I immediately reacted in complete disbelief at what I had heard.

"What? What do you mean, married?" I almost shouted. "Of course he isn't married. Where in the world did you ever hear that rumor?" I demanded to know.

She looked so forlorn as she attempted to convince me. "Yes, Leta, it is the truth. He really is married, and you can't see him anymore."

That was the first "you can't" I had ever heard coming from either of my parents.

I refused to believe what she told me; and there was only one way to find out the truth. My hands shook as I picked up the telephone and called the State Police Barracks where Michael worked. The policeman on desk duty informed me that he was out at the time, but that he would give him a message for me. I said, "This is Leta. Please tell Michael I need to talk to him as soon as possible; it is urgent."

Memories of the day I overheard my classmates talking on the playground near the outhouse, at the one-room schoolhouse in Reading Junction, returned. But this time I didn't run away; I waited, counting the tick-tocks coming from the wall clock, until Michael's phone call finally came. On the first ring, I picked up the phone and asked him to please come to the house right away, that I had something to tell him. He said that he would come as soon as possible.

Michael arrived about an hour later, and before his finger could depress the button on the doorbell, I opened the door.

"Let's go somewhere where we can talk," I said.

He didn't ask what was so important that he had to make a special trip to my house, which I found very strange. We drove into the country and ended up parking in some church parking lot. It was dark. That was in my favor. I didn't want to see his face when I confronted him about what I had heard.

"Michael, are you married?"

It was a grievous inquisition. I waited for an admission . . . or an accusation hopefully denied.

"Leta," he said, as he reached for my face and drew me close to him.

"No, no, I don't want to know." I begged him not to tell me.

"I knew this time would come, but I had hoped it would be much later, long after my divorce was final. It's true, I am married, yes, but—"

I interrupted, "What do you mean—but? You are either married or you're not; there's no room for a 'but' in there anywhere. Why didn't you tell me? I've been dating a married man, Michael. Please say it isn't true."

"But I love you, Leta, and more than anything I want to take care of you for the rest of your life. I didn't mean to deceive you, I truly didn't. And you might as well hear it all, I was also married before. This is going to be my second divorce."

Oh my God, I thought, *what in the world have I gotten myself in for? What am I going to do?* I had already fallen in love with him.

"I can't believe you waited all this time to tell me you are married, and you've been married twice." My heart burned like Chicago. I pounded his chest with my fists as the tears ran down my face; he just dabbed at my eyes with his handkerchief and waited.

"You know we can never see each other again, Michael. I cannot see you as long as you are still married." He reached out to me, but I recoiled, as if his touch was suddenly poisonous. So great was my sorrow and my disappointment.

"Leta, if only you hadn't found out, I would have soon been free and we would not have had to go through all of this."

"Michael, tell me, exactly when did you intend to tell me about your wives?"

"I planned to tell you everything . . . after my divorce was behind me. I know, for a policeman, that is probably a cowardly way of doing things, but I just didn't want to hurt you; I love you."

I asked him to take me home. He started the car, while I wished we were in California so we could spend three thousand more miles together before we said our good-byes.

We drove in silence. My tongue occasionally licked a salty tear from the corner of my lips. I sat in a state of disbelief, unable to comprehend all that had happened. I had been so excited about my new job, about plans for a future with Michael, and for the goals that I had set for myself. Now there was no joy or expectations, only an emptied tomorrow.

When the car came to a stop in front of my house, the last words we would say to each other seemed frozen in time. There didn't seem to be any right words for an unhappy ending. I was not ever going to see Michael again. Even after his divorce became final, I didn't know if I could ever trust him again.

I don't remember how long we sat there, and my mind refused to take note of his leaving, but I clearly remember his promise to watch over me. In light of all that had happened, it didn't seem to me that he would make a very good guardian angel. I was certain that he would continue patrolling my neighborhood, my house and my car . . . a constant reminder of his presence in my life. He didn't disappoint me. I was frequently aware of his patrol car passing our house and behind my car coming home from work. I knew that it was his way of hoping to reunite with me somewhere down the road. He called many times, but I refused to talk to him.

Disappointment was beginning to be one of life's staples . . . and I resented it. I resented not having a close relationship with a real mother and father with whom I could share the trivial experiences of my life, as well as my deepest concerns . . . and in return, receive the wisdom of their many years of experience. And even though my foster mother was good to me, I blamed her, my dad, and everyone else for my unhappiness. I was particularly reminded of those things every time I felt rejection, as though life had dealt me someone else's hand.

Consequences of my own rebellion, disobedience, and selfishness were yet to come.

. . . NINE . . .

It didn't take long for me to discover that Armstrong Cork Company had an active thespian group. I made it a point to convey my interest in acting to several co-workers who were involved with the theatre group, however, and much to my disappointment, the major parts had already been filled for their upcoming production. Only mildly appeased, I was given an opportunity to audition for a singing and dancing part in the same show.

My name appeared in fine print under "others" in the playbill that was handed out to hundreds of people as they entered the door of the theatre for Opening Night. I had never been satisfied being number two in anything, let alone number fifty-two in a row of singers and dancers! But number fifty-two danced and sang her heart out!

Apparently I made some kind of an impression, besides the one I left on the floor when I fell during one of the first rehearsals, because they asked me to read for a part in the next production. I was so excited. I found acting much more gratifying than taking shorthand.

Working with girls that had far more experience in just about everything than I did laid the groundwork for some bad choices in behavior and my selection of friends. I soon accepted invitations to go out after work with a group of girls to a local bar and have my share of sloe gin fizzes. It became my favorite mixed drink. I can only conclude that the spiritual seeds planted in my life earlier yielded some good fruit, sparing me from abusing alcohol. In addition, I added Kool cigarettes to my repertoire of unhealthy habits. Learning to smoke, and then "inhaling" (which I admit doing) turned out to be a sick-inducing, self-abasing experience. Why I ever put myself through that is beyond me. The pain far outweighed the pleasure, as you will see.

Feeling accepted was something entirely new to me and I did not handle it well. I was easily persuaded to join in activities that I would have otherwise avoided, had I not gotten involved with friends who were about as spiritually removed as witches from prayer meetings. But I was slowly being inducted into the "in-crowd."

It was an enormous honor the day I received my first invitation to the Armstrong trainees' mansion party. It was an evening to remember.

The music was great, and we all Bunny-Hopped around the piano in the great room. Never had I been in the presence of so many handsome men at one time. I even got to dance my first dance with a local judge's son. It was a male smorgasbord! There was no promiscuous behavior that I witnessed, just a lot of fun. I returned to that mansion many times thereafter to join in festivities of one kind or another. A lot of future world-traveling businessmen came out of that group of Armstrong trainees, one in particular with whom I've stayed in touch over the years. As a matter of fact, he married one of my closest friends (the same friend who fell into a barrel of rotten potatoes while playing OFFS) and who, many years later, put up a tremendous battle against cancer, and lost.

*   *   *   *   *

One day while working on reports for Mr. Thatcher, the buzzer, beckoning me into his office, interrupted me. He politely informed me that there was a position available as secretary to two men in the Packaging Department, located in a building some distance from the main office where I had been working, and he was going to personally recommend me for the job.

I never knew for sure whether or not I got that job as a result of my adeptness at fulfilling double secretarial assignments, or the fact that he had simply been concerned about me. The older employees definitely had some influence on me, and I wanted to believe that Mr. Thatcher was exercising a fatherly regard for my well-being. Either way, I found myself in the employ of two very busy department heads. It was all I could do to keep up with my work. One of the good things that came from the move, however, was my introduction to twin sisters who were just a little bit older than I was and whose family owned a number of riding horses. They lived in nearby Columbia and boarded their horses a few miles away at a local farm. When I finally got an invitation to go riding one Saturday afternoon, I realized the horse I chose to ride was a far cry from my daddy's back. Not to be outdone, or out-jumped, I followed the leader and jumped my horse over every obstacle that got in the way, much to my demise. I was not oblivious to the upcoming tree that had fallen across the path, just simply too proud to go around it. As it turned out, I jumped the tree, and the horse remained behind. It was a rough landing. All I had to show for my horseback-riding expertise was a broken collarbone. *El fin.*

*   *   *   *   *

It soon became apparent that I would have to buy an automobile, especially since I hadn't gotten very far on a horse. The old family Pontiac just wasn't up to going all the places I wanted to go. Every time Mother or Daddy wanted to go anywhere, I had to be somewhere else. It seemed like an opportune time for me to invest in an automobile. I couldn't afford a new one on my salary, so I was compelled to consider a used car, and financial help from my foster parents.

The Saturday morning after I expressed my desire to purchase a car, my dad and I went car shopping. Our first and last stop was at a local Chrysler-Plymouth dealer, located several blocks from our home on Fulton Street. As soon as we drove into the parking lot, a bright red 1947 Plymouth convertible caught my eye. By all appearances, it was evidently well loved by its previous owner . . . or the car dealer did a very good job at making it look that way. I only hoped that it was a car I could afford to make payments on. The salesman met us in the parking lot. "He's already counting his sales commission," my dad said, as the young man came out the door of the showroom.

In less than two hours, I became the proud owner of a bright red Plymouth convertible. I already saw myself, blonde hair blowing in the wind—in a bright red convertible—getting more attention than was good for me . . . and I liked the feeling.

I could hardly wait until the next day when I could show off my new purchase to my fellow employees. Naturally, everyone fussed over it and thought it was the perfect car for me. It also was the only thing on my mind that day, and my work suffered for it. I couldn't wait until five o'clock to get behind the wheel.

You know, I truly believe "God'll git ya' for the things you don't git yourself." "Pride cometh before the fall" is written in the Bible, but in my case, it "cameth" before the crash!

I was distracted as I backed out of my parking space that day. With my car in reverse, and forgetting to look both ways in a crowded parking lot, I suddenly heard the most disturbing sound. "Oh my God!" I said out loud. "I hit that car! The first day I've driven my new car to work and I've just wrecked my car!" I was devastated. Sure enough, when I got out to examine the damage, it was extensive. I began to cry. There was only one thing for me to do: wait for the person whose vehicle I had hit to come out from work, and hopefully I could win his sympathy. I did not want him to call the police, and I sure had no intention of calling them.

While I sat waiting, I thought of calling Michael, but then I realized that the area was out of his jurisdiction. But, oh, how comforting his presence would have been at that moment; he would have known what to do. I would just have to wait, I decided. With my luck, I figured the person who owned the car would be working late and I would have to sit and wait for several hours. And that is exactly what happened.

An older gentleman who appeared to be a salesman in a three-piece suit, carrying a briefcase, was walking in the direction of my car, and I was sure that he was the man who owned the automobile I had hit. I immediately got out of my car and met him face to face. But before I could say a word, he exclaimed: "What in the world happened here? I just picked up my new car yesterday."

"Yes, well, so did I," I replied. "Mine may not be the latest model like yours, but it's just as new to me. I'm sorry." I continued to explain. "I was distracted and didn't realize I had turned the wheel as far as I had; please, do you think we can take care of this without calling the police?" I begged.

"Of course. I don't see any necessity for reporting it since it happened here in the private parking lot, but I must have your insurance information."

I immediately introduced a little salesmanship of my own.

"Would you consider allowing me to pay for the damages without reporting it to the insurance company? I know the cost of my insurance will really go up if they know I've been in an accident that was my fault."

After I gave him a little of my life's story, just enough for him to take pity on me, he agreed to those arrangements.

I really dreaded to go home that night. But where else was I going to go? All my friends had already left their offices, so I had no choice but to go home and face the firing squad. Thankfully, my car could still be driven, as could the gentleman's car that I damaged.

All I had to do was walk in the back door, and Daddy, who was sitting in his assigned seat at the kitchen table reading the evening paper, looked up at me and asked, "Well, how bad is it?"

I was dumfounded. I had never credited him with extrasensory perception before, but you better believe, I was reconsidering.

He walked outside with me to view the damage. I explained how it happened, expecting to be lambasted out of town; instead, he simply said, "Well, I know this guy at the other end of town who they say is one of the best auto body men anywhere. I'll tell you where he is and you can do the rest. You can also pay for it."

I was relieved, to say the least, that Daddy hadn't ranted and raved as he sometimes did, but I suppose the fact that I was out in the world earning my own money determined where his responsibility ended and mine began.

The following evening, on my way home from work, I decided to scout out the body shop Daddy had referred to. I did not expect it would be open after five, so I felt safe in cruising by the place.

As I turned off Main Street into a somewhat desolate alley, I thought, *Boy, this guy's business sure is hidden away.* I checked the address again on the piece of paper I had on the passenger seat, and it appeared to be the right address. Halfway down the alley, I saw several men standing over the most unusual-looking car I had ever laid eyes on, and one very intimidating-looking German shepherd guard dog. My eyes focused on the shepherd's teeth, which displayed an impressive gum line. As I pulled my car to the side, my hesitation in opening the door began attracting some attention. Soon a crew cut, coverall-clad man ordered the dog to retreat to a spot inside the door of the building. With that danger removed, I proceeded to exit my vehicle. My first question was not, "Is this Brogan's Body Shop?" Instead, I asked, "What kind of car is that?"

My question seemed to humor the male spectators. They laughed, as if to poke fun at a girl asking about a man's automobile, something they obviously believed I knew nothing about. You would have thought I asked to see the hair on their chests, the way they had responded. But the crew cut, coverall-clad man seemed interested in satisfying my question.

"It's an Allard," he answered. "Have you ever seen one before?"

"No, but it sure is different looking. It looks like a fast one."

"Oh, no doubt about that," he said, with a proud grin on his face. "It is as light as a feather and has a big Chrysler high-powered engine beneath its hood. It's fast all right."

The car really reminded me of a casket with three wide leather belts around it to insure that the body didn't escape. It was a shiny chrome casket on four large thick wheels. Its appearance was demonic. But it apparently was something very special.

I had almost forgotten why I was there, as I stood admiring the Allard. But I was soon reminded.

"What can I do for you? Not that I need to ask," he said, as he looked at my car.

"Well, I just bought this car, and the first day I drove it to work, wouldn't you know, I was distracted and I turned my wheel too far and sideswiped the car next to me. My dad said that Mr. Brogan is the best body man in town, and I thought I would check the place out on my way home from work today. I didn't expect it to be open. Is the owner around?"

"I'm Brogan," he said.

Just then, something I had heard came back to me. I recalled some of my girlfriends from Bucherville talking about a Mitch Brogan. They said he drove fast cars, had lots of money, could date any girl he wanted to, had his own automobile dealership, was a decorated war hero, and was engaged to the same girl for at least seven years, but she still hadn't been able to get him to marry her. There had been two such men in Bucherville, they reported; both were good-looking, unmarried, owned businesses, and both considered to be "good catches." I was pretty sure that this was the same Mitch Brogan they had talked about. The other name mentioned was Gene Norton. *Well, the girls and I will have something to talk about now,* I thought.

All of these thoughts were going through my head while Mr. Brogan was examining my car. He rubbed his hands over the car the same way you would caress a woman. He didn't stop at just the damaged area, but was rubbing his hands back and forth over the hood, the trunk, and then the roof of the car. "Gosh," I said to him, "I didn't come for a complete physical examination. I hope the whole car doesn't need painted. Please tell me you musn't paint the whole car."

"No, but your car needs wax very badly."

With that, he went into his place of business and came back with some kind of form in his hand. He began writing down some figures, presumably what it was going to cost to have my car repaired and waxed. I waited for the unfavorable news.

"Well," he said, "it looks as though it will cost you about two hundred and fifty dollars to have that crunch repaired."

My mouth must have dropped to my chest. "Two hundred and fifty dollars?" I exclaimed. "There is no way I can afford that."

At that moment I must have looked shocked . . . as well as poor.

"Well, I'll tell you what I'll do," he said. "If you buy the cleaner and wax for your car, and you clean and wax it yourself after I repair your damage, I will see what I can do about the cost of repairing your car. Only under one condition—that I get to check out your wax job after you've finished it."

Why would he do that for me? I wondered. It sounded like I wouldn't have to pay for the repairs, or at least, not very much . . . and all I had to do was wax my car.

"That sounds like a pretty good deal for me. Are you sure you want to do that? I know I can't afford to pay those repairs on my salary."

"Where do you work?"

"Armstrong Cork Company," I replied.

He handed me a copy of his estimate. I noticed that he had my name written down at the top of the form. How in the world had he known my name, I wondered. He hadn't even asked me what it was, and I hadn't volunteered it. Before I could ask him, the shepherd came out of the building, protesting my presence and my closeness to his master. After that unexpected interruption, he told me to drop the car off that night and put the key in the door slot, or I could drop it off the following morning, whichever suited me. Then he focused on the shepherd. I took that as my cue to leave.

I was greatly bothered by the body-man's obvious familiarity with my name. But my questioning would have to wait until another time. I was just relieved that perhaps I wouldn't have to pay two hundred and fifty dollars to have my car repaired. I also knew I had my work cut out for me. I had never cleaned or waxed a car in my life.

For as long as my car was indisposed, our neighbor, Mr. Foster, again offered to pick me up each day for our ride to Armstrong Cork Company.

*   *   *   *   *

One day while I was working, I was browsing through the Lancaster newspaper in the ladies' lounge, and an announcement caught my eye. Franklin and Marshall College Greenroom, one of the best theatrical organizations of its kind in the area, under the direction of the brilliant Darrell Larson, was announcing tryout dates for their upcoming production of "By Hex," a musical folk-play. The article included names such as: Howard Blankman, John Rengier (attorney and writer), Jan Forry (choreographer), Cardell Cook, and Don Trostle (accomplished musician), all well-known contributors to the art and entertainment world.

I read the ad with great interest . . . then I read it again. I cut out the announcement and stuck it in my pocket. Then I questioned myself: Would I be good enough to perform for such well-known and experienced entertainment people? I was not very hopeful.

Up until then, I had gotten every part I had ever auditioned for, as well as having been asked to read for the next Armstrong presentation. So I decided that the only way I would ever know was to answer the newspaper ad.

I called the listed phone number. I was told that I had to set up an appointment for an audition. I was instructed to provide the sheet music for any song that I would enjoy singing, and also to be prepared to read for several parts. I was so nervous when I hung up. *How in the world will I ever be able to audition in front of all those notable people?* I asked myself. It was different than the Armstrong show, "Girl Crazy"; there I seemed to blend in with all the other singers and dancers. Fortunately for me, my audition was not scheduled for several weeks. That would give me time to rehearse in front of a mirror, and also time for my car repairs to be completed. I wasn't sure that my dad would be willing to escort me to a play audition. My parents weren't exactly thrilled with my interest in the theatre, unlike when I was a young girl on the makeshift stage in Reading Junction.

A week passed, and I still hadn't heard from Mr. Brogan about the status of my car repairs. However, I did hear from Michael.

He stopped by the house one evening while on patrol. He said he liked my new car, and he was sorry about the accident. He asked me why I hadn't called him. I wanted neither the police or insurance company to know about the accident, yet he seemed to know all about it.

"How did you know about the car and my accident?" I asked him.

"You forget, I inspect garages, along with arresting speeders and criminals," he explained. "I stopped in at Mitch Brogan's garage and saw your car there. He told me what happened. Not to worry, I won't reveal your secret. And if you recall, I promised to always protect and watch over you, and I am keeping that promise."

"Oh Michael, I certainly didn't think you were serious about that." As a matter of fact, I had believed him.

"I was very serious; I am still serious. You're my life, Leta, always remember that."

With that, he touched my face with his black-gloved hand and smiled so warmly that I wanted to run into his arms. But I dared not.

...Ten...

It was Monday evening of the third week since taking my car to Brogan's Body Shop. I was becoming a little more than anxious. My audition with the Franklin and Marshall Greenroom was scheduled for the end of the week.

Having grown impatient, I decided to check on the progress of my car, but I did not want to reveal my impatience by running into Mr. Brogan, so my plan was to observe Brogan's Body Shop from a street that paralleled the alley where the shop was located. As I approached the alley from Main Street, my eyes caught sight of a beautiful maroon Porsche convertible sitting in front of a restaurant. For some reason, cars had always fascinated me, especially sports cars, and I could name almost all of them . . . with the exception of the Allard, of course. I even wondered at times whether or not I had petrol, instead of blood, running through my veins; that's how much I loved automobiles. I also toyed with the idea that perhaps I had inherited my love for driving from my birth father . . . still an unknown part of my life.

The restaurant was about a half block beyond the turnoff to Brogan's Body Shop; the extra steps didn't deter me one bit, not when it came to a fine-looking sports car. When I reached the Porsche, I stood marveling at the sleek beetle-shaped lines. I leaned over and smelled the seats. *Real leather,* I said to myself, *no doubt about that.* The car was impeccably clean. I looked up the street, and then down the street, like someone who was planning to steal something. Not seeing anyone around, except for the traffic normally found on a main thoroughfare, I decided to open the unlocked passenger door and slide in. No harm in getting a little taste of affluence, I rationalized.

In the midst of my covetous thoughts and meddlesome behavior, I nearly fainted when I heard a deep voice from above. At first I thought it was God Himself. He began to reprimand me for my forwardness in sitting in a car that did not belong to me. At first I thought he was angry, but then his voice took on an amused tone. Too embarrassed to look up, and hoping I would not be recognized, I sat motionless, expecting to be lifted up by the collar, hoisted out, and deposited on the sidewalk. As I proceeded to exit the car by my own volition, I looked up and into the face of none other than Mitch Brogan himself.

"Mr. Brogan, I am so sorry," I sputtered, "but I just couldn't resist sitting in this Porsche." As if it would make a difference, I offered yet another explanation. "I didn't know it was your car . . . honest. That was a very bold thing for me to do, but I just love sports cars; I am so sorry."

"Well, now that you've warmed the seat, how would you like to go for a ride?"

"What . . . are you serious?" I asked, thinking he was just trying to make me feel really bad about what I had done.

"Of course I'm serious. Come on, get in."

I had completely forgotten about my car by then.

He held the door for me as I climbed back in. I was almost afraid to look at him; but when I did, I couldn't help notice how neatly he was dressed. His clothes appeared starched, pressed, and very carefully chosen. His hair had been freshly cut, but there wasn't very much of it; it was very short and it looked like how you would expect a teddy bear to feel. He looked over at me and smiled. He had caught me looking at him.

We took off down the street, and I mean, we TOOK OFF down the street! My head flew backwards as he accelerated out of the parking space. I grabbed hold of the "sissy bar" that was located at arm's length from where I was sitting and held on for dear life.

We ended up on the Pennsylvania Turnpike, traveling at speeds I had never driven before. The song "Teach Me Tonight" was playing on the radio. He told me it was his favorite song, and that I should listen to the words. I did, and that song came to have special meaning to me several months later. I was also thinking about words from another song: "Oh, what a night it was, it really was, such a night," words sung by Johnnie Ray, the same ones I had written over and over again on a sheet of paper as punishment for skipping school to attend his concert. Those lyrics came close to describing just how I felt that night. The ride lasted longer than I anticipated and turned out to be the "mother of all rides." By the time we got back to the body shop, my long hair was a tangled mess, and I was all but numb from the experience. I felt like I had just completed the Indy 500, and won.

"Here," he said, as he handed me a large yellow comb from his glove compartment, "you can use this one."

"How very convenient. What else do you carry in there?" I asked, a little sarcastically.

He just smiled.

It took me some time to remove the tangles; it also gave me an opportunity to take stock of this man who had just given me the ride of my life. His eyes were as dark as his hair, and his skin was very tan. He also had an abundance of muscles . . . someone who obviously worked out on a regular basis. I had no idea how old he was, but I found him rather good looking, and he certainly seemed to fit the available bachelor description my classmates had given me at one of our pajama parties . . . which I had long forgotten about.

Remembering why I had walked to the body shop in the first place, I finally asked Mr. Brogan about my car. He said he would deliver it to my house the following night, and reminded me of our deal; he also asked me to call him Mitch, instead of Mr. Brogan. I hadn't forgotten about the "deal"; the "Mitch" part, however, was a little harder to remember.

He offered to drive me home, because it had grown late and dark. As he pulled into our driveway, I noticed a police car sitting across the street about a half block from my house. I knew it had to be Michael. I thanked . . . Mitch . . . for the great Porsche ride, and told him that I would look forward to getting my car the following evening. He drove off rather slowly . . . understandably so, and disappeared.

I had forgotten to ask him how he had come to know my name.

*   *   *   *   *

The police car pulled into the space where Mitch's Porsche had been. I waited.

Michael rolled down the window of his police car and looked warningly into my eyes.

"Leta, I have some advice for you. You won't live long if you continue riding with Mitch Brogan. He is a wild man in an automobile. I have arrested him many times for speeding. He does things in an automobile even race car drivers aren't crazy enough to do. You'd be doing yourself a favor, and me, if you didn't make a habit of that, especially if you're interested in staying alive."

"Michael, I know you have been looking out for me, and I really do appreciate it, but I can take care of myself." I don't know why I felt I owed him an explanation, but I continued. "He was just bringing me back from checking on my car repairs." I wasn't being quite truthful, but I thought that explanation would prove a bit more palatable.

"O.K., if that's what you say. But I'm telling you, you better think twice about being seen with him."

"Michael, no pun intended, but I don't think you are the person to be issuing that kind of warning to me."

"I care about you, Leta. That's all that I'm saying."

It was difficult for me to believe his sincerity; after all, he was the same person who had deceived and hurt me. I still cared for Michael, I had to admit, but I just couldn't allow myself to give in to him. Dating him had already caused minor character damage to my life, since apparently I had been one of the few who hadn't known he was married. I was determined to have my reputation . . . and my car . . . repaired to their original condition.

"Michael, you must stop following me," I warned. "I know you don't look at it like that, but I do. You were very good at looking after me, Michael, and I did feel secure with you once, but I can't see you any more, not after what happened; don't you understand that?"

I half pitied him; the other half I used to feel sorry for myself.

"Guess I'd better get back on the streets, Leta. Sleep warm and safe."

I felt awkward standing alone in the middle of the driveway watching his car disappear. My throat burned. I couldn't hold back the tears. I had a difficult time getting to sleep that night.

*   *   *   *   *

The phone rang Tuesday night. It was Mitch. He informed me that my car was ready to be picked up. He said he was unable to deliver it, but that I could pick it up after eight o'clock that night. My dad agreed to drop me off at the body shop around eight o'clock, as Mitch had suggested.

There was only a dim light coming from the office of Brogan's Body Shop. But the same German shepherd's teeth and gum exhibit was still showing. I didn't expect Mitch to be anywhere around, since he said he was unable to deliver my car, but much to my surprise, he came walking out of the building, and with a one-word command, the shepherd cowered and backed into the building. *Wow,* I thought, *his dog is really obedient, and obviously very afraid of him.* But I was grateful that he had been there to intercept the animal. My eyes immediately caught sight of my Plymouth. Together, we walked over to the car. I was impressed. I really didn't know too much about auto body work, but there was absolutely no way you would have guessed that my car had been damaged. It looked terrific. I was all the more impressed when he told me there would be no charge.

"No charge at all?" I replied. "Are you sure I don't owe you a little something?" I felt a trifle guilty . . . just a trifle.

"No," he said, "we had a deal. You can pay me for this wax and cleaner and I'll explain how you go about using it; remember, you promised to show me the car when you're finished."

I paid for the materials, took the bag containing the wax and cleaner, and then asked for the keys to my car.

"What are you up to tonight?" he asked.

"Nothing in particular. Just picking up my car, then home to rehearse for an audition that I have with Franklin and Marshall Greenroom on Friday."

"Would you like to go for a ride and get something to eat or drink? I don't have any plans either."

I thought about what Michael had said. I thought about the girlfriend and what she would think if she knew her boyfriend was riding around with some young girl while she sat home alone. But for some reason, I really wanted to go with him.

"Sure, why not?" I replied.

I followed him into his garage where his beautiful Porsche sat. There wasn't a speck of dust on it.

"Boy, you must spend all your time cleaning your car. I can't promise you mine will look like that, but I'll do my best."

"I'll make sure yours looks as good as mine, how's that?"

Is he flirting? Yes, I believe he is, I thought.

The convertible top was down. He opened the door for me and helped me into the car. He lifted the manual garage door, got into the car, and drove it outside. He returned to close the door, and we were gone.

He looked at me and said, "Until we're out of town, keep your head low so no one can see you."

I could only guess that he didn't want anyone to know he was with another girl. I obeyed . . . just like his dog. After leaving town, I was told it was safe to sit up.

I was amazed how he took the corners of every turn with the expertise of a race car driver. He knew exactly when to shift gears. As a matter of fact, he was so good that he could shift gears without depressing the clutch. He obviously had a love affair with his car. I loved the throaty sound of the Porsche engine.

We arrived at a bar-type restaurant in Yorktown. Because it was dark, I didn't recognize any of the buildings from the short time I had spent in that town with Jean Marlow and Bassie. I did mention to Mitch, in few words, that my birth mother lived in Yorktown, but he didn't seem particularly interested in that bit of information. Instead, he assured me that the place we were going to eat had the best burgers anywhere, and great beer. I opted for my favorite, sloe gin fizz.

"Oh, what a night it was, it really was." Just like in the song.

*   *   *   *   *

I learned more about Mitch Brogan than I really wanted to know. He told me he was engaged to the same girl for seven years, and that she expected him to marry her, but that he had been less sure about making a lifelong commitment. He told me he had been a paratrooper in World War II, but not "just" a paratrooper—a 101st, 506th paratrooper. He had been awarded the Purple Heart for the injuries he sustained during the liberation of Holland, France, and Belgium. He told me how he and his fellow troopers had been preparing to jump out of a transport plane while flying over a specified drop zone during the war, when all of a sudden they became the enemy's target. He showed me scars on both sides of his nose where shrapnel had gone in one side and out the other. He said he considered himself very lucky, since he was one of the few who lived after jumping out of the plane that day. He said that nearly his entire platoon was killed before they even jumped that day.

He told me how he had shot a young sniper out of a church bell tower in St. Marie Eglise, France, where she (yes, she) had been "picking off" American paratroopers as they hung in trees by their parachute chords. They died before they had a chance to cut themselves free.

He told me how he wanted to go back to Germany and look up the shop owner whose leg he had shot off, but hadn't killed, during that terrible war. He was confident that he would one day locate that man and they would sit and exchange war stories.

He wanted to revisit the place where his best friend and fellow paratrooper's English girlfriend had worked, in hopes of finding her.

He was also confident that he would one day locate an unexploded grenade he had tossed at a German tank. He said he had taken a mental picture of where it fell, and he vowed to return to find it one day.

But most moving was his story about the young man who had saved his life. The one who had stood up from his bunker and had taken a round from a German tank after telling Mitch and his men to take cover. The men whose lives that young man saved planted the dead soldier's gun in the ground like a flagpole and placed his helmet on top of the gun as a monument to his bravery and in memory of the sacrifice he made. Mitch was determined to go back to Holland to see if the monument still stood where he had helped plant it.

He told me how he had been riddled with shrapnel, and that some of it had actually ended up in his heart, unable to be removed without endangering his life. It was likely that his life expectancy would be shortened as a result, he told me.

Suddenly, I found myself in awe of Mitch Brogan. As we sat eating and drinking, I developed an almost idol-like admiration and respect for this brave, courageous, good-looking man. It was unbelievable that I was fortunate enough to be sitting there in his company. He was tough. He was a protector. He also had impeccable manners. All I had to do was just sit there and look pretty. He did all the rest, from ordering my food, to instructing me from which side of a T-bone steak to eat first. I was overwhelmed, to say the least.

The one thing that still bothered me was how he had known my name, long before I had given it to him. I decided to find out.

"Mitch? There is something I have been wanting to ask you ever since the day I brought my car in to be repaired."

"Ask away."

"How did you know my name when you prepared the estimate on my car?"

"That's a good question. I just don't know if I want to tell you just yet."

"Why? Is the reason indecent or something?"

"Some might think so."

"Come on, that's not fair," I begged. "You can tell me; it couldn't be all that bad, could it?"

"Well, I guess not."

I braced myself, not knowing what to expect. I almost wished that I hadn't asked him. But my curiosity had to be satisfied.

"Well, I have known about you for some time now; for several years, as a matter of fact. Ever since you started coming to the church where I go, I have been watching you; you've turned into a very pretty young lady, too, I might add. I used to say to myself, Mitch, one day you are going to marry that girl."

"What? You're kidding."

Just then, someone put a quarter in the jukebox, and the song "Teach Me Tonight" began to play. He took my hand and said, "Come on, let's dance. They're playing our song." We joined several other couples on the dance floor. That's when I remembered hearing that song playing on the Porsche radio the first night I went for a ride with Mitch Brogan.

I was still in a state of disbelief as he took me in his arms to dance. This older man had said he was interested in marrying me, I mused. *Surely that must be one of his lines,* I thought to myself. But by the end of the song, I had reason to believe he had meant every word.

We remained on the dance floor as the song repeated itself several times. He held me very close, and although I considered myself a great dancer, he was much greater. Never in all of my short life had I ever danced with someone who moved like he did. He had such natural rhythm, and his moves were flawless, almost as if they had been purposely choreographed for that night. The tempo changed when someone else selected another song on the jukebox. A perfect jitterbug song began to play. I thought, *This is where we sit down.* I loved to jitterbug, but I was sure that that type of dance wouldn't appeal to Mitch Brogan. I was wrong! Before long, everyone else sat down, leaving only Mitch and myself on the small dance floor. The applause was unending. I found myself being lifted over his head, swung between his legs, and spinning like a top, a human yo-yo in his hands. He never once tramped on my feet to move them, nor did he have to announce his next move. I felt it. At the end of each dance, our audience coaxed us on to the next one. He was obviously pleased with my performance, and that's exactly what it felt like, a performance. We danced until very late that night. When we were ready to leave, we were told that the drinks were on the house. They invited us back to dance again, which we did many times thereafter. It became our "haunt," as they say.

As we drove home in the wee hours of the morning, I rested my head on the back of the seat and peered into the star-filled sky. Mitch's hand left the steering wheel and took mine. He gently squeezed it, then released it.

When we got within a few miles of Bucherville, he said he noticed what appeared to be a car following us. My first thought was, *Michael*. He said, "Hold on, we're going to lose him, whoever it is." I held on to that now familiar sissy bar, while we drove at high speeds through the country trying to lose our pursuer. The Porsche literally slid through the corners sideways, but at all times, Mitch was completely in control. He owned the market on cornering.

Mitch finally told me that he had managed to lose the other sports car, and that he knew it had been one of his friends trying to see who was in the car with him. After all that intrigue, I was more frightened of being discovered with Mitch Brogan than of any mad-car maneuvers he made that night.

When Mitch dropped me off at my house, he asked to see me again. However, he told me that when he came to pick me up, he would park at the end of my street and blink his lights, and I was to walk to his car instead of him coming to pick me up in front of my house.

As I thought about this plan, I could only conclude that he did not want anyone to know he was seeing me. So I decided to broach that subject the next time I was in his company. I was reminded that he didn't owe me an explanation, and I certainly had a choice with regards to seeing him again; nevertheless, I agreed to do what he said.

Two days later, Mitch called to tell me that he had been arrested for speeding by Sgt. Michael Banks, and that Michael told him that he would be watching his every move, and also that the State Policeman had mentioned my name. Mitch wanted to know how I knew Michael Banks. Michael apparently had visited Mitch's garage many times because of Mitch's garage being a state inspection garage.

I told Mitch about the accident I had been in while in high school, which of course he had known about, but he hadn't associated Michael with the accident. Now he knew the whole story. I also knew Michael meant what he said: Mitch would have to keep his eyes on the rearview mirror from now on.

The next time Mitch and I met was at the end of Fulton Street, in response to his blinking light signal. I felt as though I was doing something terribly wrong. There he was . . . a prominent "engaged" businessman, carrying out a covert rendezvous . . . and there I was . . . a willing participant in that unscrupulous plan. I wondered how long it would be before Mother and Daddy would be waiting for me at the kitchen table and it would all end, just like it had between Michael and me.

*   *   *   *   *

Friday came and I awakened with butterflies in my stomach. It was the day of my audition with Franklin and Marshall Greenroom Productions. I had rehearsed the song "Tea for Two," a light and easy song to perform for the audition.

Mitch called me early in the morning before I left for work and wished me good luck. He had expressed his dislike for the theatre, but knew he had little, if any, influence over my decision to audition for "By Hex."

Based on the show's name, I had practiced speaking with a Pennsylvania Dutch accent every day at work, much to the amusement of my fellow employees, who placated my theatrical obsession by permitting me to practice on them.

I was feeling a lot more comfortable with my music and my accent, as the time to audition drew near. I was not a very good secretary the day of the audition; I was sure my bosses were hoping I would not make the cut and return to the job I was getting paid for. But I felt differently; I was fairly confident I would get at least some part in the play.

*   *   *   *   *

The auditions were being held in a room at a local hotel. When I arrived at the hotel, I found a ground floor parking spot and took the elevator to the fourth floor and to Room 403. As I gently knocked on the door, it opened. Inside I joined an eclectic group of individuals; some were dressed all in black, some in colors that didn't match anything; others were hardly dressed at all. A large piano sat in the middle of the room. Chairs were provided for those of us waiting our turn to sing. As the line grew shorter, I grew more terrified.

Very conspicuously planted in one corner of the room like a fica tree needing water, was a flamboyant (and some might say eccentric-looking) gentleman smoking two cigarettes. *And I thought I was nervous!* I said to myself. This most unusual character turned out to be the eminent director himself.

As I listened to the others taking their turns singing and reading, my confidence slowly returned. I was certain I could do as well, if not better.

Then it was my turn.

The piano player took my sheet music and played it through one time. After a brief introduction, I was instructed to begin singing. After hearing the songs sung by the others, I realized then that perhaps I had decided on the wrong song. Their music was much more upbeat than the traditional "Tea For Two"; nevertheless, I sang it with sparkle and ease.

I was unable to tell whether or not the music director liked my rendition of the song, or if, in fact, he even liked my voice. Instead, I was immediately directed to go into an adjoining room and read for a part.

The "Fica Tree" followed me into the next room, with only one cigarette in his mouth, but that one he had in backwards; he was struggling to light the filtered end. With a smile, I boldly took the cigarette out of his mouth and turned it around. Without so much as a word, he handed me a script and asked me to read the part of Lydia, the lead female comedy role. I became a bit unnerved when he didn't react to my good deed for the day. I thought, *Well, I guess I just blew my big chance.*

The Dutch accent came naturally; I had been talking like that since responding to the newspaper audition ad. I read several pages. The director said, "Enough, enough; we'll be in touch with you." There was nothing left for me to do but go home.

As I drove back to Bucherville, I debated with myself. *You got the part . . . well, maybe you didn't . . . but you read well . . . but maybe someone else read better . . . but you got that accent just right . . . the song . . . maybe that was the problem . . . I didn't have the right song . . . I should not have turned his cigarette around . . . that probably did it.*

Mother and Daddy were waiting to hear the outcome of the audition. I detected a hint of pride and curiosity.

"How did you make out?" Mother asked.

"I don't know; they said they will be in touch with me. That is what they always say; that usually means you won't be hearing from them, but I'll just have to wait and see."

"Did anyone call for me tonight?" I inquired.

With a questioning look, Mother replied, "No, were you expecting someone to call?"

"Not really. I think I will go out and get something to eat. I am starved."

*　　*　　*　　*　　*

As I headed for the Milk-Bar, a local gathering place, by way of Brogan's Body Shop, I noticed a car with a bubble on top, following me. I pulled to the side of the street and parked. I could only guess that it had to be Michael.

He opened the passenger side of my car and got in.

"Michael," I said, "are you following me? You know you can't keep doing this."

"Leta, I love you. I can't think about anything else. Please, can't we at least go out somewhere some night and have dinner and just talk?"

"Michael, what you really want is to get Mitch Brogan; am I right?" I asked, changing the subject.

"Someone should. He drives like an absolute maniac."

"But that's not even what this is all about, is it? You think that he and I have something going, don't you?"

"And you don't?"

"No, we don't." And that was the truth.

But I still didn't want Michael to single out Mitch for speeding just because of me; I didn't want him to catch us together either. Michael had the power to act. All I could do was react to his infringement on our privacy. I decided to plead with him not to stake out my house and to please leave Mitch Brogan alone.

His reply caught me a little off guard, and for some reason I tucked it away in my memory.

"One day, Leta, you will look back and remember how I cared about you and how I wanted to protect you. I will do as you ask, but always remember . . . you can call me anytime and I will be there for you. No matter where I am, no matter who I am with, you can count on me, do you hear me?"

"Yes, I hear you, and I love you for caring so much about me, I really do, but I hope that will never become necessary. I really do wish things could have been different between us, but I felt so deceived, Michael."

His hand touched my face, and for a brief moment I wanted him to hold me, but he got out of my car. As he walked toward his patrol car, he stopped and looked over his shoulder. I read the words "I love you," coming from his lips, as he got into his car.

I began to cry.

... ELEVEN ...

Michael's unexpected visit in the front seat of my car left me confused and extremely melancholy. I spent most of that night wrestling with my bed sheets into the wee hours of the morning. As dawn approached, I got up, wrapped myself in a terrycloth robe, and went into the kitchen. On the way, I reminded myself that feeling blue was not an excuse to eat; that kind of response had been my routine antidote for pain before, and I did not want to revisit those days. After my skirmish with the refrigerator, I laid my head on my folded arms on the kitchen table, the place where all the big decisions were made, and fell asleep.

The smell of coffee filled my nostrils; I inhaled the delicious aroma. Never had I smoked in front of my parents, although Daddy smoked two packs a day, but at that moment, a cigarette was just what I needed to go with my coffee. Instead, I managed to prop my head up on one arm on the cool Formica-top table and gulped down my first cup of morning coffee.

Mother was concerned. She asked me if I felt all right.

"I'm fine," I assured her. But it wasn't the truth.

Michael . . . Mitch . . . Mitch . . . Michael; my head was spinning.

Mother sat down beside me and we drank our second cup of coffee together. I wanted more than ever to be able to talk to her about my personal life and then be comforted by her; I was in a dilemma and I needed direction, but I did not know how to initiate that kind of exchange with her. I reached over and took her hand. It was an awkward show of affection, but something I thought she might respond to. So many times while growing up, I would have given anything, to have anyone . . . other than Dolly, put their arms around me and tell me they loved me, but it was never to be . . . not then . . . and not that morning either.

*   *   *   *   *

I thanked God for Saturday morning. At least I could just hang out in my robe for a while. I was unable to resist the piping-hot chocolate and buttered toast that Mother put in front of me. She had always made breakfast for me, just as she had done for all of the foster kids, even though I was capable of preparing my own, and I followed her example throughout my years as a mother and wife.

*   *   *   *   *

Saturday night came and went. I watched television, unable to focus much on anything. I pictured Mitch Brogan with his girlfriend; after all, Saturday night was date night, and I wasn't his girl. I tried to remember Michael's schedule, but soon gave up on that too; I wasn't his girl either.

I had wanted to smoke a cigarette all day, so I told my mother that I would be back in a little while, that I just wanted to take a little drive.

When I returned home, my mouth was filled with peppermint gum. I knew if my mother found out that I had taken up Daddy's dirty habit, it would break her heart.

Then it was Sunday.

*   *   *   *   *

I thought about staying home from church. But I wanted to see if Mitch and his girlfriend would show up together. I thought about what Mitch had said, about having noticed me in church, and wondered how much of what he said was true. Had he really seen me for the first time in church and decided he was going to marry me? I questioned. His explanation had sounded so preposterous.

Finding a parking place at the United Brethren Church in Bucherville, which was located in the center of town, was a test of faith. You just had to believe that you would find a spot somewhere . . . and eventually you did.

I entered the church from a side door, instead of the usual front entrance. I felt more conspicuous than spiritual that Sunday. As I walked through an overflow area into the main sanctuary, I felt like someone was breathing down my neck. I took a seat about six rows from the front of the church, where I spotted Dolly and her family sitting.

As we began singing the first hymn, I looked to my left and into the front row of the overflow room that was easily visible from the main sanctuary. I saw Mitch first, and then I looked at the girl sitting beside him. She was very attractive and considerably younger than he was. She wore a broad navy-blue picture hat with a white flower that matched her beautiful white linen dress. Seeing them together produced a globe-sized lump in my throat. Mitch looked up from the hymnal he was sharing with his friend. Our eyes met. I looked away. I tried to remember what I had on just then. Oh yes, I was sporting a small black hat with a broad black feather that curled down over my forehead. Compared to Mitch's friend's hat, mine resembled a dead crow that had fallen on my head. I was wearing a simple, straight black dress; I was no match for Mitch's sophisticated girlfriend. *If her hat was any bigger, they could use it as a golf umbrella,* I commented to myself. I wanted to run out of there, but for the sake of Dolly and her family, and to avoid looking more conspicuous than I felt, I persevered through the entire service.

When the service ended, and while I stood talking to Dolly and her family, my eyes caught a glimpse of Mitch and his girlfriend as they were preparing to leave. The girlfriend, whose name was Michelle, walked ahead of Mitch. That gave him an opportunity to glance back at where I was standing. Our eyes met for the second time that morning. Why, I asked myself, would he bother with me at all? Michelle was lovely. I had no explanation at the time as to why I felt so ruffled over seeing the two of them together. I reminded myself that we had only danced together . . . there had been nothing more than that. In my opinion, I looked like a kid compared to Michelle. I could only surmise that Mitch's interest in me stemmed from his being bored with dating the same girl for seven years.

Mitch and Michelle left by the side door of the church. After shaking hands with Reverend Tobias, I exited the front door, and walked into a bright sunny afternoon.

*　　*　　*　　*　　*

I spent the remainder of the afternoon at a local park feeding the ducks. I envied the resiliency of their feathers as I watched them bathe and preen in the pond of shallow water. I absorbed life . . . that made me vulnerable, not resilient.

My heart was in deep water.

*　　*　　*　　*　　*

Monday morning I went to work with Mitch Brogan on my mind. I decided that I had to know what was happening between us. I was never one to just take things as they came. I had a need to identify beginnings and justify ends; that is what I set out to do with regards to Mitch and me.

There was a party that night at the mansion, or Armstrong Manor as it was formally called, and I thought about going, but I was afraid I would miss a call from Mitch. I expected some comment from him regarding our Sunday meeting.

When one of my fellow workers asked me if I was going to the party at the Manor that night, I declined. Instead, I drove directly home that evening in anticipation of a call from Mitch. But my mother met me at the door with a different message.

"Leta, you got a call from the Franklin and Marshall Greenroom. They said to tell you that you got a lead role in the play. Here is the number they left; you are to call them tonight."

I had all but forgotten about the audition.

Just then, the telephone rang.

It was Mitch. He asked me if we could meet down the street about nine o'clock that night; he would flash his lights and I would respond by walking down the street to his waiting Porsche.

Mother had prepared a nice evening meal, but food was the farthest thing from my mind. However, Daddy hadn't shown up for dinner, so I sat down and ate with her. I wasn't going to abandon her too. We ate, and we even laughed some. She seemed proud that I had gotten the part in "By Hex" and promised to come and see me perform "at least once," she teased. I helped her with the dishes and told her I would be meeting a friend to go to a movie later that night.

She caught me by surprise when she asked, "Isn't your friend a bit too old for you, Leta?"

I gulped.

Just as Daddy had known about my automobile accident before I ever told him, Mother now seemed to exhibit that same kind of extrasensory perception. I tried to wiggle out of a direct reply.

"What are you talking about?"

"Mitch Brogan," she replied. "We know you have been going out for rides with him."

"Thanks to the neighbors peeking through their curtains," I replied.

"It doesn't matter, Leta, how we found out, but Daddy and I think he is much too old for you."

"Well, just how old do you think he is?" I asked her.

At that moment, I too wondered how old he was.

"I don't know," she answered, "but he already served in the war and had time to build a good business; he must be in his mid-thirties at least, and you are only nineteen."

"Well, you needn't worry, we've only gone for drives in his Porsche. He knew I loved sports cars and he just thought I would enjoy a ride or two."

She didn't say another word after that. I think all she wanted me to know was that she knew.

"Mother, when do you think Daddy will be home?" I hadn't said that to change the subject. I was truly concerned. She had wanted so much to travel and go on vacations, but Daddy was opposed to traveling long distances, wanting to stay home instead. Of course, his idea of staying home was not leaving Bucherville. Mother longed to go to Israel for as long as I could remember, but Daddy refused to go. I suggested a bus tour with other ladies, and she seemed to like that idea. They had once planned to go to Florida with two friends of theirs, but Daddy had backed out at the last minute, and another couple had gone in their place. Everyone in the car burned to death when an eighteen-wheeler crashed into the back of their car in thick fog on the way south. That pretty much put an end to Daddy's future traveling plans; it was one trip Mother was glad Daddy had backed out of.

Mother couldn't disguise her pain when I questioned her about Daddy's absence. I detected moisture beneath her eyes as she turned her head slightly to the side to avoid looking directly at me.

"It doesn't get any better," she explained. "I never know when he is coming home. I only hope that one day he stops his smoking and his drinking. One of these days, the police will be bringing him home; that's what I'm afraid of most." She was right. The police did bring Daddy home one evening; it was a very sad time. I remember putting my arms around her and we cried together. There were some things I couldn't tell my mother, incidents involving my dad and his drinking problem. There were some things I couldn't tell anyone. *Some things are better left unsaid . . . to fade . . . or perhaps, even to die.*

* * * * *

At nine o'clock that night, after signaling me by blinking his Porsche headlights several times, I met Mitch at the end of Fulton Street. I determined it would be the last time we would meet under those arrangements. If he was ashamed of meeting me in public, then he shouldn't have been meeting me at all, I decided.

He leaned across the passenger seat and opened the door for me. I slid into the leather bucket seat. The tantalizing aroma of soft leather was pleasing to my nostrils. I recalled the same enfolding sensation when I sat in the overstuffed chair at Blairsouth Estate when I was very young.

Before I could even say hello, he made an unusual observation.

"Has anyone ever told you how much you look like a German or Swedish girl?"

"No, I don't think so. What would make you think that?" I questioned.

"The color of your hair, and especially the way you are wearing it tonight."

I was wearing my hair in two pigtails, fastened on the top of my head with a satin ribbon. He seemed very pleased.

"So . . . are you hungry?" he asked.

"Not really, thanks. I ate dinner with my mother."

I hunched down in the Porsche, hoping no one would recognize me until we were out of town, something I now did automatically.

Mitch was impeccably dressed and his breath smelled strongly of Sen-Sen.

We drove to Yorktown to our favorite restaurant.

There didn't seem to be an end to the wad of money Mitch carried in his pocket. He told me that when he was a young boy, his family was very poor. He even had to wear his sister's clothes to school sometimes. For that, he received more than his share of badgering. His only defense had been his fists, he told me. Much later, his mother told me that he never came home from school with all of his buttons still on his shirt, or without a note saying that he had beaten someone up for teasing him. At fourteen years of age, he had worked for a garage in the middle of town where he was paid to wax and clean cars. He had grown up loving cars and soon became an expert on nearly every aspect of the automobile. He knew at an early age that his life would always revolve around automobiles. He was one of the first dealers selected to sell a small, funny-looking, popular German automobile that led to a love affair between a man and his car. In fact, the demand for the car was much larger than the supply, creating endless waiting lists, from which Mitch benefited. He also shared with me his intent to become the East Coast distributor for the more expensive French, Italian, and German automobiles. However, that had not yet come to fruition.

I looked across the table at Mitch drinking his Lowenbrau beer; I was so impressed with his manliness. He possessed a commanding, and somewhat militant, disposition; yet he displayed enough gentleness to win my affection. There appeared to be two sides to Mitch's personality, but that night I sat on his gentle side. I saw a man who appeared wise, experienced, and protective.

The bar was becoming crowded and smoky. Mitch reached over and held my hand. I let him. Although he didn't realize it, his next comment was more like a warning than merely an observation, to me; it came after a woman sitting across from us lit her cigarette.

"Boy, if there is anything I dislike," he said, "it's a woman with a cigarette in her mouth. That has got to be the dirtiest habit anyone could have."

"Yes, I agree," I replied.

Oddly enough, a cigarette was exactly what I thought would have tasted good about then.

When Mitch took me in his arms to dance that night, he held me so close I could feel the throbbing of his heart. He kissed my cheek and ear. When the dance was over, we left the floor and headed for our table. I watched him as I sipped my sloe gin fizz, and I thought, *At some point tonight, I am going to have to discuss our relationship.*

Sitting in the Porsche beside Mitch, somewhere between Yorktown and Bucherville, I asked him how old he was.

"Age?" he said, a little startled at my question. "Now what does that have to do with anything?"

"Well, you know I'm nineteen years old, but I haven't a clue how old you are."

"I am thirty-four," he said. "Now don't go fainting on me."

I thought about that for a minute; he was fifteen years older than I was.

"Leta, our ages are unimportant," he rebutted.

"But Mitch, you are engaged to be married to someone else," I argued. "How can we continue doing what we're doing? I know I don't intend to hide till we're out of town every time you want to be with me. Either you want to be with Michelle, or you want to be with me, but you can't have both. So which will it be?"

"I won't see Michelle anymore. That is not a difficult decision, O.K?"

"Are you saying you are going to break your engagement with Michelle?"

"I'll take care of it."

*   *   *   *   *

I introduced Mitch to my mother and dad first. However apprehensive they may have been regarding the difference in our ages, they seemed to like him.

The discreet meeting arrangements ended.

He took me to meet his mother and father. It had never occurred to me that he lived at home with his parents, especially at his age. But he did.

His mother was a very tiny woman, with white hair and a crippled back. She was one of the sweetest women I had ever met. I noticed an open Bible on the table as she put her arms around me and hugged me and asked me if I knew the Lord. Even though I was a Christian, I was surprised at being asked that question on our first meeting.

"Yes," I replied, feeling a little guilty; mostly because I hadn't been living like one. "I'm a Christian. I know the Lord."

"Good, I am glad to hear that."

I wondered if Mitch had shared his mother's faith. He went to church, that much I knew, but he never talked about it. As a matter of fact, I hadn't shared my spiritual experiences with him, either.

Mitch looked like his father. His father was a heavy smoker and a hard worker. He ran a small gas station in Bucherville. Their backyard contained a menagerie of eatable fowl: tame rabbits and home-raised pigeons, just to name a few. Mitch's home was where I was first introduced to "squab under glass," which simply meant, "pigeon on a plate." The Brogan family also introduced me to quail eggs, eggs that resembled large marbles and so small that you had to eat about of dozen of them to feel like you had breakfast.

The Brogans lived in a modest row home in the center of Bucherville. Mitch's bedroom was on the second floor, in the rear, overlooking the mini-barnyard. There were pictures of Indians hanging on his walls, which he explained by saying that he was part American Indian. His skin was unusually tan, so I believed him. Once I got to know his mother better, she said it was a cruel joke, that his tan came from spending a lot of time in the sun.

Mitch had two sisters and several nieces. I got to know them at a family dinner several Sundays later.

There was one thing that captivated me: it was the way their family hugged and kissed one another. Affection in their family was liberal and genuine. A hug came with every hello. I gorged myself on their affection. I wanted to be part of that family.

By the time we left the Brogan home that day, I felt accepted. Good-byes also came with a generous share of embraces. I could hardly wait to return.

When we were in the car, I said to Mitch, "Your family is so affectionate. Is that the way it always is?"

"Yep. There is no shortage of love there. Of course, once you get to know Dad, well, he is different. He is a little hard on my mother. Because of the hard times they've been through, and because of her back, she never gets out much. She spends most of her time with my sisters, and, of course, praying and reading her Bible."

"Well, to tell you the truth, I must say I was a little surprised by the question your mother asked me. But it was a good reminder for me. I became a Christian when I was sixteen, but I admit, I've lost that 'first love' feeling. Other things have become more important. I've considered going to some kind of church where they teach more from the Bible. But we'll see."

"No question that they liked you, that's for sure."

"I'm glad."

I decided to change the subject. I was pretty sure that Mitch didn't want to discuss religion.

"Mitch, have you told Michelle about us yet?"

I saw the answer in his face.

"No, but I will. Don't worry."

I wasn't at all comfortable with that revelation. I insisted that he take care of that, since it was neither fair to her, nor to me.

*   *   *   *   *

That night we drove to Obie's Steakhouse, one of Mitch's favorite restaurants in Lancaster. We dined on succulent T-bone steaks and vintage wine. It occurred to me that each time we ate there, Mitch ordered the steaks for both of us; he always suggested that I eat the large section of the steak first, saving the small piece for last. That way, he explained, he could help me out by eating the smaller portion of the steak if I was unable to finish the whole steak. So each time I had a T-bone stake, I ate the large side and Mitch ended up eating the small piece that was left over. There was something strange in being told from which side of the steak to eat, but I was falling in love and so I didn't make a big deal over it.

He told me that the following Saturday night he had made reservations for dinner at the Log Cabin, a favorite hangout of the Sports Car Club members. He said that he wanted his racing friends to meet me. It sounded exciting, but I admit that I felt a little peculiar, since they obviously knew Michelle. I wondered how they would receive someone fifteen years younger than their friend and, most likely, younger than most of the club members themselves.

It occurred to me that I had not yet broken the news to Mitch concerning my role in "By Hex" with the Franklin and Marshall College Greenroom. So many other things seemed to be happening, I had almost forgotten about it myself.

"Mitch, do you remember wishing me good luck on my audition for that show 'By Hex'?" I asked him.

"Yes, I remember. How did you ever make out?"

"Well, I'm proud to say, I got the female lead comedy role. We start practice next week."

"Good for you. Will you have to practice every night?"

"Yes, because we only have two months before opening night."

"Where do you have practice?" he asked.

"It's a real neat barn in Lancaster. We do all the rehearsing there until time for dress rehearsal at the theatre."

He wrote down the address in a little book he carried in his breast pocket.

"There won't be a whole lot of time to spend with you," I explained, "except for Sundays, I'm afraid, at least until after the show closes."

"Where is the show going to be held?" he asked.

"They're working on that. Depending on the weather, I think they would like to have it outdoors, somewhere in Ephrata, a more central location that would accommodate more people. They are looking at a two-week run, ending in early August. The writer's goal is to have the show end up on Broadway. Can you believe that! That means the show will no doubt run until the beginning of August."

Mitch motioned for the waiter. I found it odd that he hadn't commented on any of the information I had given him. Instead, he asked for the check. The owner of the restaurant met us at the door and said that he would look for us at the Log Cabin Saturday night. Apparently the owner was a member of the Sports Car Club as well.

It became clear to me that no matter where we went, Mitch was usually recognized . . . and catered to. It wasn't long before I became the recipient of that same kind of attention.

When we got into the car, Mitch unknowingly allowed me to peek through a hole in his personality. I thought of my foster mother, peeking through the hole in the covered bridge at my father, seeing more than she wanted to see.

"You know, Leta, I'm not into theatre or those involved in them," he finally responded. "The men are so effeminate, and the women look like a bunch of Bohemians."

"That's not fair; how many actors and actresses have you met?"

"None, and I really don't care to meet any, thank you. I find it hard to believe you would get yourself involved in that stuff."

"I'm really sorry you feel that way, Mitch, but this is something I have always wanted to do. When I was a little girl, I spent hours playacting beneath the forebay on our farm; I even performed, along with other friends, on a makeshift stage built by my dad. We put on real shows for the people in our neighborhood. I even wrote short plays for high school productions while I was in high school. It must be in my blood. I only wish you would be happy for me."

"I am, if that is what makes you happy. But it doesn't have to make me happy, right?"

"No, I guess not."

*   *   *   *   *

Perhaps I should have picked up on Mitch's indifference to my interests, and how he expected me to be involved in his. However, his persuasiveness overpowered me, and my own identity was lost in the dust. We talked endlessly about automobiles and ice hockey, conveniently sidestepping things that interested me. It wasn't long before I joined his political party . . . but I refused to share his prejudices. We discussed (and quite fervently at times) his opinions regarding people of other color and nationality. Giving in so readily to someone else's convictions exposed my own intellectual weakness and insecurities. Clearly, I was not a challenge for Mitch's persuasive and dominant personality. *Ah contraire*; I endorsed it. I only saw someone caring enough to exercise control over me; something a father might do . . . something I had never experienced. I would realize later, however, that that was not Mitch's role to play; the time of discipline for me had already passed.

*   *   *   *   *

Alone in my bed, I thought of all the opportunities that were mine. I envisioned myself becoming a film star, CIA or FBI agent, playwright, or novelist. Then there was the role of wife; one I had not yet played, even beneath the forebay in Reading Junction. Was Mitch really going to ask me to marry him one day? I wondered. Then I thought of Michael, and I wondered how he would react if he knew about Mitch and me.

*   *   *   *   *

The struggle with what to wear Saturday night dominated most of my week. In anticipation of meeting all of Mitch's friends at the Log Cabin, I decided to treat myself to a new outfit. To this day I can give a detailed picture of my purchase. It was a two-piece, black and white Anne Klein II pants suit. The sleeves, lapel, and collar were trimmed in white stitching. The pants were slightly bell-bottomed and the neckline was modestly revealing. My waist was notably small; the choice I made emphasized that fact. Because I knew Mitch loved my hair braided, I decided in favor of the German-looking coiffeur.

Mitch was pleased with my appearance.

He looked equally handsome in his white pants and black shirt. Although we hadn't planned to dress alike, we came dangerously close to looking like two teenagers who had arranged to wear matching outfits the night of basketball playoffs.

I confessed to Mitch that I was a bit apprehensive about the impending introductions to his sports car club friends. He tried to put me at ease by telling me how beautiful I looked, "just like a German *fraulein*," he said. I was slowly getting the impression that he probably would have been happier with a German girl instead of the American apple pie variety.

We arrived at the Log Cabin about seven-thirty. I noticed a small gathering of people outside the restaurant in the woods. Was this the welcoming committee? I wondered. I began to perspire; I realized that I had worn too much perfume.

"You smell like a million bucks," Mitch whispered, as he parked his Porsche far from the possibility of unwanted scratches. My eyes couldn't stop racing up and down the parking lot, taking in all the different sports cars. There was a Jaguar, Mercedes, Alfa Romeo, MG, TC, Morgan, several Porsches, Aston Martin, Austin Healy, and some I didn't recognize. It looked like a stack of money on wheels to me.

Mitch opened the door, and I stepped out. Nearly every head, except for those engrossed in car conversation, turned to take a look at Mitch and his new friend. Within moments, the introductions began. As we entered the restaurant, there were several others at the bar ready to make my acquaintance. They were all friendly, accepting of the new face in the club.

Mitch ordered the usual T-bone steaks, potatoes, salad, and wine. We sat with two couples who would later become close friends to both of us. There was another couple there I didn't get to know, at least not very well that night. That unfamiliarity would change drastically in the years that followed. I instantly adored the Jewish couple who appeared to be closest to Mitch, as well as another couple who sat at the same table. It didn't take long until I felt right at home with his friends. When it came to discussing fine foods and exotic automobiles, I was out in the cold. But I warmed up when the questions changed to my being chosen for a role in "By Hex." Everyone promised they would come and see me perform . . . at least once! It was a show of acceptance, and it meant the world to me . . . for Mitch's sake, and mine.

Not once had anyone mentioned Michelle, Mitch's former girlfriend. Years later, however, they confessed to me that they thought he had robbed the cradle; the second time I was linked to cradle robbery.

It had been a lovely evening, and I looked forward to being in the company of Mitch's friends soon again.

When we arrived in Bucherville after our dinner at the Log Cabin, Mitch said he wanted to stop at the shop and pick something up, and if I would mind if he stopped before taking me home. "Not a problem," I replied. It was late when we drove up in front of his place of business. He parked and ran into the office, and was back in less than five minutes. I didn't realize it then, but the purpose of stopping at the garage was just to get me alone, away from everyone else. When he got into the car, he took me in his arms and kissed me. That kiss led to a discussion of marriage and divorce. I believed in marriage, I told him; I did not believe in divorce, for any reason. I also made it absolutely clear that I intended to remain a virgin until after I was married.

We sat in his car for a long time before he finally drove me home. I think my declaration to remain pure caught him off guard. When I exited the Porsche, he told me he would call me at my office, that perhaps since the theatre was going to occupy most of my evenings, we could at least have lunch together during the week.

For the first time since we met, he told me that he loved me.

Leta sweeping the sidewalk at the Carpenter farm.

Another baby arrives at the Carpenter farm. Leta gets to hold Sally's doll for this photo.

Leta and Dolly— friends day and night.

Jean Marlow and Leta. Leta cut off Bassie's head in this photo.

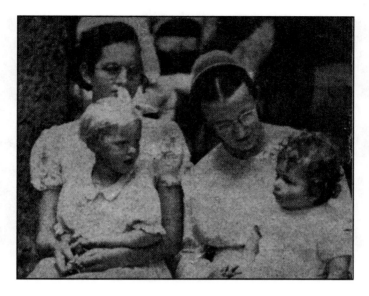

Back row, left to right: Rose and Grace Carpenter holding, left to right: Leta and curly-head Sally.

Early Bible School class with Leta, far left, in the second row.

1941 family outing.

Grace Carpenter with (left to right) Leta, Doris, and Jean—two new foster girls.

1953 accident where God spared Leta's life.

Leta growing up.

Leta's 1953 graduation picture.

Grace Carpenter, Benjamin, Sarah, and Leta beside the Mercedes Benz.

... TWELVE ...

Mitch's proclaimed love for me hadn't hidden the fact that he failed to mention my seeing him and Michelle in church that Sunday, nor had he mentioned anything about attending church with me the Sunday following our night at the Log Cabin. But I was still reeling from his disclosure of love, so I didn't think any more about it until the alarm sounded at eight o'clock Sunday morning.

I dressed for Sunday School, a class that preceded church services and was made up mainly of people age thirty-five and under. It was a lively group that engaged in in-depth discussions on how to apply biblical teaching to everyday life. I hadn't been attending on a regular basis, but when I had shown up for the class, I really enjoyed it. When Mitch didn't call me that morning, I gave up all hope of joining him in church.

I took great pains to look particularly feminine that morning. I chose a red and white Swiss polka dot dress, and a large red hat. I hadn't thought about the maroon choir gown that would hide my carefully chosen attire that morning, when I joined Dolly and her sisters in the choir.

It was after nine o'clock in the morning when I arrived on the second floor of the church building where Sunday School class was being held. I arrived about ten minutes late. That left me with two options: a front seat by the window, or another front seat by the wall. I opted for the wall seat. There was the usual chitchat and interrogations going on over Saturday night activities. As I looked to my left to engage in conversation with the person sitting next to me, I suffered a stroke . . . of bad luck. There on the opposite side of the room sat Michelle, Mitch's ex-girlfriend. The bright sun caught the large diamond engagement ring still on her finger, and she maneuvered the small penetrating spot across the ceiling, down the wall, and directly into my eyes. Other than facing the wall flat on, I was unable to avoid the spotlight announcing that she was still engaged.

After class was over, my heart struggled to keep up with me as I walked into the choir loft with Dolly, her sisters, and the rest of the choir. In spite of the sunny day, the notes on the pages of my sheet music grew cloudy. Fighting back the tears, I gazed straight ahead, focusing on a stained glass window heads above the congregation.

Church finally ended, and I removed my cumbersome gown; but I was unable to remove from my mind what had happened in Sunday School class that morning.

*   *   *   *   *

I did not want to go home.

I drove to the duck pond and sat on the wooden bench and watched the white swans glide toward me, in anticipation of a meal of stale bread.

It's time to be realistic, I said to myself. *Do you really think Mitch was serious when he told you he loved you? He hasn't even broken his engagement.*

As I sat pitying myself, the old familiar pattern of self-debasement and insecurity returned.

And a little boy cried when a large swan stole a piece of bread he had intended for a tiny duckling. "That's how life is," I said to him, under my breath.

*   *   *   *   *

Eventually, I drove home to find a message from my mother on the kitchen table. It read:

> *You are to call Mitch at home as soon as you can.*
> *We went visiting. Be home later.*
> > *Mother.*

I picked up the phone and dialed Mitch's number. His mother answered the telephone. My heart was beating so fast it could have whipped cream.

Mitch came to the phone and asked if he could come and talk to me. But I couldn't wait. "Mitch, what is going on?" I asked. "You told me you were going to break your engagement."

"How do you know I didn't?" he asked.

I told him what happened that morning in Sunday School class. He obviously hadn't attended services that morning; conveniently so, I thought.

I had barely hung up the phone when he drove in the driveway.

Before he had two feet in the door, he said, "Leta, I am so sorry. I can't believe Michelle would deliberately do that to you. She knows about us, but I didn't tell her. She found out through someone else. It won't be necessary for me to go through the whole thing with her now."

"But that isn't right, Mitch," I pleaded. "You owe it to her to explain why you are breaking your engagement. She is still wearing your ring; she thinks she is still engaged to you."

"It's not necessary to hurt her any more than she's already been hurt, that's all I'm saying. It's better left alone."

I could see that I was not going to change his mind, and before I could say anything further, his arms pulled me close to him, and his kiss was more reassuring than any words he could have spoken. While his lips were still on mine, I wondered how long it would be before Michelle would remove her engagement ring. It was something that continued to bother me, but I knew better than to broach the subject again.

We agreed to meet the following day for lunch.

*   *   *   *   *

Mitch waited for me by the main entrance of Armstrong Cork Company where I worked. The convertible top was down on the Porsche and he looked as handsome as ever with his summer tan. As I approached the car, he got out and opened the door for me. Dozens of young women exiting the front door on their way to lunch took turns exclaiming over the car and, later, over the man who had picked me up. I felt proud and important . . . and envied.

We enjoyed a famous burger at Stan's Restaurant and Bar. He had a beer; I was not able to drink while on the job. We ate and held hands. I loved him very much.

He tried to talk me out of going back to my office after lunch, saying that I didn't need to work now that I had him to take care of me. But I couldn't allow him to support me, not just yet.

As he left me at my office door, he reiterated his displeasure that my evenings were going to be spent rehearsing for the F & M Greenroom show. I assured him that weeknights away from him would only make our weekends doubly pleasurable. That seemed to appease him.

*   *   *   *   *

Wednesday night when I arrived for rehearsals, Director Larson was especially portentous. He demanded that every word and action convey perfection. It was a grueling night for all of us. But I enjoyed it. We worked hard and late, sometimes ending in the wee hours of the morning. He did not intend it to be one of those "fly by night" productions. With every expectation that the show would end up on Broadway, Director Larson was inflexible in his effort to present a flawless presentation of "By Hex."

Somewhere around midnight, we took a soda, coffee, and cigarette break. I decided to go outside with several other cast members and smoke a cigarette. As we leaned against the barn wall, a car approached from a narrow hidden street. I hadn't thought much about it, until I realized that the sound was unmistakably that of a Porsche. I tried to hide my cigarette behind my back, but I had been too slow. Mitch took one look at me, and just that quickly, he was gone.

"Who was that?" asked one of the other actresses.

"It was my boyfriend, and I'm in trouble."

"Why, what did you do?"

"He told me once that he hated women who smoked. He said it was the dirtiest habit anyone could have, and I agreed with him."

"So, big deal. Is he going to throw you out of his life just because you were smoking a cigarette?"

"Yep, probably."

The call to return to rehearsals was given and we walked back into the barn. But my throat burned and my voice cracked as we repeated several scenes. Director Larson called time out and told us to come back the following night with our heads on straight and to be ready to work overtime.

*   *   *   *   *

It was Friday night, and I still hadn't heard from Mitch. I couldn't decide whether or not to call him. I had hurt him deeply. Furthermore, I had lied to him. I feared that I had seen the last of Mitch Brogan.

The noonday sun filtered through the venetian blinds as I greeted Saturday morning with a yawn. My eyes were swollen and pasty from crying myself to sleep. I pulled the covers over my head and opted for one more hour of uninterrupted oblivion.

I heard the phone ring once. Then it rang again . . . and again. There didn't seem to be anyone else in the house, so I slowly began to make my way toward the phone table. From the living room, I could see the kitchen clock. It was one-fifteen Saturday afternoon.

"Carpenters," I answered, barely recognizing my own voice.

"Leta, this is Mitch."

"Mitch!" I replied, and then I began to cry.

"Listen, Leta, I haven't been sleeping well, and I thought we better talk about the other night. How about if I pick you up around seven tonight and we can go get something to eat, O.K?"

"O.K.," I said, "but I just want you to know how sorry I am for misleading you about the cigarette thing."

My fellow thespians would have defended my right to smoke, followed by a recommendation to get rid of the guy. But I had been wrong to mislead Mitch and I wanted to make it right, regardless of the outcome.

Over dinner, I was given an ultimatum: cigarettes or Mitch Brogan. He emphasized that he wasn't about to marry a woman who smoked.

"Marry! Mitch, are you serious? You want to marry me?"

"I chose you when you were about sixteen years old. Now it's your turn to choose."

We had known each other less than a month, and already he was asking me to be his wife. *He must really love me,* I thought; I was flattered.

"Of course I choose you, Mitch."

"Good choice," he responded, thoroughly pleased.

It was good. But whether or not it was the right thing to do, well . . .

"As soon as that show closes in August, we'll get married. How does that sound to you?"

"Sounds fantastic," I said, "but how can I plan a wedding in two months when I will be spending most of my time working and performing for the Greenroom? I don't know if I can pull all of that off."

"Not to worry, we'll go to Maryland and get married. We won't have to wait, and we won't have to spend all that money on a wedding, either."

"I thought only pregnant girls run off to Maryland and get married. And that couldn't be further from the truth in our case."

"It's just such a waste of time and money to do that whole church, gown, and tux thing. We could use the money we would spend on a wedding to get a nice place to live."

I thought that perhaps he was just being considerate of my parents and me, knowing we would never be able to afford a big church wedding. It sounded reasonable, so I agreed.

"Well then, if I'm engaged, shouldn't I be wearing a ring?" I asked.

"How about if we just get wedding rings and forget about an engagement ring. There again, we could use that money toward a house. With plans to enlarge, or maybe even relocate my business, it's going to require a good bit of extra cash, so I think it would be wise not to spend the money on a wedding, and instead, use it for the business. We certainly ought to be able to sacrifice some things to be together, don't you think?"

We left the restaurant arm in arm and headed home to break the news to my parents.

My mother and dad showed little emotion when we shared our plans with them. Only after Mitch had gone home did they express their deep concern over my wanting to marry someone I had known for less than a month. However, they seemed quite confident that he would be able to take care of me. They readily admitted that he was a successful businessman, and although his reputation for fast cars and numerous arrests for speeding had preceded his good looks, he had the means to provide a good living for their foster daughter. They just asked that I give it some more time. I made no promises.

*   *   *   *   *

For the next month, I spent all non-rehearsal time with Mitch.

Most memorable was the night I left the rehearsal barn in the early hours of the morning on a foggy rain-soaked route home. I had been exhausted. I had thrown my three-inch-thick script across the front seat of my car as I crawled in behind the wheel. As I drove home, my eyes closed, and then opened again. *I'm just going to rest them,* I told myself. And so they rested.

When my eyes opened again, I found myself being hurled into the passenger side of the car. The steering wheel was no longer in my hands. The car and I had come to an abrupt halt.

"Oh, no," I yelled, "what have I done?"

My head hurt, and the three-inch script that I retrieved from beneath my buttocks, looked like an accordion. The car seemed to be leaning to the right. I had no idea where I had landed. Realizing that I was not critically injured, I managed to open the door, only to discover that I had left the road and was planted running-board-deep in mud, between rows of corn stalks. As I stepped out of the car, I could see the wheels of my beautiful red Plymouth convertible buried hubcap-deep in mud. As I looked across the field I saw that I had just missed hitting a telephone pole and several huge trees. A porch light went on at a nearby farm. I headed toward the light. My feet made a sucking sound with each step, as I lifted one mud-laden foot in front of the other.

Not to frighten anyone living in the farmhouse, I had gently tapped on the door. A farmer, dressed for barn chores, looked out the window. The porch light had illuminated my face, and apparently what he saw had not posed a threat to him or his family, for he opened the door and asked me if I needed help. I said that I had slid off the road due to the rain and could not get my car out of the mud, and then I asked him if I could please use his phone to call for help. The farmer kindly invited me in. I removed my mud-covered shoes and he directed me to the phone. I called Mitch's number. He had been sleeping. After asking me approximately where I had driven off the road, he agreed to come and rescue me.

The first questions he asked were whether or not I had smashed the car and if I had been injured. Thankfully, I could answer "no" to both.

It seemed forever had come and gone before I finally heard Mitch's Porsche. Everything seemed fine once I was in Mitch's arms. I remember him surveying the damage with two wide-eyed halogen Porsche headlights; that's when he decided that he would come back in the morning, after the sun came up, to pull my car out of the mud with a tow-truck.

When he asked me how it happened, I told him the truth.

He said, "Well, I bet you'll never do that again."

He was right. I not only consider myself one of the most wide-awake drivers on the planet, I'm even afraid to blink.

*   *   *   *   *

Our weekends were spent making up for lost weekdays. We generally headed for the Hershey Park Ballroom, a partially open-air building that housed a spacious dance floor bordered by a large swimming pool. It was the best of both worlds. You could swim a while, shower and dress, and then end up on the dance floor. Hershey Park Ballroom attracted big band names like Stan Kenton, Ralph Flannigan, Billy May, Tommy Dorsey, Count Basie, and Lionel Hampton. Mitch and I were usually found standing directly in front of the stage absorbing the big band sounds, or we were in the middle of the dance floor showing off.

Nights at the Hershey Park Ballroom are probably still on the top of my "things I would want to do again" list. To this day, my mind dances when I pass the place where the ballroom once stood. Some things you really should be able to bring back.

*   *   *   *   *

Mitch and I set our wedding date, the day after the last performance of "By Hex." All I had to do was get a blood test. Mitch said he would take care of everything else.

*   *   *   *   *

Each passing day brought us closer to opening night. The air was filled with excitement, and our stomachs were filled with butterflies. We had done a good job, according to Director Larson, and he was ready to present "By Hex" to Broadway by way of Franklin and Marshall College Greenroom Productions.

The show opened the first week of August to a sold-out crowd. The band, the backup singers, and the actors and actresses were all on board for an expected ride to stardom.

After an unexpected standing ovation, the first night's performance ended. When the crowd dispersed, I could see Mitch and quite a few of our Sports Car Club friends standing together in the rear of the outdoor theatre. When I reached them, Mitch hugged me and said, "Good job." The rest congratulated me on a great performance and said they would come again the following week. I was elated.

I introduced some of the cast to Mitch and our friends, but much to my surprise, Mitch remained aloof and unfriendly. It was obvious that he was not comfortable around theatrical people. Embarrassed, I explained to my fellow cast members that he was into cars, not plays. Gratefully, they hadn't taken offense.

For the first time since those "way-off" Broadway shows in Reading Junction, I was having the time of my life.

Marsha and Irv, members of the Sports Car Club and two of our closest friends, informed me that Mitch agreed to go to the show with them on the last night of the performance. That was welcome news to me, particularly since he hadn't said very much about the show after opening night.

I had spent considerable time organizing my life to accommodate the show and my wedding day. My classmates from Bucherville High School, with whom I kept in close touch, had a surprise bridal shower for me. Aunt Mabel, my dad's sister, hosted a second bridal shower. There was no turning back after that. Was I having second thoughts? You better believe I was. If the show hadn't occupied most of my time and my thoughts, I would have seriously considered having a nervous breakdown.

*   *   *   *   *

In that place reserved for private thoughts, lived a fear of the first night of our honeymoon. My husband would be the first man with whom I would become physically intimate, and I hadn't a clue what to expect. Call it naiveté, but we just didn't discuss those kinds of things when I was growing up. The "Birds and Bees Story" wasn't read in our house. Oh sure, we had Health as a subject in high school, but that was for teeth-brushing and underarm deodorant instructions. The subject of intimacy wasn't even discussed among my friends. It truly was considered sacred territory, and rightly so.

*   *   *   *   *

Because cast members were required to arrive at the theatre early before each night's performance, I usually drove alone. The last night of the show was no different. As the last actress arrived backstage, Director Larson made his appearance. He told us all to have seats, and then proceeded to make an announcement.

"The show has been a tremendous hit, as you know," he said, "and we haven't had one empty seat for two weeks. I am going to announce tonight that we will be extending the run of 'By Hex' for at least an additional week. Does anyone have a problem with that?"

Everyone was excited over the news, except me.

"Mr. Larson," I hesitantly replied, "I don't personally have a problem with holding it over for one more week; however, I think my fiancée will have a huge problem with it. We're planning on getting married . . . TOMORROW!"

"YOU'RE DOING WHAT TOMORROW?" he bellowed.

"I am getting married. I didn't think to tell you because I was sure the show would be over. We planned on leaving for Maryland tomorrow night, and that's where we're getting married."

Director Larson motioned for the rest of the cast to leave the room.

Nearly all of the cast members knew about our wedding plans, but when Darrell Larson ordered them to leave the room, you could see the suspense rise when they did.

Completely out of character, Director Larson used the gentle approach in convincing me to change my wedding plans and continue my role as Lydia for one more week. He promised that he would go directly to Mitch after the show that night and talk to him personally. He was sure Mitch would understand. I hoped he was right.

After the last act of the last scheduled performance and predicted standing ovation, Director Larson made the unexpected announcement that the show would be held over for one additional week due to popular demand. That same evening, he had also broken the news to us that a producer of several New York Broadway shows would be in the audience the following week. We knew this was the big moment Director Larson and the producers of "By Hex" had been waiting for.

As the theatre grew quiet, and the other cast members were greeting their friends and families in the front of the theatre, a terrible scuffle was taking place far behind the last row of seats, and half way into the parking area. The voices were loud and threatening. One of the cast members said they thought that Director Larson and my boyfriend were in the middle of a fight. I rushed down the aisle to the back of the outdoor theatre to find several of our friends holding Mitch down in an attempt to distance him from Director Larson. It was obvious from their shirttails that a confrontation had taken place. I ran to Mitch's side.

"What in the world is going on, Mitch?" I questioned.

"Don't you realize what he has just done to our wedding plans, Leta?"

"Yes, Mitch, I do. But will one week make that much of a difference? I really don't mind, and I am enjoying the show so much."

"How can you take this so calmly? Aren't you the least bit upset?"

"Yes, but it isn't worth fighting over, that's for sure."

Mitch had rearranged Director Larson's clothes and face. Flushed and red from the confrontation, the director expressed shock and bewilderment. I walked over to where he sat. I apologized for Mitch's behavior. I wanted him to know that he could count on me for another week.

I learned later, from our good friends who managed to disengage Director Larson from Mitch's hold, that Mitch had called Director Larson a "fag" and then proceeded to rough him up a bit.

Mitch and I had a long discussion that night. Driving home alone, I had time to think about what had happened, and although I never succeeded in convincing Mitch that what he did was wrong, he did concede to postponing the wedding until later that month. Perhaps my biggest misjudgement was due to my interpretation of the event. I saw his not wanting to postpone our being together for the rest of our lives as an expression of Mitch's love for me. I did not consider four things I already learned about the man I was going to marry: He had an explosive temper; he disliked Afro-Americans, Jewish people, and the effeminate. He respected our Jewish friends, that was evident, but never revealed to them how he really felt about their nationality. Years later, he befriended a black man, which was a rare exception for Mitch. He called his black friend his "bodyguard." But the one thing that stood out above all the rest was the exceptional fondness he had for Germans.

My motive for marriage, and total acquiescence when it came to Mitch, mystified even me. Apart from loving him, I had many other reasons for wanting to spend my life with him. I felt secure, important, and needed. Those may have been all wrong reasons, but I felt deserving of them all. Cost consideration was never my strong point.

We managed to get through the last week of the show without incident.

To commemorate the success of the show, we were invited to attend an elaborate party in our honor, at an exclusive downtown hotel. I couldn't wait to tell Mitch about the party. But my joy was shot down at point blank by Mitch's refusal to attend. He suggested we have our own private celebration with dinner and the most expensive bottle of wine available. Again, I considered his proposal a romantic gesture, a gold-embossed display of love. In truth, he didn't want to rub shoulders with anyone connected with "By Hex"; his distaste for theatre was that vehement.

*   *   *   *   *

It wasn't long before Mitch acquired box-seat tickets for the Hershey Bears' American League Hockey Team games. I did not care much for the sport, but out of love for Mitch, I learned to tolerate the twice a week habit that lasted twenty-some years. My enjoyment of the sport began when Frank Weder, former piano player for the well-known Billy May Orchestra, and I corroborated in writing the music and lyrics for the Hershey Bear Theme Song. Together, we continued to write music and lyrics for songs played and sung by numerous big bands during that era. Frank Weder and I became close friends, but he and Mitch had been friends for many years. Mitch had gone to see Frank play with the Billy May Orchestra at every opportunity. Frank was as talented then as any musician is today. We bonded immediately, most likely because of our mutual love for music and the talent for putting that music to words. On several occasions, he tried to discourage me from getting married, but had never actually said why. I always believed that Frank saw behind door number one, but he never told me what was there. In addition to Frank's mastery of the piano keys, he also had an innate ability to handle a sports car, not unlike Mitch; consequently, the three of us spent a lot of time together. If we weren't involved in some sports car race in Sebring, Florida, or Watkins Glen, New York, we were planning trips to the Grand Prix of Le Mans in France.

Once again, I was aware that Mitch and I spent most of our time involved in all of the things that he loved. Our conversations centered on the 101st Airborne, cars, hockey, and fine wines.

The curtain closed on my love affair with the theatre.

... THIRTEEN ...

Somehow I had managed to do the things one does to prepare for marriage. In our case, that happened to be very little. Eloping required more spirit than customary planning.

Mitch met me under an overcast August sky. We stuffed an insubstantial amount of luggage into the cramped trunk quarters of the spit-polished Porsche. With the top down, and dressed like we were just going out to dinner, we waved good-bye to my mother and dad, who stood on the small front porch, unable to change the course of events.

We headed for the state of Maryland and to the home of a Baptist pastor and his wife. The wedding rings had been tucked away safely in Mitch's pocket. The "after the ceremony" plan, according to Mitch, was to find a place that night on our way to Virginia, and then spend the remainder of the week in the pits (no pun intended, but not too far from the truth). We were expected to join one of Mitch's racing friends who happened to be racing that weekend in a National Sports Car Race. The team's pit happened to be their predetermined meeting place. It was not my idea for the perfect honeymoon.

As the pastor stood with his back toward the imitation fireplace, his pleasant robust wife by his side, he opened the Bible, the Book of unchanging words and love. He hesitated, as if to give us a last-minute opportunity to change our minds. I half suspected that he was also deliberating with himself as to whether or not he was doing the right thing as well. He asked me if I would take Mitch to be my husband, in good and bad times, in sickness or in health, and for richer or poorer. For a brief second, fear rushed to my lips and they began to form the word "no," but they quickly reverted to the expected "yes." *Oh, Lord, what have I done?* I asked myself. *Please help me get through tonight, Lord. I am so scared.* I was not surprised when God didn't answer; I would probably need to reintroduce myself to Him again one day, I thought.

Mitch took me in his arms and kissed me, as we were pronounced man and wife. I was now Mrs. Mitch Brogan.

After some expected formalities, the pastor and his wife wished us Godspeed. I smiled and thought to myself, *Speed was one thing Mitch managed all on his own.*

We left the pastor's roadside home and headed toward Virginia. Close to Mitch's intended stop for the night, it began to rain. He explained that due to the aerodynamic design of the Porsche, no matter how hard it rained, we would not get wet, as long as we didn't have to stop. As soon as those words were out of his mouth, the traffic stopped, right in the middle of the downpour. My beautiful new dress and his Brooks Brothers suit were totally drenched. We reached over the back seat of the car and pulled the folded top over our heads. Fortunately for us, the motel where Mitch had made reservations for the night, a motel owned by a relative of his, was located several miles down the highway.

I was about to share my life, and my whole self, with another person. Mitch realized that I was about to give him a very precious gift, one that I had never given to anyone else.

After a hearty breakfast the following morning, we left for the state of Virginia.

*   *   *   *   *

The smell of race car fuel entered my veins just the way big band music had done at the Hershey Park Ballroom. The sounds, smells, and speeds of the race car engines provided instant gratification. It didn't take long for me to get caught up in the excitement of the race car world. After four days of watching bright red Ferraris race around the tracks, and often in the company of the men who drove them, I learned more about cars than I did about love.

The honeymoon was over, and I returned home a different person.

*   *   *   *   *

Plans for our own home did not materialize. Instead, Mitch informed me several weeks before our wedding day that we would temporarily reside with his parents. He wanted us to take our time, he had said, to find a nice apartment until we could see our way clear to buy a home. Somehow I was under the impression the purpose of us forfeiting a church wedding and engagement ring was to enable us to put that money towards a new home. But as always, I accepted his explanation without question.

The benefits I derived from spending time in the company of Mitch's precious mother far outweighed the disappointment of not having our own home. Because of her, I renewed my relationship with God. Watching her faithfully read her Bible every day, and always with a cup of hot water with fresh lemon slices beside her, awakened a sleeping desire to start reading my own Bible again.

After we had been in Mitch's parents' home for several months, his mother took my hand one day, as we sat side by side on the living room sofa.

"Leta, Mitch will be a wonderful provider for you and your children, should God bless you with children, but I'm afraid he will not make the same kind of husband or father."

Had that information come from anyone else, I would have let it roll off my back (a lesson I learned from the ducks), but the words had come from Mitch's small gray-haired mother, whom I had come to know as a spiritual giant. *How can she say that about her own son?* I thought. She shared the many letters with me that he had sent her when he was a paratrooper during the war, and they were filled with affection and concern for his family, especially his mother. I loved him for that. But he was thirty-four years old and still living at home, surely she knew him better than I did. I did not discard her words; I kept them to myself.

As soon as we returned home from our honeymoon, Mitch had asked me to resign my job at Armstrong. By that time, I was so distracted by my relationship with Mitch, that when I told my employers that I was planning to resign, one of them said, "Well, the way things have been going, if you hadn't resigned, we would have fired you." I was mortified. But thinking back, they were right. I hadn't been getting enough rest, and with my role in "By Hex," and all the makeup hours spent with Mitch, I knew I had not been doing my job, but I hadn't wanted to admit it.

Those were lonely days and nights, as we sacrificed time together so Mitch could continue building his pyramid to success. During that time of loneliness, I joined a Bible Study and came under conviction regarding drinking alcoholic beverages. I listened to alcohol-related horror stories and how its consumption had literally torn good families apart. I thought of my own foster parents, and what it had done to their relationship. I did not want that to happen to us. Just like an ex-smoker, I became totally intolerant of other people who did not have that same conviction. Mitch had great difficulty understanding my position, but as long as I did not infringe on his freedom to drink, the subject lay dormant between us.

One evening Mitch came home with an invitation to meet with an automobile importer in New York City. He asked me to accompany him. It was the most exciting announcement since our wedding date. He gave me money and told me to go to a well-known dress shop in Ephrata and buy a beautiful suit. He also planned to do some shopping for the occasion. Mitch had one more request. He asked me to wear my hair the way he loved it best . . . in two long braids pulled together on the top of my head. Each time I wore it that way, he would call me his beautiful German *frau*.

We drove to New York City to meet Maxwell Albrecht, a major importer of foreign automobiles. His office was located on Park Avenue, high above the noise of the streets below. As we exited the elevator, I realized that the entire room was surrounded by glass. I looked out over the tops of skyscrapers and nearly lost my breakfast. An attractive receptionist directed us to a room with real overstuffed leather chairs, where fine china cups on saucers were filled with freshly brewed coffee. "Or," she said, "would you care for some cognac instead?" We decided on the coffee. It wasn't long before we were escorted into an ultramodern office to meet Maxwell Albrecht. He shook Mitch's hand; he kissed mine.

"I see, Mr. Brogan, you have a lovely German wife!"

I wanted to correct him, but refrained from doing so when Mitch didn't respond to his comment.

His accent and mannerisms revealed his own German origin.

"My guess is, you are Austrian; am I right?" Mr. Albrecht asked me.

"No, actually you are off by about three thousand miles and eighteen hours by prop-plane."

Mitch looked dreadful. I could almost see him thinking, *If I wanted to make an impression with Mr. Albrecht, this wasn't what I had in mind.*

"Well, Mr. Brogan, you certainly have a charming wife. I can see she will be an asset to you and your business. And, hopefully, to *our* business."

Mr. Albrecht's reply seemed to alleviate some of Mitch's concerns, and his smile returned.

At the end of the day, and over a fabulous lobster lunch at the renowned Palm Restaurant, a deal to distribute some of the world's most expensive foreign automobiles throughout the East Coast was consummated between Maxwell Albrecht and Mitch Brogan. The income potential was enormous. It was one thing to be the dealer of one of the most popular German cars in the world, but an East Coast distributorship was an even more lucrative position to be in.

The decision to expand beyond the formidable Bucherville alley, the current location of our business, was the major topic of discussion on our way home from New York City. Because things were happening so fast, Mitch decided, and I agreed, that we should not concentrate on our personal needs at that time, but wait until we had seen monetary returns from our contract with Maxwell Albrecht to proceed with our plans to look for a home.

Mitch praised me for the way I had handled myself with Mr. Albrecht. He handed me fifty dollars and told me to buy something nice for myself. Since my name wasn't on the checkbook, and my weekly allowance didn't allow for extras, I naturally accepted the money with gratitude. Mitch's compliment, however, indicated to me that he considered my personality purposely designed to impress Mr. Albrecht. Mitch didn't know that entertaining conversation, and humor, served as barbed-wire fences around my heart. It came naturally. If anyone had taken the time to scale the wall of my heart, they would have gotten a panoramic view of pain and rejection, but to that point, I had managed to keep it well hidden. What I didn't know was, the fifty dollars Mitch gave me was only the first of many monetary rewards for a "job well done." It was one of the few ways I accumulated money of my own. The fact that I was not permitted to write a check, and no longer had a job (at Mitch's strong insistence), made it difficult, if not impossible, to keep up with Mitch's expectations of me. It wasn't long before Mitch found it necessary to hire additional employees. That freed him to concentrate on the distribution and sale of automobiles throughout the East Coast. As an East Coast Distributor, we began making regular trips to New York City, where we would meet Mr. Albrecht, who would generously wine and dine us and welcome us to his New York City penthouse, or to one or more of his magnificent homes outside of the city.

As a local dealer for the small German car, we were invited to join other dealers on our first European trip by chartered plane to Frankfurt, Germany. Since Mitch was one of the first such dealers in the United States, we were extended special privileges, such as choice seats on the airplane, and VIP attention by the distributor and his entourage. If the wine didn't go to our heads, the attention surely did.

Before our trip to Germany, I made the decision to introduce Mitch to my birth mother. He knew very little about the person he had married. In truth, the person he married knew little about herself as well. Perhaps it was my apprehension about flying, and the possibility of my dying in an airplane crash, that made me feel so strongly about the decision to have Mitch meet my birth mother. I hadn't heard from her since she decided to disown me, neither had I tried to get in touch with her; it was going to be a crapshoot at best.

When I approached Mitch about visiting my mother and half-sister, he was intrigued. He said he thought it was a good idea.

We drove to Yorktown on a Saturday afternoon, about a month before our trip to Europe. I had no idea if we would find my mother living at the same address, but at least it was a starting point.

There was no recollection of fond memories as we ascended the steps to her flat. I did not know what to expect, but with Mitch by my side for moral support, we knocked on the door of the apartment where we had hoped she still lived. We stood there for some time before we heard footsteps approaching the door.

Bassie opened the door, just wide enough to see who was on the other side. From the look on her face, seeing me must have catapulted her back three years of yesterdays.

"Hi, Bassie. It's me . . . Leta," I said, just in case she hadn't recognized me.

As she opened the door a little further, I could see beyond her into the living room, where Jean Marlow, my mother, was sitting on a large sofa. She appeared ill. Muttered words echoed hollow as they reached the door. I could see that my mother was upset by my unannounced visit.

"Bassie, I just wanted you both to meet my new husband. I thought perhaps time had made a difference in how Mother felt about me, but I can see that I have upset her."

Jean Marlow's weakend arm motioned for Bassie; we stood waiting for Bassie to return. Mitch insisted that we leave, but I wanted to hear what my mother had said to Bassie.

When Bassie returned, she relayed my mother's message.

"I'm sorry, Leta, but she wants you to leave and never come back. She said she doesn't consider you her daughter any more, and she has no interest in seeing you, and she doesn't want to meet your husband."

I could see that Bassie didn't exactly share my mother's sentiments, but she remained loyal to my mother, at the expense of her own feelings. I introduced Mitch to Bassie and assured her that I would honor my mother's request to never come to see her again.

It was the last time I saw my birth mother.

The identity of my birth father remained a mystery.

*   *   *   *   *

Having experienced the ravages of war himself, Mitch recognized a wounded soldier when he saw one. In the personal war with my past, I had been critically injured. If God ever blessed us with children, they would never know their real grandparents; I felt very sad about that. Grace and James Carpenter would be the only grandparents my children would ever know. Despite my foster dad's shortcomings, I was confident that they would make wonderful grandparents.

I decided that I would never get divorced; I would never do to my children what my mother had done to me.

*   *   *   *   *

Looking like wealthy world travelers dressed in the latest fashions, Mitch and I finally ascended the stairs that led to the belly of the

Lufthansa airplane and our assigned seats for my first trip to Germany. Mitch had seen Germany from an entirely different perspective during the war. Because it was a chartered flight, we had met the plane's captain and the crew earlier in the VIP lounge. There were bottles of champagne and trays of delicacies for our enjoyment. The obnoxious behavior of some of the dealers and their wives, resulting from overindulgence in alcohol, began long before we had ever left the ground.

I knew before we took off that I was not going to love flying. But I tried very hard to be brave. The distinct odor that reached my nostrils when I entered the cabin of the plane was the first clue I had that I was not the only apprehensive flyer. The unusual odor permeated every inch of the plane. When we finally took off from Idlewild International Airport, we were given more food and more alcohol. It seemed to me that half the passengers were already drunk. I clutched the arms of my seat until my knuckles lost their color. As the plane climbed high enough for a brush with Heaven, Mitch tried to calm me with some less than reassuring words. "Don't be such a baby; get hold of yourself," he said. And then his final sarcastic remark, "Do you want to get off?"

I squeezed back the tears and continued to look straight ahead.

Not long into our flight, a couple from New York who happened to be sitting behind us got into a shouting match. They began to physically abuse each other. The husband picked up a bottle of champagne with every intention of using it as a weapon to injure his wife. But instead, the bottle hit the window of the airplane, and a piece of glass hit the back of my neck. As I looked around, I saw the couple engaging in a literal fistfight, throwing curse words at each other like darts. The man was on top of his wife, punching her over and over again. I realized then that I was bleeding from the glass that had punctured my neck. When Mitch saw my wound, he got up, took off his suit coat, and walked back to the seat where the fight was taking place. He grabbed the man by the collar, disengaged him from the hold he had on his wife, and with one blow, knocked the man out cold. The flight attendants came running, with the captain not far behind them. Together with the help of the crew, and Mitch's powerhouse of strength, they transported the lifeless man to an area near the galley and restrained him for the duration of the flight. When we landed in Germany, the annoying couple resumed their disagreement, but with much less gusto. That evening, at a beautiful reception for all of the dealers, that same couple acted more like newlyweds than we did.

It was a vivid and lasting picture of how overindulgence of alcohol could affect a relationship, and I wanted no parts of it. As a result of my abstinence, I was one of the most popular people on the trip. Everyone wanted to sit beside me so they could drink the beer and wine that I refused.

Alcohol changed how my father treated my mother; the airplane experience was just another example of its poisonous sting.

*   *   *   *   *

We toured Europe in an elaborate coach, far exceeding the comfort and luxury of any tour bus I had ever seen in the United States. The driver was a handsome blue-eyed blonde man who kept trying to flirt with me through his rearview mirror. One of our first stops was the famous Beer Garden in Munich, where I could all but tolerate the carousing atmosphere. The idea was to drink as much beer as you could, all in one gulp. Naturally, I abstained. But as I sat and watched all the merriment and the flirtatious exchanges between my husband and the German *fraulein* waitresses, with their overexposed bosoms, the more annoyed I became. His fixation for German girls and Germans in general, was as clear to me as the *Glockenspiel* chimes.

I soon began to emulate German women, in order to please Mitch.

Before we went to sleep that night, I asked him a question.

"Mitch, I don't know how to ask you this, and I hope it won't make you angry, but would you have rather married a German girl instead of me?"

His answer hurt me, but it didn't surprise me.

"You look more like a German girl than some of the German girls themselves. And once I buy you some German clothes, who'll know the difference? A good leather coat and a dirndl dress with puffy sleeves should do it, don't you think?"

"And I guess you want the low neckline, too, huh?"

He realized then that he had hurt me, and he said that he was sorry; he said he had meant it as a complement. That is when he explained something that I have never forgotten.

"Leta, just because we are married doesn't mean we will never be attracted to other people. Sure, I was attracted to that one waitress, but that's all. I married you. You will also be attracted to other men, but it doesn't mean that you have to do anything about it. It just stops there."

I thought about what Mitch said. Then I thought about the bus driver.

Several days later, while we were having dinner at another popular German restaurant, I was coming out of the bathroom located in the rear of the building when the blonde bus driver approached me. His English was flawed, but I understood him very well.

"You are a beautiful American girl," he said, then he put his hand across his chest, indicating that I had touched his heart. Mitch had been right. It stopped there. For the rest of our tour, I made a point to avoid the handsome bus driver, but several times I caught him looking at me through his rearview mirror.

Mitch had been serious when he mentioned all the German clothes he intended to buy me. By the time we left Germany, I owned one of everything, it seemed. Each time someone mentioned how European I looked, it brought a proud smile to Mitch's face. I continued to wear my hair in braids and I wore the clothing that Mitch purchased for me . . . that was how much I wanted to please my husband.

*   *   *   *   *

When it was time to board the plane for our flight back to the United States, I was petrified. The experience coming across the ocean had heightened my fear of flying. And again, I was subjected to unwelcome comments from my husband. I cried some of the time. Other times, I just held on tightly to the arms of my seat.

It was good to be back in the United States without incident, but Mitch was already planning our next trip to Germany. "The next time," he said, "we are going to try and find some of the things I left behind after the war." He mentioned the wounded storekeeper whose leg he had shot off; the grenade he had thrown at a German tank, still lying unspent along a hedgerow somewhere; his friend's girlfriend; and the dead soldier's marker he had helped erect somewhere in Holland. We also planned to visit Omaha and Utah Beaches to view the field of crosses, memorials to the many dead Americans who had fought and died for the freedoms we were enjoying.

The thought of returning to Europe by airplane was a recurrent nightmare for me.

*   *   *   *   *

The year 1954 ended, and a new year began.

I spent more time with Mitch's family than I did with Mitch. I longed to be alone with him, instead of simply shutting a bedroom door and calling it home. But I knew he was working very hard and I wanted to be a supportive wife, and so I tried not to complain.

One morning in January, after walking into his parents' kitchen, I became very ill. I could barely stand the smell of Mother's freshly brewed coffee. I raced to the bathroom praying to throw up. When I was again able to join Mitch's mother in the kitchen, I explained how I had felt, and she smiled. I questioned why she would smile when I was feeling so poorly.

She suggested that I might be pregnant. *Oh my goodness*, I said to myself, *I never gave that a thought.*

I visited the doctor the following week, after my morning sickness had not improved. The result of that visit was a positive one. We were going to have a baby. That evening when Mitch came home to his reheated platter of food, I broke the news to him. He was thrilled. Of course, he wanted a boy; I wanted a girl. Each day we played the name game until we decided to just be thankful for a healthy child no matter what the sex happened to be.

Realizing how difficult it would be to rear a child in shared living quarters with his parents, Mitch began to actively search for an apartment. It didn't take long before he took me to see a second-floor, one-bedroom apartment on Main Street, very close to the restaurant where he had caught me sitting in his Porsche that night, and about a block and a half from where our business was located. It wasn't long before we were climbing a seemingly limitless number of steps to our new apartment. For the first time since we had married, we were alone in our own home . . . even if it was just an apartment. Our furniture and dishes were borrowed; the owner of the building provided the appliances, but the curtains were brand new. I was finally playing house.

An adjoining apartment was occupied by Ken and his new wife, the friend with whom I had been in the fatal accident in high school. Because we knew each other so well, we kept the adjoining door to our apartments open, except at night. We carried on a sort of dual living relationship. We shared food and laughter. Because Mitch was not at home much of the time, I was happy to have them so close.

Our first apartment guests were Mitch's airborne buddies and their wives. If it had not been for the *Mennonite Cookbook*, we would have starved. I had never observed my mother first hand while she was cooking, but I was up front and center when it came to consuming the food she had prepared. I was more occupied with playing OFFS or choosing up names for some physical sport. In retrospect, I sure wished Mother had insisted on my learning some household skills; it would have served me well during my first year of marriage.

By the end of my first week at keeping house, my *Mennonite Cookbook* had become seriously floured and egg stained. With the exception of liver failure (preparation of that tasty organ), I learned to cook fairly well.

*   *   *   *   *

Until my marriage to Mitch, there were a lot of guests in my life, people who spent time with me but hadn't stayed very long. I determined to make my marriage something secure and permanent. In the name of submission, I forfeited my own interests and lived to please my husband. He reciprocated by generously providing for my material needs.

The closer the time came to giving birth to our first child, the more time I spent reading my Bible. God's promises were a constant source of comfort to me. We began attending another church so we would not aggravate the still sensitive issue of his unbroken engagement to Michelle. As far as I knew, Michelle was still wearing Mitch's engagement ring. She was also making regular trips past our apartment. On many occasions, I would see her Buick convertible, the one that Mitch had picked out for her when he was still dating her, drive by the apartment when I was getting into my car or walking from our apartment to the business. Because of that constant reminder, I began feeling guilty about the part I played in breaking up their seven-year engagement. I was sure she had been deeply hurt. I tried not to think about it, but the thought just stood in line until it was at the front of my mind. I knew I had to talk to Michelle, if not for her benefit, certainly for mine. I did not tell Mitch what I planned to do.

I took a plain piece of paper and a pen, not wanting to convey any subliminal message by using our personal letterhead, and spent an entire afternoon compiling a letter of sincere apology for my part in causing her pain. I told her how much I loved Mitch, but that I was sure she had felt the same way about him. I told her I hoped, in time, that she would forgive both of us; however, I spoke only for myself. I also wrote that had I known I would end up causing anyone such marked suffering, I would not have done what I did. I shared with her the disappointments and pain of my past and said that I wouldn't have wished that kind of pain on anyone. By the time I had finished the note, I honestly wished I hadn't married Mitch. My last words to her included the fact that Mitch and I were expecting a child.

The summer months were unbearable as I waited to give birth to our first baby. The seventeenth of October of that year, a beautiful baby girl occupied the little blue-and-pink-trimmed bassinet. After seventeen hours of absolute torture, Sarah entered the world knees first. She was healthy, dimpled, and blonde. Mitch was hesitant about picking her up, afraid that he would break her. But in time, he did his share of rocking; but when it came to diaper changes, he emphatically proclaimed, "That's a woman's job." I proclaimed that there would be no more babies.

During a very bad case of the common cold, something that seemed normal for a small baby, Sarah was given a prescription for nose drops by our family physician. In trying to help, Mitch misread the dosage when administering the drops, and hours later, I discovered Sarah's head had grown much larger, and she wasn't breathing normally. I was frantic. The doctor urged us to get to the hospital as soon as possible, that she had apparently been given an overdose of the prescribed drugs. It was a life-threatening situation.

I watched as our dear little Sarah, the one I had held to my breast, lay small and helpless in an oxygen-fed hospital unit. It took a special phone call to Mitch from our family physician, to convince him of the urgency of the situation before he reluctantly left his office to transport us to the hospital, with little time to waste. I never left Sarah's side until she was able to return home. I think I skipped several years of my life during that emergency. I thanked God that there were no residual effects from the unintended overdose when Sarah finally recovered.

It wasn't long before Mitch decided that the apartment was just too small for the three of us. Sarah was growing, and by January 1957, we were expecting our second child.

Mitch came home one evening at eleven o'clock, having kept the shop open late, accommodating everyone but his family, and announced that he was purchasing a small parcel of land across from the shop. He asked me what I had thought about house trailers. When I questioned him about getting our own home somewhere else, he said the decision to buy a house trailer was the wiser of the two options.

I learned later that plans were already made to build and relocate our automobile showroom in another town in the near future.

*   *   *   *   *

Lovely dinners at the Hotel Hershey preceded our faithful attendance at all of the Hershey Bears' ice hockey games. We became regulars at the hotel by that time and were given a reserved parking place at the main entrance for our bright red Ferrari. I coveted those evenings with Mitch. But most of our dinner conversation centered on cars.

It was during one of those infamous hockey games that I was introduced to another side of Mitch Brogan. He had known most of the players, the coach, and the owner of the team. Mitch would become exceedingly annoyed when anyone from the opposite team would rough up one of our players. Quite frequently, Mitch found his way onto the ice, or halfway over the protective glass barrier, with fists flying, scoring one hit after another in order to defend his hockey buddies. I sat helpless, embarrassed, and stunned. Some cheered him on, while others discouraged that type of retribution, particularly the arena police. Mostly, he was considered a hero by the fans and the players.

*   *   *   *   *

During that summer, and before our second child was born, we attended a sports car race in Bridgehampton, Connecticut. Being pregnant, I tried hard to avoid the crowds of drinking spectators. To preserve energy in the heat of the day, I leaned on a fence post to watch and smell the Ferraris accelerating out of the "s-turns." It wasn't long before some big overbearing guy pushed his way next to me, and his twelve-ounce plastic cup of beer spilled all over me. With lightning swiftness, Mitch was by my side. His fist sent the guy reeling backwards into the ground.

I gained a fearful respect for Mitch as a result of those racetrack and ice hockey experiences.

... FOURTEEN ...

Mitch and I were blessed to have Fannie, an unmarried woman, as our housekeeper and babysitter. It was important that I not be too encumbered by children and housework in order to free me to accompany Mitch on business trips, to social events, and to sports car races. Fannie was dependable, trustworthy, and totally charmed by Sarah's tiny smile. She began her employment with us shortly after Sarah was born.

In October 1956, Benjamin, our second child and every bit as charming, was born. We had already moved into our new house trailer directly across from my husband's car dealership and body shop. It was beginning to look like a baby a year for us, and I could already foresee another move in our future. The house trailer had bunk beds in one room, to which we added safety bars so the babies wouldn't fall out of bed. The slightly larger room became our bedroom. This was our home for the following two years.

Living at arm's length from my husband's place of business had advantages and disadvantages. The disadvantages became evident all too soon. Mitch continued to maintain a state inspection station that required periodic checkups by the Pennsylvania State Police. The officer most often performing those checks was none other than Michael Banks.

As a diversion in my daily routine of being a mother and wife, I decided to resurrect the oil paints and easel that I had buried in the attic. In addition to acting, I was also blessed with some artistic talent, and I decided it was time to put that gift to use. While the children were taking their afternoon naps, I would often set up my easel and paint for several hours a day. My first large project, in addition to the children's portraits in charcoal, was a large painting of a Civil War battle scene. It was the most detailed and difficult painting I had ever undertaken. As I stood back and scrutinized my brush strokes, I was transported from my living room into that blood-soaked war. I could actually feel the pain of death as I looked at the fallen soldiers and horses that covered the canvas battlefield.

A dark shadow approaching the steps that led to the glass door of our trailer home distracted me. It was Michael Banks. I assumed that

Mitch was across the street at the business, so I didn't feel threatened by Michael's appearance.

Numerous times, when I got into my car to run errands, I had found notes under the windshield wipers of my car. Each brief note read the same.

Checked your house last night, and all is well.

Without question, it was Michael who had written and left those notes. I found it somewhat comforting that he had still been looking out for me. Mitch, on the other hand, was so busy attending to his growing business that he somehow overlooked those notes, until they began to appear more frequently. When he finally approached me regarding one that he had found on my car one morning, I denied having received any other notes. I didn't want to engage a sleeping steamroller. I was all too aware that Michael had the wherewithal to put Mitch behind bars, and Mitch had the wherewithal to disfigure Michael's face.

"Michael, how are you?" I said as I greeted him at the door. "Have you seen Mitch?"

I had asked that question in hopes of dispelling any assumed improprieties between Michael and me.

When he didn't reply right away, I began to feel uneasy about Michael being in the house, and yet I felt confident that Mitch must have given the green light for the visit.

The reply came after his eyes had made a quick journey around the room.

"Your husband is busy selling cars," he responded.

And then he immediately changed the subject.

"Hey, that's really good, Leta," he said, as he looked at the nearly completed painting. "I didn't know you had such talent. If you don't have a buyer, I'm interested."

"You must be kidding, Michael," I replied. "I don't sell my work. This is just for my own pleasure."

"Well, it would give me pleasure to buy it. How much do you want for it?"

"No, really, Michael, I've never sold anything I've painted, and it's not even finished yet."

"Well then, consider this your first sale."

I thought about it and decided, *Well, why not?*

"O.K., Michael, you win," I answered, "but I can't let you buy it; when I complete it I will give it to you as a gift."

"Absolutely not," he said, as he pulled a one-hundred-dollar bill out of his pocket. "I know it's probably worth a whole lot more, but you know we troopers don't get paid what we're worth. Just don't forget that it belongs to me."

"Michael, I can't take your money."

But he did not allow me to return the money.

"Leta, how are things between you and Mitch? Are you happy?"

"Yes, Michael, I am very happy," I declared. "Lonely, but happy. If it weren't for the races and the hockey games, I would get to see very little of my husband, I'm afraid. Moving across from the business has helped a little, and sometimes he even takes time out to have lunch with us, but most of the time he is busy selling cars, just like you said."

"Talk about timing; I get divorced and you get married, and here you are with two children already; boy, you haven't wasted any time, have you?"

I wasn't about to let him off that easily, and so I reminded him of the inaccuracy of his statement.

"Divorced? Don't you mean divorced again, Michael?"

"You're right," he admitted. "I've always regretted that I wasn't honest with you. But there's little I can do about it now, I suppose. I just want you to know that I still love you and if your husband ever does anything to hurt you, you know my number at the barracks. You be sure to call me if you need me, understand?"

"I don't think that will be necessary, Michael, but thanks for your concern. Now I must get back to painting because the children will soon be awake from their naps."

"Just remember what I said, O.K?"

"Yes, Michael, I'll remember."

Agreeing with him seemed the quickest way to discourage a lengthier visit. I really didn't want Mitch to think that Michael's stay indicated any further involvement on my part with his archenemy, so I was relieved when he finally left the trailer.

Mitch spent long hours away from the house, and although I could see him working at times, I missed having him with me. He began to spend less and less time with the children and me. My companions were mostly books and music. Occasionally I would watch television, but I much preferred reading. I began to write poetry as a way of expressing my loneliness. The pages were filled with sentimentalism and discontent.

One night, long past eleven o'clock when Mitch finally came home from the office, I decided to confront him concerning the time he was spending away from the children and me. When I accused him of loving his work more than he loved the children, he became very angry. He claimed that he had to work as hard as he did to support the family, and he accused me of being unappreciative of what he had already accomplished on our behalf.

What started out as a simple explanation for my loneliness ended with a slap in the face. Ending up on the floor in fallen disbelief, I apologized and begged his forgiveness for bringing up the subject. Of course, I did appreciate what he had done for us, but I was young, already the mother of two children, and I just wanted to spend more time with my husband. I wanted to know the deep and shallow parts of him. Instead, I began to realize that I really didn't know him at all. My face stung from the swiftness of his hand. I had begun to cry, which only made things worse. He admonished me for crying, followed by the same familiar comments he had hurled at me on our harrowing trip across the Atlantic Ocean.

The fact that we knew very little about each other, I presume, was due mainly to our brief courtship. In all fairness to Mitch, he couldn't have known the amount of attention, affection, and reassurance I would require to feel loved. And little did I know that my needs as a woman would become a means of provoking Mitch to react abusively. In the future, I would have to be very careful not to discuss my feelings with him. I accepted full responsibility for what had taken place.

Even with Mitch's arms around me that night, his way of reconciling differences, I was unable to fall asleep. Afraid, and not wanting to withhold myself from him, I nevertheless responded somewhat begrudgingly to his overtures. Many future altercations were resolved in like manner.

The next morning, Mitch told me he loved me and gave me a little extra money to buy something "nice," as he referred to it. That was his way of saying, "I'm sorry."

*   *   *   *   *

Another distressing indicator of a marriage in trouble was the untenable strictness with which he governed the children and me. Toddlers ordinarily attract dirt like flies to flypaper, but when our children got dirty, it was considered a criminal offense. Because I knew the consequences of mud-stained clothes, I took great pains to discourage the children from normal outdoor activity. The children were expected to remain presentable at all times. We bought the children expensive and stylish clothes, and even as toddlers, they looked like miniature fashion models. Their manners were impeccable. Whenever we visited friends or went out to eat at a fine restaurant, the children always received compliments on their behavior. Our lives were spent standing at attention.

*   *   *   *   *

March of every year, Mitch and I would head to Florida for the Sebring, Florida, Grand Prix car races. Fannie was left in charge of the household. Generally we were gone for about two weeks.

The Sports Car Club took up nearly one whole floor of rooms at the Lake Wales Motel. My fondest memory during those times was when I got to pick fruit from the trees behind the motel and ended up gorging myself on delicious grapefruits and oranges. Fragrant gardenia bushes pervaded the air surrounding the grounds, just like the smell of Ferrari fuel permeated the racecourse on the day of the big race.

There were countless activities during race week. Banners hung all over town advertising every beer and fuel oil additive ever made. Car lovers from far and wide filled the streets, motels, and restaurants. We touched shoulders with some of the biggest names in the sport, eventually becoming close friends with several of the well-known drivers.

Mitch had his own Ferrari, plus numerous other exotic cars, and I had the pleasure of driving a large black Mercedes sedan with real white leather upholstery. But we still lived in a house trailer. Outwardly, we appeared to be happy and successful; or, as someone put it, "You two are the perfect couple."

During the Sebring races, Mitch and I spent more time together than at any other time. The children accompanied us to Florida on several occasions, but generally not during the Sebring Grand Prix. As the children got older, they began to travel with us more frequently; and because of my fear of flying, they eventually took my place on trips to Europe with their father.

*   *   *   *   *

Mitch's business continued to grow, and it wasn't long before an expansion was necessary to accommodate the BMW East Coast Distributorship. Mitch purchased a large building one block from our home and converted it into a showroom and offices for his new enterprise. The demand for Mitch's time increased.

We found ourselves spending more and more time in Maxwell Albrecht's New York City office. A considerable amount of time was also spent in his New York penthouse apartment and his breathtakingly beautiful rambling home in Rye, New York. Servants, chefs, and the finest things money could buy surrounded us on every one of those occasions. I would accompany Madeleine, Mr. Albrecht's wife, to Tiffany's where armed guards stood watch over a pearl and diamond necklace, an anticipated birthday gift from her adoring husband. I felt a little envious.

I especially recall, and quite vividly I must say, the time I mentioned to Madeleine that I was looking for a special dress. She took me to an exclusive Madison Avenue dress shop. Upon entering, nothing yielded a clue as to what was being sold there. Beautiful sales women greeted us at the door. They asked what the occasion was that warranted one of their exclusive designs. As a result of the information I provided, they produced several selections from the back room. The first dress was exactly what I would have loved to own, but when she told me it was fifteen hundred dollars, I immediately found ten things wrong with it. The second choice was no better. Red faced, I admitted to Madeleine that I was thinking more in terms of seventy-five dollars. Only then did she realize she had misjudged my purchasing power; she suggested Macy's as a possible shopping alternative.

When I shared that experience with Mitch, he said that I, too, would be able to spend that much on clothing some day. "That is why I spend so much time working," he explained. Somehow I didn't think affording me a fifteen-hundred-dollar dress was his sole reason for working overtime, and it certainly wasn't for our children's college education; he was against any of his children becoming "college brats," as he called them. Only after much cajoling by me, did he permit our daughter Sarah to attend a dental assistant education school in Pittsburgh. He said that if any of "his" children ever wanted to go to college, they would have to pay for it themselves. In his opinion, the only children worth taking up space on the planet were career military sons and daughters. But even those aspirations for his children came with strings attached: they had to become Screaming Eagle, 101st Airborne, sons and daughters. Early on, I suspected that if our children did not pursue military careers, they might possibly find themselves disowned or even disinherited. *You may want to take a note of that educated guess at this point.*

The more time Mitch and I spent with people of enormous means, the more Mitch's desire to become successful and rich increased . . . and it was contagious.

We traveled as far as Montreal, Canada, to buy clothes for our whole family. One of Mitch's favorite men's shops welcomed us with small Waterford glasses filled with topaz-colored cognac, followed by a couple thousand dollars' worth of sales. No one would have imagined that the same people who lived in a two-bedroom trailer home would be spending thousands of dollars on imported clothing. The reason for our humble dwelling was that most of our money was being directed toward numerous building projects for Mitch's automobile business.

*   *   *   *   *

In January 1958, Thomas, our third child and the second of our two sons, was born. A child a year, and another move, hadn't been an erroneous prediction.

When I was released from the hospital, I came home to a surprise. A new and larger trailer home stood where the smaller trailer home had been. The new trailer even had a small Franklin fireplace in the living room. It was obviously a step up from the dining car appearance of our former trailer home. Between Mitch's family and mine, they had transferred all our belongings into the new home, leaving me searching deep and wide for our daily staples.

We had three of the most precious children ever born. Sarah, with her large blue eyes, dimples, and blonde hair, was irresistible. Benjamin had a gentle manner, inheriting his mother's people-pleasing nature at an early age. Thomas, on the other hand, had all the makings of another Mitch Brogan, at least in temperament. When I tell you that they were the best-behaved children around, it is not an exaggeration. But they didn't have a choice. The rod was not spared in our family, and the children remained unspoiled. Never, in all the years of rearing our children, was it necessary to remove one treasure from the coffee table in order to avoid breakage. Although that was good . . . in retrospect, they really weren't permitted to be children.

*   *   *   *   *

We enjoyed our new trailer home, but it still wasn't large enough to comfortably accommodate our family, so Mitch hired a young German man named Klaus as an auto mechanic, who, along with his connatural automobile talents, also happened to be an accomplished builder. It also raised the number of Mitch's employees to five. It wasn't long before Mitch hired Klaus to build an addition to our trailer home.

After living in small quarters for four years of our marriage, the addition of a large living room, finished basement, two bedrooms, and a large bathroom felt like we had moved into a mansion. I converted the old living room, with the Franklin fireplace, into a dining room, which enabled us to entertain more comfortably, and it provided more room in which the children could play. We appeared to be the perfect little family.

*   *   *   *   *

Mitch's abusive behavior surfaced again, when late one night he came home with alcohol and tobacco on his breath.

The children were already in bed, and I had spent most of the evening watching the clock. It was winter, and it had been snowing since late afternoon. As I waited for Mitch to come home, the snow grew deeper, until it was hugging the tires of the cars lined up outside of the dealership. Then it suddenly stopped snowing, and a light wind began to blow the snow into small mounds against the cars until they were partially hidden; then I heard the sound of his car. He walked in the door, but gave no excuse for his late arrival. And although I still remembered what had happened to me the last time I questioned his whereabouts, I did not expect the same response twice.

Before I could say anything, Mitch warned me not to start interrogating him. I assured him that I did not consider my concern for his absence an interrogation, but I did think that he owed me some explanation for coming home at two o'clock in the morning. He said nothing. Instead of letting it go, something I found almost impossible to do, I insisted that he explain his whereabouts. After some unpleasant exchanges, I still hadn't received a satisfactory explanation. I began to cry. Out of sheer frustration with having to account to me, his wife, he grew increasingly angry, and before I knew what happened, his open fist came smashing against my face. Drops of blood covered my bathrobe and I felt an excruciating pain across my nose. I touched my face and my hand was covered with blood. *Oh my God,* I thought, *he broke my nose.* All I could think of was how to get away from him. I ran out the door in my slippers and bathrobe, without a coat, and my hand over my bleeding nose. I ran three blocks, in the snow, to the home of Mitch's parents. I did not have time to look for the keys to my car; furthermore, I knew that if I remained in the house, he might possibly hit me again. When I reached his parents' home, I kept banging on the door until his mother finally came to the door.

"Please let me come in, Mother. Mitch hit me," I begged.

Unfortunately, she suggested that I return home to Mitch, saying that she didn't want to interfere in our marriage. "It just wouldn't be right," she said. She allowed me in the house only long enough to supply me with extra tissues and a coat, before convincing me to go back home. I disagreed with her reasoning, but I knew that it had been a sincere conviction on her part; thus, I never held it against her or my father-in-law for not coming to my rescue.

My bedroom slippers were wet, and I was very cold.

I was relieved to find the door of our trailer home unlocked. I used the same caution to enter my own home as a burglar uses to enter the home of a stranger. Mitch was nowhere in sight. Shivering, I managed to make it to the bathroom without incident. It was apparent that Mitch had already gone to bed. My nose had stopped bleeding, in part because of the outside temperature, and because it really wasn't broken. After I had taken a warm bath, I crawled into bed, beside Mitch.

There was no mention of the previous night's event as we shared the breakfast table with our unsuspecting children, who, innocently enough, had slept through the whole disturbance. My nose was very sore and had already begun to turn a dingy shade of gray. I knew I would have to fabricate a reasonable explanation for the discoloration later that day when I visited my parents.

Mitch bent to kiss my forehead as he excused himself from the table. He rarely spent time with the children, and that morning was no exception. He patted them on the head, reminded them to be good, and was off to the office.

Mitch was unduly rough with the children, even when he spent time playing with them; usually one or more of the children ended up getting hurt. Ben's gentle demeanor earned him the name "sissy" from his father, something I strongly took objection to. He was a loving and sensitive young boy, undeserving of that label. He was forever offering extra pillows to his Grandma Brogan for her crippled back in order to make her more comfortable. But the name calling continued.

In spite of a hearty breakfast, we were starving . . . for Mitch's attention.

When the children and I arrived at my parents' house, Mother discreetly questioned me regarding my black and blue nose. The children had settled on the living room floor to play with their favorite toys, consisting mostly of clothespins and pots and pans. Expensive toys did not hold the same fascination for them. I began by explaining to my mother that I had not been paying attention when I opened a cupboard door, and I hit myself in the nose with it. There was no way of telling whether or not she believed me, but my experience with her in times past told me that she probably didn't. But like my mother-in-law, she would never have interfered in our personal affairs.

*   *   *   *   *

It wasn't long before I suspected I was pregnant for the fourth time. I didn't want to have any more children. But birth control, like divorce, hadn't been one of my options. I figured God had already numbered the children I would have.

After carrying the baby for six months, I unexpectedly broke out in a rash all over my body. I went to the family physician, who in turn had me admitted to Lancaster General Hospital. After a considerable number of medical opinions, it was determined that the baby had literally disintegrated within my womb, and there was no way to put it back together again. I was told it was the hospital's first such case, with a name I didn't understand then, nor am able to provide now. The only choice available under such circumstances was to perform a legal abortion; to do otherwise would have put my life in jeopardy.

Paper was spread out beneath my body in preparation for the deluge of matter from its place of warmth and security, onto a cold, uncertain resting place. I cried. Not for me, but for the tiny baby that was unable to complete his journey into life.

It took a long time for me to mentally recover from that experience.

... FIFTEEN ...

The distributor of the world's best-selling German automobile met with Mitch and me for the purpose of determining the location for Mitch's new automobile dealership. As a rapidly growing business, it quickly outgrew its cloistered location in Bucherville. The supply and demand sales status of the popular bug-sized vehicle had granted Mitch ample time in which to design, build, and open his new dealership.

As we sat with the distributor, we were given two possible relocation choices: south of Bucherville in a growing metropolitan area, or in a less populated blue-collar area north of Bucherville. Since the distributor played an instrumental part in determining the relocation of the business, they continued to meet with us on a regular basis until the appropriate site was chosen.

I had been introduced to, and in the company of, the vice president's family, long before that particular meeting ever took place.

Vanessa, the vice president's wife, and I had already become friends. She told me that her husband thought I had displayed a keen sense for business, was exceptionally supportive of my husband, and equipped with the survival skills needed for an enduring business venture. Perhaps that is why I didn't think it strange when I was asked to express my opinion on a prospective location for the business.

The southern location, known as Lancaster, with its increase of new businesses, industry, new homes, and a large college campus, was easily my relocation choice. Having worked in Lancaster before marrying Mitch, I had found it to be a very progressive city.

In what I believed was an attempt at pulling rank on my opinion, and to show his displeasure at my being included in such an important decision, Mitch chose the northern location. He gave numerous reasons why he thought that location was the more lucrative of the two locations. Primarily, his argument appeared logical. Minden, in contrast to Lancaster, was a small town whose populace was less affluent. "What better place to sell an economic automobile?" he said. But I remained convinced that the southern location would transport itself into the future with much greater potential.

As the years proved, Lancaster would indeed have been the more ideal location, financially speaking; nevertheless, following the distributor's building guidelines, we broke ground for our new dealership in Minden, north of Bucherville.

*   *   *   *   *

Shortly after the ribbon cutting, an East Coast dealers' meeting was scheduled for Nassau, in the Bahamas Island. Thinking it would make a nice family vacation, we planned on taking our children with us on our Bahamian cruise. It turned out to be an eventful cruise. The seas were greatly disturbed . . . making it a very rough crossing. I realized then why God had given me arms and legs, and not webbed feet and feathers.

As we left the cruise ship and set foot on shore, we were captivated by the island's carnival-like atmosphere. An unusual calm pervaded the air between Mitch and me, broken only by an annoying cough that began plaguing me during our brief water voyage.

While visiting the beautiful Bahamas Island, Sarah discovered the miracle of the iguana. She made a valorous attempt at capturing one of the creatures and, in the end, was left holding only its tail in her hand. Unknown to Sarah and me, God had gifted the iguana with the innate ability to drop his tail in order to evade capture; then he would go off and grow another one. Sarah's face was covered in tears; she thought she had dismembered a helpless creature . . . a fitting picture for the *National Geographic* magazine. An accommodating native Bahamian explained to Sarah why the iguana had dropped his tail, and only then was Sarah able to recover from that experience.

My persistent cough made sleeping nearly impossible for all of us. We finally found a drugstore where we purchased a strong liquid cough suppressant. But the cough accompanied me back to New York City and home to Bucherville.

One of the first things Mitch mentioned when we returned from our cruise was his plan for us to spend some time in Europe. Had it not been for my fear of flying, I would have welcomed that news. As it was, I thought of nothing else but how I was going to avoid going on that proposed vacation.

Several weeks after that, I visited the doctor's office for a medical opinion regarding my severe coughing spells. The doctor listened to my chest and suggested that I get a chest x-ray done as soon as possible.

Several days before we were scheduled to leave for Europe, the phone rang. It was our family doctor, the same one who had delivered all of our children and who knew me very well. The news he delivered that day was unpleasant and unexpected. Always direct and to the point when it came to breaking bad news, he said, "Leta, this is Dr. Scott. I have some unpleasant news for you." I waited as he continued. "The x-ray indicates a very suspicious spot on your right lung. How soon can you leave for Temple University Hospital in Philadelphia?"

Not completely comprehending the urgency of his call, I replied, "We have plans to leave for Europe in two days, Dr. Scott. Can't it wait until we come back?"

His reply indicated the seriousness of the findings.

"No, this cannot wait," he assured me. "If it is what we suspect, there is a fifty percent chance your right lung will have to be removed. So how soon can you be there?"

"I will have to discuss this with Mitch. I will call you back."

The feeling in my stomach was mixed. I had to think about how Mitch would accept the news, since he had so much looked forward to going to Europe. But I could not ignore the consequences of putting off such an important matter.

When Mitch came home for lunch that afternoon, which was a rare occasion, I took it as an endorsement to announce the bad news. His response left me stunned and heartsick.

"Ah, it's probably nothing; you can drive yourself to Philadelphia, and I'll just go to Europe by myself. I sure wouldn't want to lose money on two tickets."

"But I may have to have my lung removed," I explained. "You mean you would go to Europe while I'd be in the hospital having such a serious operation?"

"Hey, you'll have the best doctors; you won't need me there, too. Anyway, they always make things sound worse than they really are."

Mitch had the greatest respect for our family doctor. As a matter of fact, after his medical discharge from the 101st Airborne, he had driven ambulance for the Bucherville Fire Company. He had said that our family doctor, formerly a military doctor himself, and with whom Mitch worked during his time on the ambulance crew, had been one of the few accompanying doctors that hadn't poked fun or made derogatory remarks about individuals being taken to the hospital. The news concerning my lung came from that same respected physician, so I was more than surprised at Mitch's blasé attitude. I hadn't wanted him to think that I was a sissy too, so I held back my tears until after he left to go back to work.

I called the doctor back and told him what Mitch had said. He was furious. But his next words accompanied and encouraged me on my long drive to Philadelphia and Temple University Hospital.

"Leta, I am your friend and your doctor," he said, "and you will have excellent doctors at Temple University Hospital. Remember: God's in Heaven, and I am here, too. Let Mitch go. We don't need him."

With the children under the care of my parents and Fannie, and Mitch already in the air, heading for Europe, I packed a small bag and left for Philadelphia. During the drive, I repeated the doctor's words over and over again in my mind. I spent all my amassed courage driving into the city of Philadelphia for the first time in my life. I had a full tank of gas, an empty wallet, and absolutely no clue what to expect when I arrived at the hospital. And, I had absolutely no idea that I would need some kind of proof of medical insurance coverage once I got there. Mitch had always taken care of everything.

A guardian angel led me to a public parking lot not far from the hospital. I later realized it hadn't been the right place to park when being admitted to Temple University Hospital, but I knew better than to admonish an angel. Had it not been for a very sympathetic parking attendant, I might have spent my last night at the hospital sleeping in the lounge.

After presenting some paperwork from my family doctor to the admissions office secretary, I discovered that I had absolutely no insurance information to offer. Nevertheless, I gained unwanted entrance to Temple University Hospital.

My visit consisted of standing on my head; swallowing cups of play dough; being poked with enough holes to water a garden; ogled by dark-skinned, bearded, turban-headed strangers; and a female doctor who slipped a disc while giving me an examination. I had to use my personal call button to announce that one of the hospital's doctors was in my room, had bent over, and literally couldn't get up.

After innumerable tests, it was determined that I had contracted a serious lung disease, generally caused by overexposure to fowl droppings, smoke, aerosol sprays, paint fumes, and asbestos. Determining which of five culprits had contributed most to the diagnosis had been relatively easy. I had grown up playing in chicken houses; I lived in a town where the chief industry was manufacturing asbestos; and I also had to admit to smoking for a brief period of time in my life. As well, I had a can-of-hairspray-a-week beehive coiffeur. Most certainly, all of them contributed to my unhealthy lungs.

It took nearly a week before a decision was finally reached regarding the removal of my right lung.

In place of the warm breakfast tray I was expecting, three doctors entered my room looking more like shepherds bearing news of a lost lamb. Contrary to my assumption, the doctors offered me a number of suggestions regarding my health situation: I could begin a rigorous exercise program consisting of daily jogging; avoid all types of smoke; move to an asbestos-free environment; and eliminate hairspray from my beauty routine. To adhere to those guidelines would discourage the growth of the disease, I was told. If I did none of the above, they said, the only option left was to remove my right lung. It wasn't a very difficult decision for me to make.

While in the hospital, I received daily calls from Mitch, but those calls did not replace his personal presence by my side. The fact that he had left me without the necessary insurance information for my hospital admittance, and money for the removal of my car from the parking garage angered me. But I blamed myself for not having had the foresight to think of those things myself.

After seven days in the hospital, I was discharged, lung intact. I was directed to undergo yearly examinations, including chest x-rays and blood work. That was the easy part. Getting out of the hospital was a formidable task of another kind.

I called the manager of our business, requesting the insurance information needed for my dismissal from the hospital, and the money to pay the concerned parking attendant. Without explaining why, our manager refused to forward the necessary items. I did not know what to do. After much deliberation, I asked to speak to someone in charge of discharging patients. Gratefully, the man with whom I spoke had the authority to discharge me despite the absence of the necessary items the hospital normally required, but he made it very clear that I had to send them the information as soon as my husband returned from Europe. I agreed to do just that.

After I returned home, I began implementing an exercise program that included running five miles a day. I became addicted to running, and regardless of the weather, I never missed a day.

Mitch returned home from Europe.

When I relayed his manager's unwillingness to provide the insurance information necessary for my dismissal, he defended the manager by saying that he probably had only been teasing me. When the hospital called and talked to Mitch requesting the information, he then believed my version of what had taken place. The manager was neither fired nor reprimanded. Several years later, he resigned. I never found out why he was unwilling to help me in my hour of distress.

*   *   *   *   *

Another unforeseen event surfaced three weeks after I returned home from the hospital.

New renters moved into an apartment house at the end of the alley where our trailer home was located. In fact, the end of our small yard practically joined the apartment house property. It didn't take long for me to recognize our new neighbors. It was a cousin to Michelle, Mitch's former girlfriend.

One day as I glanced out of the window, I observed a pair of binoculars observing me from the second-floor window of the apartment building. I felt the eyes of those binoculars on me everywhere I went. I was also fairly sure that Mitch's every move was being observed as well. Michelle had obviously not been receptive to the note I had sent her some time earlier and was apparently still having a difficult time putting her relationship with Mitch behind her. I did not, however, appreciate being subjected to such an invasion of our privacy. I was forced to keep my drapes closed on the side of our house facing the apartment building, causing a hovering gloom over half of our living room.

Michelle had also gotten married, I learned, and she and her husband and two children had moved into a row home that was located about three blocks from our house. It puzzled me why Michelle was still interested in our lives when she had a family of her own. But of all people, I knew something about the lingering nuisances of requited love, and I did not harbor any animosity towards Michelle for her actions. Instead, I felt sorry for her. I had not liked being spied upon, but I thought that perhaps in time, her interest in our lives would wane. I was so wrong.

Sarah and Benjamin attended grade school on the street where Michelle and her family lived. It wasn't long before I became suspicious of the time it was taking the children to walk home from school everyday. So I decided to conduct my own surveillance. And what I discovered outraged me. Michelle had been inviting our children onto her porch for cookies and milk after school. The time had come for me to take action.

After school had ended one day I approached her home, catching her completely off guard. Her eyes were as big as Frisbees when she saw me on her porch. Because the children were present, I reserved my condemnation for another time. I gathered my children and simply told them that it was time to go home.

That evening when the children were in bed and Mitch was still working at the shop, I walked up to Michelle's home. Confident their children had also gone to bed, I confronted her at the door. With few words, I warned her never to speak to my children or invite them onto her property again. My words of warning were underlined and spoken in red. She acknowledged her wrongdoing and agreed never to do it again. I also reminded her of the intrusion into our private lives by using a pair of binoculars to spy on us. For that, she doubly apologized. I took her at her word when she promised never to engage in those types of activities again. I accepted her apology.

*   *   *   *   *

I did not tell Mitch about some of the things that had taken place involving his ex-girlfriend. But one day I finally broke down and decided to give him the details of what had been going on. Instead of taking my side, he accused me of being jealous of Michelle. Not wanting to involve the children, I opted not to bring them on the scene as witnesses, especially with regard to Michelle intercepting them on their way home from school. I felt hurt and defeated. Nearly every time I shared my concerns with Mitch, his defense would go up like the American flag on Memorial Day. After that, I began to pray that we would move away from Bucherville, and God answered my prayers.

Before settling on a beautiful one-story stone and redwood home overlooking a man-made lake, halfway between Bucherville and our new business location in Minden, Mitch and I had another physical confrontation.

It was the first time I felt the necessity to take Michael up on his offer of help. When I called the State Police Barracks after Mitch had left the house, I asked to talk to Michael. It just so happened that he was in the office at the time and he came directly to the telephone. When I told him that Mitch had hit me, he asked me if it was the first time he had done that to me. I told him, "No." Then he asked me if I owned a gun. I'm confident that Michael wasn't suggesting that I shoot Mitch, but he was concerned that perhaps one day I might be faced with a life-threatening situation and have no way of defending myself. He asked me if I wanted him to come and get me.

As I mentioned before, the police were not quick to interfere in anyone's personal life in those days. What Michael was suggesting was personal intervention on my behalf. I wanted to feel the comfort of Michael's arms around me, but I didn't trust myself, plus the fact that I feared leaving the children alone with Mitch. I had left them with him once before during such an episode, and although, at least to my knowledge, nothing ever happened, I was never going to do that again. Instead, I asked Michael to please patrol our house more frequently, that I needed to know he was there for me. He agreed to do that much. But he had wanted to do much more.

There came a time, however, when I did call upon Michael to help conceal my whereabouts in order to avoid physical retribution by Mitch. I considered Mitch's threats of abuse at that time to be life threatening . . .

and with nowhere else to turn, I turned to Michael.

The reason for the fray that left me with another black eye and nose several months later eludes me today, but it took place during the summer; that much I do remember. The reason I recall the season is that the day after the violation, I took my children to the Bucherville community swimming pool.

Maureen, an attractive and friendly girl from the south, whom I had met at one of our Sports Car Club gatherings, and whose child had been sharing the baby pool with my youngest son, came over to talk to me. Recognizing my unhappiness, along with my visible skin discoloration, she quickly engaged me in personal conversation. Her words were probing, but with genuine concern.

"Hi, Leta," she said as she proceeded to plop down beside me. "Do you mind if I join you? We can both watch our children from here."

Of course I had no objection. I was actually glad for the company, but fearful that she would notice my bruised face. My fears were soon confirmed.

"Are you all right, Leta?" she asked.

Signs of sadness and discontent had not gone unnoticed by many of our friends, but Maureen was unusually perceptive.

Exposing her sensitive side, she asked, "Would you rather not talk about it?"

I thought about it for a few minutes, then replied with honesty, "No, I need to talk to someone about it."

I confessed to her, with tears in my eyes, that Mitch had been hitting the children and me. I recall admitting that I didn't know what to do and that I hadn't been able to talk to Mitch without provoking him to acts of violence. I told her that I had tried every approach, thinking that perhaps it was the way in which I had presented my objections or questions that warranted his violent responses. She asked me why I was blaming myself for something Mitch had done. All I knew was that I had blamed myself for everything. She was right; there was something wrong with that kind of thinking. It was then that Maureen and I began an inseparable forty-five-year friendship.

I learned that Maureen had been brought up in foster homes after her mother had died. Maureen suffered physical and mental abuse herself, until she finally married. While still pregnant, her husband had deserted her and the marriage ended in divorce. She was left to raise her son alone. She shared with me how she had nearly starved in order to feed her son, working long hours and making very little money. When she remarried, it was to a man who became her best friend. He provided a good home for her and her son. Maureen understood all that I was feeling.

It was easy talking to Maureen; she was blessed with that southern charm you hear so much about. I even told her about Michael and the loves of my past. She in turn shared some of her most personal experiences as well.

* * * * *

My relationship with Maureen brought back memories of my friendship with Dolly. But as so often happens, time has a way of putting distance and circumstances between friends sometimes. Dolly and I stayed in touch over the years, and in my heart, her family was still my family. Unfortunately, we just didn't see much of each other any more, until 1999, when I was invited to join the Witman family at a yearly Christmas celebration . . . a blending of times past. It was a glorious time. At that celebration, I read portions of One Came To Stay *while it was still in its infancy. At a dinner hosted by Don Witman, Dolly's brother, and his wife Barbara, I came to know my dear friend Laurette, a published author and a great source of inspiration and encouragement to me while completing this novel.*

* * * * *

Maureen and I talked on the phone at least twice a day—sometimes more—or I would visit her in her home, which sat on a hill overlooking the town of Bucherville. Many were the times we sat at her small kitchen table drinking coffee and sharing our lives with each other. When her husband's job dictated an out-of-state move, we continued our long-distance friendship. Our phone bills were of colossal proportions, something Mitch was not at all happy about.

Although Maureen could scarcely endure seeing the children and me mistreated, she also understood my reasons for staying in the marriage. She knew what it was like trying to raise one child on her own, let alone three. She was also aware of my spiritual convictions regarding divorce.

* * * * *

In January 1965, nearly eight years since our last child was born, we made plans to introduce some variety into our vacation time. With Fannie still faithfully attending to the housekeeping and the children, we made some alternative plans for our yearly trip to the Grand Prix of Sebring, Florida.

I was extremely fond of fishing and had done so many times in a creek near our Reading Junction farm. After much consideration, Mitch allowed me to precede him to Florida, by way of Marathon in the Florida Keys, to enjoy some deep-sea fishing. There I met up with some of our Sports Car Club friends who also had a fondness for the sport. Mitch planned for me to pick him up at the Miami Airport a week later, just in time for the races. Fishing was not Mitch's idea of a good time.

My first stop on the way to Marathon was the South of the Border Motel between North and South Carolina. There, I looked forward to an evening meal of chicken, ribs, and my favorite side order of hush puppies. The drive south was an enjoyable time for me. I was given the gift of an entire week alone, and I spent most of it fantasizing on what it would have been like to have a husband who enjoyed doing some of the things I enjoyed.

The ocean was therapeutic to my soul. Except for the time when, on a dare, I dove into the shark-infested waters of the Atlantic Ocean to prove an old sea captain's claim that if you didn't have an open wound on your body, sharks would never harm you. I came out unscathed.

As I entered the state of Georgia on that particular trip, with my long blonde pigtail flapping in the breeze, a Georgia state trooper pulled me over. At his insistence, I produced my driver's license and questioned why I had been stopped. While looking at my license, he asked me where I intended to spend the night (which I thought was an unusual question to ask). I informed him that I had already made my stop and was driving through to Marathon in the Florida Keys. Up until that time, he still hadn't given me a reason for stopping me. He finally stated that for me to avoid being written up for speeding, he was going to make me a proposition: I could either pay a steep fine for a vehicle infraction, or I could stay in Georgia for the night and have dinner with him. I couldn't believe what I heard. I reminded him that not only was he out of order, but that I was a married woman, and if he even tried to arrest me he would be answering to his superiors. He then threatened to have me stopped down the road if I didn't accept his invitation, and that he would take me in for disorderly conduct and for disobeying an officer.

I began to laugh, thinking that he had to be joking. I told him I would not accept his proposition, and that I was going to continue on my way, and that if he stopped me, I would immediately report him. When I put the vehicle in gear, he stepped out of the way. I drove with one eye on the road and the other one on the rearview mirror. He followed me for what seemed to be a very long time, but eventually, no doubt uncertain as to how I would handle our brief but bothersome encounter, he turned around and drove off in the opposite direction. It was one of the few times that I wished Mitch had been there to protect me.

Once settled in my motel room on the small Key of Marathon, Florida, I looked forward to the chartered fishing trips that took us some twenty-eight miles out into the Atlantic Ocean. Generally there were about seven of us who charted the *Salty Dog* fishing vessel, and at the helm was Captain Tom and First Mate Rob Benson, who was also the singer and piano player in the dining room area of the motel where I stayed. Rob, an actor and writer, had been married to a well-known movie star, divorced, and then had taken to working as a first mate on a fishing boat as a way of gathering inspiration for a book of poetry he was compiling. I had the opportunity to read some of his work, and it was exceptional. He even wrote a poem for me that I cherished, but lost. Had I not been married and surprisingly pregnant with our fourth child at the time, I probably would have taken up with Rob. He was sensitive and romantic, and very easy to talk to.

Then there was our captain, a distinguished-looking man who nearly caused my death.

While trolling in the ocean, waiting for the catch of the day, a rather strong wind came up, and despite an earlier warning of possible high seas, he opted to continue on. I was feeling a bit queasy, so he invited me to climb up the outside steps of the fishing boat for a breath of fresh air, which by the way, was on a simple rope ladder leading to the top deck of the fishing vessel. When I had nearly reached the top step, the boat hit a wave and almost turned on its side, the side to which I hung for dear life. My back hit the water, (that's how far the boat had tilted) and it took all my strength to just barely hang on.

When the boat was upright again, Captain Tom reached for my hand and pulled me onto the deck. It was undoubtedly the biggest fish story I ever told, but it was true.

The view from the top deck of the fishing vessel rendered me speechless. It was an orchestra seat in the ocean's theatre. I saw turtles as large as elephants (well, almost), schools of huge fish, and every fisherman's dream . . . a beautiful sailfish just asking to be displayed over the fireplace in a bragger's den. There was an endless parade of spectacular sights and discoveries. I fell in love with the sea.

Arriving back at the pier, Captain Tom broke open a six-pack of beer. He offered everyone a can of the just newly-introduced Colt 45. His glowing description of the flavor made me curious. I did not drink alcoholic beverages; however, after some coaxing, I eventually agreed to take a sip from his can. It was just another beer. But you would have thought it had won the Blue Ribbon of Beers Award from the way everyone was exclaiming over it. A couple of sips had been enough for me.

Later that evening, we all met down by the dock to watch the beautiful sky, still unmatched by any other I have ever seen. In the small tackle shop located next to the pier, I overheard a discussion about how sick Captain Tom had become after he returned from our fishing trip that day. He had been rushed to the hospital, the man in the tackle shop said. Fatigue and discoloration of his skin led them to suspect a serious ailment. All I could think of was, *Oh no! I drank from the same can he drank from this afternoon!* But after that, I no longer thought much about it. He was still hospitalized when I left Marathon for Sebring the following week. We had sent him a card wishing him a full and speedy recovery.

Except for one bad seafood experience, my stay in Marathon was relaxing and thoroughly enjoyable.

After a week of sun and fun, I met Mitch at the Miami Airport. When I met him at the baggage claim area, he did not recognize me. My hair had turned three shades lighter and I was sporting a beautiful dark tan, something rare for natural blondes. When he did realize it was his wife, he said that I looked fantastic and then told me he would send me on ahead of him next year. I did not object.

While at the races in Sebring, Mitch and I seemed to get along just fine. We enjoyed the festivities, the dinners out, the encounters with numerous famous race car drivers, and the time we spent by the pool at our hotel in Lake Wales. Mitch seemed more relaxed and less intimidating when he was away from home and business. Being in the warm climate and knowing it was cold and snowing at home, seemed to lighten Mitch's spirits and mine. The smell of gardenias floated through our bedroom window and all seemed well at last.

... SIXTEEN ...

The necessary paperwork for the sale of our trailer home was finalized as our family planned its next move to our newly purchased mountain resort home overlooking Laurel Lake. The house, suitably tucked away amidst dogwood trees and mountain laurel and located midway between Bucherville and Minden, was going to be quite different from our trailer home existence. At the same time, another set of plans, to build a large showroom and distribution center for BMW automobiles, was also taking place.

Laurel Lake had been one of my favorite teenage swimming hangouts, and even back then I had dreamed of perhaps living there one day.

To say it was a busy time in our lives would be a gross understatement. Because of his business expansion plans, Mitch had no time to help in the moving process, and he wasn't in favor of hiring a moving company to do the work, and so the responsibility became exclusively mine. With my pregnancy and my still-lingering cough, I could barely get through a day. I single-handedly planned, packed, and executed our move to Laurel Lake. As a result, my health was profoundly affected by overexertion. I was utterly exhausted. I could no longer even hold a broom in my hand without struggling to get my breath . . . and I was too tired to eat. When everything had been transported from Bucherville to our new home in Laurel Lake, I went to bed and I did not get up again.

The children prepared their own meals as I surrendered to total exhaustion. Mitch attributed my lack of energy to the move and said that once we were settled, I would soon recover. But that did not happen.

Maureen, whom I still considered my closest and dearest friend, was the first visitor to our new home. She arrived in the afternoon one day. I still had been unable to sit up and take nourishment and had remained in bed. She took one look at me and said, "My God, Leta, you're bright yellow!"

"What do you mean, I'm bright yellow?" I questioned.

"I don't know, but your skin is not a normal color. I am going to call your doctor."

Shortly after she had spoken with the doctor, I was admitted to Lancaster General Hospital, and she and my family were inoculated against hepatitis. Back then, the disease didn't come with letters of the alphabet; it was simply referred to as hepatitis. It was later determined that I had either contracted the disease from sharing someone else's drinking glass, or from spoiled seafood. Since the information I gave to the state examiner included eating a good number of raw oysters and clams, and drinking from Captain Tom's beer can during my recent trip to Florida, they were able to draw conclusive evidence regarding my illness. It was determined that both could have easily contributed to my malady.

During my time in isolation, the hospital staff attended to my needs looking more like nuclear and chemical weapon inspectors than doctors and nurses. When I finally could eat, after having been fed through a tube for a large portion of my confinement, I was fed at arms' length from a long-handled pizza baking board. I had lost a lot of weight, and the little solid food I could swallow returned on a round-trip ticket.

The fact that I was pregnant was of the utmost concern to the attending doctors. Most certainly, since I had hepatitis, the baby more than likely had it as well. At that point there was some discussion about aborting the baby because the baby's heartbeat could no longer be heard. After a brief meeting with my family physician, who believed that a mother knows her body better than anyone else, I decided against another legal abortion. The doctor asked me if I felt the baby still moving inside my womb; I had to admit that I had not felt movement for some time. There were no outward signs of poisoning to my system as I had previously experienced, and so I elected to carry the baby full term if possible. However, in doing so I was forewarned that should the pregnancy go full term, it was pretty much agreed upon by the doctors that the baby would suffer some serious defects, if it lived at all. But I refused to change my decision. I even went so far as to promise God that if He let the baby live and be normal, I would devote the rest of my life to Him.

I remained in the hospital so long that I actually had trouble walking when I was finally allowed to return home. Eventually I regained my strength and returned to my normal activities.

Maureen was furious. She never forgave Mitch for ignoring my deteriorating condition during the move to Laurel Lake. She never understood that Mitch had somehow managed to overlook the sick person she had seen lying helpless and pale.

*   *   *   *   *

We hadn't been in our new home very long when I got a call from my foster dad asking me to please come to their home quickly. He said that my mother had just been run over by an automobile in her own driveway and was being taken to the hospital by ambulance. Fortunately for us, we had gotten to know a retired military officer and his wife who lived several doors from our home. I called them and asked if they would please keep our children while I went to my parents' home to find out what had happened to my mother. They kindly offered to take care of our children.

When I arrived at my foster parents' home in Bucherville, our family physician was waiting for me. He took me aside and told me that Mother was in critical condition. He said that he had had to crawl beneath the car to administer morphine, and that by the time I would reach the hospital, it was possible she would no longer be alive. He told me how a friend of hers had come to pick her up and had pulled her car in the driveway behind my mother's car. She had blown the horn to let my mother know she had arrived, and then waited for my mother to come out of the house. As my mother walked between the two cars on her way to the passenger side of her friend's car, her friend inadvertently engaged the forward gear. She ran over my mother, driving my mother's body beneath her own car, where she remained trapped until they could extricate her.

I did not cry until I walked into the hospital room and saw my mother's body. She had blown up like a balloon and was barely recognizable. But she was still alive. I felt, however, that it was going to be my last look at her before she died. Daddy was totally incoherent. He wouldn't come into the room to even see his wife. He just sat there crying outside her door. When the doctors suggested some invasive procedures that might save her life, Daddy was unable to make the decision, passing the responsibility on to me. They informed me that my mother would die if they did not take invasive steps, and even then, it might not be enough to save her life.

One possible life-saving option was to drill a hole through the top of her head to release the pressure that was obviously causing the swelling. By the time I reached the hospital and had spent some time in the waiting room with my dad, the medical staff had already cut Mother's body open from top to bottom. She had a cracked skull, split liver, and every rib broken, plus numerous other injuries.

I personally talked with the surgeon who would drill the hole in my mother's head. He assured me that the operation was totally necessary, but that there was no guarantee of success. He suggested that we go home, get some sleep, and come back in the morning. He did assure me that my mother had no idea what had happened to her and would not regain consciousness again that night, if at all. So I took Daddy and we went home.

Early the next morning I received a phone call from the surgeon with whom I had spoken the night before regarding the invasive procedure. His words more than surprised me. What he shared later convinced me that divine intervention and answered prayers were still alive and well.

He said that he could not explain, at least in medical terms, why, through pure premonition or some other strange phenomenon, he had been influenced by a vision he had that night to withhold drilling a hole in my mother's head. Instead, he said he believed she would regain consciousness that day.

I knew many people, along with myself, who had begun to pray for my mother, and I believed that God had truly intervened, and that He had somehow spoken to Dr. Ruben in a vision on my mother's behalf. I told him what I believed had taken place and that I would support any decision he made regarding the procedure, regardless of the outcome.

After talking with Dr. Ruben, I left for my dad's house. When I arrived there, I told him about Dr. Ruben's vision, but he appeared oblivious to anything that was going on. I suspected that he was either in a state of shock or denial, but nevertheless, I had to ask him if he wanted to go along to the hospital. He replied that he had not wanted to go. He said that he didn't want to see her in that condition. *Well, I guess not,* I thought. *He surely must be feeling some kind of guilt about how he treated her now that this has happened.* So I drove back to the hospital alone. Mitch had inquired about the accident, but he continued working, just as he had done when his father and mother died. It was business as usual, and hardly a day wasted on mourning. Although Mitch and his sisters sang at their father's funeral, and for the first time I had actually seen tears in Mitch's eyes, he had missed the smile on his mother's face as she greeted the angels who had come to take her home. I wanted to be with my mother when she went home to be with the Lord.

When I reached the hospital, I didn't know what to expect. I certainly didn't expect to see my mother propped up in her bed, eyes open, and actually talking, but that is exactly what I found. It had truly been a miracle; for whose benefit, I wasn't quite sure. But Dr. Ruben's vision, or whatever it was, had been right. Although my mother wasn't totally coherent, she at least was talking, and it was usually about a man in her room whom she imagined was using her bathroom. Of course, there was no such man.

As the weeks went by, Mother began forming sentences and recognizing visitors. I was finally able to convince Daddy to visit his wife, but it turned out to be a painful visit. Again, I witnessed the absence of any kind of affection. *How sad to live without hugs and kisses,* I remember thinking at the time. I, on the other hand, thrived on affection and physical contact, and I counted on Mitch to provide both. I worked so hard to earn every touch. That is why it was so difficult for me to find rest in the security of God's love. His love was free. I didn't have to earn it, work for it, or pay for it. That kind of love sounded so un-American . . . a peculiar kind of love.

My heart delighted in seeing my mother recover and return home to start her second chance at life. Daddy seemed grateful to have her home as well. He gave up smoking and much of his drinking ceased.

*   *   *   *   *

In October 1965, I entered the hospital to deliver our fourth child. The likelihood of complications due to my bout with hepatitis was evidenced by the presence of every doctor who had visited me while being treated for hepatitis. As my family physician indicated earlier, they were not expecting me to give birth to a normal child, and they did their best to prepare me for their expected outcome. But unknown to them, I had struck up a deal with God, and I somehow felt that He was about to hold me to it. God knew my heart better than anyone did and I felt confident that everything would be just fine. And it was.

Luke Brogan was born without complications and immediately announced his arrival with an overwhelming overture of wails. We were all smiles, including those of the doctors.

Mitch was not present for the delivery.

Following the birth of each of my children, I had asked my doctor, "Does the baby have red hair?" And in each case, his answer was "No." This time, however, he announced, "You finally got your strawberry blonde."

When I held Luke for the first time, I thought of my birth mother and her auburn hair, and for a moment I thought, *Oh, if only she could see her grandchildren.* But I knew that would never come to be.

Sarah and Ben could hardly wait to play Mommy and Daddy to little Luke. Thomas was only eight years old at the time and the parenting side of his brain hadn't developed yet.

Mitch enjoyed being called Daddy by his beautiful, well-disciplined children, but he spent little quality time with them. To make up for his absence in our lives, he provided us with an exceptional amount of material goods.

Attending worship service every Sunday was a given, but I believe that routine was more for the purpose of pleasing his dear Christian mother than out of a desire for spirituality. In spite of any wrong motive on Mitch's part, God used that regular church attendance to remind me of the promise I had made to serve Him, if He allowed Luke to enter the world without complications.

It was a difficult time for all of us. Mitch wasn't home very much, and even with four children keeping me busy, I still felt very lonely. A discontent ran through me like an undercurrent ready to break on a strange but waiting shore.

Our children were exceptional, by demand. They had such a fear of being punished for any wrongdoings that they were usually always on their good behavior. Thomas, however, was just a little more adventurous than the other three; he decided that his behavior was his alone to determine. He generally did what he wanted to do, then proceeded to pull down his pants and get ready for his whipping long before his daddy ever got near him. Thomas had the personality and disposition of his father. There was a hint of Mitch in Sarah as well, but because she was a girl, it was a little harder to detect. She was unbelievably beautiful, that Sarah. When she was in her teens, friends tried to persuade us to send her to modeling school, saying that they thought she had the makings of a supermodel, but her daddy would have no parts of it.

As we settled in our new house, it was beginning to feel more like home. Unfortunately, Mitch began spending even more time away from it, devoting the majority of his time to the two businesses. Although we were already making plans for another trip to Europe, and planning several dinner parties as a way of introducing our new home to friends and associates, we remained remarkably detached from one another.

When Mitch hired an attractive secretary whom I had to go out of my way to meet, I began to feel seriously threatened and became increasingly insecure about my relationship with my husband. I was very relieved when she began dating our manager.

We owned a Ferrari, Maserati, BMW, Porsche, Jaguar, Lancia, DKW, and a Mercedes Benz. We bought skis and began taking skiing lessons. But that didn't last long; one mishap involving Mitch and a pine tree, and that ended that sport. We had the best clothing money could buy . . . and yet . . . my name still didn't appear on our bank checks. Instead, I continued to receive a weekly allowance for food and clothing. My primary jobs were to entertain business associates (domestic and foreign), care for the children, and stand ready to accompany Mitch on business trips at a moment's notice. If Mitch had known how many times his German associates had tried to win my affection, he wouldn't have been so hospitable, and most certainly he would never have allowed them in our home. Quite honestly, I welcomed the attention, as I was beginning to feel unattractive and unloved.

At one point, Mitch and I were in partnership with a handsome German man in the hotel business near Idlewild Airport in New York. We attracted a large number of airline travelers and the crews of those airlines to our hotel. It was an exciting time. But I knew that that kind of living was not going to keep me faithful to my husband for very long. The attractions were too numerous and the temptations too hard to resist. I soon stopped accompanying Mitch to the hotel. He was not happy about that, as he considered my presence advantageous to his business dealings.

A dozen potential affairs loomed in the distance, beckoning me to take what I thought I deserved; only by the grace of God did I manage to escape.

Before we departed for our next trip to Europe, something very unpleasant took place.

*   *   *   *   *

We had gotten to know our next door neighbors very well. The introductions were made when our children began playing together. The Ross family had four children. Mr. Ross was an attorney, and his wife was a very friendly person. It wasn't long before we became friends; not like the friendship Maureen and I shared, but we enjoyed having coffee together in each other's homes, and that led to a number of invitations to their home for social gatherings. On one of those party events, I walked out of their house because a hired guitar player was told to sing and play dirty songs. It was clear by the way the musician reacted when he got the request, that he didn't want to play those kinds of songs either, and he told Mr. Ross that he wasn't going to comply with the request. An argument soon ensued, ending in a verbal battle involving four-letter words. Whereupon, the guitar player walked out of their house as well, throwing all the money he had been paid out of his car window as he drove down the street and away from the Ross home. I said to myself, *Hooray for that talented college student with uncompromising convictions!* Needless to say, the children thought it had rained money during the night, when the following morning on their way to meet the school bus, they began stuffing their pockets with the paper money they found hanging from the bushes and trees that lined the road.

When I left the party that night, I explained to our host and hostess why I was leaving the party. Mr. Ross hurled some very unkind words at me, but I turned my back and walked out the door and down the path leading to our house; Mitch wasn't far behind me. We decided not to attend any more of the Ross parties.

The next day a dozen roses came to my door with a note of apology from Mr. and Mrs. Ross. *Alcohol and money do strange things to people sometimes,* I thought. I accepted their apology and we remained friends. The incident never repeated itself.

But a much more devastating event was about to take place between us.

*   *   *   *   *

Early one Saturday morning the telephone rang. The phone seemed to be a routine conveyor of bad news for me. One of the Ross children called to ask if Thomas would be allowed to come over and play at their house. I confirmed the invitation with June Ross, and soon Thomas was running out the door.

The Ross family had a very large house overlooking Laurel Lake, with a large recreation room in the basement. They also had an equally huge Saint Bernard dog.

Thomas hadn't been gone for more than ten minutes when the phone rang again. I picked it up and heard a breathless June Ross on the other end.

"Leta, you had better come over here. Thomas was bitten by our dog."

She didn't sound overly excited, so I assumed it was just a nip somewhere on his leg or arm, so I said I would get some clothing on and be right over. It was one of those lazy Saturday mornings, and I was still in my bathrobe. Mitch had gone to work hours earlier, and I had extended my morning with an extra cup or two of coffee. But June's next words had a much more urgent appeal.

"Just grab something, Leta. We need to rush him to the hospital right away; it is really serious."

With that, I grabbed a pair of sweats and a shirt and ran over to their house.

When I arrived, I saw Mr. Ross and a friend of his, who had come to play golf, carrying a large blanket that obviously held the body of our son Thomas. They instructed me to quickly get into the car so we could head for the hospital.

"How bad is it?" I asked, as I crawled into the back seat.

"Very bad," said Mr. Ross's friend. "You don't want to see your son right now."

In the meantime, all I could hear were little moans and groans coming from beneath the blanket. Soon I could see patches of blood seeping through the blanket. *Oh my God,* I thought, *this is really bad!*

When we got to the local hospital, they put Thomas up on a table and removed the blanket. I happened to be standing right beside the table. When I saw that little face with his nose nearly torn off, and his eyes swollen shut with large bloody bites all over his face and head, I nearly fainted. But I did not cry, mostly because I didn't want Thomas to know how badly he had been bitten. After a brief observation by the attending nurses, they covered him up again. It appeared that there were no doctors available at Minden General Hospital at the time to assess my son's injuries. When I finally found a doctor sitting in a nearby office, he claimed he didn't know the boy and wouldn't be able to comment on his injuries. I became enraged at that point and made a call to our family doctor, who in turn talked with one of the nurses on the floor. Following that exchange, Thomas was immediately rushed to Lancaster General Hospital by ambulance, where they assured me that a well-known plastic surgeon and his staff would be waiting. In the meantime, I contacted Mitch at his office and told him what had happened. He said that he couldn't go to the hospital immediately, that he had someone in the office at the time. I did not have time to think about Mitch's reaction; all that I could think about was our son, whose face had just been mangled by a dog.

When the ambulance arrived at Lancaster General Hospital, Dr. Lu, a very well-known plastic surgeon, and his staff were waiting as promised. Thomas had already lost a lot of blood and was immediately rushed into surgery.

I waited for five hours or more until Dr. Lu finally came into the waiting room to give me a report on Thomas. He said that Thomas had done very well, and that the surgery was a success; however, a determination would be made later as to how much additional surgery would be required. He said that I was permitted to go into the room to see my son. He told me that I would find Thomas's whole face bandaged, and that he wouldn't be able to see very well due to the swelling and the number of stitches required in closing his wounds. Even so, I wasn't prepared for what I saw when I walked into the room. Thomas's head was completely bandaged, as Dr. Lu had said, but it looked more like a huge cabbage sitting on top of his shoulders, with one tiny peephole in it. I was very careful not to make him talk, so I just held him and told him it was going to be all right.

Mitch did not arrive at the hospital until much later that day.

While at the hospital, Mr. Ross explained to us how the accident happened. He said that his children had been chasing their dog in and out of the rooms in their den before Thomas entered the picture, and they had gotten the dog overly excited. Subsequently at the sight of a strange person walking down the basement stairs, the Saint Bernard dog had lunged at Thomas, took Thomas's head in his mouth, and proceeded to gnaw on his face and wouldn't let go. The men were somewhat apprehensive in their attempt to get the dog off Thomas, for fear of being bitten themselves, which gave the dog even more time to inflict damage on Thomas's little face.

ONE CAME TO STAY ~~169~~

It was sad that they had to lose their family pet, but the state thought otherwise and ended the dog's life. They performed an autopsy on the dog and discovered that he had a large brain tumor, and the excitement had only aggravated the situation.

Mr. Ross, being an attorney, was quick to offer an out-of-court settlement long before we had time to even consider any such action. Since I had nothing to say in the matter, Mr. Ross and Mitch agreed on payment for all medical bills incurred, plus ten thousand dollars to be put in a trust fund which would be available to Thomas when he turned twenty-one years of age. With wise investments over the years, that ten thousand dollars would provide some recompense for all the pain Thomas experienced.

Thomas never saw the ten thousand dollars. Mitch claimed the bank invested the money unwisely and had lost all of it in the stock market, and that was pretty much where the discussion ended. I don't know what really happened to that money, but to me, there were only two possible explanations: Mitch told the truth about the bank making bad investments; or, as trustee of those funds, Mitch appropriated the money for another use.

Thomas had been inundated with gifts from friends and family during his stay in the hospital, and when he finally came home, he expected those gifts to continue. All the attention had spoiled him. He recovered nicely in spite of his harrowing experience, and surprisingly enough, he never had a fear of dogs. There were a few bullies in school who called him Frankenstein, but that didn't seem to bother him one bit.

As a mother, Thomas's accident was a devastating experience for me, too. When I left the hospital the night of the accident, I went home and immersed myself in a bathtub of hot sudsy water; only then did I break down and cry.

Mitch visited Thomas in the hospital, and although he expressed sadness over what had happened, nothing seemed to touch his heart like cars and ice hockey.

*   *   *   *   *

Filled with anger and hurt, I broached the subject of Mitch's lack of concern and unavailability regarding our family once again, However, I didn't choose the best of circumstances to introduce the subject. I had just excused myself from the dinner table to nurse Luke, after one of our shared evening meals, when I decided to express how I felt. He responded by verbally assaulting me, accusing me once again of being unappreciative and selfish. When I responded in kind, he slapped me so hard that it caused Luke to fly out of my arms onto the floor. When I leaned over to pick Luke up off the floor, he grabbed me and threw me across the living room head-on into a large sauerkraut crock that stood in the corner of the living room. Dazed and unable to get up, I looked across the room at the children sitting at the table, witnesses to what had just played out before their small eyes, and I was mortified. I had failed in my attempt to convince Mitch that we needed him more than we needed his money.

But over the years, it was precisely money, and the security it provided, that kept me with him.

*   *   *   *   *

It was difficult for me to comprehend the changes that had taken place in Mitch's personality . . . and probably in mine as well, as a result of putting everything but God first in our lives. I do know that I no longer felt connected to Mitch. Our line of communication was all tangled up and I wanted to cut myself free. But for the sake of our children, I could not.

The next day when I visited our family doctor, he recorded the injuries he observed. He asked me then why I hadn't left Mitch. I replied, "Where would I go? How would I ever support four children?" He told me to let him know every time any of us were abused in the future. He wanted to talk with Mitch, but of course Mitch had no intention of meeting with the good doctor. Mitch never considered his actions wrong.

Maureen was justifiably concerned. She approached the subject of leaving Mitch time and time again, saying that she couldn't stand to see the children or me hurt any more and that she would support me if it became necessary to leave. Without her friendship during those times, I am convinced I would have ended up in a hospital for the mentally disturbed, or I would have committed suicide. She reminded me that she had avoided being emotionally hurt by simply turning people and situations off like a faucet, but I never believed her.

*   *   *   *   *

Maureen's concern for our safety was justified. After every incident, I grew increasingly fearful of my husband. I believed with all my heart that he had the capacity to seriously injure any one of us, at any time. While I spent hours laboring to bring each child into the world, Mitch spent his time involved in numerous fistfights. Excuses from being run off the road to a dirty look from a driver in a car next to him was all Mitch needed to engage in hand-to-hand combat. Once, while I was giving birth to one of our children, he slammed a man's head between the man's own car door, and then he proceeded to throw the man's keys as far as China, just because the man had tailgated him. And yet, I believe that when he mistreated the children and me, he was genuinely remorseful; he just wasn't able to convincingly convey any degree of contrition. Instead, he continued to offer me money after every such incident, and I continued to take it as payment for what he had put us through. That was my mistake.

During my stay in the hospital, while I was recovering from my bout with hepatitis, there was an incident involving a male patient in another room. The gentleman caused quite a ruckus when he insisted on coming into my room, announcing that he "wanted to see the blonde who lived next door." The nursing staff had great difficulty restraining the man, so Mitch restrained him for them. It ended in a puddle of blood. Mitch had knocked the guy out cold.

Mitch and I spent a great deal of time outrunning cops, avoiding road barricades, and hiding in the garages of strangers to avoid being arrested for speeding. Driving 125 miles per hour on super highways and negotiating s-turns on rural roads going sideways was considered normal. Mitch was an outstanding driver, that I must say. He taught me driving skills that hopefully I have since passed on to my children. We both seemed to have inherited the ability to control an automobile. Hopefully, there are a lot of things that I have taught my children not to do in a car as well.

On one of our trips to Europe, Mitch and I accompanied an automobile manufacturer's test driver to the company's test dome. It was a place where sheer speed and centrifugal force enabled the driver to take his hands off the wheel of the car as it reached speeds that I determined were solely for orbiting purposes. Needless to say, I couldn't stand up after that ride, and I never did it again. Conversely, Mitch was the personification of speed, and I lived with "Speed." To this day, if you ask anyone who has ever driven with Mitch Brogan how they felt sitting in the passenger seat of that car, they would tell you unequivocally that it was probably the most paralyzing experience they have ever had.

Maureen and I each owned our own motorcycles, not a hard thing to comprehend since her husband owned a motorcycle sales and accessory business after he retired. As the result of a bet between our husbands and us that we couldn't pull it off, the two of us toured the Blue Ridge Mountains and Skyline Drive alone, on our bikes. It was quite an experience. Maureen wore a protective helmet and had a nice large windshield on her bike; I had neither. By the end of the day, I had more bugs in my hair than follicles. The danger we could have been confronted with, just two women traveling alone on motorcycles, had not intimidated us in the least. For me, it represented a very calm interlude in an otherwise turbulent environment that I called home.

*   *   *   *   *

Maureen and I often discussed the missing pieces of her past and mine. I often wondered about the identity of my birth father and why my mother had chosen to keep Bassie and had given me away. Had I been nothing more than mere happenstance? I asked myself many times. My inexhaustible need for reassurance, love, and recognition, I eventually learned, was directly related to my feelings of rejection as a child. With so many instances of abuse in my marriage, I felt totally worthless, which made me work all the harder to gain acceptance. I was often willing to settle for bad attention rather than no attention at all. And yet, during my teenage years I had an overwhelming amount of attention; I practically had to hang out a "no vacancy" sign on the door of my heart to discourage relationships. But now my heart felt empty. I longed for gentleness, kindness, and understanding from Mitch. Instead, I received much of those tender ingredients from my children, and flirtations with other men. But it was the coveted love of a husband that my heart truly desired.

I imagined myself being involved in theatre again, having moved to a resort area that had a popular playhouse and an active summer stock theatre group. Among the stars that had gotten their start on stage in Laurel Lake were well-known celebrities such as Charlton Heston and Bernadette Peters. But my idea to act again was shot down by Mitch like a pigeon in Hegins (a place in Pennsylvania where they make sport of shooting pigeons over the protests of animal rights activists).

*   *   *   *   *

Maureen was expecting her second child, and together we shared in all the hoopla of her new arrival. For a time, it took some of the attention off my own problems. We shopped with our children, stood in line at petting zoos, and watched our children play as we sat and drank coffee together during the winter months, and sipped iced tea in the summer. I depended on her for so much. We depended on each other. There was nothing known or felt that we hadn't shared. I enjoyed making her laugh, and she enjoyed laughing. Her newborn daughter was the crystalline jewel of her life. She loved her son, too, but there was an extraordinary closeness between her and her daughter.

. . . SEVENTEEN . . .

Grace and James Carpenter loved their grandchildren, and for that, they received generous portions of love in return. I was very grateful that our children got to feel the texture of love, something I did not experience as a child. I received a tremendous back-payment of joy as I watched the interaction between our children and their grandparents. I can't say with certainty, but I suspect Mitch took those tender moments as an opportunity to suggest to Grace and James Carpenter that they consider formally adopting me as their daughter; until that time, my maiden name remained Marlow. I was unaware of the plan until my parents approached me and asked me if I wanted to take their name through the legal adoption process. What purpose changing my name to Carpenter would serve escaped me. They told me that it had been Mitch's idea, and that it was something they wouldn't mind doing . . . if I had no objection. Believing it to be one way of paying them back for all they had done for me, I agreed to appear in court to consummate the adoption.

It didn't occur to me that new information regarding my past might possibly reach the floor of the adoption court, but when it did occur to me, it put a curious new face on the entire process. Reluctant as I was to give up my name, albeit marriage had already changed it from Marlow to Brogan, I began "courting" the unknown.

Memories of another marbled-floor corridor momentarily distracted me as I walked toward the adoption courtroom; I thought about Michael. I wondered how different things might have been if I had married Michael instead of Mitch. I had learned through Michael's sister-in-law, with whom I still corresponded, that Michael was considering leaving the State Police to rejoin the Marine Corps to fight in Vietnam. The thought of Michael not being there for me was not welcome news.

I had to abandon my private thoughts when Mitch took my arm and guided me through the door of the courtroom. My foster parents, who accompanied us to the courthouse that day, had been unusually quiet. I wondered if they, too, anticipated something unexpected to turn up during the court proceeding.

My mind focused on the gavel as it brought the court to order. The only people present were my foster parents, a lawyer, the judge, and Mitch and me. There was no opposing attorney present to represent my birth parents. I concluded that no one planned to argue against my name change. It was a sad and dismal moment for me.

When the adoption was finalized and my name legally became Leta Carpenter Brogan, I felt as though I had been stripped of my only true identity. I had liked the name Marlow.

It was only the second time that I recall seeing tears in my dad's eyes, but I don't think they were tears of joy. Rather, I believed them to be signs of a conscience in mourning. In the quietness of that courtroom, I knew he had to be reflecting on that deep, dark well, the mad rooster, and many other incidents that had taken place over the years.

At the conclusion of the adoption, the judge presented me with an unexpected ultimatum: "You are entitled to know the name of your father, Leta," he announced. "And," he continued, "I have the liberty to provide that information to you; but it comes with strings attached. Should you want to have that information, I must ask that you never try and locate your father."

He may as well have handed me a life sentence than confine me to those terms, I thought. But knowing full well that you don't argue with a judge any more than you do with a policeman, I was willing to bargain for the name of my father. I waited while he repeated the conditions, especially the emphasis on the part: "You will regret it should you ever try and locate your father." That part unnerved me. What danger would that present, and to whom, remained unanswered questions. My word was all the judge had to affix that agreement. For a moment, I thought about ignoring his warning, but the look on his face pretty much squashed that plan.

Immediately, my imagination gland was activated. I had my father on America's Most Wanted List; a maximum security prisoner in a state penitentiary; and even a card-carrying member of La Cosa Nostra. Better still, he may have been a well-known dignitary or politician, and his name would have been changed to "mud" if his illegitimate daughter entered the scene.

My musings ended when I thought of something my foster dad told me when I was a little girl watching the trains pass through Reading Junction: "Wait for the caboose," he had said. "It's a very important part of the train. When the caboose passes, the railroad worker will then switch the direction of the track and point the train in another direction." Why his words occurred to me just then, I do not know, but its correlation was the blueprint I used to redirect my intended inquiry into my past, without breaking the agreement I had just made with the judge.

I was then handed a piece of paper containing the name of my birth father. I carefully guarded the document, out of fear that it might self-destruct. An endless array of questions and scenarios began to leap into my head.

As I read the name out loud, I couldn't help thinking what a lovely name it was. It had an intriguing ring to it, even bordering on mysterious . . . and a little romantic. I repeated it over and over again. "David L. DuLaney . . . David L. DuLaney." I was sure there had to be a story behind that name, but I had no idea where to begin my search.

Confronting my birth mother, even if she were still alive, or my half-sister, who by that time had probably married and had a different last name, were all eliminated as viable directions to go in my attempt to gather information about my father. By example, I had to switch tracks and go another direction if I ever hoped to learn more about my birth father.

* * * * *

With the adoption behind me, and Mitch's plan for us to spend an extended vacation abroad ahead of me, I had precious little time to resurrect someone from my past.

I did not discuss my intentions with Mitch, as he would have dismissed them as ludicrous. I didn't even tell Maureen what I planned to do; she would have advised me to leave the past behind and just let it go and turn it off, like a faucet. No, this was a journey I was going to have to take all by myself.

* * * * *

Blairsouth Estate, a place I had visited with my birth mother many years before, seemed to be the most logical place to begin.

Mimmie, the Blairs' maidservant, was kind and sympathetic to me as a young girl; she also appeared to have a telltale camaraderie with my mother. She seemed to be the most likely person with whom I could make contact. *If only I could locate her whereabouts,* I thought. *Funny what observations you make when you are young.*

I picked a warm sunny day for my trip to Yorktown. The children were staying with Fannie, so there was no reason for my hasty return.

Mitch had gone to New York to Maxwell Albrecht's office on business. He had wanted me to accompany him, but I used the children as an excuse not to go, though I admit, I always enjoyed going into the city. As a matter of fact, the last time I had gone to New York City with Mitch to Herr Albrecht's office, I mentioned the fact that I thought it would be fun to have Mr. Kenneth, Jackie Kennedy's hairdresser, do my hair. It wasn't long before Herr Albrecht was on the telephone with the famous salon, telling them that I was the German Ambassador's wife, and that I would be coming to the salon immediately to have my hair done. Of course, that produced some menacing, if not dangerous, complications. I spoke very little German, and although Max's limousine would provide a convincing presentation, it didn't override my fear of imprisonment for impersonating an ambassador's wife. But at Mr. Albrecht's insistence, and under the pretense that I spoke very little English, I spent one of the most pampered days in the history of my life. But the ensuing adventure I was now about to embark upon was just as, if not more, jeopardous and tantalizing, and I doubted that I would feel pampered if I succeeded in unearthing any amount of dirt from my past.

It didn't take very long after arriving in Yorktown to obtain directions to Blairsouth Estate.

It had been nearly twenty years since I put my hand in Mimmie's hand and accompanied her on a tour of the Blairsouth mansion. As I parked in the cobblestone courtyard of the estate, I removed my hands from the steering wheel of my Mercedes and found them wet with perspiration.

It took several minutes to compose myself before finding my way to the door of the Blair mansion. The door appeared much larger than I remembered. It also occurred to me just then that the appropriate thing would have been to precede my visit with a telephone call, but that opportunity had already come and gone. My hand was already on the huge horse-head doorknocker. I moved the bit in the horse's mouth up and down, hoping to arouse someone inside the mansion.

A much older Mimmie, but with the same charismatic personality I rememberd as a young child, opened the door.

"Hello, Mimmie," I said.

With a smile and an inquisitive look on her face, she asked, "And who may I say is calling?"

"Leta . . . Leta Marlow, Jean Marlow's daughter."

At once, she reached out for me, took me in her arms, and gave me a huge hug.

"So what in the world brings you to Blairsouth? Let me look at you. I can hardly believe my eyes. Please, please come in."

Even though Mimmie hadn't recognized me at first, she was obviously happy to see me. She offered me a glass of lemonade, the same treat I remembered from another afternoon on the stone patio at Blairsouth Estate.

Nothing much had changed inside the mansion. During our walk through the majestic rooms to the patio outside, I learned that Mrs. Blair was visiting a friend in Europe, and that she was not in good health. But mostly, Mimmie wanted to know about me. After giving her an abbreviated version of my life before and after Mitch, and bragging about my children with pictures and stories, we sat down to the reason for my visit.

*   *   *   *   *

"Mimmie," I began, rarely taking a breath, "can you tell me anything about my father? How he and my mother met, and why she decided to get rid of me and keep my half-sister Bassie? I will not hold you responsible for revealing information to me," I promised. "It's just that there are some things I'd really like to know. I have these conjured-up unreliable theories about what happened, and they're driving me crazy. I have been warned not to try and find my birth father by an adoption court judge, but he didn't say I couldn't inquire as to what kind of person he was."

I handed her the piece of paper revealing the name of my father.

"The judge gave me this," I told her, "but it still doesn't provide closure in my life, Mimmie. I thought that perhaps you, or Mrs. Blair, would know something about my father and the circumstances surrounding my birth."

She appeared to be giving it very serious consideration. Finally, she agreed to share with me what she knew about David L. DuLaney and Jean Marlow. But first, she asked me to promise her that I would not contact my mother or Bassie. As you might guess, that just made it all the more curious. There seemed to be so much secrecy surrounding my existence. Mimmie further explained that my mother hadn't been well and that Bassie had literally sacrificed her own personal life in order to take care of Jean. I believed Mimmie, so I gave her my word that I would honor her request not to try and contact either one of them. She and my mother had been close friends, she said, and she wouldn't have wanted to do anything to ever hurt her.

Mimmie began by telling me that my mother had great difficulty dealing with her past. (*She's not alone there,* I thought to myself.) She said that my mother could have gone to New York City and opened a business of her own, completely financed by Mrs. Blair, but because of the friendship that had developed between Jean and David DuLaney, Jean had chosen to remain in Yorktown.

"Your mother was a well-known milliner, Leta; she designed hats for some very rich and famous people, but she fell in love with David DuLaney, the Blairs' chauffeur, and quite a handsome man he was at that! But more of that later," she said.

"Your mother was deeply hurt, not once, but several times, and she tried so hard not to be vulnerable again. As you may know, Leta, Bassie's last name is McFarland, not Marlow."

"No, I didn't know that, Mimmie," I replied.

I probably looked semi-comatose as Mimmie continued.

"Your mother married John McFarland, a handsome, but very impetuous young man. Bassie was born less than nine months after their marriage. Then he left her for another woman. She was nearly penniless and completely brokenhearted. To this day, she still wears the locket around her neck that he gave her when they got married. Your mother felt absolutely unloved during the years that followed. And even though Bassie reminded her of sadder days, Bassie became her everything."

As she continued, I began relating, in a new way, to the pain my mother must have undergone having to rear a child by herself, compounded by the loss of the man she loved. The sympathy I was building in support of my birth mother toppled, as Mimmie revealed more of my mother's personal life.

"After Bassie was born, your mother involved herself in a period of indiscriminate dating, resulting in several illegitimate children. Obviously, that means you have several half-brothers, in addition to your half-sister Bassie, but few people knew about them. She put the boys up for adoption before she ever laid eyes on them. I was told that one of them became a doctor, and the other one was killed, but I can't tell you how; I've never been able to confirm either report. Jean hadn't wanted to know anything about them, so I've never discussed that information with her, or anyone else, until now."

After digesting all that Mimmie had told me thus far, I didn't see how I would be able to swallow one more tidbit of information. And yet, I hungered for the rest of the story surrounding my mother's relationship with my father, and it looked like Mimmie was going to supply that information.

"During each period of time after Jean had given up each of the boys, she immersed herself in her work. Mrs. Blair had a passion for style, and she was your mother's favorite client, as well as a good friend. Soon Jean was designing hats for many prestigious women throughout the country. She would never admit how talented she really was, especially her potential as a big fashion designer; instead, she would say, "Oh, it's just a dream." She had only herself to blame for that, and I would tell her so. She passed up many opportunities to expand not only her business, but her social life as well; but then, she had already met David DuLaney. I saw how attracted they were to each other, and how that attraction grew with each visit to Blairsouth Estate. I already knew she had vowed never to allow her heart the freedom to love again, but David was so handsome, and his French accent and gallant manner only made it more difficult for your mother to resist. David was born in France, in case I hadn't mentioned that; he came to the United States for a better job opportunity. Leta, I would watch the two of them walk from this house out to the limousine; I thought they made an attractive couple, and I will admit, I was even a little bit envious. Well, it wasn't long before she whispered to me that she and David had gone out to dinner together. When I reminded her of the promise she had made to herself not to get involved again, she said that I shouldn't concern myself over it, that she and David were just friends. I knew better, Leta.

"Now for the part you really came to hear."

She gave me a hug as I braced myself for the next background installment on my life. A watery shine filled Mimmie's eyes. I realized then, that what she was about to share was as hard for her to tell as it was for me to hear.

"One very misty night as they were walking to his car, after their first date at David's favorite restaurant, he confessed his love for your mother, she told me. He told her that the first time he ever opened the limousine door for her, she had stepped out of the car and into his life. It sounded so romantic. But of course, David DuLaney himself was very romantic. I even had a crush on him for a while; but that's our secret, O.K?"

A flood of sympathy began to flow from me to Jean Marlow, and Mimmie hadn't even finished telling me all she knew. Noticing that Mimmie hesitated before continuing, I encouraged her to go on.

"Well, as you might expect, when David took Jean home that night, he invited himself in for a glass of wine. She told me that they had had a few glasses of wine at the restaurant, but that the wine hadn't necessarily been an invitation for David to join her in her flat. Bassie happened to be spending the night with friends at the time. However, Jean said it was not her intention to spend the evening alone with David in her flat; much to the contrary, she said she had settled that dispute with herself before that evening had ever begun.

"But, Leta, your mother just wanted to be loved, that's all."

Unaware of my own thoughts and equally insatiable appetite for affection, Mimmie continued.

"To abbreviate what happened, skipping the passion that obviously accompanied that night, David and Jean ended up spending the night together. They announced their engagement shortly thereafter. They wanted to spend the rest of their lives together. Or so it seemed. He even told Jean that he considered Bassie an added benefit of their impending marriage. Jean was extremely happy.

"Several months later, after Mr. and Mrs. Blair left for vacation, Jean came to see me. She was obviously distressed. God only knows why she chose to seek my advice; I had little experience in those kings of things, but as a trusted friend, my shoulder was always there when she needed it.

"I couldn't tell at first whether her tears were of joy or of sorrow . . . and then they turned out to be both. She told me she was pregnant. My first thought was, *Oh no, not again.* But instead, I waited until she told me how she had felt about the situation she was in. She said she was so happy, but that she hadn't told David or Bassie about the expected child. She thought that maybe she could hide her pregnancy until after they were married. But David had to return to France for some reason, and so she decided to tell him about the baby right before he left. She was confident that the news would hasten his trip back to her and Bassie. Unfortunately, that's not how things turned out.

"David left the United States with more than a suitcase of clothing. He left knowing he was the father of Jean's child, and that was just enough to send him packing . . . forever."

I couldn't keep silent any longer. I had to respond to what Mimmie was telling me.

"You mean my father never came back to my mother and the baby?" I asked the question as if the baby was someone other than myself. And I already knew the answer.

"My God, how could he do such a thing? And all because of me."

"Now, don't you go getting upset," Mimmie advised. "You had nothing to do with that whole situation, you hear? Just because he was a deserter, that's no fault of yours; you've got to believe that, Leta."

Sure, I thought. *How could I not feel responsible. I became the paramount reason for my mother's unhappiness.* But Mimmie kept right on talking.

"Anyway, Jean was unable to deal with the pain of David leaving her. She loved David with all that was left in her. As a result, your mother spent a short period of time in a hospital; you know, one of those places that deals with emotionally disturbed people. When she was discharged, Mr. and Mrs. Blair came to her rescue. They helped her out financially, and they insisted that she keep the baby, but Jean had already decided on going the same route she had gone with your half-brothers. I mean, your mother was not a real young woman any more, and it would have been quite a responsibility to support another child.

"On October 27, 1935, she gave birth to a seven-and-a-half-pound baby girl; that baby was you, Leta. Unlike the two boys, whose faces she never saw, she couldn't resist looking at you, Leta."

With that, I gave up tears reserved for sadder things and indulged myself in a double portion of self-pity.

"She did love you, Leta. She wouldn't allow them to take you away until she had decided on a name for you. And just like that, she named you Leta Marguerite Marlow. I never thought to ask her why she gave you that name, but she seemed confident that the name belonged to you. So, I'm sorry that I'm unable to tell you how you came by that name. But once you became Leta, she put you in the arms of a Children's Bureau caseworker, then she turned her face away from the door and cried."

"Mimmie," I said, still teary-eyed, "I was never adopted until just a few weeks ago, and thankfully, at least I was never handed off from one family to another, either. I stayed in the home of James and Grace Carpenter until I got married. And did you know that when I was little, my mother and Bassie came to see me at the Carpenters' home pretending to be friends of theirs?"

"Yes, I knew, Leta. She told me what a beautiful child you were and how difficult seeing you had been for her. But somehow, seeing you helped alleviate the lingering ache in her heart as a result of David's betrayal. Of course, she never fully accepted her share of responsibility in the matter. She never dated again, and she never heard from David. She continued designing hats though, until just recently, when she became very ill. She loved your father, Leta, and she will probably die wondering why he never came back to her."

Of course, I knew the reason: *Me.*

"Mimmie, the judge told me never to try and find my father. Why do you suppose he made that stipulation before giving me his name?"

"Well, all I can say is, rumor had it that he became a fairly prominent person in France, a far cry from being a chauffeur. Everyone around here just didn't mention his name any more, and no further information was sought, or for that matter, attainable. So, the mystery remains. I wish I could tell you more about your father, but I just don't know any more about him."

"It just seems strange, Mimmie, that I was made to promise not to try and find him. I mean, he is my father. I get to Europe at least once or twice a year, and it wouldn't be that difficult to trace him down, I would think. I mean, how many David L. DuLaneys could there be? Of course, I wouldn't know where to begin."

"I really don't think it would be a good idea to try and locate him; after all, he may not even be alive any more. It's the same with your mother; contacting her again would only cause her more pain, and she has had quite enough."

"Quite frankly, Mimmie, she wouldn't want to see me again. She made that blatantly clear; and I have no desire to see her, either. I neither love nor hate her. I don't feel anything. But what you've told me certainly sends a distress signal to my own feelings of rejection and insecurities."

Mimmie seemed genuinely surprised and hurt when I told her about the letter I received from my mother in which she declared her repulsion for me and vowed to disown me. But I began to see more clearly how that revulsion may have been directed at my father, and not at me.

It was getting late in the afternoon, and I wanted to return to Laurel Lake before Mitch arrived home from New York, and I had to take Fannie back to her home in Bucherville, so I prepared to leave Mimmie and Blairsouth Estate.

Instead of walking through the house to the front door, we followed the outside garden path leading to the courtyard circling the entrance to Blairsouth. I could almost picture David DuLaney, handsome and gallant, escorting the fashionable Jean Marlow up the cobblestone steps to the door of the Blairsouth mansion. But it wasn't a fairytale. It was a true story—not completely told, not completely known.

Mimmie had given me a small picture of my mother and Bassie. They were standing together in the front lawn of Blairsouth Estate. I later cut the head off of my sister and stuck the remaining portion in my wallet. The significance of that exercise is best left to the experts. My greatest misfortune was that Mimmie had been unable to come up with a picture of my father. I would have given anything to see his face, even in a picture. To this day, I wonder what part of my appearance or my personality is David DuLaney. I see more vividly the part of me that is Jean Marlow.

Exhausted, I drove back to Laurel Lake, some emotional distance from Blairsouth Estate. It was as though I, too, was stepping out of one life and into another.

To resume any normalcy after my meeting with Mimmie, I would have to adopt Maureen's philosophy: Just let it go, and turn it off, just like you do a faucet.

I made a valiant attempt at doing just that.

... EIGHTEEN ...

The past hastily became the present, and back again, when on his return from New York, Mitch displayed two plane tickets to Europe, accompanied by an itinerary as long as the Nile River. The plan to revisit the war-torn fields of his past, and the liberated towns of Western Europe that he so vividly remembered from his tenure in the Army would finally come to fruition.

The children were to remain behind in Fannie's capable hands.

I became more aware of my children as individuals since my visit to Blairsouth Estate. Each one had a personality and character distinction that set them apart from the other, formed by God and circumstances. I loved them so much, and I was going to miss them when we left for Europe. I had never before been away from them for more than two weeks at a time. Their protection was of utmost concern to me; I wanted so much to protect them from the pain that love sometimes brings. But unfortunately, it was a little late for that; they had already witnessed love's bruises, firsthand.

Had I been able to see beyond the years, I probably would have done things a whole lot differently. *Instead, I walked each day . . . but rarely by faith.*

*   *   *   *   *

On a breezy day in September, we landed in Frankfurt, Germany, via Lufthansa Airlines. I had held my breath and the armrests of my seat, the entire length of the Atlantic Ocean. I hadn't eaten, or slept, throughout the entire flight. Mitch, on the other hand, assumed his all too familiar "I don't know you" position in a seat close to the wing section of the airplane, anticipating my "over-reaction" to the slightest hint of turbulence. I resumed breathing after I felt the wheels of the airplane touch down on the Frankfurt runway.

It was early morning in Frankfurt, Germany.

We rented a BMW and headed for our hotel.

Flower boxes on the windows of nearly every home spilled over with cascading red geraniums and white petunias. Regardless of the size or age of the quaint houses, each one looked like it had just been freshly painted. The aroma of fresh sausages cooking floated out of every door. As soon as we could, we found ourselves sitting at an outdoor café, sipping coffee and feasting on spicy hunks of sausages and freshly baked bread. In the afternoon, we drank cold beer and devoured freshly baked German soft pretzels.

The following day, we drove to Munich, Germany, the city that eventually became our home away from home. We checked into the Four Seasons Hotel, the best hotel in Munich, and quite possibly in all of Germany. It was an elegant hotel, boasting of impeccable service. Fresh fruit and flowers graced a small table in our room. The linens were made of the finest cottons, and at night, petite chocolate mints were placed on the fluffy goose down pillows like a goodnight kiss. Robes and slippers were as customary as a bar of soap at the Four Seasons Hotel. In the ensuing years, the famous chefs at the hotel became acquainted with our children, and as far as we knew, they were the only children permitted to enter the kitchen area of the five-star restaurant inside the hotel.

While I was asking, "*Was ist das beste Stuck, die beste Revue, Operette* in town," Mitch was reveling in the fact that there was no *Hochstgeschwindigkeit* (maximum speed limit) in the country. He was barely able to contain himself, in anticipation of driving the BMW flat out on the *Autobahn*.

We used our three weeks in Europe to visit East Germany, Belgium, France, Holland, Italy, and England.

Armed soldiers, more than willing to shoot us as we toured the poverty-stricken Communist country of East Germany, escorted our vehicle everywhere we went. Buildings that had been reduced to rubble during World War II still remained the same. It was a devastating sight. I watched families line up for blocks waiting to purchase their daily ration of meat and bread for their evening meal. It had a profound effect on my psyche, and it multiplied my gratefulness for living in a land where we undoubtedly threw away more than that country ever had. I returned to West Germany with a new understanding of Communism and human suffering.

On our visit to Einhoven, one of the towns in Holland Mitch helped liberate, we trampled field after field in search of the gun and helmet Mitch claimed he had helped erect in memory of a fellow soldier who had given his life to save Mitch and his platoon. The soldier had taken a full hit from a German tank, allowing time and opportunity for Mitch and his men to escape. Within hours of thinking that we had been on a wild goose chase, we came upon the exact spot Mitch had told me about. There among the brush and stubble stood a solitary gun, permanently stationed in the ground, a helmet placed on top of it. I was so touched, mostly I think, because I knew the story and how it related to the monument. Mitch remained unusually quiet. We spent another hour or so preoccupied with the circumstances of that war, which had called upon a soldier to give his life so that others might live. It was the perfect analogy of what I believed Jesus did for me, but little did I realize then that I would turn my back on that   Person, just as so many had done with regard to the soldiers who sacrificed much for their freedom.

During our stay in Holland, we felt privileged to be invited as special guests to a ceremony commemorating the liberation of Einhoven by the allies during World War II. It was an emotional display, as we stood listening to the show of appreciation by the Dutch people for the allied men and women who had sacrificed their lives for them and their countrymen. All I knew about the war was what I had read in history books and from Mitch's firsthand accounts. That day in Einhoven, I felt as though I had been in the battle.

France was of special interest to me. The romantic allure of Paris, from the buildings and cafés to the people themselves, remains unmatched by any other. Whether touring the French countryside or gazing at the Eiffel Tower along the Champ-Elysees, I managed to conjure up visions of David DuLaney. As a recipient of the infamous French "pinch," I couldn't help wonder how easily I would have been enamoured by a smooth-talking romantic Frenchman myself. But it was useless entertaining any thought of finding my birth father, though to this day, I regret not having at least tried. I loved Paris, but it was disheartening to find that Paris didn't feel the same way about me. The French were not at all happy to have Americans visit their country, and they made sure that by the time you left their country, you were fully aware of that fact. Aside from that, Paris was by far the most beautiful of cities.

In St. Marie Eglise, France, we visited the church bell tower where a young girl, armed with a weapon, had hidden during the war, a position she used to shoot and kill American paratroopers as they hung by their parachute strings like Christmas tree ornaments. Mitch himself had parachuted close to the church, but landed without incident. He instinctively reached for his weapon and shot the young girl out of the church bell tower. Why he wanted to revisit that site puzzled me, but after giving it some thought, I understood clearly why sometimes you are compelled to revisit the pains of your past.

We shared our next memorable event with the French Gendarme.

Unable to locate a particular French town in our tour booklet, we stopped at a local French police station for directions, and as the saying goes, we were at the right place at the wrong time. What we hadn't known at the time was that a faction of renegade Algerians had been randomly terrorizing police stations in France, and quite unexpectedly, we found ourselves in the midst of one of those skirmishes. At the first sound of gunfire, we were quickly escorted into an inner room of the police station to safety. Unscathed, but still a bit anxious, we got out of that place fast. We were able to obtain directions, and we continued on our way. It was only after we returned to the United States that we realized the seriousness of what had taken place. Similar attacks, as reported in national newspapers, had occasionally resulted in death. You can be sure we talked about that for a long time.

It hadn't taken much coaxing by Mitch, after our experience in France, for me to imbibe in a glass or two of wine. I believe that was when I became more tolerant regarding the moderate consumption of alcohol.

Our visit to Einhoven had been memorably heartrending, but nothing compared with the fields of white crosses overlooking Omaha and Utah Beaches. Hundreds of rows of white crosses marked the graves containing the bodies of soldiers who had died for their countries, and whose heroism had been taken so much for granted. That image was forever branded in my mind. I watched as busloads of people, foreigners to me, placed hand-cut flowers on the graves of American soldiers as a way of expressing their continuing gratefulness for what they had done. Sunday after Sunday, and year after year since the end of the war, I was told, the people of that area faithfully repeated that ritual. I felt ashamed.

I had no flower to give.

I didn't remember the war . . . but I shall never forget those fields of white crosses.

*   *   *   *   *

Before, and after, marrying Mitch, I would accompany him to the yearly 101st Airborne Reunions throughout the country. I had memorized the horror stories and felt the pain of the veteran amputees as they relived the war all over again. We entertained many of those veterans in our home. I had talked personally with General Westmoreland and General Taylor, two respected World War II military leaders. I felt immensely appreciative for what Mitch and his fellow paratroopers did for our country, even more so after I visited some of the same areas that I heard them talk about so much. The gratitude I felt for Mitch's service to his country, and the sympathy I felt for him because of his impoverished childhood, came to play an important role in a decision I would make many years later.

*   *   *   *   *

Rome, Italy, had its memorable moments as well.

While having a late breakfast one morning in a well-known hotel in Rome, I noticed a familiar face across the room. It didn't take long to discover that it was none other than Joe Namath, the famous football star. He happened to be making a movie in Rome, co-starring Ann Margaret, at the time. After my attempt at secretly photographing him was exposed, he approached our table and offered to accommodate the "novice photographer" (as he graciously put it). When we told him that we were from Pennsylvania and touring Europe for three weeks, he said that he, too, was a Pennsylvanian. That began a very congenial exchange between us. It was one of the more pleasant memories of our stay in Rome.

What disturbed me most about our visit to Rome were the apparent riches of a particular area, while its sovereign landscape remained blanketed in poverty. But in spite of that finding, Rome was one of the most exciting and fascinating cities I have ever had the opportunity of visiting.

With one unvisited country left before leaving Germany for our return to the United States, we made plans to fly to England.

As we boarded an airplane that looked as if it had been borrowed from the museum of ancient history, I noticed several men in work coveralls standing in the galley brandishing some VERY LARGE TOOLS. That didn't surprise me, considering the airplane's appearance. Since my fondness for flying hadn't yet turned to love, I considered their presence highly suspicious and somewhat disconcerting. It wasn't long before my suspicions were confirmed. One English mechanic looked at the other English mechanic and said, "I say . . . this bloody thing should have been mothballed long ago!" With that, I told Mitch I refused to fly on that rattletrap of a plane, knowing full well that something was not working properly. I felt like I was about to board a bird with a crippled wing. But of course, my request to disembark was denied.

The flight to London turned out to feel like the bumper car ride at Hershey, Pennsylvania's amusement park . . . with several differences: I couldn't get off the plane, and we paid a lot more for the ride. The plane sounded like a container of empty soda cans being thrown into the back of an early morning garbage truck. To make matters worse, we still had to fly back to Germany before taking our final flight home. In my mind, I had already given up flying, and not just for Lent.

After several days of exploring England, we successfully located the town, and post office, where the girl who had fallen in love with Hudson, a United States military officer and close friend of Mitch's, had worked during the war. Mitch repeated the story to me, how his friend Hudson and this girl had fallen in love. When the war ended, the girl had been unable to join Hudson in the United States for reasons unknown to Mitch. They remained apart for a very long time, Mitch told me, and because of Hudson's obligation to his ailing parents to take over their cattle farm in Kentucky, the two of them eventually lost contact with each other. Sadly, we failed in our attempt to locate the woman. However, when we visited Hudson in Kentucky the summer following our visit to England, we learned that not long after the war, he received a letter from his wartime girlfriend telling him that she had married someone else. Hudson had been devastated by the news; subsequently, he never dated another woman, remaining unmarried for the rest of his life.

Mitch and I were treated like royalty in the local pubs on the outskirts of London, especially after they found out that Mitch had been a member of the 101st Airborne Division. We spent afternoons in cozy, secluded English pubs, sipping dark beer and reminiscing about the war. My participation was limited to sipping.

Apart from my fear of flying, Mitch and I spent a memorable, and generally amicable, three weeks in Europe.

*   *   *   *   *

It was time to leave Germany for our flight home to the United States. I hadn't slept all night just thinking about it.

When we arrived at the airport in Frankfurt, we learned that all flights across the Atlantic, except the one we were scheduled to take, had been cancelled due to inclement weather. Because of my acute fear of flying, I decided to conduct my own mini-investigation. I talked to several people who had just arrived in Frankfurt from New York City. The man that I questioned appeared hesitant in revealing the conditions through which he and his wife had just flown, but his wife was much more eager to give me a report.

"Honey," she said, "I don't blame you for being concerned; that is some storm out there. I didn't think we were going to make it. But those pilots know what they're doing, so I'm sure you don't have a thing to worry about."

Still unsatisfied and twice as fearful, I approached several other passengers who had been on the same flight, and their opinions confirmed what the first couple told me.

By the time we were called to our gate for boarding, I was sick in my stomach and near tears. I asked Mitch if we could please cancel our flight and go home another day, but he was adamant about returning home as scheduled.

I looked around the airport as though I was looking at it for the last time. My throat burned and I wanted to cry, but pride wouldn't allow me that luxury, at least at that time.

I boarded the airplane an emotional cripple. I heard others discussing the option of remaining behind, even as they searched for their assigned seats. I had already counted myself among the missing, confirmed by the announcement on the late-breaking news the following day, after word that our plane had gone down somewhere in the middle of the Atlantic Ocean. It wasn't long before the plane's mouth closed around us and we were swallowed up much like Jonah in the belly of the whale.

Mitch exchanged places with me when he discovered a very attractive girl occupying the window seat in the row where our seats were assigned. He suggested that I sit next to her, hoping that she and I would be good company for each other on the long flight home. So I exchanged my aisle seat for the one between the two of them. What I really needed was to be reassured by Mitch that things were going to be fine . . . not a seat next to a total stranger. I was very aware how much my fear of flying frustrated Mitch . . . with my constant need for reassurance. But his hand in mine would have been a welcome show of love and support at that time.

As we waited for the plane to take off, I decided to strike up a conversation with the attractive girl beside me. She told me her name was Susan Bally; I told her about my fear of flying. She began by saying, "No matter how rough a flight we might encounter, it's nothing to be concerned about." She told me she had flown in all kinds of weather conditions and that she had lived to tell many stories. The meaning of that statement became all too apparent later in our flight.

The large Lufthansa airplane taxied down the runway, and shortly thereafter, its nose pointed toward Heaven.

After we had been in the air for a short period of time, we were informed that our first stop would be Gander, Newfoundland, where we would be refueling. But as the plane gained altitude, it began to shake and quiver like a belly dancer. The captain assured us, on the intercom system, that we would be flying above the existing weather conditions, but that we were to keep our seatbelts fastened until we reached our intended altitude. As the plane continued to climb, I prepared to meet God. The plane never managed to rise above the storm. Suddenly, everything that hadn't been securely fastened came flying through the airplane. The plane was being tossed back and forth like a paper airplane between two boys in their backyard. Unfortunately, our plane had an ocean, and about thirty-five thousand feet, beneath its wings.

There were several Catholic nuns on our flight, and they had already begun to pray their rosaries. I, on the other hand, was no longer in a praying mood. I was angry that Mitch hadn't agreed to cancel our flight and return home another time. Mothers who had small children waiting for them at home began to cry; they were sure they would never see their children again. The mighty and brave . . . like Mitch, sat unemotional, accepting their tempestuous plight. Repeatedly, a voice from the cockpit assured us that we would soon be out of the storm; but that wasn't the truth.

With clenched teeth and sweaty palms, I held on to the arms of my seat and fought to hold back the tears. My mind began to visualize our funeral: no bodies . . . just empty boxes covered in flowers, and Fannie beside herself as she agonized over what to do with the children. At one point, I, too, thought we would never see our children again, to which Mitch replied, "Don't be ridiculous; you always make things worse than they are. Planes are made to withstand things like this; they don't just break apart and fall out of the sky; get a grip." I would have gotten a grip, but by that time I was paralyzed and couldn't move a thing.

At first, I thought it was Mitch who reached for my hand . . . only to find out that it was Susan who took my hand in hers.

"It is going to be all right," she said. "This is pretty bad, and I'm afraid too, but let me tell you a story."

If I had been used to bedtime stories when I was a little girl, I would have thought I was revisiting those moments.

"Some years ago," she began, "I was secretary to an ambassador, and we were on a flight between two countries, flying over a thick jungle, when the plane developed engine trouble. The pilot had no choice but to crash-land the plane in the jungle below. When I regained consciousness, I was lying beside the airplane unable to move, but I was still alive. We were in the jungle many days before a rescue team located us. Not everyone lived through that disaster; I was one of the fortunate ones. So you see, I have been through a whole lot worse than this, and I have lived to tell the stories."

After Susan shared her story with me, I reminded myself that it was impossible to add one more minute to my life . . . if God had other plans. But there was still that old argument: What if the pilot's time is up, and not mine; would I have to die with him?

Susan, my unexpected (or perhaps God-sent) source of support, continued to talk to me, hoping to distract and comfort me. But I was not easily comforted.

Stewards and stewardesses alike remained strapped in their seats, evidence of how serious the situation was. They eventually began to pass small bottles of liquor down the aisles of the plane, hoping that the alcohol would soothe the nerves of their passengers.

Occasionally, the captain came on the intercom with an update on our situation. I observed the reactions of the other passengers, as the explanations were given in their languages first; then I heard the same explanations in English. With few exceptions, we were all deathly afraid. I was petrified. Even the crew admitted that they had never been in a storm quite like that one. People were getting sick and the aisles were strewn with food and personal effects.

After many hours on that agonizing flight, the captain's voice came on the intercom once more; and just as before, his message was in several languages, English being the last.

"Ladies and Gentlemen, may I have your attention please. We have been in touch with Gander, Newfoundland, where we were to have refueled. Unfortunately, we've been informed that due to severe weather conditions, we are unable to land in Gander, so instead, we will be flying directly to Idlewild Airport in New York City. Thank you for hanging in there with us in these unusual circumstances. We will inform you of any changes in our flight plans as they occur."

I found that information extremely bothersome. *If we were to have refueled in Gander, Newfoundland*, I reasoned, *where is the fuel going to come from to enable us to fly directly to New York City?* But my question simply made room for more unexplainable events that were to follow.

Many tears later, following Mitch's admonishment for my open display of fear, the captain interrupted with yet another announcement.

"Ladies and Gentlemen, may I have your attention please. We have some bad news for you."

I was convinced right then and there that we were surely going to die, which made me listen all the more intently, as he continued.

"New York is experiencing the same severe weather conditions that exist in Gander, so we are unable to land at Idlewild Airport as planned. The same is true of Boston, Atlanta, and other East Coast airports. We will continue communicating with other airports until we find one that will give us clearance to land. We will be back to you with further information as soon as it is available to us. Thank you."

I don't know how that news affected the others, but I do know that it took an all-consuming toll on me. I clenched my teeth harder and harder, until they had literally come loose in their sockets. I could take my fingers and move every tooth back and forth with my fingers. *Oh my God,* I thought, *I am going to lose my teeth and my life over this!* But before I could shed any additional tears over the latest news, the voice on the intercom asked for our attention once more.

"Ladies and Gentlemen, I would like to have your attention. This is your captain."

I considered it totally unnecessary for him to keep introducing himself to us; goodness knows he had been talking to us often enough.

"We are having a difficult time locating an airport that isn't experiencing severe weather conditions. We have been unable to get landing clearance from any East Coast airport. In the meantime, we have been evaluating our fuel situation and the wind velocity. Based on our findings, we have decided to return to Frankfurt, Germany. We will be taking the necessary steps to lighten the plane for fuel conservation in order to assure us all a safe return. Thank you for your understanding. We believe that what we are doing is in the best interest of our passengers and its crew; we apologize now for any inconvenience to you and your travel plans."

I couldn't help wondering whose luggage or what kind of cargo was going to free-fall to earth in order to lighten the plane. Since we had not refueled in Gander, extra fuel wasn't likely one of those dispensable items. The announcement made it pretty obvious that we were in big trouble. *I prayed.*

We landed safely in Frankfurt, our original point of departure, amidst emergency equipment, newsmen, and food. The extravagant selection of comestibles may as well have been fish food for all the interest it held for the nerve-wrecked passengers of that flight.

After refueling and taking on a fresh crew, we boarded the same plane and flew directly back across the Atlantic Ocean for the third time. Not everyone joined us, however; some had been too sick to travel; others had opted to spend some additional time in Germany until they had recuperated from the harrowing experience.

Fortunately, the storm had abated considerably by that time, albeit it was still a rough ride home. As far as I was concerned, anyone who had a fear of flying and still got back on that plane qualified for a Purple Heart.

I began the second trip to New York with several strong drinks, but my teeth were so sore that I had to drink though a straw. At that moment, I made my final decision: I was never going to fly again . . . or laugh, since I was sure that all of my teeth were going to fall out.

When we landed at Idlewild Airport, I knelt unashamedly and kissed the macadam. As I sat on a suitcase outside of the Lufthansa Arrival Terminal waiting for Mitch to retrieve our car from the long-term parking area, a handsome uniformed man approached me.

"Hello there," he said, "were you a passenger on the flight that made two trips across the Atlantic in that terrible storm?"

"Yes," I said, quite weakly.

"I was your captain on the second crossing. Are you going to be O.K? Will someone be meeting you?"

"Yes, thank you," I said, confident that he hadn't wanted to die any more than I did.

Mitch and I drove home in silence. He said that he was ashamed of my behavior; that I was a grown woman and should have been able to control my emotions. I was deeply hurt, and ashamed of myself. *Mitch is just going to have to get used to traveling alone in the future,* I thought to myself.

What should have produced endearing memories from our three weeks together in Europe reminded me instead of what a disappointment I was to my husband. I couldn't wait to feel the arms of my children around me, welcoming me home.

A letter from Lufthansa Airlines, explaining what had taken place and why the crew made the decisions they did, remains in my personal belongings to this day.

Occasionally, I take it out and read it and thank God that I am alive "to tell the story," as Susan Bally had so aptly put it.

. . . NINETEEN . . .

As the children grew older, depending less and less on me, I began to depend more and more on them to fill the void in my life. Mitch continued to devote most of his time to cars, hockey games, and trips to Europe; but it was entirely my decision not to accompany Mitch on any more of his planned trips abroad. I devoted my time to our children and to our home.

Although the children's involvement in school sports was limited, I made every effort to attend each and every one of their activities. I was also present for most parent-teacher meetings. I had been unsuccessful in getting Mitch to attend those events with me.

When Ben qualified for the wrestling team, Mitch agreed to attend one of his meets, but afterwards, I wished he had never gone. He referred to Ben as a "sissy" when Ben didn't respond to his opponent the way Mitch thought he should have. It wasn't long before Ben dropped out of wrestling and switched to playing cymbals in the school marching band.

Sarah's favorite sport was trying to hide a relationship she was having with a young man, one whom she was sure would not meet with our approval. She also had plans to someday attend a dental-assistant training school. Her father discouraged both. Thomas liked cars . . . and that came as no huge surprise . . . seeing how much he took after his father. He was also the only one of our sons who had shown any interest in serving in the military. Mitch lauded that prospect!

Luke was still making school friends, and it paid off for him. He and his best friend, Frank, his friend since kindergarten days, remained close throughout their college years and beyond. As a matter of fact, they served as best man at each other's weddings.

Mitch never went to any of the children's graduation ceremonies, and that was entirely his decision. He was especially disturbed that Ben's commencement speaker was a black woman. I found his objection a little like the person who complains about the President of the United States when he never even voted in the election; his opinion doesn't count.

*   *   *   *   *

With the new businesses organized, in full operation, and in the good hands of capable managers, Mitch indicated to me that he would soon be returning to Europe. In my stead, the children started taking turns accompanying their father on his trips.

Our children had become world travelers by the time they were teenagers. Our youngest son, Luke, experienced the thrill of flying to France on the Concorde shortly after its maiden flight, and he exclaimed for days over the gourmet food they had been served on that flight.

Unless we traveled by automobile, ship, or train, I remained a stay-at-home mom and wife.

*   *   *   *   *

During the summer of 1972 while Mitch was in Europe combining business with pleasure, disaster struck home.

It began to rain quite heavily one day, and it didn't stop. The deluge of water that fell over several days became known as the Flood of '72.

The first indications that it was a serious rain were the sounds of trees plummeting into the lake near our home. The water pummeled the ground, taking down everything that stood in its way. I was so thankful that our home sat on high ground overlooking Laurel Lake.

It wasn't long before the phone rang, and on the other end of the line was the panic-stricken voice of one of our Minden employees. He talked so fast that it was very hard for me to understand him.

"Mrs. Brogan," he said, as if he was trying to catch his breath, "you won't believe what has happened! Everything is lost! The water is . . . is rising . . . fast, and . . . and . . . we're trying . . . as . . . as . . . hard as we can to get . . . ah . . . all the cars out of . . . the . . . ah . . . building, but the . . . oh my God, I've gotta get out of here!"

After that, I heard crashing glass and nothing more . . . just a deadening click.

I had to get to Minden, I decided, but how? . . . that was the question. Fallen trees and high water had blocked most of the roads, but I knew I had to try. Before I reached the door, the phone rang again. It was one of my husband's salesmen.

"Leta," he said, sounding stunned and in shock, "don't even think about coming in here. They won't leave anyone near the place. You'll have to wait for the water to recede, but I thought I'd better prepare you before you do come. Everything is gone. The cars that are still standing on four wheels are filled with water, and I can't even begin to describe the rest.

It's terrible. I can't believe it. There's got to be eight feet of water inside the building."

I couldn't imagine the magnitude of the destruction he described.

"Where are you calling from, Paul?" I asked him.

"I went to a restaurant in another part of town that still has use of their telephone. You had better wait until you see this place before you call Mitch."

"I will," I promised. "There's nothing he can do anyway. And I doubt whether he would cut his trip short to rush home, but thank you. It looks pretty awful here, too."

"What do you think we should do?" he asked.

"Well, if you can contact the rest of the employees, tell them to come in tomorrow and we'll just continue to pay them while we sort things out and decide what to do. They're not to worry about losing their jobs, just assure them of that."

The weight of that devastating act of God had not yet fallen on my shoulders.

Another phone call came shortly thereafter from our manager in Bucherville. His report was equally depressing, echoing the horrors of yet another business and its contents destroyed or damaged by the flood-waters. He told me that they had managed to get most of the cars to higher ground, but the building had at least seven feet of water in it.

Fortunately, our recently built distributorship, located between Bucherville and Minden, had suffered only moderate external damages.

That night, as I waited for the water to recede before going to Minden, I got a glimpse of the widespread destruction on the television evening news. The camera zoomed in briefly on the corner where our business stood, and longer on the ravaged scenes throughout the small town of Minden. Our place of business was barely recognizable. I began to sob. How was I ever going to describe to Mitch what I had just seen on television when he was so far removed from the disaster?

When I reached the overseas operator, I explained that I had to get in touch with a family member in Germany immediately. Much to my surprise, she replied, "I am so sorry, but we are unable to put your call through at this time. The United States has just experienced a flood disaster, and service has been temporarily disrupted; please try your call again later."

The following day, after dozens of phone calls from friends expressing sorrow over our loss and offering to help in any way they could, I made another failed attempt at contacting Mitch . . . then I left for Minden.

When I reached the road just beyond our home, I was overcome with sadness. Huge majestic trees that had withstood the ages were not splintered and broken . . . their roots protruding from the ground. How often I had heard the expression: "If trees could only talk." The stories those trees could tell would now remain forever untold.

The bridge I normally crossed to reach the main highway was impassable. I turned the car around and took another narrow road that eventually led to a secondary road leading to the main highway some miles down the road. I maneuvered through an obstacle course of downed trees and wires (dead and alive).

As I entered the town of Minden, not far from where our automobile business was located, several policemen stopped me. Recognizing me, one of them said, "You can go through, Mrs. Brogan, but take it easy. I'm really sorry about your place. Go on, I know you need to get there, but I would advise you not to try and go inside of the dealership. There are hot wires and glass everywhere."

In spite of our employees' warning, I wasn't prepared for what I saw.

From a distance, I could already see the dealership. I saw cars turned upside down, nose sides up, and on their sides. Nothing had been spared. The storm had visited havoc all over town. I parked the car some distance from our business and walked the rest of the way.

As I got within a block of the building, Paul, the salesman who had alerted me on the phone to what I would find, rushed to meet me. His arms went around me, and he comforted me. A number of our faithful employees came walking up the muddy street to meet us, and together we walked toward the flooded business. When I was in full view of the devastating sight, I could not hold back the tears. And once more, Paul's arms were around me.

The first thing we did once I regained my composure was to send the employees to buy as many buckets, rags, shovels, thigh-high fishing boots, and rubber gloves as could be found. While several of the employees were off on that scavenger hunt, a van of Amish folks pulled up to where we were standing. They proceeded to unload cleaning equipment and freshly baked bread and pies. I was moved to tears once more as the Amish people went to work on their hands and knees to clean an entire apartment house that sat on our property in order that the people who rented the house could move back in.

When it came to the business, it was hard to know where to start. The cars were covered with mud; the showroom floor was thick with slime-covered papers and human waste. Because of health concerns, free medicine and services were offered to anyone in town who was involved in the flood.

For the remainder of the day, we shoveled mud and debris . . . making sure to avoid live wires and shattered glass. The children, with their shovels and brooms, worked their hearts out as well to help put a dent in the surmounting work ahead of us. At the end of the day, we went home exhausted and prepared to spend the next several weeks continuing the cleanup process. It was bad enough losing one business . . . but we had lost two. Our good fortune was that our home had been spared, which was more than a lot of people could say who suffered through the Flood of '72.

My next stop was Bucherville; there I found the same kind of destruction I had seen in Minden. Bucherville was a much smaller community, and after the water had receded, the town appeared desolate. A large percentage of it was mud filled and in total ruin. Mitch's manager assured me that he had everything under control; he had saved the inventory of cars that were to be distributed throughout the East Coast . . . and according to him, we were still in business. I was grateful for his optimism.

On my way back to Laurel Lake, I stopped at our new distributorship and found that we had suffered the least amount of damage in that location; another redeeming factor in what could have otherwise bankrupted us for life.

The third night following the flood, I was finally successful in reaching Mitch in Munich, Germany. I had carefully prepared the words I would use to tell him about the disastrous flood and our losses. But when I heard his voice on the phone all the way from Germany, I couldn't remember one word that I had planned to say.

"Mitch, have you heard about the flood that we had here in the United States?"

"Yes," he said, "I was just told by the operator that there was a disaster there. What happened? We're only getting bits and pieces here."

I began telling him all that had happened. His reaction took me by surprise. He calmly told me to call the insurance company right away and have them come in and estimate the damages on all three business. I was to let them decide what to do about getting rid of all the flood cars and that he would return home as scheduled. He asked me what I had done about the employees, saying that he wanted to keep them working because they had families to support. I assured him that I had kept them working and that they had been very grateful. And that was the end of our long distance conversation.

When the insurance representatives arrived to estimate the damages, I was told that I would have to decide what to do about getting rid of the cars; so with their help, I made contact with a company in California known for purchasing flood-damaged cars. They obviously refurbished the vehicles and resold them at reduced prices. The following week, car carriers arrived to transport the flooded cars to California. They were no longer my responsibility.

That evening, Paul, the salesman who had comforted me during that distressful time, and I decided to meet for pizza. We had worked very hard, and it was a well-deserved respite for both of us. We revisited the damaged areas where the evening breezes hadn't yet dried the memory of the rain-soaked fury that had left hundreds homeless and many businesses destroyed.

"You've done a fantastic job, Leta," he told me. "I know few women who could have taken over like you did in such a crisis. You deserve a lot of credit. You should get a medal from Auto America, and from that husband of yours."

Auto America was the East Coast distributor of the small car that we so successfully marketed after it was first introduced into the United States, and the president and vice president of that company, along with other members of the organization, had come to view the flood-damaged property in Minden. I remember well, and with pride, how I felt when they told me that I had done a good job.

In its infancy . . . while we were still in the process of building our little automobile empire, I felt like I was an integral part in everything that took place. I was even told by many of our friends and business associates that I had greatly contributed to Mitch's business success. But after the completion of those projects, I wasn't even allowed to have my car washed in the wash bays of any of our three dealerships. I don't know why, but after the flood I thought Mitch would be proud of me, but nothing changed.

Paul asked me if he could share a personal observation with me.

"Sure," I replied.

"Well, quite frankly, and I have to be honest, Leta, I don't think your husband appreciates you. If you were my woman, I would not treat you the way he treats you."

I was flattered by Paul's words, seeing they had come from a man some fifteen years younger than myself. He was a very good-looking young man and had served some time in the Army before coming to work for my husband. But the Army hadn't affected him the way it had affected Mitch. One reason, of course, was that Paul hadn't seen action in a world war as Mitch had.

"Thank you, Paul," I replied, "you don't know how much I needed to hear that, but you really don't know the half of it."

"Maybe I know more than you think I know," he replied.

Believing that he did know more, I found myself telling him about the abuse that had taken place in our home, making sure that he understood our conversation was to be held in strict confidence. I told him how the children and I had been mistreated . . . that I was concerned for our safety, and how I feared that one day it would get completely out of hand.

I told him how a friend of mine had even suggested that I purchase a gun for protection, and that another friend had suggested I leave Mitch.

Paul sat dumfounded. After a little while, he looked in my eyes and said, "Leta, I suspected things were not good, but I had no idea about the abuse. I just thought about how he travels without you and how I've seen him treat you when you've been at the dealership. I can't believe that he actually hurt the children and you. My God, what are you going to do?" he asked.

"Nothing. What can I do?" I said, not really expecting him to come up with an answer, and not quite sure I had done the right thing by sharing my heart with him in the first place. "If I threaten him in any way, Paul, he would definitely kill me." Of course, I never really believed that Mitch would go that far.

Paul's look was beginning to warm me; I knew I was in dangerous territory. Here I was, having dinner with someone other than my husband; if Mitch found out, he probably would kill me. I justified our meeting by telling myself that we had been working so hard for the last few days, so what harm could a little innocent conversation produce. But I was sure that Mitch would never have understood. Instead, on his return the major part of the devastation would have been cleaned up, and he would have little or no appreciation of what we had been through.

As we were leaving the restaurant, I told Paul that I really did feel better since talking to him. He thanked me for paying the bill, which was the least I could have done for all the help he had given me. When we reached my car, he opened the door for me. As I reached for the handle of the car to pull the door closed, he stopped me and put his hand over mine. I looked up into his face and thought how easy it would be to turn this one time into another time.

"Leta, don't leave just yet. You must know how I feel about you . . . I've felt like this for some time. I don't know why I am telling you this now, except for these last few days . . . working beside you . . . I think I'm falling in love with you."

"No, it's not possible," I argued. "This is not what tonight was about." Or at least I didn't think so. "I feel close to you, too," I admitted, "but I think it's because we've spent so much time together and under such traumatic circumstance; and I'm lonely, but that is as far as it goes."

"But I can't pretend I don't feel this way. I want to hold you in my arms and love you."

My insides churned. *If he only knew how much I want to be in his arms now,* I thought, *he would not leave me off so easily.*

"Looks like I won't be convincing you to meet me again, huh? I hope this doesn't end our friendship, Leta. I would never forgive myself for disclosing how I felt about you if that happened; and worse, I would really hate myself if you didn't feel comfortable facing me again."

"Don't worry, Paul," I said with a smile on my face, "as a matter of fact, I take it as a compliment. Even if I don't understand what a young man your age would see in an old woman like me."

"I think you're beautiful, Leta . . . and you're not old."

"Sure, I know . . . it's that crush thing," I said, trying to make light of all that transpired.

When the car door finally closed, I found myself guilty of flirting outside of marriage.

As I pulled onto the road from the parking lot, I looked in my rearview mirror and saw Paul still standing where my car had been. Suddenly, I felt sad . . . and desirable. I had to remind myself that I was a married woman with children.

Although I needed so much to be loved . . . like in everlasting, I could not justify being unfaithful to Mitch. But those old archenemies—rejection and self-pity—were waiting to be used as an excuse to sin, and I was tempted to accommodate them. Michael claimed to have had that kind of love for me once, but he soon found love in the arms of someone else. He told me that there would never be anyone who would mean as much to him as I did, and I held on to that belief for a long time . . . quite foolishly, of course. When I was younger, I thought I felt that kind of love for Bill Casset . . . but young love grows up and moves on to other things, and other people.

I had to surrender my thoughts. I wasn't going to look for love in the arms of someone else no matter how much I believed I deserved it. My sin was that, in my mind, I had already been unfaithful.

*   *   *   *   *

Mitch and Luke returned home.

Immediately, Mitch became involved with the reconstruction and remodeling of the businesses.

When Luke and I were alone one evening, he told me something that made me very angry.

"Mother," he said, "Daddy forced me to finish all my food one night at a restaurant in Germany, and I felt so sick. I told him I couldn't eat anything because I was afraid I would throw up, but he made me put more food in my mouth. I kept asking him not to make me eat any more because I felt sick. But I was afraid, so I took the next bite and then I really got sick. He was really upset with me, but I didn't try it. I knew I would get sick, and I told him so."

I hugged him and told him that it wasn't his fault. With that, he seemed to dismiss it from his mind; however, years later it was the one story he repeated when he reflected on his trip to Europe with his father.

*   *   *   *   *

After the businesses were remodeled and things were nearly back to normal, Mitch came home one evening and asked me if I would like to have a diamond ring. He may as well have asked me if I'd like to have a cup of coffee for all the enthusiasm he displayed. My first reaction was to question what I had done to deserve a diamond ring. After all, he hadn't thought I needed one when we got married, so of course I thought it had to do with something he wanted me to do. But I was pleasantly surprised when I found out that Auto America had wanted to contribute quite a nice sum of money toward the purchase of a diamond ring for me, as a token of their appreciation for what they had told me was a "job well done." But my joy was short-lived when Mitch told me that Auto America had shamed him into "springing" for the other half. The purchase was obviously going to be an unwilling expenditure for Mitch. I somehow understood his reluctance to spend that kind of money, after having to take out several loans following the flood.

"Yes, I would love to have a diamond ring," I replied.

We made arrangements to purchase a flawless three-carat diamond ring from a jeweler in Lancaster. I proudly placed it next to my simple gold wedding band. I couldn't take my eyes off of it. It captured every sunbeam, sending luminous dots everywhere. I couldn't help thinking about Michelle and the time she used her diamond ring to nearly blind me as a way of reminding me that she was still engaged to Mitch.

I met Maureen the following day for coffee and showed her my beautiful ring. We both took it as an encouraging sign that perhaps Mitch was having second thoughts about our relationship, particularly because of what I had done to keep the businesses going while he was away, and which Auto America so generously chose to recognize. But it was a misplaced hope.

*   *   *   *   *

The same day I met Maureen with the exciting news about my ring, I ran into another friend who lived in Bucherville. After exchanging some news regarding a fellow classmate, she said she really had to tell me something, and hoped it wouldn't upset me too much. I didn't know what to expect, but it was easy to tell it wasn't going to be good news.

"Leta, I saw Mitch sometime last month standing in front of Michelle's mother's house talking to Michelle. They talked for a long time. I was across the street at the shoe repair shop, and I just stayed there and watched. I don't know why, but I did. When they had finished talking, he put his arms around her and kissed her on the cheek. I was going to call you, but I didn't want to cause any trouble, but it sure looked like more than just a friendly exchange, if you know what I mean."

My heart broke open. Then I thought about the dinner I had had with Paul. What right had I to say anything to Mitch about what my friend had just told me, I asked myself, when I had gone out to eat with one of my husband's salesmen. In the back of my mind, where there was mighty little storage room left for any more rejection, was the unsubstantiated belief that perhaps Mitch wished he had married Michelle instead of me. My diamond lost some of its sparkle.

For a period of time, Paul became a haunting presence in my life, just as Michael had been. But I confess, I thrived on that attention. As long as there was always someone who cared about me, even thinking they were in love with me, I was able to cope with the way Mitch treated me.

. . . TWENTY . . .

It wasn't until Mitch left on another business trip to Europe that fate, in cahoots with my thinking, provided me an irresistible opportunity.

A considerable amount of time had gone by since I picked up my artist's paintbrush to put something on canvas, and my love of acting seemed to be a thing of the past, but having been taught that idleness is the devil's workshop, I decided to renew my interest in both; I didn't want my marriage to be one of the devil's demolition jobs.

I had little doubt that, when I responded to an ad in the local newspaper requesting interested parties to audition for an upcoming Mt. Pines Summer Stock Theatre Production, Mitch was going to be more than annoyed. Although the majority of actors and actresses usually came from New York, local talent was sometimes solicited for numerous bit parts.

The outdoor theatre in Laurel Lake had many successful seasons, attracting busloads of people from as far away as New York, Philadelphia, Maryland, and Washington, D.C. It boasted of having given Charlton Heston and Bernadette Peters their first break in theatre . . . and rightfully so. Charlton Heston never forgot about his early acting career in Laurel Lake, returning as recently as the late nineties, with his wife, to perform "Love Letters" on the Mt. Pines Theatre Stage.

I loved the theatre, and I couldn't help thinking how much fun it would be to appear on stage again. Confidence and an adventurous spirit preceded me as I joined several rows of total strangers who had apparently come to the Mt. Pines Theatre to audition as well.

One by one, we were singled out to read for a very small part. When my turn came, I was asked to read the same part . . . three times; I apparently hadn't done a good job the first two times. To my surprise, the director asked me if I would be willing to read for another part . . . a less significant role, I presumed. I didn't tell him so at the time, but I would have read for the part of a boiler-room attendant, just to get a part in one of their productions.

The story line revolved around a Jewish family, and I was asked to read the script with a Jewish accent. I smiled as I thought about the time that I had impersonated the German Ambassador's wife in New York.

"I can do that!!" I replied, enthusiastically. The director handed me a rather thick script. He then motioned for Ms. Claypool, the leading lady, to come forward. A handsome young man, who obviously had the leading male role, quickly took his place beside Ms. Claypool. I was then asked to begin reading the part of the leading lady's sister, who, by the size and content of the script, enjoyed a major part in the story.

After we had read several pages of the script, the director called a halt to the session. He looked at the leading lady and man; several nods were exchanged, and then he addressed me: "Can you show up for rehearsals on Monday morning?"

It was only then that I realized the significance of what I had just done . . . yet in spite of the looming consequences, I decided that what I was about to do was going to be good for my marriage. I would just have to figure out a way to make it palatable to Mitch.

"Yes, Mr. Coughlin," I replied, "I will be here on Monday morning."

Whether it was simply a case of paranoia resulting from what happened when the show "By Hex" was extended by a week, I don't know, but I had to make certain this show would not go beyond the planned two-week run. When I asked the director if there was any possibility of that happening, he assured me that the lead actor and actress had to return to New York for other commitments at the end of the two weeks.

By the time Mitch returned from Europe, the show, "Dear Me, The Sky Is Falling," was a little more than two weeks away from opening night.

With all the fervor of someone fighting for her life, I presented my case to Mitch. I pointed out the many diversions he had enjoyed over the years, such as cars and hockey games, while I had been able to pursue very few of my own interests. I gave him my word that I wouldn't read for any more shows in the future. He thought about it for a few minutes, then agreed to the "just this once" part of the deal. As sad as I felt at the time, promising never to "do it again," as though I was a very bad girl who had done a very bad thing, I was relieved and grateful that confronting Mitch hadn't resulted in another physical fray.

As a result of my name being mentioned in the newspaper as the local actress who would be playing a leading role at the Mt. Pines Theatre, all of my friends, past and present, showed up for opening night. The same Sports Car Club members who had witnessed Mitch's shocking behavior years before, when I had appeared in "By Hex," also attended opening night. They even talked Mitch into bringing the children to the show.

Opening night awakened so many memories in me, especially the days when Mitch had been so in love and he had been so proud of me—or so I thought. So much had changed since then; I was no longer sure how Mitch felt about me.

After a successful and gratifying two-week performance, the show closed and another one began. My artistic appetite returned, and I wanted to feed it again. But as far as Mitch was concerned, my acting career was over. And so I exchanged my passion for acting for a blank canvas and a three-legged easel.

*   *   *   *   *

Several weeks following the close of "Dear Me, The Sky Is Falling," and with nerves still extremely fragile, a family squabble ended in serious injury to our son Ben. Too many years have passed to repeat verbatim the words exchanged between Ben and his father, but it resulted in Ben getting kicked in the stomach, causing injury to his appendix and subsequent hospitalization to have his appendix removed. My intervention only resulted in another slap in the face.

After that altercation, I wanted to get the children and myself as far away from Mitch as possible, but I didn't have the courage to do it. Not only did I have a convincing fear of Mitch, but I also knew that I would not be able to support four children on my own, and I was even surer that Mitch would never provide any kind of financial help. Because of those reasons, I chose to do nothing, only to discover that in a circular course, the wind returns.

What both amazed and puzzled me was that, in spite of their being physically mistreated, the children loved their father. But I did not share my children's dedication; it was my need for security that kept our marriage together, for better or worse.

*   *   *   *   *

Frequently I will be asked, "Which is easier to rear . . . a boy or a girl?" My reply never changes: "Boys, most definitely."

Unquestioningly, Sarah was our biggest challenge while growing up. She had such an angelic face; she was our firstborn—our only little girl—and we trusted our angel (she never gave us reason not to).

As I slept one night, I was suddenly aroused by what I thought was a strange noise outside the house. Being a light sleeper (a distinguishing mother-mark), I immediately arose and switched on the outside lights, illuminating the woods surrounding our home, but I didn't see anything of a suspicious nature. Before I went back to bed, I decided to peek into each of the children's rooms. Sarah's room was empty. It had been a good bit past midnight and, even though she was a teenager (and then some), she was never permitted to be out at that hour. Furthermore, she hadn't been away that evening, as far as I knew. Kidnapping was the first thing that entered my mind as I awakened Mitch. Under normal circumstances, waking my husband would have been the right thing to do, but in our situation, it was the worst thing I could have done. In doing so, I unknowingly compromised the welfare of my daughter and myself.

After ruling out a break-in, we waited for Sarah to return home.

She entered the house through her bedroom window. After questioning her whereabouts, she admitted that she had been rendezvousing with a young man she was bound and determined to continue seeing . . . against our wishes. How long she had been climbing out of her window for those secret meetings, we didn't know, but this time she got caught.

The horror of that night, the injuries Ben sustained at the hand of his father sometime earlier, and Thomas's nearly fatal dog wounds were almost more than I could bear. Luke, our youngest son, had thus far been spared anything harsher than a pat on the fanny and a few scowling words. But how long would it be, I wondered, before he too would be the recipient of his father's wrath.

It all happened so fast. Mitch's hands were around Sarah's neck before she or I could utter a single word. He slapped her across the face so hard that she fell backwards against the bedroom wall. Her nose started to bleed badly. Mingled with blood, tears, and saliva, her small mouth fell open in a helpless attempt to beg her father not to hit her again. With that, I grabbed Mitch and yelled for him to stop. I stood in front of him, blocking his way, which just aggravated him more. After grabbing me tightly around the arm, he told me to get out of the room and warned me not to interfere. I was more afraid for Sarah than I was for myself, and so I made another attempt at intercepting another blow intended for Sarah, but he shoved me out of the way and proceeded to strike Sarah again. I threatened to call the police, but that didn't seem to deter his fury; Mitch knew that I would never do that, for fear of the consequences that would be meted out on me if I had. So I just stood there—scared, helpless, and defeated.

When Sarah was curled up in a ball on the bedroom floor, her hands covering her bruised and bleeding face, Mitch demanded that I bring him a scissors. When I asked him what he was going to do with the scissors, he said, "I'm going to cut off all of her hair, then we'll see just how pretty she is!"

Sarah's hair was long, silky, and blonde—a girl's crowning glory. She begged him, in spite of her swollen mouth and face, not to cut off her hair.

I rushed for the scissors, thinking that cutting her hair would be a whole lot better than having him hit her again. I cried as I watched him haphazardly cut her hair within an inch of her scalp, ending in jagged pieces going every which way. The added pain of embarrassment, as she felt her head, left her worn and fragile. She looked like a human rag doll.

Sarah's heart, and mine, suffered irreversible damage after that episode, and I relive that night every time I look into my daughter's eyes.

Satisfied that he had made his point, Mitch told her to clean herself up and not to ever let him see her with that boy again. Not surprisingly, what took place in the wee hours of that morning only intensified Sarah's interest in the young man.

We hadn't known much about Jeff, whose love she nearly paid for with her life, but his shoulder length hair and "hippie" appearance were two good reasons why we tried to discourage their friendship early on.

Mitch made Sarah attend school the following day. He counted on her feeling embarrassed when her classmates saw her ugly hair and black and blue marks; he was just as confident that his punishment would serve as a deterrent against her sneaking out of the house again.

The obvious signs of abuse and Sarah's inch-length hair caught the attention of not only her classmates, but the school counselor as well. Unfortunately, school officials were not quick to report suspected abuse to the authorities in those days, so it went unheeded. Many years later, however, that same school counselor came to me apologizing for not having intervened in what he thought would have been a legitimate intervention case. He told me that he had literally lost sleep over not reporting the abuse and that he has never been able to forget what he saw. He asked me, at the time, whether or not we had all experienced abuse, then decided that he already knew the answer to his question. He has apologized no less than a dozen times since then.

Today it is easy to see why Sarah was so attracted to Jeff. He was just the opposite of her father. It took a long time, but I slowly began to see Jeff through Sarah's eyes. He was a gentle, soft-spoken, modest, and somewhat passive young man . . . and eventually, he was to become Sarah's husband.

Early on, it appeared that Sarah and Jeff had taken a vow to live a very simple life, as a way of rebelling against the so-called establishment, I supposed. But to this day, they continue living a sacrificial life, doing without what most of us slave for—and a great deal of what they do possess is spent helping the less fortunate. I am fairly certain that Sarah's experience with abuse made her exceptionally sensitive to hurting people. Their goal to minister to, and live with, the poor Native Americans came near to fruition when they began spending their vacations on an Indian reservation in New Mexico several years ago.

Sarah and Jeff have two adopted children, four dogs, one cat, two parakeets, two ducks, and a brood of chickens. Not having been able to have children of their own, they consider their two adopted children as gifts from God. My granddaughter, who was born in Cambodia, is severely handicapped and spends most of her days in a wheelchair; but in spite of her disability, she is a beautiful young lady with a tender loving heart. My grandson, born in Korea, is a very ambitious and extremely intelligent young man. His chess accomplishments and his knowledge of the Civil War are quite remarkable.

It was a long time coming, but when I realized that there were other hands directing my children's lives . . . that I could only guide and hold what God owned, and that I might even have to watch them fall into a pit before they experience the peak, I was able to "let go and let God." While I haven't always condoned their behavior or agreed with the choices they've made, I have always been able to love them unconditionally. I am sure, as their mother, I have not always pleased them either.

*   *   *   *   *

When I married Mitch, I had promised myself that if and when we had children, I would provide them with all the love and acceptance that I had never had. Instead, I watched my children suffer the greater pain.

Every attempt was made to hide most of what was happening in our family from friends, relatives, and neighbors—mostly because I was sure that Mitch would have made everything look like my fault.

Whenever the raging fury in our family subsided, a coveted tranquility would come over our household. We would then, in effect, lead another life.

Our family had some very good times. We traveled; we had family picnics; we ate in the best restaurants; and we went to sports car races with the children. Our children even grew up on a costly diet of hard shell crabs from Maryland on a regular basis. On the best days, everything except affection was ours in abundance.

Mitch had invested a large portion of his generosity in little league baseball and ice hockey sponsorships. Other things were of little importance to him. For a period of time, my foster parents even supplied all of our bedding, because Mitch wouldn't give me money to replace worn sheets and pillowcases. Expenditures generally were based upon whether or not they would benefit Mitch or the business . . . and so, after eight years of living in our first home in Laurel Lake, Mitch decided he wanted to build a new and larger home—one that would accommodate overnight business associates. I argued that it would make more sense to enlarge our present home, since we had the choice location overlooking the lake, but I was overruled.

Our new home was to consist of a complete guest area with its own game room. The plans also called for a large kitchen with a wall-to-wall fireplace, surrounded by a full-size sofa and fireplace chairs, while the table, chairs, and latest appliances would occupy the other end of the kitchen. A laundry, powder room, generous den, formal living and dining room completed the first floor of our newly proposed house plans. Each child would have his or her own bedroom and bath. The master bedroom would be spacious, with a large bathroom and several large walk-in closets. It certainly was intended to make a statement, just by the mere size of it. As a matter of fact, after completion of our new house, out-of-town tourists often mistook our home for the Mt. Laurel Hotel.

I was going to miss our small comfortable home overlooking the lake.

It wasn't long before Mitch produced three or four building sites for consideration. I chose one about three miles from Laurel Lake. It sat very high on the side of North Mountain, overlooking the town of Minden and beyond. It would have been a beautiful location. I could just imagine the panoramic view of tiny fireflies flickering in the dark forest-nights in the valley below, just like another night when I sat close to Michael Banks on top of another hill many years before.

After lengthy deliberation, the building lot Mitch chose was three lots from where our present home stood; it was located around the bend and some distance away in an overgrown area of virgin woodland. Mitch then hired a local building contractor to begin building our new home. The project proceeded with very few hitches.

During the building process, we became close friends with the contractor and his family. We visited their beautiful home often and our children became friends with their children. Of course, the biggest draw for our children was our friend's impressive backyard in-ground swimming pool. The men, on the other hand, shared similar interests in automobile racing and the four of us enjoyed many trips to Maryland for hard-shell crabs.

The fall season arrived and after many months of construction and unforeseen expenses, we moved our family and our problems into our new home. If I thought a new home (not unlike the reason some people have a baby) would make a difference in Mitch's and my relationship, I was sadly mistaken.

We were just traveling in circles, substituting love with "things" on the way.

*   *   *   *   *

Fortunately for me, and unlike our move from Bucherville to Laurel Lake the first time, my life was made a little easier when we traveled south to a number of leading furniture manufacturers, where we picked out new furniture for the entire house and had it all delivered.

Our lake home had already been sold to one of Mitch's managers. And as much as I hated to leave our cozy stone and redwood rancher, I was caught up in the excitement of moving into our new white stucco and dark wood-trimmed Bavarian chalet, an exact replica of a large Austrian farmhouse. It sat like a tower of pride on top of what we called Alpine Hill.

A ritual of Nazi marching tunes, with speech excerpts by Adolph Hitler, resonated through the rooms of our new home. From the time we moved to Laurel Lake from Bucherville to our new home on Alpine Hill, Mitch had continued to add to his collection of German marching songs. In his raspy authoritative idiosyncratic style, Adolph Hitler managed to drown out the voices of our children. When I protested, Mitch responded by increasing the volume on the stereo set. Several of the children vividly recall the unwelcome presence of Adolph Hitler's voice in our home. Mitch was fascinated with Hitler, "for his influential mastery, and not for the man himself," he would assure me. But I often accused Mitch of being just like Hitler. Those accusations usually ended with another unwelcome confrontation. I never believed that Mitch condoned Hitler's commitment to annihilating the Jews; I do believe, however, that Mitch's admiration for various aspects of Hitler's personality traits helped him form unusually low opinions of certain groups of people. At one point, we even joined the John Birch Society—an organization I suspect did not represent love and toleration. I never researched the organization and, thankfully, our membership was short lived.

*   *   *   *   *

As so often happens, we had no sooner moved into our new home than Sarah expressed a desire to move out on her own. When she finished high school, her intention was to further her education by attending a school in Pittsburgh specializing in dental-assistant training.

When the time came for Sarah to leave for Pittsburgh, Mitch was overwrought concerning her living arrangements. "There is no way she is going to be allowed to live in an apartment alone, or with other girls, or guys, and end up pregnant," he said. And so we inquired about alternative living facilities in the area and found that there was a Catholic school nearby that had boarded young ladies attending various other schools in the area. Having Catholic nuns as guardians was a much more appealing scenario to Mitch than some dingy third-floor apartment with an easy-access fire escape. So we traveled to Pittsburgh where Sarah enrolled in dental-assistant school, and we moved her into the Catholic boarding house.

The fact that Sarah decided to move into her own apartment as soon as she completed high school indicated to me how much she wanted to get away from us, her parents. While appearing serene and loving on the outside, Sarah, I knew, was emotionally scarred inside, and I couldn't help asking myself: Would she forever blame me for not succeeding in stopping the abuse or for not taking her and her brothers away from their father? Or would she blame me all the more if I left her father? I do know that, as time passed, we grew further and further apart.

After Sarah was out on her own and living in an apartment, she spent many wasted years in rebellion. But in the end, and with our reluctant blessings, she and Jeff decided to get married. Years later, a miraculous transformation took place in the lives of Sarah and Jeff, but first God had to literally burn down their home for them to see Him in the charred debris of their lives.

To see one's child snatched from the hands of evil is a beautiful thing.

*   *   *   *   *

After nearly a year of living in our new home at Laurel Lake, Mitch accused me of entertaining a man in our home, which I had not done. He threatened to disfigure my face so I would not be attractive to another man. Quite surprisingly . . . until then . . . I wasn't aware that he had even noticed the interest other men paid me. I was certainly guilty of some serious flirtations, and there were relationships between some of our friends and myself that could have been regarded as indiscreet, but with regards to that particular accusation, I was completely innocent. As a result of Mitch's accusations and his threats of bodily injury, and after freeing myself from Mitch's grip, I grabbed our youngest son and ran to my car. After quickly locking the car doors, I managed to start the car, and Luke and I headed for my parents' home in Bucherville. Much to my surprise, Mitch did not come after us.

I dropped Luke off with my parents, telling them that I would be in touch with them, and to just please take care of Luke for me. I spent the next few hours at the home of a lady friend, and the next three days and nights were spent in a cold transient motel room fearing for my life.

Maureen's husband had warned her not to get involved in our skirmish, as it may have put them in danger as well. So I wasn't able to count on Maureen's help, other than phone conversations with her during those three days. I called my mother from the motel, out of concern for the children, and to let her know that I was safe, but I did not tell her where I had been staying. She finally admitted that she and Daddy had felt so badly that they hadn't come to my aid before that time, and that they hadn't wanted to believe that my bruise marks had come from Mitch. Mitch had done so much for my parents and I knew they hadn't wanted to wrongly accuse him. They promised me that they would look in on the rest of my family and see that they were being taken care of. Then I called a police sergeant friend of ours and told him of my predicament. By that time I no longer knew Michael's whereabouts, and I didn't want to involve him, because Mitch would have totally misconstrued my motive had he ever discovered Michael had come to my defense.

When our policeman friend arrived on the scene with a bag of personal items that I had requested, and a promise not to disclose my whereabouts to Mitch, he found me in a state of hysteria. He remained by my side until a phone call came from Maureen telling me that Mitch had called her and asked her if she knew where I had gone. She said she hadn't told him where I was staying, and that he promised not to harm me if I would just come home. On the third day, another phone call came from Maureen telling me that Mitch had given her his word that he would not harm me if I came home right away, and that I was to return home for the children's sake. He told her precisely what he had told me many times, that if he ever laid a hand on me again, he would leave the house and never come back. I knew that it wasn't Mitch who wanted me home—it was Mitch's pride. For his wife to walk out on him was the supreme pride buster.

After a considerable number of discussions between Maureen, our policeman friend, and me, two of whom believed that Mitch wouldn't dare lift a hand to hurt the children or me now that others knew about the abuse, I agreed to return home.

Mitch appeared extremely apologetic and promised that he would never resort to physical abuse again. As a part of the agreement, I suggested that we seek marital counseling with a professional, or at least go see the pastor of our church. But Mitch was reluctant to go that far. I was the one who went to see a lawyer friend of ours who in turn recommended a counselor with whom I made an appointment the following week.

After spending some time with the counselor, he asked me if it was possible for my husband to come and see him. I said that Mitch thought all counselors were "crazy" and I didn't think that he would come. But I agreed to at least ask him.

I approached Mitch with extreme caution, and at arm's length. I threatened that our marriage could not be saved unless we both received professional help. I was still blaming myself for the abuse and hadn't excused myself from needing some kind of counseling myself. Mitch finally agreed to go, but he was not at all happy about the visit.

At my next appointment with the counselor, I found out that Mitch had indeed made an appointment with him, had broken it twice, but had kept the third. Unfortunately, the counselor said that the meeting had been less than congenial and that it hadn't gone very well, and that Mitch said he had no intention of making another appointment. The counselor indicated that he held out little hope that Mitch would ever change and that I would have to be the one who did all the changing. He questioned me on whether or not I considered myself equipped to return to the work force if need be. I told him that I didn't think so, and that I would just have to stay put regardless of the situation. He assured me that Mitch would undoubtedly resort to violence again. He said he had met too many men like Mitch, and those men were convinced that they, too, hadn't needed help, and that everyone else was to blame. That was not encouraging news to me.

The counselor assured me that my need for security, recognition, and love was perfectly normal, but that I lacked self-confidence and self-esteem. He said that my lack of self-esteem resulted from my believing, from the very beginning, that I was not a significant person because my mother had given me away. He convinced me that I had the wherewithal to stand on my own, and that I even had the potential of becoming a successful businesswoman if I put my mind to it. He reminded me of the things I had done to help promote Mitch's business, and how I was instrumental in the decisions that helped Mitch realize his dreams. He suggested that I think seriously about getting my family out of that situation, but that he was not permitted to recommend taking that kind of action. But his suggestion did help set the thought in motion.

Since our last encounter, Mitch seemed to become less combative, but still resistant to change. I suggested a joint checking account, which would have enabled me to purchase certain things, like groceries and clothes, without his consent. After all those years together, he finally agreed to do that; however, the account would still be controlled by him and he would limit the amount of money in the account so I would not be able to make large purchases without his prior approval. For the first time, I truly felt like Mitch's wife, and not his daughter or charge. That is when abuse of another kind began.

It had been so long since I had the option of purchasing clothes, or anything else, without Mitch's approval, that I found myself deeply in debt at a local clothing store, thinking that I could always pay the bill the next time Mitch put money into the account. But Mitch wasn't contributing enough to the account to enable me to do that. Subsequently, I was forced to go to him and tell him that I was in serious debt and wasn't able to get out of it. He was furious. He said that that was exactly why he hadn't allowed me to have anything in my name; he was afraid I would do just what I had done. He cleared the debt for me and warned me never to charge another thing again. My name remained on the account, but the account contained enough money to buy our food, and little else.

Extravagant spending became an addiction for me in the ensuing years. I just couldn't satisfy my desire to purchase "things." I knew I had a serious problem.

... TWENTY-ONE ...

In the resort village of Laurel Lake there stood an old Victorian building known as "The Gift Shop." All winter long, Mt. Pines Theatre, the Pavilion Restaurant, The Gathering Place (where banquets and cultural events were held), and The Gift Shop stood cold, barren, and boarded shut, waiting for the budding trees of spring to proclaim the beginning of another season of summer activities.

From Memorial Day to Labor Day, tourists from far and wide visited the enchanted village of Laurel Lake. The quaint cottage porches, dressed in latticework of many colors, made all the more charming by a variety of high-back rocking chairs beckoning one's presence into the past, engaged many a curious passerby. But over the years, due in part to extensive media coverage, Laurel Lake changed from a village of cane-driven retirees to a community of sophisticated cultural-minded driven professionals.

Modest Victorian summer cottages, made of wood and stubble, with ne'er a straight board between them, and squeezed together as if they were trying to keep warm, were refurbished and turned into year-round residences. The charming cottages bordering the narrow walking paths stood sadly small and largely threatened by a shift in time.

I rarely visited the yellow-gold building with its high columns, wrap-around porch, and floor-to-ceiling windows known as The Gift Shop; but my interest in the aging historical building peaked each time I had occasion to drive by it.

One day, I decided to inquire into the possibility of purchasing The Gift Shop, but much to my disappointment, I learned that all of the commercial properties were either owned or managed by a board of directors from the community, and that they would never be sold. But, I was told, "from time to time, a building is vacated for one reason or another and then made available for lease to the public." The board member assured me that, should The Gift Shop become available in the future, I would be one of the first persons contacted. I didn't have the slightest idea what I would do with the building; and the likelihood of Mitch supporting me in a business venture of my own was something I hadn't even considered when I made the inquiry. I held out little hope that I would ever get the opportunity to rent the building, and so, for the most part I forgot about The Gift Shop.

It would have been presumptuous of anyone to think that my interest in procuring The Gift Shop was a deliberate plan on my part to lay the groundwork for self-support, should I ever decide to leave Mitch. Living independently of Mitch Brogan was not even a consideration at that time. But, with his hating the theatre as he did, I thought perhaps another less-threatening type of involvement on my part might win his support. I hadn't thought about the fact that the Mt. Pines Theatre sat directly in front of The Gift Shop.

When I gathered enough courage to tell Mitch about my desire to start my own business, he said, "Good, I'll set you up in a retail-wholesale tire business."

"That wasn't exactly what I had in mind," I replied. I had to laugh as I thought about how dissimilar a tire business and gift shop were. That ended my plan to go into business.

*   *   *   *   *

An invitation to dinner with Doris and Sam Hancock, owners of a local radio station, produced an even more unexpected development. While the four of us were having dinner together, Sam said that he thought I would make a great radio advertising salesperson. He claimed that I possessed the personality and intelligence to communicate well with people. Coming from Sam, the idea earned some credibility with Mitch. Sam Hancock was a very persuasive man, and Mitch respected him. But somehow, I couldn't imagine myself, the wife of a successful businessman, knocking on doors and begging people to buy radio ads. But the thought of earning spending money of my own more than intrigued me. However, I was sure that, had Mitch detected any positive response from me, it would have been the end of that proposal, and so I remained purposefully disinterested.

Sam suggested that I stop by his place of business for a personal tour sometime and give him an opportunity to explain what went on inside a popular radio station. I calmly accepted Sam's invitation, which astonishingly enough received Mitch's blessing.

Not long after I was introduced to the radio station and its personalities, Sam offered me a job. He said that I would be given a company car, a salary based on a draw against commission, and that I would be able to make my own hours, depending on how successful I wanted to be and how much money I wanted to make. The job description had mouthwatering income appeal.

I had reason to believe that Mitch and Sam covertly coerced me into accepting the job with WRAT Radio, if just for the sole purpose of teaching me a lesson. I was sure that Mitch thought that once I understood the time and energy it took to make a comfortable living, I would be more inclined to appreciate the time he spent away from our home and family. But as so often happens, covert actions sometime backfire.

I began my job with WRAT Radio selling commercial air time to local businesses, along with promoting the ever popular and controversial "love him or hate him" personality of the infamous talk show—"The Fred Williams Show." Advertisers clamored to buy time on Fred's show, which made it relatively easy selling lengthy contracts for that time slot. In my travels for the radio station, it was not uncommon for me to pass road crews with their truck doors flung open and their radios tuned in to the "Fred Williams Show," much like the Rush Limbaugh talk show of today. I would usually blow my horn, wave, and then smile as I thought about cashing my weekly paycheck.

Working for a successful broadcast company provided an abundant amount of experience, self-confidence, and personal satisfaction at a time when I needed it most. I don't think either Mitch or Sam ever counted on me enjoying the job as much as I did.

As time passed, I filled Sam Hancock's desk with twelve-month contracts and creative ideas for promoting the businesses they represented. After proving myself competent as a salesperson to Sam Hancock, he began grooming me to handle several national accounts. Negotiating with large companies made me feel important, but more than that, I was happy that I had lived up to all of Sam's sales expectations.

What I hadn't counted on were the accusations being made against me by an unidentified caller to my husband. The anonymous caller claimed that I had been involved personally with Sam Hancock . . . a completely false allegation. Thankfully, Sam's wife, who was still a friend of mine, believed me when I denied the accusations. However, some years later, Sam and Doris divorced as a result of his apparent involvement with someone who had an uncanny resemblance to me. After many years, and as a result of those allegations, plus the increased demands put on me to overperform by continually increasing my sales-goals, I tendered my resignation from WRAT Radio Station.

The income I generated while working for Sam Hancock had not precipitated any divisive plans on my part to leave Mitch Brogan. Although I had become somewhat more independent during those years, I still longed for a strong, but compassionate, leader in our home. I wanted that person to be my husband. It was not a role I wanted to play. I enjoyed being a woman.

The need to be significant in someone's life remained constant. I tried very hard to win and influence people and to be accepted by everyone. I no longer permitted myself to make mistakes, unless I left a trail of excuses behind them. Self-confidence became the trajectory for uncontrolled perfectionism. It became increasingly difficult for me to accept mistakes made by others, let alone the ones I made. I measured my worth by performance . . . not by how God saw me. But then, I hadn't thought much about God anymore.

*   *   *   *   *

With Sarah off to school in Pittsburgh, Ben in the process of receiving an appointment to the Air Force Academy, and Thomas still struggling to get through school, my involvement centered on the children.

When the notice came for Ben to report to the Air Force Academy for a physical examination, having set his heart on becoming a pilot, he was already flying above the clouds. The fact that Ben wanted to be an Air Force pilot, and not a paratrooper, disappointed his father greatly. Thomas and Luke remained Mitch's only hope for an airborne clone. I, on the other hand, encouraged Ben to pursue his love of flying. I even talked Mitch into giving Ben a gift of flying lessons for his birthday. Unfortunately, Ben returned from the Academy—rejected and dejected. He had flunked his physical examination. As if grasping for a buoy in an ocean of disappointment, Ben abruptly announced that he was going to pursue a carpentry apprenticeship in Germany.

Ben learned the art of woodworking, but his love of flying never ceased.

*   *   *   *   *

As difficult as it was, our family persevered in spite of what had happened to us. But I felt as though I had betrayed my children. I had not been able to stop the abuse.

If our children were provoked to anger, they never allowed that anger to show. I was very concerned that they were stockpiling their emotions and would some day release them, causing injury to others, or even to themselves. But there was little, if any, evidence of revengeful spirits in any one of them.

Thus far, Luke was the only one who had escaped Mitch's wrath. I prayed that he would never have to go through what the other children had gone through. He was still very young, but I began to fear for him. With Mitch's promise to leave me if he ever laid a hand on any one of us again (and there had been witnesses to that promise), I hoped it would be enough to discourage any further abuse. There were a couple of times when he came close to raising his hand against me, but I had held my breath and then reminded him of his promise. It seemed to be working.

*   *   *   *   *

Having learned more about my birth mother and father, and assuming the children were now old enough to understand what had taken place during my childhood, I shared the newly-acquired information with them. Ben, being the gentle concerned soul he was, thought I should hire an investigator to find out "the rest of the story." But for me it was simply an opportunity to discuss with them why, under some circumstances, mothers must give up their children. It was something I never imagined myself doing, but in all honesty, I had to ask myself, *Exactly what difference is there between giving up one's child and divorce?* In either case, the child becomes the victim . . . at least to my way of thinking. It was also my personal opinion that the Children's Bureau . . . at least while I was under their jurisdiction . . . could have done a much better job of placing children in foster homes and in matters of adoption. I shared with my children how I had experienced first hand the residual effects of being separated from my birth mother and father, and how it related to just about everything I did or thought since that time.

*   *   *   *   *

Eventually, I moved into the guestroom of our house, and I no longer accepted dangling fifty-dollar bills as a substitute for "I'm sorry." But I was very lonely.

Once again, I directed all my unspent affections and energy toward the children.

After Ben returned from Germany, it was time for Thomas to graduate from high school. Thomas was adamant about joining the tank division of the United States Army—another disappointment to Mitch. But Mitch said he'd rather have him in the tank division of the Army than not to have him become a soldier at all. Thomas's motive for joining a tank division, however, was rather bizarre. He figured an impenetrable tank would be the safest place to be when the predicted notorious killer bees arrived in the United States. We laughed about that, but Thomas was dead serious; it wasn't long before he was off to basic training. Sarah, on the other hand, was already in school learning to be a dental assistant.

As we sat on the bleachers at Thomas's military graduation ceremony, I watched him as he displayed his adeptness at dismantling a gun, then putting it back together again at lightning speed before a military review stand. Mitch wasn't able to disguise the pride he felt as he watched along with me. But he continued to remind Thomas that he still hadn't joined the elite branch of the Army to become a paratrooper, as his father had done. I think, at the time, Mitch's comments hurt me more than they had hurt Thomas.

Before Thomas left for his first tour of duty in Germany, he spent some time at home with us in Laurel Lake. The memories made during that time were the kind you wish you could forget.

*   *   *   *   *

Cars were so much a part of Mitch's existence that, at times, it seemed he valued them more than he did human life. To some extent, I understood that, mostly because his love for cars began at a very early age—about the same age that I fell in love with acting—and a love like that is not easily annulled.

Once, when the children were small, I had taken them to Minden for ice cream cones. The only car available at the time was Mitch's special BMW, which I generally was not permitted to drive. I had dropped the children off in front of the ice cream store and told them to go in and order their cones while I parked the car. I happened to have some mail that I forgot to drop off at the Laurel Lake Post Office, and decided to drop it in a mailbox located near a telephone pole several parking areas away from where I had just parked the BMW. After depositing the mail, I began walking back to the ice cream store. When I looked up, I saw Mitch's BMW charging towards me. I had obviously left the car in neutral and had failed to engage the emergency brake. All I could imagine at the time was a crinkled BMW and a face to go with it. In split-second timing, I stood sideways against the telephone pole hoping that I had sufficiently braced myself for the painful encounter with the vehicle. When it hit me, I felt my blood vessels explode like party-poppers. The impact sent the car—the driver's door wide open—down Main Street and into oncoming traffic. Realizing that I was still alive, I ran as fast as I could until I caught up with the car. I dove headfirst into the driver's seat, feet and legs dragging on the macadam, and with all my strength, managed to pull on the emergency brake. Embarrassed beyond words, I gathered the contents of my purse, that had fallen out of the car, and drove back to the ice cream store.

The children stood with their mouths wide open, the melted ice cream running down their little arms, as they watched in disbelief as another scene played out before their tiny eyes.

Later that same night, as I was undressing for bed, having sworn the children to secrecy regarding what had happened that day, Mitch walked into the room. He immediately began to question me about the huge black and blue marks on my body. With little time to concoct a lie, I had no choice but to tell him what happened. He called me stupid, ignorant, and foolish—words relatively harmless compared to the physical abuse I had expected. But he was extremely happy that his BMW had not been seriously injured.

In looking back over that event, I'm not so sure that what I did should have been categorized as stupid, especially when I consider the injuries I could have suffered, had Mitch's car sustained damages equal to mine.

*   *   *   *   *

Thomas was enjoying his time with us at home and the opportunity he had to visit school buddies before leaving for Germany. He had a car of his own, and like his father, he was equally proud and protective of it.

One evening, when Thomas came home from visiting a friend, he entered the den where Mitch and I were sitting. The look on his face was one I had seen on my own many times . . . one of fear and uncertainty. He asked his dad to follow him outside.

The very next thing I heard was Thomas's voice coming from the garage. "No, Dad! Don't, please don't!"

I ran into the garage and found Mitch with a hockey stick in his hand beating Thomas across the back and neck with repeated blows that were meant to do damage. Without thinking, I ran to Thomas's side, grabbed the stick and tried to get it away from Mitch, but he was much too strong for me. He pushed me against the wall and told me to go back into the house.

I was more than a little surprised why Thomas, who was much leaner and meaner since basic training, had not retaliated or even tried to stop his father from hitting him.

When I saw blood coming through Thomas's shirt, I ran into the house and picked up the telephone and called the police. Just as I had finished describing the scene to the dispatcher and had given him our address, Mitch was behind me. He grabbed the phone out of my hand and slapped me across the face as hard as he could; but I hadn't felt a thing. For once in my life, I knew I had done the right thing.

Within ten minutes, the local police arrived with their clubs drawn, and one had his hand on his holster. Mitch ran upstairs, but not until he made sure he left me with something to think about. "I'll take care of you later," he warned.

The police entered our home and observed Thomas' injuries. They ordered Mitch to return downstairs, and they told me to pack my bags.

"You will be pressing charges against your husband, won't you?"

Quickly recalling what Mitch had said about taking care of me later, I replied, "No, I know exactly what I must do, and I am no longer afraid to do it. Thomas will be leaving for Germany soon, and out of harm's way," I told them, "and I have made a long overdue decision."

Before the police left, I looked directly at Mitch. "Mitch, you know I am going to have to do something to prevent anymore of this abuse, and if that means leaving you, or asking you to leave us, then that is what must be done. You apparently never meant what you said about leaving us if you ever struck anyone of us again, so now I am going to have to take things into my own hands."

I don't know why, but for some reason I wasn't intimidated by Mitch, feeling quite confident as I spoke . . . partly, no doubt, because the police were still in the house and had witnessed just a small portion of what had taken place in our home many times.

Because of my unwillingness to press charges, the police had no choice but to leave the house. They assured me that they would remain in the area should I have need of them again that night.

Mitch went directly to bed without another word.

I apologized to Thomas for his father's behavior. I then questioned why he hadn't tried to defend himself. He explained that it would have just made the situation worse and that he hadn't had the heart to inflict injury on his father, whom he loved.

How often, I thought to myself, *have I hurt my heavenly Father Whom I claim to love?* It was a hard parallel to swallow.

The following day, instead of a fifty-dollar bill, Mitch promised me the choice of any car I wanted, a bank account of my own (with money in it), and anything else that would keep me from doing something as "foolish as leaving" him, as he put it. He said that he hadn't blamed me for being fed up with how things had been going, and like so many times before, he promised never to do it again. When I asked him if he would be willing to get counseling, he once again replied, "No!"

For the next several weeks I would lie awake thinking of how in the world I was ever going to leave my husband when I hated even the thought of divorce. I believed once married, always married. And I still believe "until death" is how long marriage should last. But I was unable to reconcile that thinking with some of the things that had taken place between Mitch, the children, and me. Then I had an idea. Maybe, just maybe, Mitch would agree to a temporary separation, something I felt might benefit both of us. But when I mentioned it to Mitch, he boldly threatened, "If you leave this house, or me, you leave for good. You will never be allowed back into this house! When you're gone, you're gone!" In addition, he vowed that he would burn down the house before he would ever allow us to return. He also said that he would never give us one lousy cent to live on. I believed him. No matter what happened, I knew there would be no turning back once I left Mitch.

*   *   *   *   *

With three of our children pretty much on their own by that time, my immediate concern was for Luke. *How can I break up our home?* I asked myself. No matter how bad it had been at times, I still believed it was better for our children to live in an unhappy home than to try and survive a broken one. (To this day, I am not sure where I stand on that issue.) I can only say that leaving my husband was one of the hardest decisions I've ever had to make, and the effect it had on our children was devastating.

I kept telling myself that I deserved to be happy, but I was so busy blaming myself for the predicament I was in that I never stopped to consider how to go about achieving that kind of existence. I couldn't imagine how I would ever get along without the material security that my husband provided. Instead, I buckled under the slightest threat by Mitch—doing anything to keep peace in the family, particularly for the sake of the children. After all, it was in "my" nest the babies were fed and I wanted desperately to protect them. Perhaps those were some of the same reasons Nicole Simpson found it so hard to leave O.J., and my reason for understanding her reluctance to do so.

In retrospect, part of the problem, at least in my case, was not recognizing in myself that ever prevailing affliction of women called co-dependency—a debilitating disorder that, if unidentified, can, and often does, lead to self-destruction.

But fear . . . ah . . . that was the hardest part to overcome.

*   *   *   *   *

Maureen and I spent hours formulating possible plans that would enable me to leave Mitch; but it always came down to the reason I couldn't leave—*money*. Then the thought occurred to me. *Selling my diamond ring would be the quickest way to acquire instant income. At least it would be enough to help pay rent on an apartment until I find a suitable job.* Luke was twelve, and he no longer needed a babysitter, at least during the school season, so I was able to bypass that expense. But just the thought of being on my own overwhelmed me.

The contractor who built our home in Laurel Lake also built several apartment complexes on some land near Laurel Lake. They were lovely apartments, but very expensive. Nevertheless, I decided that that was where I would begin my search for a place for Luke and me to live. Remaining in Laurel Lake, I felt, was the best option with regards to Luke's welfare. He would at least remain connected to his friends, and would still have easy access to visiting his dad. Maureen also thought that a lake apartment was an excellent idea. I contacted our friend and, in confidence, shared with him the plans I had to leave Mitch. He said he would be happy to help us out and would rent an apartment to us right away. He expressed his regrets when I told him about the abuse but, for some reason, when he hadn't appeared shocked, I felt he already knew what had taken place in our home. In a community the size of Laurel Lake, nothing remained secret for very long.

In the meantime, I sold my diamond ring—the one I had worked so hard for. When the jeweler handed me the check, I left the store in tears.

I never told my mother and dad about my plans to leave Mitch, and I had no intention of doing so until after Luke and I had moved into our new apartment.

Mitch began making plans for his next overseas trip, and Ben decided to accompany his dad for the two-week stay in Germany. As he mentioned the dates in passing, I took note of them.

While I was making plans to move into the apartment when the right opportunity presented itself, Maureen was scanning the newspapers, looking for cottages for sale in Laurel Lake. She was very much a business woman and her opinion was that I would be much better off using the money from the sale of my ring to put a down-payment on a small cottage instead of throwing money out the window (which she rightly referred to as "paying rent"). But that option presented too great a financial responsibility for me. I didn't have a job, and my lawyer was advising me to remain unemployed. Buying a home sounded so "permanent," and I was thinking "temporary." I was hoping that our separation from Mitch would serve as a stepping stone to reconciliation, but it wasn't long before the decision on where to live was made for me.

The week before Mitch and Ben were to have left for Germany, our contractor friend called me. He said that Mitch had contacted him and warned him not to rent an apartment to me if I called him. So now our friend was telling me that he was very sorry, but he could not rent the apartment to me after all.

Fear had spread beyond our household.

That's when I reconsidered Maureen's idea about buying a cottage somewhere in Laurel Lake.

Maureen picked out several cottages she thought were worth looking at. One in particular was located in the old section of Laurel Lake and had just been remodeled. It was love at first sight! Maureen offered to help me out financially until I was able to get on my feet; she loaned me several thousand dollars, in addition to the money I had received from the sale of my ring. She never said that I had to pay her back; it was just something I eventually planned to do. Unfortunately, that time came sooner than expected. She said she was concerned that her husband would find out that she had given me money . . . something she didn't want him to know, so she asked me if I would pay back the money as soon as possible. Somewhat disappointed, I gave the money back to her long before I could afford to do so. I was now left with only the money I had gotten from the sale of my ring, and very little of that would be left after putting a down payment on the little cottage.

Just before Mitch and Ben left for Germany, I began making arrangements to purchase "Tumble Inn," a cozy reverse-board and batten-cottage, nestled among the trees. A young couple, who had just acquired a large portion of land outside town, where they intended to build a new home, were the owners of the cottage I planned to purchase. The transfer of property took place in secrecy and in total confidentiality. I was scared to death!

My worst fear was that the children would hate me for breaking up their home. No matter how much I thought I was doing the right thing, the same security that blanketed me had also blanketed them.

... TWENTY-TWO ...

Bowers Moving and Storage Company backed their medium-sized truck up to the door of our large home. Maureen and I directed the moving crew to load only those things marked with a red tag, leaving behind most of the beautiful furniture, family heirlooms, and all of the appliances. I took two beds, two chests of drawers, a sofa, two living room chairs, a phonograph-player, a radio, a small table, and two chairs. In retrospect, I left empty-handed. We loaded boxes of dishes, photographs, and books of poetry that I had either collected through the years, or had written.

I looked up into the half-empty truck and saw twenty-three years of my life in the unused portion of that moving van and wondered what would fill the next half of my life. *Mitch certainly wouldn't be able to accuse me of robbing him of everything we owned*, I thought.

The house appeared untouched and still looked like home, which helped ease the guilt I felt about my decision to leave it. But I was confident that Mitch, when he found out what I had done, would realize just how much we meant to him, jolting him into reconciliation and badly needed counseling . . . and yet, I didn't believe it somehow. My move was intended as a temporary arrangement, a sort of tourniquet on our life until our bruised marriage had time to heal.

I made several trips back and forth to our new cottage before Luke was scheduled to arrive home from school. My heart was already hurting for him. This was the day he would come home and find out that he no longer was going to live in the big house with his mommy and daddy.

Anticipating Luke's arrival, I wore a smooth path on the driveway stones from my repeated pacing. Then I heard his small voice announcing his arrival as he came skipping happily up the driveway. Immediately, I sat down with him on the front porch steps and explained to him that we were going to be living in a new and different home for a while. I told him that his daddy and I had had some serious disagreements which we hadn't been able to work out and that I thought it would be the best thing if we just moved into another house until things got better. Hopefully, I told him, it wouldn't be for very long. But I had serious doubts about that statement.

Luke never said a word, but the weight of his silence crushed me. I hadn't known what to expect, but I did not expect him to quietly accept what I had taken great pains to explain. He simply got into the car and, in complete and utter stillness, we drove to our new home.

I struggled to hold back the tears as we traveled the short distance from our big house to the cottage. Finally, I took Luke's hand and said that I hoped he would like his new home. But there was no response. A root of guilt wrapped itself around the trunk of my heart, suffocating to death any kind of righteous justification I had for my actions.

When Luke looked at his new surroundings, he asked me if he could please use the telephone, as if the phone belonged to someone else. "Of course," I said, "this is your home and you can use the phone anytime you want to." I listened, as he tried to explain to his friend Frank how we had moved away from our big house and were not going to live there anymore. Then he asked his friend if he would come over and see his new house.

I don't know how things would have turned out had Luke's little friend not shown such enthusiasm. When he arrived, he began by exclaiming over and over how neat he thought the little cottage was. They discovered small hidden areas in and under the house, and I could slowly see Luke's countenance begin to change. They played together for several hours before Luke too admitted that he thought the cottage was pretty neat.

I was not fooling myself. The worst was yet to come.

*   *   *   *   *

In less than a week, Mitch and Ben would be arriving home from Europe. Mostly, I was concerned that Ben would be terribly upset when he found out that Luke and I were no longer living at home. He was the most sensitive of the children, and although he was a young man by that time, I didn't want him to hate me. There was no easy way to break the news to any of the remaining children; I could only pray that they would forgive me and would even understand why I had to move away from their father.

It occurred to me that Mitch's manager had also accompanied them to Germany on that particular trip. I cared very much for Mitch's manager and his wife; they were a special couple and very good friends. It so happened that the manager's wife was a counselor for a local school district, and I thought it might be a good idea if I informed her of what had taken place; surely she would understand. I explained to her in detail why I had decided to leave Mitch. She was not totally ignorant of our situation, nor was she shocked by my news. She knew both of us well and was aware that we struggled through our marriage; but neither she nor her husband had ever brought up the subject in our presence. She was supportive of me, yet very concerned regarding the children. She suggested that perhaps, when her husband called her from New York upon arrival, she would tell him what had happened and he, in turn, could prepare Mitch and Ben for what they would "not find" when they arrived home.

As it turned out, telling her what I did was probably one of the best things I could have done under the circumstances (the best thing being hard to identify at the time).

The day of Mitch and Ben's return came all too quickly.

*   *   *   *   *

Luke and I were sitting at the table eating our dinner when, out of the corner of my eye, I saw a loden-green cape-draped figure walking across the porch towards the dining-room door. It was Benjamin.

I quickly got up from the table and opened the door, anxious to take him in my arms for an emotional reunion. But before I could say a word, several large Parisian fashion magazines, like the ones I always brought home as souvenirs from my trips to Europe, were thrown in my face, along with some injurious words.

"How could you do this to us? I never want to see you again, ever!"

With that, Ben walked off the porch and out of our lives.

As I lowered my head to prevent Luke from seeing my tears, he got up and came over to me; he put his arm around me and said, "Don't cry, Mother. It's all right; he didn't mean it. Don't cry."

Mounds of comfort came in that one hug and those few words that evening and they had come from a twelve-year-old child whose life had been uprooted and transplanted in strange ground. He had tried his best to make *me* feel better . . . the one responsible for all the changes.

It wasn't long before the other two children became aware of my move . . . but all I could do was wait for their responses; I hoped they would understand.

At that moment, I realized that I had been no better than my birth mother. She hadn't been able to deal with her circumstances either, and she made decisions that affected her children as well and, as a result, at least one of them ended up hating her. To expect more from my children seemed downright presumptuous. No matter how I justified my actions to myself, it didn't alter the obvious: the children loved their father. Regardless of what they had been through, it was apparent to me that having their parents together at any cost was far more important to them than having them apart for peace-sake.

*   *   *   *   *

I had yet to hear from Mitch. When he finally called, he accused me of deserting our family, along with a dozen other first-degree charges. His biggest concern, however, was that he still be able to see Luke. I verbally agreed that visits with Luke would not be withheld, but that the agreement came with a warning. The minute he laid a hand on Luke, as he had done with the other children, I would never permit him to see Luke again, at least if I had anything to say about it. His plan was to pick Luke up every other weekend, which seemed to please Luke and Mitch.

It took some time, but eventually Ben paid me a visit, as did the rest of the children. In spite of what happened to them, Ben and Thomas remained living with their father until they moved away from home. It is possible, I suppose, that their reason for doing so was based on Mitch's ability to provide for them materially, but I cannot validate that supposition. But I do know that over the next twenty-some years, I became extremely materialistic; I thought it would buy me the same family loyalty privileges.

I never got over feeling like the poor ogre in the family, but at the same time, I derived a sense of peace and contentment in my modest habitat, even while struggling along on twenty-five dollars a week, and literally not knowing where our next meal was coming from.

When I approached Mitch concerning some financial support, he laughed in my face. I took that as a "no." When I asked him if he would be willing to talk to a minister or a counselor regarding our situation, the answer was the same. He assured me that he would never give me one red dime and would still burn the house down if I tried to take that from him. He ended with words I will never forget: "I never want to see your face again!" And yet, years later, I was told that he cried when he asked a mutual friend of ours what he could do to get me back again. That information was strangely unconvincing, since his conversations with me were not only consistently hostile, but it was rare that a word was exchanged between the two of us. I knew his pride was hurt, but more than pride suffered as a result of our circumstances. For the life of me, I couldn't understand how someone with so much to lose could be so stubborn and unrelenting . . . except for pride.

I did not want a divorce. Mitch didn't want a divorce. But neither did he want to make the necessary changes needed to save our marriage. I will be the first to admit: no one party is completely innocent, or guilty, in the breakup of a family, and that was no less true of us. I was certainly beset with my own shortcomings, but I still would have done anything to save our marriage. I have little doubt that pride contributed immensely to the breakup of our marriage.

*   *   *   *   *

Social pleasures, to Luke and me, meant having a good piece of chocolate now and then and an occasional fast food meal. The fines imposed on me for not having my car inspected—the necessity of which never crossed my mind—eventually erased even those few luxuries from our social calendar.

It was very different being alone. I knew I would not be able to continue much longer without getting a job. The bills began to mount, and I had no way of paying them. It was easy for my attorney to advise me not to get a job; he wasn't the one starving.

Having had previous sales experience, and contrary to the advice of my attorney, I applied for a job in a men's clothing shop. It was a fine haberdashery. Two Jewish men owned the clothing shop and they quickly took me under their wings and groomed me to be their bookkeeper and office manager. The elder of the two gentlemen helped me out financially and we developed a close friendship. He was an excellent arbiter, and he managed to get my home mortgage interest reduced considerably through his personal bank. He was like a father to me—a very special person.

*   *   *   *   *

Ben continued to agonize over not being able to fly. I suggested that perhaps he try his hand at becoming a flight attendant since I knew how much he loved airplanes. A fellow classmate of mine was a captain for Pan American Airlines, so I decided to contact him. In turn, he sent an employment application to Ben. However, it happened that they were not hiring at the time, so I suggested he contact several other airlines. Eventually, he presented for an interview with another major airline and began training as a flight attendant. To this day, Ben works as a flight attendant for a major airline, but he also went back to school and became a registered nurse.

Thomas served with a tank division of the United States Army. He spent time in Germany and Korea. Several life-threatening incidents took place while he was on tour of duty with the United States Army.

One evening, I got an unexpected overseas call from Thomas. There was tremendous fear in his voice. He told me that several superior officers were threatening his life because he refused to become involved in drug trafficking. The individuals had armed themselves with chains and were in hot pursuit, threatening to beat him. He didn't know where to turn, because he didn't know whom he could trust. He managed to allude his pursuers and got to a telephone where he made his phone call home. My recommendation to him was to go to the military police or the highest office he could find and, in the meantime, I would see what I could do from my end.

At once, I contacted one of our Pennsylvania's State Representatives; his response was immediate. He set the military machines in motion to get Thomas out of Germany. When it didn't happen as fast as I thought it should, I contacted the Chief of Staff of the Army at the Pentagon. Within several days after speaking with the Pentagon, and after threatening to contact "60 Minutes" regarding some of the things I knew were happening in the military regarding drug trafficking, Thomas was flown home to the United States. Actually, I had known very little, except that which pertained to Thomas's situation, but I was a desperate mother trying to rescue her son.

Some years later, Thomas experienced another life-threatening event.

*   *   *   *   *

After my separation from Mitch, I eventually appeared in court for support for Luke and myself. Since my earnings were minimal, the court awarded me a small amount of support to be paid on a weekly basis. There still hadn't been any talk of divorce, but I was sure that, had I filed for one, I would have received a whole lot more money. But since divorce and money were not my reasons for leaving Mitch, all I wanted at the time was some financial assistance to help provide for our needs. I still had the notion that one day Mitch and I would resolve our differences and we would be together again.

*   *   *   *   *

One day, as I was working in the men's clothing store, a man came in to purchase some merchandise—a man I happened to know from our mutual attendance at ice hockey games. He and his family had box seats not far from ours during the years that we faithfully supported the sport. He bought several pairs of trousers and several shirts and ties that day. As I helped him match ties with the shirts he selected, something not required in my job description but which I did simply out of familiarity with the gentleman, he asked me a question.

"Have you been dating anyone since you and Mitch separated?"

I told him that I had not been dating and expressed my surprise at his knowledge of my situation. At first, I thought he was making a pass at me; however, he continued to explain.

"Oh, I wasn't asking for myself," he said with a smile. "My son Jon just moved back home from California and he is quite lonely since he's been back. Most of his friends have gotten married. He would really enjoy meeting someone who plays tennis, or someone to go to a movie with now and then, or just someone to talk go. Why don't I tell him to give you a call sometime?" he suggested.

"No, I don't think so," I replied. "I'm not divorced, and I am not really interested in dating," I assured him.

Then the thought occurred to me that his son couldn't be much older than my own children were, so I decided to mention that to Mr. Matthews.

"How old is your son?" I asked.

"He's young. But don't worry, you aren't old enough to be his mother," he chuckled.

"What makes you think he would be interested in meeting me? I'm forty years old."

"Well, what could it hurt then?" he responded.

"No, don't tell him to call me," I insisted. "I'm absolutely not interested."

With that he paid for his purchases and left the store.

I was hoping he wouldn't have the audacity to bring his son into the store to meet me.

*   *   *   *   *

The weekends Luke spent with his father were the loneliest times for me. I missed his company so much, and yet, I didn't want to convey dependence upon him. Surely, if he were anything like me, he was already thinking he had done something to cause his parents' separation. That is one of the sad residuals of a broken family.

I was not at all comfortable with Luke spending weekends with his father, but I thought it was the right thing to do, and unless he was being abused, I intended to honor our visitation arrangement.

Returning home after spending one of his weekends with his dad, Luke appeared extremely exhausted. I asked him if they had been up late the night before. Generally, I never questioned what they did or what they talked about. But Luke seemed particularly tired, and it concerned me. He ended up telling me that on the weekends he was with his dad, the two of them would go to a restaurant in a nearby town, where they would stay until the wee hours of the next morning.

I knew the restaurant. It was an exclusive restaurant and a place Mitch and I had eaten many times. Luke said they would sit there until he could no longer hold his eyes open and he would fall asleep at the table. He said they had been doing that on a regular basis. I was furious. To keep a young boy up so late at night, sitting in a restaurant, just didn't make any sense to me. It wasn't until much later that I learned the real reason for the extended stays at the restaurant. Apparently Mitch developed an interest in the manager's wife, an Austrian-born woman with a German accent irresistible to Mitch. I recalled having met the lady's husband on several occasions; he happened to be the chef at the restaurant, and a very good one at that. He had come to our table quite frequently to inquire whether or not we were pleased with our food, but I never recalled meeting, or ever seeing, his wife.

I didn't want to get Luke into trouble by revealing what I now knew, but neither did I want him to be subjected to those kinds of hours and situations again. So I decided to confront Mitch.

I weighed my words as carefully as ingredients for a special recipe. I simply requested that Luke get more rest when he spent weekends while staying with his dad, that he had shown extreme exhaustion the last few weekends. Otherwise, I would have to reconsider my decision to let Luke visit him, apart from a court order. I did not betray Luke's confidence by revealing to Mitch what I knew about his nights at the restaurant. Thankfully, and according to Luke, the routine ceased. But the Austrian woman remained in the picture, making reconciliation between Mitch and me highly unlikely.

*　　*　　*　　*　　*

I had been working at the clothing store for over a year when I received a phone call from someone I had never bet before. He introduced himself as Mr. Wayne Barrick, general manager of Cable AdNet (Cable Advertising Network). He explained that he had been told about my successful sales record with a former station, and he wondered whether or not he could interest me in having lunch with him. He said he had wanted very much to talk to me about cable advertising. I figured I had nothing to lose in hearing what he had to say, so we arranged a luncheon meeting the following Saturday afternoon.

I met and immediately liked Wayne Barrick. He was straightforward in his approach, and he impressed me as a fair and honest businessman. His sales expertise did not go unnoticed. He was notably well versed regarding his product, and he was also very skillful at using his charming personality as a very persuasive tool. I mentally bought everything he was selling. The income potential was undeniably greater than that of the radio station, and leaps beyond my current income at the clothing shop. I agreed to give his proposal serious consideration and told him I would contact him within several weeks. He seemed pleased with that arrangement. We came together as strangers, but I felt we parted as friends.

The thought of informing my current employers, who had been so good to me, about my new job opportunity, was very difficult. Not only did it take me the entire two weeks to come close to considering the job with Cable AdNet, but I also begged an additional month from Wayne Barrick in order to prepare my proposed resignation. I wanted to give my employers ample time to find a replacement for me. The fact that Mr. Barrick understood my situation convinced me he was a man of integrity, one with whom I could work. And so the way was prepared for me to leave my position at the clothing shop and accept employment with Cable Advertising Network.

*　　*　　*　　*　　*

Stepping out of the familiar and into the unknown necessitated a withdrawal of small amounts of confidence I had banked when making my decision to leave Mitch, and my stress level began moving up and down like Wall Street. I tried very hard to suppress the terror I felt about my new job, and about being the main financial provider for Luke and myself. In addition, I still anticipated some kind of revenge from Mitch, revenge that had the potential to cause bodily injury or even death. I just didn't know what form that revenge would take, but as certain as putting my feet on the floor to walk, I knew it would happen.

One day, I ran into a long-time friend of Mitch's, and I shared my concerns about that expected retribution. He said that he didn't blame me for leaving Mitch; he was all too familiar with Mitch's volatile disposition, but he told me he was equally confident that Mitch would never fatally injure any member of his own family. He also said I was "to get on with my life."

Some months later, I found myself occupying a seat in the Minden Courthouse sitting face to face with Mitch, as the case for support was presented to the judge on my behalf. Maureen sat behind me and occasionally touched my shoulder as a show of another kind of support. The judge ruled to increase our support. And although I was relieved, it was just a sample of things to come, should it be necessary to meet again on a divorce and property settlement. I prayed that would never happen. But, being realistic, it looked very much like that was the direction we were headed.

The increase in support was still not enough to support us in the manner to which we had become accustomed, and so I did not change my plans to begin working for Cable Advertising Network.

*   *   *   *   *

Suddenly, there I was, briefcase in hand, off to a new job in Minden.

Evidently, local cable advertising was something new since the proliferation of cable stations and cable home subscriptions. ESPN, CNN, and USA networks came through a little black box that sat obtrusively on top of nearly everyone's television set. They were showing up in homes all over the country, making it very attractive for businesses to advertise their products in a very specialized and direct market. If sporting goods was what a company wanted to sell, ESPN and USA were natural places to advertise. Some businesses were more suited to advertising on CNN where you could watch twenty-four hours of news every day of the week. Specialized cable programming was on the move, and we were right behind it. Our general manager was a progressive-thinking man with great ideas. He needed us to sell businessmen and women on the advantages of advertising on cable television.

Generally, the job allowed me to be home when Luke arrived home from school. But my main concern was what to do when he was not in school during the summer months. I was always a supporter of mothers being home for their children, even if it meant changing their lifestyles to do it. Of course, over the years, the cost of "needs" (though more often luxuries and wants) necessitates both parents working in order to keep up with the cost of living, and the neighbors . . . and it shows. There are many more divorces, a decline in morals, and an increase in drug-dependent children and adolescents. I was so afraid that I might become one of those statistics.

My first job review by Wayne Barrick was positive and encouraging. My first three months proved financially rewarding, and I was confident that I could do an even better job. I wanted to become a sales manager and I worked hard toward that goal. Cable AdNet grew like dandelions in a field of advertising opportunities. I felt fortunate to be part of that exciting time.

Cable AdNet's offices were soon moved from Minden to Hershey, Pennsylvania. The advertising business grew beyond anyone's expectations, and within a short period of time, I became sales manager for Minden and Lancaster Counties, eventually opening an office in Minden to exclusively serve those two counties. I enjoyed the fruits of my labor and had a great sales team to thank for our successes.

Then something even more exciting happened.

Following a phone conversation with Laurel Lake's resident historian, I learned that The Gift Shop—the one I had driven by on a daily basis and dreamed of leasing one day—might possibly become available in a year or two. His inquiry was primarily to find out whether or not I was still interested in the building. I assured him that indeed I was still interested, though I hadn't the foggiest idea what I would do with the place. But it sure gave me something other than myself to think about. Perhaps I really would have my own business in a couple of years, I thought. That was all the incentive I needed to learn as much as I could about merchandising. I told myself that, if I could do well in someone else's business, then I should be able to succeed in my own.

As I reached for my dreams, circumstances beyond my control were waiting to ambush me.

... Twenty-Three ...

Leaves, struggling to cling to their branches, at the right time, fluttered to the ground in a heap of colors. Fall was one of my favorite times of the year, especially in Laurel Lake. The lake looked like it had been on fire, as the multicolor-reflections of the trees in the water swayed with the wind, or stood still, as if traced on the surface of the water. The leaves floated aimlessly in circles and, in no attempt to save themselves, disappeared over the small dam and were gone forever.

Hiking trails, deep in the woods, provided unlimited solitude for the thinkers and dreamers of Laurel Lake. That is where I would spend hours reading in undisturbed quietness. Sometimes, a proud doe accompanied by several of her fawns would pass close by me and never appear disturbed by the intrusion. It was also there that I wrote pages of poetry from my hurting heart . . . poetry later deemed publishable by a seasoned author from New York City. Unfortunately, the collection experienced a tragic end.

Following one of those introspective afternoons in the woods, as I fumbled with the door key to let myself into my cottage, I heard the telephone ringing. The voice on the other end of the line was unquestionable that of Michael Banks. It had been a very long time since we had spoken to one another, but his voice was every bit as distinguishable as his charm and good looks.

He said he had heard that Mitch and I had separated and he wanted very much to see me. He sounded quite nervous, until I realized that he had probably been drinking. In defense of my suspicion, he said that he had made a wreck of his life, and that he had drunk enough vodka for courage to call me.

He talked. I listened. He told me he had just completed a tour of duty in Vietnam as a sergeant major and had left the State Police force for good. He said his experience in "Nam," as he called it, had been enough to drive any man to drink. Since then, he claimed he had been trying very hard to get his life back together. I couldn't help wondering what part he expected me to play in accomplishing that feat.

As much as my heart touched his, especially after he told me I was the only woman he had ever truly loved, and that he would never be happy without me, I did not allow my emotions to rule my heart. I was not divorced, had no intention of becoming divorced, and did not need another man in my life. But how was I to convey that message to him without hurting or provoking him, since he was obviously a half-dozen black coffees from sober.

As gently as possible, I explained that Mitch and I were just separated and that I hoped we would get back together at some point in the future. I pleaded with him not to call me again, or try to see me. I said I would see how things went, but that I didn't think I would ever want to renew our relationship under any circumstances. I wished him well and asked him to honor my request not to call again.

I sat for a long time thinking about how much Michael had once meant to me—my protector, my love. Now it was he who needed caring for; our roles had oddly switched. Unquestionably, we had both become by-products of wrong choices.

The calls came nearly every night . . . all night. They kept me awake, until finally I had to warn him if he continued to call, I would have my phone number changed and unlisted. Sadly, it became very clear to me that Michael was definitely dealing with a drinking problem and, although I felt sorry for him, I didn't want to encourage him. Eventually, I had no choice but to ask his brother and sister-in-law to intercede on my behalf and plead with him to stop calling me. Because of their close family ties, they were able to convince him not to call me again. And he didn't.

For several weeks, just for insurance, I turned the "phone-ringer" control to the "off" position before going to bed at night.

*   *   *   *   *

In my daily routine of housekeeping, advertising sales, and motherhood, I could not find the glamour in singleness. Everything was harder. I could barely look at two people walking down the street together, eating together, and especially worshiping together. It was a constant reminder of my aloneness.

Luke and I became active in the Methodist church located about a block from our cottage. I felt estranged from the mainstream of worshipers, even though I was asked to teach an adult class several Sundays out of the month. I felt so incomplete as Luke and I walked up the hill after Sunday services to our modest cottage. It was painful to watch couples walking hand-in-hand and families kibitzing with their neighbors. There were no family quarrels to deal with anymore, but there were no family meat-and-mashed-potato dinners either.

With little money left over for entertainment, Luke and I spent a great deal of our time at home; still, Luke did not complain.

There was, however, a kind of battle raging inside my head. *Did I do the right thing?* I would ask myself over and over again. I knew I never again wanted to live like I had been living, nor had I wanted to subject another one of my children to Mitch's tyrannical outbursts, but still I wrestled with myself over my decision to leave my husband. And yet, Mitch gave no indication that he was willing to do anything to have us back with him. By that time, I was sure he had become involved with the Austrian woman and was no longer grieving over our departure—if he had grieved at all. I conceded that there was no use lamenting over the past, so in spite of the crippling effect separation was having on my life, I was determined to persevere.

I began to read my Bible more and more, depending on the words to comfort and sustain me. Prayer also became a large part of my daily devotions. Luke joined the church and was baptized. It was a special day of celebration in our lives. I believed that his trust in Jesus offered a much firmer foundation than the one I had given him. I shared my burdens with God; I asked Him to bear the heaviest portion of my pain. I was still carrying forty-some years' worth of baggage to an unknown destination and I needed help.

Another question haunted me: Would I end up like my birth mother—in an institution as a result of not being able to cope with life? The answer to my own question was always, "No, I would not, I could not." I had enough faith to believe that, in the end, all things would work together for my good . . . that I didn't have to become a replica of my mother and her misdeeds.

*   *   *   *   *

In a show of support, many of my friends visited me on a regular basis. But one evening we had a very unexpected visitor.

Luke was watching television and was sitting close to the Franklin fireplace, which had a log or two burning to ward off the dampness of the cool fall evening. I happened to be upstairs at the time when, suddenly, I heard voices in the living room. Knowing Luke was alone downstairs, I raced down the steps in my baggy sweat suit—my unpretentious five-mile-a-day uniform—to find Luke and a tall dark-haired young man in blue jeans in the middle of the living room floor. Immediately my defenses went up, and I ordered Luke to go upstairs and stay there until I called him downstairs again. I could only hope that no harm would come to him by the intruder. Instantly, the thought occurred to me that the guy could have been hired by Mitch to frighten me. Since I was completely defenseless at that point, I decided I had nothing to lose by displaying a little courage. Except for wanting to become an agent for the FBI or CIA, I never thought myself particularly brave, but that night I decided to stand my ground. After all, it was *my* ground. I wanted to know who the intruder was and why he was standing in my house in the middle of my living room.

He said, "I didn't mean to alarm you, but I came to see my friends, Ed and Beth, but it doesn't look like they live here anymore."

I was somewhat relieved to find that he was familiar with the names of the couple from whom I had purchased my cottage.

"You are right about that," I replied, a little cocky. "I bought the cottage from them. They bought a home elsewhere."

In the event the young man's visit was innocent, I offered to give him Ed and Beth's new address and phone number. He said he appreciated the information, and that he had just moved back into the area and had been mistaken to think that they still lived at the same place. He said that they had been best friends and that, in fact, he had even helped build my Franklin fireplace and had helped remodel my cottage some years ago before he moved to California. Like a confessing criminal, he began pointing out all sorts of things that only a person who had done those things could possibly have known about. I believed him.

While I was writing down Ed and Beth's address and phone number, he sauntered over to the kitchen sink and asked if he could help himself to a glass of water. Thinking that was a rather forward request, I became agitated by his presence. After providing him with information on his friends, I asked him if he would please leave, that I wanted to resume my work upstairs. Appearing somewhat stunned by my request, he agreed to leave, saying he hoped he hadn't intruded. He continued to explain that my cottage had been like his second home at one time, which may have accounted for his familiarity with the place, but I thought it was time to end the visit.

As soon as he closed the door, I breathed a sigh of relief. He hadn't been a hit man, and for that I was eternally grateful.

I decided to call Luke downstairs and explain to him what had happened. He didn't seem to be phased one way or another about the event. But it gave me an opportunity to instruct him to never again answer the door at night without me being present.

Moments later, I picked up the phone and called Ed and Beth. While I was describing the young man I found standing in my living room, Beth began to laugh.

"Do you know who that was?" she chuckled.

"No, I never got his name; I was just anxious to get him out of here," I replied.

"That was Jon Matthews. Isn't he gorgeous? You know his parents, I think. They had box seats near you and your husband at ice hockey games. He is an old friend of ours. He helped remodel your house. He has probably spent more time there than you have so far."

"Oh my gosh," I said, "now I know who he is. As a matter of fact, his father mentioned to me some time ago, when he came into the clothing store where I was working, that he had a son who had just moved back into the area from California. He thought the two of us should get together since we were both alone, but I was not in the least bit interested."

"You really ought to reconsider, Leta," she replied. "He is so good looking; didn't you think so?"

"To tell you the truth, Beth, I couldn't tell you whether he was good looking or not. I was much too upset by his unannounced visit, and especially how forward he was."

"He's harmless, Leta. But his dad was right. He is a lonely guy. What harm would it do to just get together and talk?"

"That's exactly how his dad put it. But I think the whole idea is absurd. I can't think of one good reason why I would want to get to know him. But, I will say this. I probably owe him an apology, since I was not terribly hospitable towards him. But I think I will just call his parents and explain the situation and extend my apologies through them."

"Fair enough. But I still think you ought to reconsider."

"Beth, do you know how old I am?"

"No, but what does it matter? You certainly aren't old enough to be his mother. You play tennis, and I know he plays tennis. Why couldn't you just get together and hit some balls? But I don't know you all that well, Leta, and I'm sure you have your reasons for not pursuing the matter, so I won't say anymore."

"Good," I replied, "I am relieved to know that he wasn't lying when he said he was a friend of yours. He'll probably be in touch with you. I hope you don't mind, but I gave him your address and phone number."

"No, that's fine."

As we hung up I thought I detected laughter in the background, but I didn't think anymore of it at the time.

I looked up the phone number for the Matthews and dialed it, certain that their son had not yet arrived home. Cliff Matthews answered the telephone.

"Cliff, this is Leta Marlow," I began. "I'm afraid I was not too kind to your son this evening. He came to my house expecting to find his friends, Ed and Beth, and instead, he found that I had moved into their home. But he never told me who he was. I spoke with Beth tonight and she told me it was your son. Please convey my apologies to him. Had I known he was your son it may have turned out differently, but as it was, he did frighten me a bit. He just made himself at home and I didn't know quite what to think about it. But Beth confirmed everything he said, so I would appreciate it if you would extend my apologies to him."

His dad agreed to pass on my apologies to his son, but he also tried to convince me that he still thought it would be a good idea if the two of us got together. He even went as far as to say he was going to tell his son Jon to call me sometime. I found it useless to argue; instead, I thought perhaps that if I didn't protest so strongly he wouldn't pursue the issue.

*　*　*　*　*

Luke continued to visit with his dad every other weekend. He always had to walk to the corner of another street to meet him because Mitch wouldn't drive within seeing distance of my house. That bothered me, only because I didn't like Luke waiting on the corner of some street until his dad arrived. Thankfully, I could see the corner from my living room window, and I watched until I knew Luke was safely in the car. It seemed so unfair that Luke had to divide his time and affections between Mitch and me. *Children somehow always end up being pulled in two different directions when their parents separate or divorce,* I thought.

I was beginning to witness the traumatic effect my leaving Mitch was having on my children. How could I have known that what I chose to do, and what their father did, would affect the rest of their lives. The decision I made to leave Mitch, unfortunately, had a reversible side to it, one I didn't see until I witnessed my children's lives turned inside out. *Couldn't Mitch see the importance of making our marriage work; wasn't it worth swallowing some pride to seek counseling?* I asked myself. I could not hold the marriage together by myself, and I did not want to return to a house full of contention.

*　*　*　*　*

It was Saturday, and Luke was spending the night with his father. I sat alone contemplating my future.

It was an unusually mild fall evening and two years since Luke and I had moved into our cottage. The white wicker furniture was still on the porch and, apart from an occasional pile of leaves scattered over it, the porch was still a welcome place to sit and enjoy the cool evening breezes.

It was still early and I had nothing to look forward to, except the rest of the night. As I was about to vacate my favorite rocking chair and go inside because it had started to feel a bit chilly, I heard the telephone ring.

Not expecting anyone in particular, I tendered my usual, perhaps somewhat despondent "Hello."

"Hi! This is Jon Matthews. Remember me?"

"Yes, I certainly do." And I most certainly did.

"Dad told me you called, and I wanted you to know that I accept your apology."

"Oh, you didn't have to call," I assured him. "That wasn't necessary." Somehow, I didn't think that was the intention of his call.

"What would you say if I brought out a bottle of wine and we could sit on your porch and talk. I really don't have many friends around here anymore, and I would really appreciate the company. I understand that you play tennis. Maybe we could get together and play sometime."

"I really don't think that is a good idea," I replied. "I know there's nothing wrong with wanting to get to know someone, but I think you would have a lot more in common with someone your own age."

"You make it sound like you're an old lady, and I hardly think that's the case. Doesn't my idea interest you at all? Are you busy tonight? Do you have a date?"

"No, none of the above. It's just that I . . ."

"I . . . don't want to hear it. I'll be there in a little while. I promise we will just sit on the porch and talk. I can tell you all about California and you can tell me all about you. I'll see you soon."

And he hung up.

No special attention was given to the house, or myself, in expectation of Jon Matthews' visit. I rather hoped he would change his mind after thinking it through. It hadn't occurred to me that Jon Matthews was a child of the fifties and more apt to arrive in a wave of feelings than a frigate of rationale.

I tried to think back and recall my first impression of the young man. He was tall—maybe over six-feet tall. He apparently hadn't shaved in a week and his hair was dark and disheveled. His jeans were well worn and his eyes were dark and probing. Yes, just like Beth said, he was rather good-looking now that I had given it some thought. But, why in God's name would he want to spend time with me? He really must be lonely, I concluded.

I went about finishing some household chores that I had started earlier, before I abandoned them for a few minutes on the porch, and before Jon's telephone call. The doors of the house stood open. It couldn't have been a more beautiful fall evening.

A Jeep-like vehicle parked in one of two parking spaces at the rear of my cottage. My heart leaped from its sitting position and stood face to face with Jon Matthews.

He was clean-shaven and positively handsome, and very young. I felt about as comfortable as a foot in a shoe three sizes too small and completely void of wiggle room. He handed me the promised bottle of wine, which I immediately placed in the refrigerator. He followed me onto the porch where I offered him a seat directly across from where I planned to sit.

Jon asked teasingly, "Are you planning to open that bottle of wine, or do you intend to save it for another occasion?"

"No, of course not . . . I mean, of course we can open the wine, but you are going to have to open it. I don't know that I have ever opened a bottle of wine before, and with my luck, the cork will end up inside the bottle."

He laughed.

The order switched, and I followed him into the kitchen. He opened several cupboard doors, finally retrieving two glasses, making himself annoyingly at home once more. I watched him as he maneuvered the cork-screw into the neck of the bottle. I had little doubt that he had done that a thousand times before. He filled the two large wine glasses, handing one of them to me. I kept my head lowered as I took it from his hand and made my way back to the porch.

We sat for several hours exchanging stories about our respective lives.

He said he had lived in California until losing a dear friend and business partner to suicide and, according to him, it was a devastating time in his life. He found it impossible to remain on the West Coast after that tragic incident, and so he had come back to Minden to be with his family. It was then that he asked if I would mind if he smoked a cigarette. I had wanted to say yes, but I knew he was sharing a very delicate mile-stone in his life with me, so I did not object.

He told me he was twenty-seven years old. I did not tell him how old I was. He admitted that he had done battle with drugs and still suffered from a sort of "hippie" mentality—the "do what feels good, man" genera-tion.

He told me how he had been drawn into numerous cults in Califor-nia and all that entailed. He had wanted nothing to do with his family during those times, a cult requirement, he said, which had broken his mother's heart. It was easy to see that his search for salvation had not ended. But if he came to me for saving, I thought, he came to the wrong person and place. My faith, faltering from years of neglect, was about as useful as an umbrella in the eye of a tornado. I had wandered a long way from the strong faith I practiced when I was sixteen years old. I was barely clinging to faith myself and I wasn't about to add any weight to my already frayed grip on God. But I was beginning to feel sorry for the young man. It would have been easy to tell him to just go to God with his problems, but I hadn't been there myself lately, so all I could do was listen.

Jon appeared genuinely touched by the story of how I came to be alone. The unique and sad circumstances of our lives, though separated at that time by the width of a country, now connected us somehow.

Jon asked me if I would mind if he changed the music on my stereo. Since he was unfamiliar with my system, and I was uncomfortable with his being in my house alone, I walked inside the house with him. As I got on my knees beside the window-seat where the stereo was located, I was profoundly aware of how close his face was to mine.

It was getting late and the sky darkened. I did not want to prolong the visit, so I explained that I had to get some rest and be up early in the morning for Sunday School and church services. He looked like a puppy being put out in the rain. *Well, he will just have to get wet*, I thought. I had no desire to see the time we spent together become more than just a visit. His dark eyes indicated otherwise. As he left, he said he would call me, that maybe we could play some tennis sometime, but then he changed his mind and asked if he could take Luke and me to a movie instead, claiming it was just the company that he wanted. I said I would have to give that some thought.

Let's see, I pondered, after he had gone. *He is twenty-seven years old and I am forty-two; that's a span of fifteen years—a whole different lifetime. Well, there was no way he's going to con his way into my home and heart; if that's what he's planning to do.*

There was no falling asleep that night, and there was no use arguing with myself about what was, or was not, going to happen; the whole situation was so ridiculous that it wasn't worth the time I was unconsciously spending on it. So I tossed and turned myself to sleep.

Not until Jon called again with an invitation to take us to the movies did I attempt to explain Jon Matthews to my son Luke. I didn't know why, but I found myself wanting to go, but at the same time, I couldn't help thinking about what my neighbors might say, since most of them were aware that I was still married. *But what harm was there in going to a movie together,* I rationalized. Following a brief embattled pause, I accepted the invitation.

It had been two years since I had done anything fun for myself. Mitch, on the other hand, had obviously gone on with his life. There didn't seem to be an urgent plea for my return, nor was there an ounce of evidence that reconciliation was in the offing. So I managed to convince myself that a movie was about the least harmless activity I could have engaged in.

*   *   *   *   *

How strange it felt sitting in the passenger's seat of a car again, having been the primary driver for the past several years. I was surprised to find out just how much I missed that part of married life. There were no more expensive dinners out and no more hockey games twice a week, and, thankfully, no more arguments. There had definitely been a trade-off in lifestyles, among many other changes. The absence of companionship in my life tore at my flesh as I looked over at Jon behind the wheel of his Jeep, and I wanted again to be a member of a "union." Dismissing that unplanned melancholy moment, I began to talk about the movie we were about to see, hoping to engage Luke in the conversation. I was also beginning to have second thoughts about the whole evening.

Gratefully, the time we spent together that night was rather benign. My faith in the innocence of that evening was restored. We returned home from the movie having stuffed ourselves on popcorn and sodas. I thanked Jon for a fun time and we said goodnight. I felt quite sure that it would only be a matter of time before he would be in touch again. He had already calculated which weekends Luke would be with his father.

As far as I could tell, there didn't seem to be one legitimate reason for continuing Jon's and my friendship. The whole thing was beginning to rob me of sleep, and I didn't like it one bit.

As I rehearsed the words I would use to tell Jon that I really didn't want to see him again, his next phone call was already on its way. He pleaded with me to let him come and talk to me, and I found myself yielding to his request.

Unlike the time before, this time he really did arrive at my front door on a wave of feelings, and with blood-shot eyes. While sitting on the sofa that evening, he began discussing those feelings with me. He said he had not slept well since we had been together and that he hadn't been able to think about anything else but me. He said he knew that his wanting to be with me was probably not right, but his "feelings" simply contradicted his better judgement.

Why is it we use "feelings" to identify truth, when they are merely shadows of what's real, such an unreliable source of permanence?

He seemed to be struggling in an attempt to share something with me. I saw tears gather in his eyes and I wondered if he had been drinking. Wanting desperately to console him, I did the motherly thing and put my arms around him and listened as he used some surprising synonyms of love to describe how he was feeling about me. He claimed that he loved me, a premature declaration of affection I wasn't prepared to return or accept. But my heart touched his. He continued with an admission that he had still been using drugs and that he didn't know what to do about it. I sensed that his pain ran deep, and it also explained why his eyes had been so red. I was completely inexperienced in substance abuse, but having been physically abused, I wanted very much to comfort and help him. I suggested that he seek professional help, and I told him that I was sure that God could give him victory over drugs, that maybe it would be good for him to talk to the pastor of the church I attended.

While holding his head in my arms, I made several decisions: I would help as much as I could by encouraging him to seek spiritual counseling, and I was not going to become emotionally involved in his life. He may have looked like Tom Selleck, the movie star, and he most certainly did, but I wasn't going to allow his appearance to reduce my good sense to nonsense.

In the end, he asked me if I would mind if he went to church with me the following Sunday. Although I didn't believe for one minute he would ever go to church, I had somewhat committed myself to helping him at that point, and so I feigned support for his palpably false intentions . . . or so I thought. Before he left that night, he told me he had planned a trip to the shore with some friends for a few days, but that he would be back in time to go to church with me that coming Sunday. It was Luke's weekend to be with his dad.

Not only did Jon call me from the shore several times that week, but he also returned bearing a gift. He had won a black and white stuffed penguin in some arcade on the boardwalk, and he proudly presented it to me, along with an apology for not having gotten me something a bit more extravagant. It was an endearing gesture, so I accepted the somewhat pathetic-looking straw-stuffed memento. He told me how much he had missed me and that he had almost come home early just to be with me, had it not been for the teasing he received from his macho buddies.

Much to my surprise, Jon kept his word and attended church with me the following Sunday. Thankfully, I was able to pass him off as just a friend to fellow worshipers, but in truth, he was becoming more than just a friend to me.

Like the pleasure and taste of sin for a season, his kiss was gentle at first. But gentle beginnings rarely end the same way.

. . . TWENTY-FOUR . . .

By what means does a relationship grow if all things go on as they are?

Wanting to keep things just as they were between Jon and me, I was relieved when he told me he had been thinking those same thoughts regarding our friendship.

Following an emotional exchange, we agreed not to see one another again.

A week of silence passed between us, evidence that our decision had grown roots. Nevertheless, I found myself lying awake at night thinking about him. Mental and emotional exhaustion finally surrendered to several nights of undisturbed rest. During one such night, I thought I heard church bells ringing, akin to some distant dream. Instead, the bells turned out to be the repeated rings of the telephone. My mind, still covered by a sleepy haze, finally began to clear.

"Hello," I said sleepily.

"Leta, it's me, Jon. I can't do this. I can't sleep; I can't do anything without you. I love you and I want to be with you. I can't do this anymore." Then he began to cry.

When I heard his voice, I knew that I had . . . for all the wrong reasons . . . missed him. The reasons for ending our friendship, on the other hand, had been right; the age difference, his struggle with drug use, and the fact that I was still married. Our equally aggrieved lives, and still unidentified co-dependent natures, were threads that bound us together.

"I miss you too, Jon," I admitted, "but it's only been a week and we're just giving in to our feelings, and they aren't reliable right now."

"I know I shouldn't feel this way, Leta, but I don't want to be without you. I must see you."

I allowed myself to believe that he really had fallen in love with me. We cried together. I was so happy that someone loved me so much. It should have occurred to me that God loved me more, but it didn't . . . at the time.

"Can we talk about it another time?" I asked.

In an almost boyish response, he said, "If that's what you want."
For reasons apparent, I couldn't go back to sleep.

*   *   *   *   *

Jon and I confirmed our close friendship by beginning to appear
in public together. We played tennis, took walks, and eventually introduced one another to our respective family members.

Jon's personality was infectious. It wasn't long before my parents
and friends accepted him without question. Maureen, who knew me best
of all, reserved her opinion for another time. Jon's mother was less receptive of our friendship, but she remained warm and gracious; she was all
too aware of the age difference between us. She herself appeared to be
only seven or eight years older than I was. His stepfather, on the other
hand, who had tried so hard to bring us together in the first place, cheered
us on from the sidelines, as if it were just another spectator sport. Luke, on
the other hand, did not appreciate another man around the house, no matter how infrequent the visits, but especially as they became more recurrent. He did not like getting instructions from Jon on any subject, and he
was quietly certain that Jon had intruded into our life, but he had yet to
share those feelings with me.

Jon tried to win Luke's affection by taking him to the frog pond
not far from our house to catch frogs, but a couple of frogs a surrogate dad
does not make. A tug-of-war for my attention began to develop between
the two of them.

It wasn't long before Jon and I became inseparable. He began coming to dinner every night, and the three of us would spend weekends together at Jon's parents' farm outside of Minden cutting wood for our
Franklin fireplace. We went target shooting, aiming at empty shotgun shells
that we would throw into a rippling stream that ran through Jon's parents'
property. Apart from the fatal car accident I had been involved in many
years earlier, it was the closest I ever came to having my face rearranged.

During one of our days in the woods, Jon handed me a 44 Mag-
num Pistol, which I proceeded to nonchalantly aim at a target, only to find
that when I engaged the trigger, the kick was so severe that my arm jolted
backwards nearly breaking my nose. I winced in pain as Jon began apologizing for not warning me about the punch that particular weapon delivered. Other than that incident, which he found somewhat humorous, some
of our most enjoyable times were spent on his parents' farm; it helped
amend the lingering negative thoughts I had regarding our relationship.

Friends kept telling me how much they envied me and that they
would have given anything to have someone pay so much attention to

them, especially someone so young and handsome. Jon couldn't keep his eyes, or his hands, off of me. The attention was overwhelming, and I was gathering it like eggs in an apron. In church, however, I felt uncomfortable. Jon's eyes focused more on me than on the pastor. Like a mother, I would have to remind him to pay attention to the speaker. Before long, I too considered myself fortunate to have met such an affectionate man. For the first time in my life, I truly felt needed by someone other than my children. Mitch had needed me once, but for entirely different reasons and, even then, he would never have admitted that he needed me.

Maureen was the skeptical one; she took her time getting to know Jon, until finally she came to the conclusion that she liked him. What she thought was very important to me. She often saw things more clearly than I did. I respected her opinions and I always believed that she wanted nothing but the best for me. We talked long and hard about Jon and me. She had to admit that Jon's love appeared genuine, and seeing me happy made her happy, she said. Jon also knew how important Maureen was in my life. She was the only family I had, apart from my foster parents and my children, and he never once tried to destroy our closeness.

Jon loved my foster mother, but he thought my dad was somewhat of a "rascal," as he put it, yet they managed to get along. Every time my mother would call me, and Jon would answer the phone, he would tease her about her sweet tiny voice. She told me once how much that had flustered her.

Despite some gentle warnings from my mother, someone I never imagined possessed an ounce of romantic insight, and from Maureen, who seemed to possess more wisdom than a dozen owls under the tutelage of King Solomon, I continued to see Jon. Neither had shared their deepest heart's concerns with me.

Using Mitch and his new female friend as a way of rationalizing my own behavior, it temporarily eased the guilt I may have otherwise experienced. I was uncomfortably aware that I was operating outside the spiritual boundaries God had set for my life and for my good. I had told Maureen early on in Jon's and my relationship that I knew there would be a heavy price to pay for my disobedience, but that I was confident God would forgive me when I was ready to ask for it. I intended to make it right someday, and I was sure God would understand. I had taught my children never to engage in the very behavior I was now involved in. *I called it love. **God called it sin.***

It no longer seemed remotely conceivable that Mitch and I would ever get back together again. That generated some energetic communiqués between his attorney and mine. Mitch made it explicitly clear through his attorney that he did not want a divorce and was not going to relinquish one cent of his money or possessions. Since I wasn't in any particular hurry to become a divorcee, we continued living in the state of separation.

I began hearing rumors that Mitch's new girlfriend, who had two children of her own, was seeking a divorce from her husband. It became fairly clear that Mitch wasn't about to agree to a divorce from me until he was ready to marry someone else. I just didn't realize how quickly that plot would unfold.

*   *   *   *   *

Jon moved out of his parents' home and into an apartment about a half-hour drive from Laurel Lake.

Weekends, when Luke was spending time with his dad, I was spending time with Jon in his new apartment. Physical intimacy seemed less immoral when it took place out of town. Although Jon wasn't entirely happy in his new apartment, it did give our indiscretions a temporary hiding place. It also provided a stepping stone for an even greater infidelity.

Not unlike college kids of today who think they are minimizing parental shock by using financial savings as an excuse for moving in with a member of the opposite sex, we, too, utilized that same logic when, several months later, Jon began moving his belongings into my cottage. At no time during that transition did I consider how that move was going to affect the rest of my life. I never anticipated the injurious ramifications of my selfish indulgence, any more than Jean Marlow had anticipated hers, only I should have known better. I had moral guidelines provided for me in God's Word. I had studied them; I believed them; and I obeyed them . . . as a teenager. They were guidelines meant to protect my heart and my life. I was now foregoing the safety of those truths to engage in an immoral relationship. Worse than that, I was exposing my son to the very things I taught him were morally wrong. But I was unwilling to sacrifice my happiness for the happiness of my son. I still hadn't learned the true meaning of love, the very thing I set my heart on.

Confusion moved in with Jon's belongings, and Luke became the recipient of most of it. I passed the baggage baton that I carried most of my life on to my son, expecting him to run with it without stumbling. He didn't know how to explain Jon's presence in our home to his friends. His friends began asking him what they should call me, Mrs. Matthews or Mrs. Brogan.

Sometimes divorce is unavoidable, but for the most part, it's a whole lot more and a whole lot worse.

I loved Luke so much, but I loved Jon, too. If I hadn't been blinded by my feelings for Jon, I would have realized the damage being visited on so innocent and impressionable a young heart and life.

*   *   *   *   *

When Jon's move was complete, the Mt. Laurel inquest began. Had I gotten married? Was I renting to someone? Was I planning on getting married? On and on it went. My separation generated more steam than the hot sticky buns served at the local coffee shop; and my new living arrangement nearly made it to the Mt. Pines Playhouse marquee.

It became increasingly difficult for me to balance Jon on one hand and Luke on the other. I was being stretched emotionally and physically. I tried to devote equal time to both of them. Sadly, I began to detect needless jealousy growing between the two.

One day, Luke presented a small school picture of himself to Jon, with these words written on the back:

> *To Jon,*
>   *You better always be good to my mother*
>   *or you will have to answer to me.*
>   *Love, Luke*

I cried when Jon showed me the picture and the message it contained. Luke had already taken on the responsibility of protector, such an unfair position for a boy his age to have.

Jon was struggling with his own balancing act as he tried to be both friend and father to Luke. There were times when I had to intervene and remind Jon that Luke was my son and that I was perfectly capable of taking care of any discipline problems Luke might have. Luke was an exceptionally well-behaved youngster, and rare was the time I had to discipline him. But these were unusual days. Should I have detected some underlying motive for Jon's constant fault-finding? Perhaps, but instead I interpreted it as Jon's way of feeling important and another way of integrating into our family.

Careful not to expose Luke to any intimacy between Jon and myself, I insisted on separate sleeping quarters. I suppose blind love deems others blind as well.

*   *   *   *   *

Just about the time we were getting comfortable with our new living arrangements and with each other, another significant equation introduced itself into our already complicated lives.

*   *   *   *   *

I received an unexpected call regarding The Gift Shop from a member of the board of directors of Mt. Laurel. It had been so long since my last inquiry regarding leasing the building that I had quite forgotten about it.

"Leta," he said, "this is Jack Collins calling."

I recognized the name immediately as the one with whom I had spoken previously regarding The Gift Shop.

"We were wondering if you still had an interest in The Gift Shop. It will be up for lease come January of next year. It would be a year-to-year lease, and the financial details can be discussed at a later date if, in fact, you are still interested in the place."

Not wanting to pass on the opportunity, I appealed to him for a little time to give it some thought, but assured him that I was definitely interested. He said he felt that that was only fair and he would call me in a week or two.

When Jon came home from work that evening, I told him about the call. We spent many hours discussing the pros and cons of going into business together. The most bothersome aspect of leasing the building was what we would do with it. After all, there was no heat and insulation in the building. It was suited solely for a summertime business. We asked ourselves what kind of business would prove financially lucrative three months out of the year. Round one of our discussions did not produce any winners. I already had a good-paying job, and Jon was working as well. A new venture would subject us to three months of additional manpower and time . . . something to consider. It most certainly would necessitate my resigning my position as sales manager for the cable advertising company.

The subject was benched while we dealt with a much weightier personal problem. . . like how the church we attended viewed our live-in situation.

The mainstream church we attended did not practice excommunication, so we felt safe there. As a matter of fact, they proved themselves unmistakably liberal when, years later, they appointed a woman as pastor. I had no spiritual credentials with which to refute church leadership anomalies, but I personally found the appointment contrary to my beliefs and convictions.

When we first began attending church together, the church had, what I would call, a conservative pastor and unquestionably a certified moderate by today's standards. Nevertheless, to our surprise, the pastor actually courted our involvement in the church. That confused me. On one hand, I was glad we were not condemned but, on the other hand, there was little chance we would come under conviction regarding our live-in situation in that kind of setting. It was as though I was waiting for someone else—reins in hand—to coax me to repentance and subsequent obedience. Instead, a defiant "it's my business" passed "repentance" by a furlong, and I was off and running toward an uncertain finish line.

Somewhere between making the decision to lease or not lease The Gift Shop and our growing involvement in the church, Jon was invited to attend a church retreat for "men only" that was being held somewhere near Bedford, Pennsylvania. The registration necessary to attend the retreat didn't come easy for him, and yet it was as though God was prodding him to go. I encouraged him to take advantage of the opportunity because, as far as I could tell, Jon was not a Christian, and I thought it would be good exposure for him. Until his move to Pennsylvania, he had dabbled exclusively in the California occult scene. I thought that perhaps the retreat would provide an open door to questions and answers, and ultimately the truth.

It is relatively easy getting to know people you meet from day to day on a casual basis, but to get to know them personally and intimately is an entirely different kinship. I had been blessed with only a few such kinships in my life. The Witman family from Reading Junction, Bill Casset, and my friend, Maureen, the one with whom I shared all things, good and bad. There were times when I was absolutely sure I would have died had it not been for our close friendship. It was rare, and it was real . . . at least to me. That is exactly the kind of relationship I experienced with God through His son Jesus when I was sixteen years old, but I began to rely more and more on my own wisdom and pretty much operated on a shoestring faith. I felt very hypocritical recommending a spiritual diet for Jon when I was not taking any serious nourishment from God's Word myself.

Before Jon left for the church retreat, we made the decision to lease The Gift Shop and to discuss what to do with it when he returned from his weekend outing.

Jon's devotion to me was evidenced by his frequent phone calls from Bedford that weekend. But one call was different from all the rest. It was twelve o'clock midnight, as Saturday turned into Sunday, and Jon's unexpected call proclaimed that he had become a new man. With tears of happiness, he explained that he decided to trust Jesus as his Savior and was confident that he was now a member of God's family, certain that when he died he would go to Heaven. We cried in celebration of his new birth as long as Bedford was from Mt. Laurel. We did not consider at the time how his conversion might affect our relationship. I had little doubt that the two relationships were going to be at odds with each other.

When Jon returned from the retreat, the three of us hugged and kissed each other. Indeed there had been a change in Jon. But the battle had only begun.

*   *   *   *   *

One day, somewhere in the middle of the week, I came home from work, put my briefcase down, and went upstairs to change clothing. I called Luke's name, but he didn't respond. I assumed that he was outside playing. He was fourteen years old and didn't always notify me when he decided to distance himself from the cottage.

When I returned to the kitchen to prepare dinner, I noticed a note on the table. I picked it up and read the words. I no longer recall the exact words on that note, but I do remember the feeling I got when I finished reading them. Luke had asked his sister to move him and his belongings back to his father's house. My heart began to pound as I raced back up the stairs to check his bedroom. When I saw the empty closets and his collection of "stuff" completely gone, I broke down and cried until I thought I was going to die. I was devastated. I loved him; I defended him against Jon's criticism; I left Mitch in order to protect him from the same kind of harm his brothers and sister experienced, but none of those things mattered anymore. He was gone.

I grieved for months as I envisioned Luke coming under the militant discipline of his father. My only hope was that, by my not being there, most of what caused Mitch to retaliate in fits of anger had been removed. Nevertheless, I thought I was going to lose my mind. Nothing would ever be the same again. Even Jon wasn't able to fill the void of Luke's leaving. It definitely began to affect our relationship.

I cherished the times when Luke would come to visit me. He was within walking distance from my cottage, and we saw each other frequently. I never interrogated him as to why he made the decision to leave. I tried, instead, to convince myself that perhaps at his age, he needed a father more than he needed me. But I had more trouble trying to figure out why Sarah had taken the liberty of removing Luke from his home without first consulting me. Having survived the horror of her childhood, I could not imagine why she was willing to subject Luke to that same kind of mis-treatment. Somehow, she must have weighed which was more likely to negatively affect Luke's life—my living situation with Jon or Mitch's abuse—which is why I am convinced that children see things a lot differ-ently than we adults do. I was confident that Mitch would never do "boy" things like catching frogs with Luke, as Jon had done. Luke, I was sure, would end up doing the things that interested Mitch just as I had done.

I learned much later that because of Jon's love and attention toward me and mine for him, Luke felt as if he had been cut out of the family picture.

Pity the children.

* * * * *

Days turned into months, and we finally came up with an idea for our new business venture. We decided to invite local artisans to display and sell their unique quality creations in our shop. We would take a commission on each sale; plus we would buy and sell our own collectibles and antiques as well. If we had calculated correctly, our commissions would pay the major portion of the lease. We would rename the shop "Mixed Blessings," mainly because of the diversified talents and items that would be displayed for sale. We thought it would be a great way to involve the community of Laurel Lake and surrounding areas by giving them a place to market their wares.

With that decision made, we signed the necessary forms for tax and name change purposes. I was beginning to feel both the excitement and the apprehension of having our own business.

Since the contract ran from January to January of each year, we had a generous portion of time to advertise for interested artists and craftspeople. We planned to clean and paint the interior of the building and begin collecting salable items with which to supply the shop. We also talked about getting married.

After being cajoled by Jon to hasten the litigation going on between Mitch and my lawyers, and to get the inevitable divorce behind us, I contacted my attorney and told him that I did not want to wait any longer for a divorce. I expressed my opinion that enough time and opportunity had passed for any reconciliation between Mitch and myself, and in the meantime, I had heard that Mitch was planning to get the divorce himself in order to marry his friend Anna. Because of my pride, I wanted to file for divorce before he did. My attorney agreed, and he began to seriously negotiate a settlement.

The unfairness to children in a divorce goes beyond description, and is inexcusable. I found that when a marriage disintegrates, the children of that marriage pick up the same weighty baggage as many foster and adopted children do, and it can have devastating consequences. I have asked myself many times since: How could I not have seen that? Revelations of that sort only come years later as you observe the lives and the decisions of those children. Because I had a close relationship with my children, the time came when they told me that nothing ever affected them more than when their parents divorced, even if the reason for divorce was a valid one.

After twenty-three years of marriage, and in spite of how bad some of those years were, I still wrestle with whether or not it was all worth it, especially when I look into the eyes and lives of my children.

*   *   *   *   *

Twice were the times I found myself staring at a judge as he presented me with financial compensation . . . the second being more heartrending.

Mitch brought the children to court to testify against me on his behalf. When I saw them walk into the courtroom, my heart sank. No matter what happened between the two of us, I would never have subjected our children to that kind of inquisition.

His lawyer flung insults at me concerning how I had cared for the children and accused me of not being a good housekeeper or mother. I was heartbroken as I sat listening to the false accusations being made. I remember watching the court stenographer, with whom I was acquainted, as his fingers moved speedily over the keys of his recorder as I tried to remove myself from the emotional scene. Now and then I would lean over and whisper in the ear of my attorney and vehemently deny the things that were being said. When Sarah was called to the stand to testify against me, she surprised everyone by telling the truth, contradicting all of the accusations that had been brought against me. I broke down and cried. I left the courtroom that day vowing that I would never return. And I didn't.

I was insistent when I told my attorney that I never wanted to appear in court again, no matter what happened. I also tied his hands when I wouldn't allow him to subpoena any of Mitch's financial records. He was forced to negotiate out of weakness. My reasoning, which my attorney found unreasonable, was simply—I pitied Mitch.

Mitch had grown up in near poverty circumstances as a child, and after a great deal of hard work and dedication (and I'd like to think with some help from me), he had become a successful businessman. He had fought hard for my freedom as a member of the armed forces, and I didn't want him to ever suffer financially again, and certainly not because of me. That was quite opposite to the "sock it to him" approach most often advised in cases such as ours, and my attorney let me know it.

Finally, an agreement was reached between our lawyers and we signed the divorce papers. Mitch never spoke to me during the entire time of litigation, which to me was a strong indicator that he considered me as good as dead.

*   *   *   *   *

Jon and I had already begun our lives together. Over the following busy filled months, we thought a lot about our new shop, and we continued to discuss marriage. However, certain developments were about to turn those plans sideways.

We worked hard all winter preparing for the opening our new business. We had more interested artists than our small shop could hold. We were so pleased with how things had progressed that we were completely oblivious to the tragic events soon to befall us.

The following year, on Memorial Day, we announced the grand opening of Mixed Blessings. A "by invitation only" mailing went out to friends and acquaintances to attend a wine, cheese, and dessert Grand Opening Celebration. It was an exciting time—marred only by Luke's leaving.

*   *   *   *   *

I resigned my job, which was not entirely due to the opening of our new business. It stemmed instead from my total abhorrence with having to sell advertising on MTV, which was and still is, in my opinion, a very real detriment to the health of every mind, especially the minds of children.

I devoted most of my newly coveted time working at Mixed Blessings, determined to make it a success.

Just when things seemed to be going in the right direction, I got a call from my dad in Bucherville, his voice indicating great concern. He said he suspected something was wrong with my mother, that she didn't seem to be breathing normally. I asked him if he had called the doctor; he said that he hadn't. With suppressed anger, I suggested he call our family physician and that I would be there as soon as I could find someone to take care of the shop. Unable to do so, I locked the doors of the shop and hung out a sign that read: "Be back later, family emergency!" I then called Jon at his office and told him what had happened.

When I arrived at my parents' home, I realized that my mother was very ill. The doctor had just arrived and had already begun putting my mother through some tests. He had instructed her to walk across the room, which she was unable to do because she had run out of breath after taking only several steps. He advised having her admitted to the hospital right away.

At the doctor's request, the ambulance arrived minus the customary sirens, and I climbed into the ambulance to accompany my mother to the hospital. Jon arrived later that night with my dad.

Mother was in her eighties and any hope of her surviving any kind of heart operation was unrealistic. My father was asked that night to make the infamous decision "whether or not to use heroics to keep my mother alive" or to simply allow her to die peacefully. My dad couldn't make that decision and he asked me if I would make it for him.

I visited a long time with my mother that night. I held a glass of water to her mouth and guided the straw to her dry, parched mouth. Jon came into the room now and then and put his arm around me, trying to provide the comfort that he knew I needed at the time, but mostly he concentrated on my dad who was having a great deal of trouble accepting the fact that his wife was in the hospital—something that meant only one thing to him; she was never going home to Bucherville again.

It was obvious that Mother was in great distress. She looked at me, barely able to claim enough breath to say, "Leta, I want to go home. The Lord is waiting for me." My eyes filled with tears, yet I didn't want her to see the hopelessness of her condition in my face.

I spoke at length with my dad regarding my mother's wish to go home to be with the Lord. He said, "Well then, tell them we've decided not to try and keep her alive with machines." And so the decision was made. Yet, somehow I believed that Daddy held out a portion of hope for Mother's recovery, and perhaps even blamed me for her death.

We left the hospital on the advice of the doctors, who had assured us that it was highly unlikely that she would die during the night.

... TWENTY-FIVE ...

An old black phone, its receiver rubbed dull from years of use, sat quietly on the shelf the way it did every day since Mixed Blessings opened its doors for business. The only difference was that, during the days following my mother's hospitalization, I watched and waited for it to ring, hoping to hear news of my mother's condition. Most of the calls turned out to be the typical "how late are you open tonight?" inquiries that came at least a half-dozen times a day.

Because of the number of tourists visiting Laurel Lake, and due to Mixed Blessings' central location, we were quite frequently called upon to provide directions to one place or another, and to share the history of Laurel Lake with information seekers. Mixed Blessings functioned more as the Laurel Lake Tourist Bureau than a gift shop at times; therefore, my mind was not always on the telephone or the news that it might bring.

The black phone may as well have been red, like the one I always pictured sitting on the desk of the President of the United States, for the message it was about to deliver.

"Hold, please, for a call from Germany," an overseas operator said as I held the receiver tightly in my hand. My chest tightened as I waited for Thomas's voice, thinking that perhaps he was in some kind of danger again. Instead, an Army doctor was urging me to make arrangements to fly to Germany as soon as possible to be by the side of my son who had been stricken with a rare, and "possibly" fatal, disease.

With two family members conceivably facing death, I had a very difficult decision to make: go to Germany to be with my son, or remain at home by my mother's side. I was grateful to have Jon's love and support during those agonizing days, although it didn't make my decision any easier.

After speaking with the doctors in Germany again that evening, and after they persuaded me that Thomas was getting the best possible care, I went to see my mother. I held her hand while she pleaded with God to take her home to be with Him. I didn't tell her about Thomas; I knew she would have scolded me for not leaving immediately to be with him. I looked long and hard into my mother's face, and I somehow knew that was going to be our last time together.

Jon's arms were around me. We left the hospital that night crying for my mother and my son. Heartbroken and exhausted, I spoke to God.

"If it's my mother's time, then please take her home, Lord, but please spare the life of my son Thomas. He is so young. Please make a way for me to get to Germany before anything happens to him. Thank you, Lord."

The absence of communication between Mitch and me, in spite of his being informed of our son's illness, continued.

As I prepared to renew my passport to be with my son, the doctor called from Germany for the third time. He said they were considering flying Thomas back to the United States to Walter Reed Hospital as soon as he was physically able to withstand the flight. They said that I was to wait until I heard from them again before making my final departure plans.

The following morning I received word that my mother had expired during the night, and they asked me to come to the hospital and view her body. Jon agreed to accompany me to the hospital.

As we stood by my mother's bed, the nurse turned down the sheet, and we looked into the face of an angel. She had left her temporary residence and had moved into her permanent heavenly home. I felt a mixture of joy and sadness.

As Jon and I rode the elevator to the main floor of the hospital that morning, he held me close as I grieved over the loss of my dear mother.

It happened exactly as my dad said it would: "Now that she's in the hospital, she won't ever go home again." He had been right; she would never be going home again—at least not to Bucherville.

Ten miles separated us from the hardest part of my mother's death—telling my dad that his wife had passed away. We used the traveling distance to discuss exactly how we were going to break the news to him. He had always counted on preceding his wife in death; he spoke of it many times, and I knew he would be angry and bitter when things hadn't worked out as he planned.

There was also the news about Thomas. We decided not to tell my dad about his illness.

Jon steered the car into my parents' driveway . . . behind my mother's car. I sat aching from the thought of never seeing her behind the wheel of her little foreign car again. At once I realized that I had not spent nearly enough time with her. *We should have had lunch together at least once a week, and I should have told her that I loved her more*, I told myself. Even though she had been a good foster mother to me, I had always yearned to have a close relationship with my birth mother; but in the end, Grace Carpenter was the one I called "Mother."

What I learned through losing my mother, and the precious moments I missed spending with her, were lessons I could not teach my children. They had lives of their own, and they would have their own regrets one day; I could not make my regrets theirs. I decided right then and there to enjoy every moment with my children, no matter how frequent or infrequent those times were, and I prayed that they would never have to grieve over wasted time as I had done.

*   *   *   *   *

Daddy was sitting at the kitchen table with the day's newspaper spread out before him, his hands holding each side as he brought the pages closer to his eyes. He looked up, as if only to acknowledge an interruption. Then he looked at my face. "Oh no," he said, as he let the newspaper fall back on to the table. "Mother is all right, isn't she?" he pleaded, as though I could change the answer he was about to hear.

"Yes, Daddy," I replied, "in a way you could say she is all right. She has gone home to be with the Lord. She is well again."

My words, however, did not stem the flow of tears, anger, and outright denial, demonstrated by the pounding of his fists on the table over and over again. The strong worn hands that once lifted heavy railroad ties could not hold the weight of his own grieving heart. *If only I could put my arms around him and comfort him*, I thought, but we didn't have that kind of parent-child relationship. I could only sit beside him and wait; I wondered about his regrets.

As expected, he angrily berated himself for not having died first. I knew he would never forgive himself for that . . . and I don't believe he ever did. The bitter aftermath of grief grew with each succeeding day.

Despite disdain for me, which became increasingly evident as Jon and I helped with my mother's funeral arrangements, I tried to remain patient and kind, attributing his behavior to the pain of losing his life-long partner.

My dad suddenly began to distrust Jon, the one person whom I depended on to help me get through my mother's death. He accused Jon of trying to steal his money, naming me as an accomplice. Nothing could have been further from the truth. I never once asked my foster parents for money; I never took a penny from them while I was at home, except for my automobile loan, and that I paid back in full. I even felt guilty accepting the meager weekly allowance I received as a young teenager. Jon was stunned at Daddy's accusations, but we again credited his behavior to his grieving state of mind.

Several months after my mother's death and my dad's refusal to allow me to help him with household chores, assist him in paying bills, or to balance his checkbook, he decided to put an ad in the paper for a live-in companion. When he told me about it, I almost yelled out loud: "You're eighty years old; you expect to find a companion from a newspaper ad!" Much to my surprise, he received numerous responses. He began sorting them out, one by one, until he settled on a lady quite a few years younger than he was. Shortly after she moved in with him, my dad put his home, and most of his possessions, up for sale, and then joined his new companion in her lovely townhouse in Lancaster County. Within months, the two of them were united in marriage.

I grew suspicious the moment I learned that my dad and his new wife were living off of my dad's railroad pension and his social security checks. The executives of my stepmother's bank were making frequent visits to their townhouse, bringing them flowers, and taking them out to lunch. I was quite certain that my dad's money didn't warrant that kind of attention!

My stepmother, whom I never got to know very well, meant the world to my dad. Because his eyesight had grown considerably worse over the years, he depended on his new wife more and more. I withheld interrogating my dad about the suspicions I had, and I refrained from accusing my stepmother of any kind of financial improprieties or selfish motives regarding their marriage arrangement, but for some reason, I felt my dad had been hoodwinked.

Not many years later, my stepmother became seriously ill and died. I visited her while she was in the hospital, but only out of courtesy to my dad. When her Last Will and Testament was read, she had left five thousand dollars to my dad and a considerable fortune (which took up nearly a quarter of a page in a local newspaper) to assorted churches and secular organizations. She had been worth millions, and my dad's modest income and savings had nearly been depleted. If that was his payback, I dreaded thinking what mine might be.

Fortunately for my dad, his thinking was no longer clear, and he never knew just how much he had been used. And if he had known, I believe he would have defended his wife to the end. It wasn't long before he lost the will to live, and his health quickly deteriorated. Unfortunately he became more and more antagonistic towards me.

As time passed, so did my plans to refute my stepmother's will, particularly after I learned that my dad had signed a prenuptial agreement: "A prenuptial agreement, at age eighty," I exclaimed to myself. "That is crazy!" I am confident that my dad didn't know he married a very wealthy woman. I also don't believe he knew what he signed when he affixed his signature to a prenuptial agreement; he just wasn't cognizant of those kinds of things. I am certain, however, that his wife's bankers knew everything.

Shortly thereafter, my dad moved into a very exclusive retirement village where he and his wife had previously arranged to live shortly before she died. He said that is where his wife would have wanted him to live, and so that is where he lived . . . and died.

His last days were spent in a blatant show of contempt for me. He told me that he never considered me as his daughter, that he didn't trust me, and that he regretted ever taking me into his home. The things I thought would give him pleasure while living alone in his small room at the retirement home, he instead found distasteful—and mostly because they came from me.

While wanting desperately to believe that Daddy never meant the cruel words he said to me, I nevertheless took them to heart, adding one more rejection to the story of my life.

*   *   *   *   *

I had to start thinking about Thomas.

Three days after we buried my mother, an Army representative contacted me and informed me that Thomas was being flown home to the States for further treatment.

Each time Thomas talked to me from his hospital bed in Walter Reed, he assured me that he was improving and that I shouldn't drive all the way to Washington to see him. He understood that I had just gone through losing my mother (his grandmother), and I thought it was just his way of trying to make it easier on me. But when a considerable amount of time passed, and he still hadn't come home, I began to wonder why he wasn't being discharged, and also why he insisted on my not visiting him. I began to suspect he was withholding something from me.

As I was making plans to travel to Washington, despite his insistence to the contrary, he arrived home . . . but not to my house. Instead, he chose his father's home in which to recuperate.

When I finally got to see my son, I nearly fainted. His skin hung loose on his bones, and the once muscular young man I knew and loved had vanished. I knew then why he hadn't wanted me to visit him. He needed assistance to walk, and he looked frail and helpless. I was sure they had sent him home to die. The disease was rare, crippling, and potentially fatal, the doctors had said.

Relapses were to be an expected part of Thomas's disease and recovery. For several months he would gain weight and actually appear healthy. Then, suddenly, and without warning, he would relapse and nearly die. It was during one such relapse that I came in contact with Mitch's wife for the first time.

The phone rang at my gift shop one afternoon, and Mitch's wife told me she thought I had better come over to their house right away that Thomas was very sick. Her voice gave every indication that the request was extremely urgent.

I contacted the restaurant across the street from Mixed Blessings and told them about the call. One of the owners came to my shop immediately and said she would take over for me and that I should go and be with my son.

As I entered the all too familiar house, the one I helped design, memories met me at every corner. The new Mrs. Brogan escorted me upstairs and into the bedroom where Thomas was lying. I had only to look into my son's eyes to realize how very ill he was. I thought the moments we spent together that day were going to be the last ones.

It was time to get serious with God. I sat by Thomas's bed mopping his brow and holding his hand . . . praying that God wouldn't take His anger out on Thomas for the choices I made. I blamed myself for Thomas's illness.

It occurred to me then that a doctor had not been summoned to Mitch's home, nor had Thomas been rushed to the hospital. It only confirmed my belief that he had been sent home to die.

While siting by Thomas's bed, between prayers, I couldn't help wonder why he chose to spend his last days in Mitch's home rather than in mine. Had I been wrong in wanting to distance the children and myself from their father's cruelty? Was an intact family unit that important to the children after all, despite everything we'd been through? I had so many questions . . . and no answers. Yet, now I was called upon to pray for my son whom I wasn't even sure loved me anymore.

God heard my prayers. Several days later, Thomas began to regain his strength, and with it, a determination to begin a rigorous exercise program to help rebuild the muscle mass he had lost and to hasten his complete recovery. He continued to suffer relapses—some very serious—but not potentially life threatening, as was the case during that particular occurrence.

God put a renewed hunger in Thomas's heart for spiritual knowl-edge following his illness. He eventually opened his own business called "The Park Avenue Gym." There he taught strength-training techniques to young athletes, and openly shared the Word of God with them. His survival was just one of God's miracles in the life of our family.

*   *   *   *   *

Sarah and her husband decided it was time to start their family, but things didn't quite turn out as they had hoped. Sarah would tell you today, just as I have shared concerning my own life, that some outcomes are based on our own disobedience.

On a number of occasions, we anxiously awaited the results of pregnancy tests. Several times, the results were positive, and we all shared in the excitement, only to have the pregnancies declared ectopic, and subsequently life threatening to Sarah. Although Sarah never gave birth to a child, God was gracious; He spared Sarah's life numerous times.

It was not enough that I nearly lost my life as a teenager, but I came close to losing a son and a daughter as well, yet the message God was trying to send me remained unopened and unread. I remained indifferent to God's goodness. "What's it going to take," God must have been asking each time a tragedy took place in our family.

After realizing that they could not have children of their own, Sarah and her husband adopted two special-needs children—a baby boy from Korea and a small, fragile girl from Cambodia—children from what seemed like another world and who have meant "all the world" to me.

Benjamin became a Washington, D.C., resident in the meantime, surviving on a major airline income, and making choices contrary to what I believe God had in mind for his life . . . and, which I am convinced resulted from not having a loving, caring father in his life. Luke, on the other hand, was just entering college at the University of Maryland, where he managed to support himself and his education with part-time jobs at the University. Luke eventually married and became a public relations representative for a major Japanese automobile company.

Mitch's second wife had several daughters from her first marriage, and Mitch quickly made them his surrogate offspring. He paid much more attention to them than he did to his own children. He was instrumental in grooming one of his stepdaughters (he never adopted them) to be the "paratrooper-son" he never had. She was the centerfold in his life . . . the son Mitch had always wanted. But that still didn't discourage his own sons from a continued relationship with him. I saw how much they yearned to win their dad's affection, but all his love was being meted out on his stepdaughters.

All of our children, with the exception of Sarah, continued to have a fairly amicable relationship with their father and his wife, but for some reason, Mitch's wife was not friendly toward Sarah and her adopted children; and they, in turn, were very sensitive to those feelings. Frequently, they were excluded from family gatherings and were discouraged from visiting the family home. It was during those times that I half expected Sarah's brothers to decline their invitations as well, if for no other reason than to show support and love for their sister; however, circumstances proved otherwise. I believe it was extremely difficult for them to turn their backs on their father's affluent lifestyle and prestigious name and stand against the injustices by Mitch and his wife towards Sarah and her family. Sarah realized that, but it didn't make it any easier for her to accept.

There was a burning desire in my heart to continue our holiday family gatherings, in hopes of keeping our family together. But the stronger my desire, the more I saw evidence of division, either by miles, circumstances, or both. I tried so hard to hold us together, but when I failed, I blamed myself. That burden, added to the baggage I was already carrying, had me teetering on the edge of destruction. Maureen warned me that the stress of the situation would eventually affect my health, but I chose not to heed her warning.

*   *   *   *   *

Sarah and her family chose to live very modestly—a lesson I could have learned from them. She had little patience with those of us that lived above . . . or even within . . . our means. She possessed a heart for the poor, the wretched, and the lame . . . and every animal that walked on the earth. She reached out to those that I could never touch—people with open sores on their bodies—the unlovely. But people caught up in the love of money and power were a much harder lot for her to embrace. However, I believe she eventually came to realize that God loves them too, and that they need love and prayers just as much as those who are physically and financially encumbered . . . if not more. And when you consider the parable in the Bible about how hard it is for the rich man to enter Heaven . . . I'm sure of it.

*   *   *   *   *

After the loss of my mother, the near fatal illness of my son, and thirty-some pounds, several of my children tried to talk me out of marrying Jon. Though they liked him, they didn't think he would make a good husband for me. But they assured me that, if Jon and I decided to marry anyway, they would give us their full support and love us through it. With that in the back of my mind, it became increasingly difficult for me to reconcile my feelings with the opinions of others, and so, for the time being, I tabled my plans to marry Jon.

A night didn't go by, as we stood wrapping antiques and collectibles for our customers at Mixed Blessings, that Jon wouldn't ask, "Well, what do you think, should we get married or not?" My answer was "yes" one minute, and "no" the next.

One evening when I was working at the shop alone, an attractive young woman came in and asked where my son was. Not knowing which one of my sons she was referring to, I asked, "Which one?"

"The one who usually works with you here in the shop, the one with the dark hair and mustache," she replied, sounding excited.

When I realized she was referring to Jon, my fiancé, I was very upset.

"He isn't my son, young lady," I sarcastically replied. "He is my boyfriend!"

She apologized twice; I forgave her zero.

It was the beginning of some real soul-searching on my part.

*   *   *   *   *

Having gone from attending a liberal-thinking church to a very conservative Bible church, we were unsure where the church stood on the subject of divorce and remarriage; but we were willing to meet with the pastor to find out. Even though I was a pretty conservative-minded Christian, my life did not exemplify the name. The church did not seem to have programs that ministered to divorced and single people . . . and those of us that fit that description felt like second-class citizens most of the time.

I couldn't believe a loving God would forbid me, a divorcee, to remarry (under certain circumstances), and then take the repentant murderer or adulterer under His wings and give them a second chance in life. But for years I sat under biblical teaching that suggested otherwise. Consequently, I debated relentlessly with God on the subject. *Oh sure*, I told myself, *I could go church shopping and eventually find a church that tickled my ears and told me what I wanted to hear*, but that would never have satisfied me. I wanted to know exactly what God had to say on the subject. But the more I researched the subject, the more confused I became. I decided that, apart from a heart conviction to the contrary, I would remain "as is"—a broken vessel, hoping that I was, in some small way, still useful to God.

*   *   *   *   *

It was a warm summer evening when Pastor Aaron came to sit on our front porch, and where Jon and I planned to introduce a list of weak cohabiting excuses to ward off the predicted condemnation. Instead, Pastor Aaron turned out to be hospitable and sympathetic. He explained that, on the subject of divorce and remarriage, left to "the flesh" (doing what he would by nature do), as he put it, he would have married us in a minute. But, in all good conscience, he said he would not be able to accommodate our marriage plans; he had to be true to his faith (according to his understanding and convictions from the Word of God) is how he explained it. "Not that you wouldn't be accepted into the fold if you decided to get married elsewhere and come back to the church," he assured us, "but you would be forever limited in your involvement in certain areas of the church."

We considered the pastor's visit informative and disappointing. It left us stranded between right and wrong . . . but we certainly knew where Pastor Aaron stood on the subject.

Not long after our meeting with Pastor Aaron, we invited two of our friends to have dinner with us in our home. Jon happened to work with his friend Paul at Envirotech, Inc., in Minden, and I had gotten to know Paul's wife Linda through attending the same church. We seldom entertained folks from the church, simply because we knew how uncomfortable it would be for them, but Paul and Linda seemed to be open to a close friendship, as well as did Shelly and Bernie, another couple whom we came to regard as close friends. Those four people, I know now, hated our sin, but they demonstrated the love of Jesus through compassion and friendship as they prayed and loved us to Jesus.

Paul and Jon decided to take a walk after dinner, while Linda and I sat on the sofa having coffee. I told her about our visit with Pastor Aaron, which gave her a window of opportunity to share what was on her heart. She asked me if I had ever considered asking Jon to move out and to find a place of his own. She felt that putting some distance and time between us would allow God to work in our lives individually. Perhaps then we would be in a better position to talk about marriage. "At least," she reminded me, "you would not be living in sin and keeping the blessings of God from touching your lives." She strongly suggested that my decision should not be based on what Jon wanted, but on what God wanted. I did not tell Linda at the time, but I had no intention of following her suggestion.

Unknown to us, Linda and Paul and dozens of others had begun praying for us to come under conviction regarding our live-in situation, and I can tell you this, their prayers were effective.

From that moment on, I had little peace about how I was living. Then God sent a messenger to my door.

The knock was timid, but persistent. A little boy I did not recognize stood on the other side of the screened-in door. His small innocent face pressed against the dusty mesh screen, and his wide eyes looked up into mine as he asked, "Lady, what am I supposed to call you? Are you Mrs. Matthews or are you Mrs. Brogan, or what?"

The example I was leaving for all the neighborhood children, and to my own children, stared back at me through those two small piercing eyes. I did not know how to answer this small tot, but I didn't want him to think badly of me, and so I answered, "You may call me Mrs. Matthews."

I lied. I was not Mrs. Matthews.

As the little boy walked down the porch steps, I could hear a voice inside of me saying, "You liar, you hypocrite!"

... TWENTY-SIX ...

Life apart from Jon . . . I just couldn't imagine it! In the five years we spent living together, he had become my best friend, mentor, companion, business partner, and my lover. He was the most affectionate, attentive, and passionate respondent of love I had ever known. Sadly, I failed to consider the cost of such a relationship.

With each passing day, the counterfeit peace I had settled for began to slip away. Then one evening as I stood talking to Jon as he sat on a stool behind the counter in our shop, his face turned intensely serious and he asked, "We aren't getting married, are we?"

"No, Jon, I don't think so," I replied.

A cloud of darkness settled in.

Even though my answer surprised me, it rang with certainty . . . without sadness or apologies. I just didn't recall organizing the words in my mind for the reply. I certainly hadn't expected the question.

The subject didn't come up again until we closed the shop that night and had gone home for the evening. With an unfamiliar calm, I explained to Jon that I wanted to get right with God, that the way we were living was entirely wrong. I sincerely believed that God would bless our relationship if we began doing things His way.

Jon questioned the feasibility of renting a place in Laurel Lake that would enable him to move out of my home and, at the same time, remain close to our business and to me (a viable excuse for inaction). There were only a few rental cottages available, and he felt the cost of any one of them was prohibitive for him at the time. What we hadn't considered was the part God had in the plan—and so the time we spent on the problem turned out to be quite unnecessary.

It was a miracle! Exactly one day later, the phone rang. It was a friend of ours looking for someone to whom they could rent their cottage . . . and it was just across the road from where my cottage was located. We were both astonished at how quickly God provided a place for Jon to live. I chose to give God the credit, believing that He had already begun to honor our decision to live differently.

The move did not take place without tears and pain, but the truth of the matter was . . . we had not really ended our relationship, merely our intimacy.

We agreed to maintain a wholesome friendship, one that would please God, and one that would perhaps eventually lead to an honorable marriage. By putting time, and a "short" distance between us (as Linda had put it), God would now have time to gain His rightful place in our lives.

The first night I spent without Jon's arms around me, I turned to God in tears. I got down on my knees and asked Him to forgive me for all the disgrace I had brought on Him through my disobedience and selfishness, and for the poor example I had been to others. I had no doubt that repentance had to begin with me. If I expected God to forgive me, then I would have to make a special effort to forgive others.

The following day I sat down and wrote a letter to Mitch asking him to forgive me for anything I may have done to cause his outbursts of anger and abuse toward the children and myself. I told him that I forgave him for all the things he did to us. I expressed a sincere desire to see him live the rest of his life contented and happy with his second wife, his stepchildren, and our own children. I encouraged him to talk to God as I had done, in a spirit of repentance, knowing full well that only God was able to move his heart in that direction. In my mind, and as I was writing the letter, I prayed that Mitch would contact each of the children and apologize to them for treating them as he had. But that, too, was something I could not control, so I sealed, stamped, and dropped the letter into the mailbox.

Several days later I received a phone call from Mitch. I was excited. For him to call me was an encouraging sign, I thought.

"I just wanted you to know that I received your letter, and I forgive you. But, quite frankly," he continued, "I never really loved you as I should have; that's why I treated you the way I did."

I thanked him for being truthful, and with that our phone conversation ended. I had done what God wanted me to do. Mitch never asked me to forgive him, and that left an open wound in my heart for years to come. We never spoke to one another at length again.

* * * * *

If ever there was a feeling of complete rejection, that was it. Going from a foster kid with ugly white hair and numerous unkind nicknames, to a woman whose husband never really loved her, took its toll on any remaining self-esteem I had left. I felt like a chocolate Easter Bunny—hollow inside.

*   *   *   *   *

Mitch continued to do battle with outbursts of temper, according to reports from friends and family, but I do believe he loved and treated his second wife and stepchildren better than he did his own children and me. Hard-hearted attitudes and unrelenting opinions were as much a part of his life as breathing. He proved to be a good friend to some, but above all, he remained true to the 101st Airborne. He was an exemplary Screaming Eagle, something that earned his full and complete loyalty; after all, that was what was nearest and dearest to his heart.

*   *   *   *   *

The separation that took place between Jon and me, I now believe, was engineered by God, and it was filled with times of testing. One such test happened to be our need to be close to one another. After so many years of intimacy, it was our greatest challenge.

I especially recall a vacation we decided to take to the Eastern Shore after we closed Mixed Blessings for the season. We rented the same condominium where we had spent a number of vacation weeks enjoying sin for a season. This time, however, we planned on spending a week just kicking back and enjoying the cool ocean breeze from our fifth-floor patio overlooking the magnificent Atlantic Ocean far from the boardwalk hubbub . . . and Laurel Lake. We made no provisions for the flesh, or so we thought.

It was during one of those star-filled ocean nights that we came to recognize our weakness, apart from super-human intervention; we were called upon to engage every weapon in our spiritual arsenal to fight the battle of self-indulgence. We decided never to put ourselves in that kind of compromising position again. Talk about sacrifice and cross bearing— obedience most certainly costs something, but at the same time, it buys an abundance of peace of mind.

We returned home questioning our commitment to live apart. We both desired purity in our lives, and yet it was so hard to do, and soon we were talking about marriage again. Meanwhile, God redirected our thoughts and our attentions on an entirely different matter.

*   *   *   *   *

As I mentioned previously, I had the good fortune of having a wonderful family physician during those days. He was thorough and unrelenting when it came to yearly physicals. He was always chiding me about missing an examination, which he claimed might very well detect a disease in its early stages, preventing further invasion of the body. He himself had lost a wife to cancer, and he was adamant about regular mammograms. As a result, I never missed my appointment, which took place in April of every year. I came to remember the date each year by telling myself that I would be a fool . . . an April fool, if I did not have the examination. I believe I dreaded part of that physical examination more than Hell itself . . . THE MAMMOGRAM! To prepare for it, I would tell myself it was a whole lot better than having my head cut off, which concurrently gave rise to a debate with myself on the truth of that reminder.

Those were my exact thoughts as the wicked nurse of the mammogram machine smiled and ordered me to hold my breath as she closed the vice over my body. *Would that I had one moment and a baseball bat alone with that machine and its operator!* I thought to myself each time I had to endure that torture. But any number of evil thoughts didn't neutralize the pain of that examination.

Afterwards, I left the hospital performing my yearly mammogram cheer. With my hand curled into a fist, I raised my knee above my waist and brought my fist down by my waist and yelled, "YES!" as though I had scored a point for some major league football team. It was over for another year!

Little did I know that several days later I would receive news that a lump was discovered on my right breast and that a biopsy would be required to determine whether it was cancerous or simply a benign tumor.

That night, Jon and I sat on the sofa in my home, alone and quiet, as though something strange had invaded our space. With his arm around me, he attempted to reassure me that he would be there for me regardless of the outcome, but that he was confident it would not be cancer. I was equally certain that the lump would be diagnosed as benign. After all, I felt great; I had no symptoms indicating any health problems. In fact, I maintained an exercise program that generally included three to five miles of jogging every day. I repeatedly told myself that the results of the biopsy would be negative.

Following the biopsy report, we sat on the sofa again, tearfully contemplating our future. The biopsy had read positive for cancer.

The impact of the news registered way off the anxiety Richter scale. I was devastated. I wouldn't say I was defeated, but I most certainly was in a state of disbelief. At the same time, I realized that there were some things I could not control, and cancer was one of them. Not that my rich food inheritance or my predisposition of genes hadn't played a part in the cause and effect of my diagnosis, but it made little difference then, as I joined many other women in the battle for life. I had no doubt that Jon meant what he said about being there for me regardless of the outcome. But for some reason, it was the "after that" that concerned me.

Jon and I sat in a small room in the surgeon's office listening to treatment alternatives. The doctor said he considered me a perfect candidate for a lumpectomy. That meant they would remove the lump and a small portion of the surrounding area. They would also test numerous lymph glands while under sedation to determine if the cancer had spread beyond its primary location. If the cancer hadn't spread to the glands, then the prognosis would be considered very good; otherwise, I stood a very good chance of having to undergo a radical mastectomy. After giving it much consideration, and taking all the doctor had said into consideration, I opted for the lumpectomy followed by six weeks of daily radiation. The cancer had not spread to any of the lymph glands. That was the good news.

The doctor spoke directly to Jon, saying, "A very important part of cancer treatment is having a loved one there for the patient during the entire recovery period, someone who would give support, encouragement, and love." Jon answered that his intentions were to do exactly that. The doctor appeared satisfied. As he was confirming a surgery date, I prayed for God to confirm His presence in all that was taking place. I asked Him to use what I was going through as an avenue of encouragement for others. He didn't disappoint me.

My daughter and her newly adopted son, my first grandchild, arranged to fly home to be with me after the surgery. That was one of the great comforts during my post-operative days. True to his word, Jon also remained by my side.

The prognosis was excellent . . . a ninety-five percent chance of full recovery. Nevertheless, as a precautionary measure, many of the glands had to be removed.

It was a precious time in my life, because I had to rely on God to get me through that difficult time. I can honestly say I entered the operating room with a smile. God provided an abundance of grace, and some of it spilled over onto the life of another young woman.

At the request of the surgeon and his staff, I was asked to speak to a young woman who was facing the same kind of operation, only she was certain she was going to die and was very fearful of the operation. They had marveled at my attitude (which, of course, I explained was not mine at all, but God working in me) and thought perhaps I might be an encouragement to this young woman named Betty. I agreed to meet with her right before she went into surgery.

It would have been impossible for me to give encouragement to Betty without mentioning the part God played in my positive attitude regarding my cancer diagnosis. As I began sharing my faith with Betty, she announced emphatically that she didn't believe in God, and admitted that if she died, she had no idea where she would go afterwards. As she spoke, I recalled the times I felt exactly the same way. I shared the good news about what Jesus had done for me and assured her that He loved and died for her as well, but she said she didn't want to get involved in that kind of stuff. She decided she just wanted to take her chances. She entered the operating room alone.

I committed myself to prayer for Betty while she was having her surgery. When she was back in the recovery room, I was there to meet her. She seemed surprised to see me, but she took my hand and I prayed and thanked God that she had come through the surgery, and that she had not died as she so fearfully expected. "Had you died," I asked her, "would you have opened your eyes and gazed into the face and arms of a loving God, or would you have tumbled into a deep dark abyss?" She said she didn't know, but that she now wanted to know. I shared with her how I had made a decision to trust Jesus, and yet had lived contrary to the way He wanted me to live, and that I had missed out on years of peace and happiness because I wanted to do things my way. She asked me to pray with her and, right then and there, on her hospital bed, Betty asked Jesus into her heart and told Him that she trusted Him as her Savior.

I left the hospital on cloud nine. The angels surely must have been rejoicing over Betty's decision, I thought . . . and more amazingly, God had been able to use me, one of His badly broken vessels. It was a very special spiritual moment in my life.

During my course of treatment, Jon moved into a new apartment south of Laurel Lake. The owners of his rental cottage decided to move back into the area, which made it necessary for Jon to find another place to live. His new apartment was very nice, convenient to the shop, and to me. Maureen made curtains for Jon's windows and helped me arrange the furniture in an attempt to make it feel like home for him. I found out later that Maureen was not at all certain during those decorative moments that Jon and I would continue our relationship. She was positive Jon loved me because, as she said, "Whenever Jon and you have a serious misunderstanding, he visits me and agonizes over how much he loves you, but he also recognizes some serious differences between the two of you." Nevertheless, she didn't discourage my seeing Jon; instead, she tried to persuade me to have Jon's name removed from the Mixed Blessings lease.

One evening while Jon and I were discussing the future of Mixed Blessings, I brought up the subject of the lease. I suggested that perhaps, since we had severed our intimate relationship, and we weren't at all certain where our lives were going, that we should review the shop lease and consider putting the lease in my name, giving our "new lease" on life more credence. Since Mixed Blessings had been my idea and my dream in the first place, putting it in my name seemed the only fair thing to do.

We began to talk less and less about marriage and, like Maureen, I was beginning to evoke some misgivings of my own. I was more than a little surprised when Jon didn't protest my suggestion to have his name removed from the Mixed Blessings lease. The only concern he expressed was to be compensated financially for the change, which meant that he expected to buy out his half of the business. We arrived at an amount wholly fair to me, and I announced that it was as good as settled. But I remained unsettled concerning why he had not protested the proposal. Shortly thereafter, the reason became unbearably clear.

After several weeks of operating the shop on my own, with the help of a part-time employee, Jon walked into the shop and asked me for the phone number of my friend who owned the condominium where we had spent many of our vacations. When I asked why he wanted my friend's number, he sheepishly explained that he had a friend who was thinking about taking her vacation at the beach, and he thought that perhaps my friend would be willing to rent the condominium to her. That sent up an alarm louder than the Three Mile Island sirens announcing an accidental escape of potentially dangerous nuclear radiation into the air. Reluctantly, I produced the telephone number. My immediate plan was to call my friend the following day and find out if Jon, or his female friend, had rented the condo.

Jon did not come to the cottage that night, contrary to his usual routine. It made me all the more suspicious about his request for my friend's phone number. Had our moratorium on intimacy given way to another relationship between Jon and someone else, I wondered. That was highly unlikely, I thought, since Jon and I still spent the majority of our time together, except for the extra time I began spending working at the shop.

The day I was to have received my final dose of radiation, I telephoned my friend.

I cleared my throat and prepared to ask my question.

"Jane, this is Leta," I said. "I'd like to ask you something if I may."

"Sure, what is it?"

I spent the next few minutes vacillating between wanting and not wanting to know the answer to my question.

"Did Jon call you and ask to rent your condo to a friend of his for a week?"

Thinking that because she was a classmate of mine, part of the group that had been meeting ever since graduating high school, she would not withhold information from me. And so I waited.

After a lengthy pause, she offered a hesitant reply. "Yes, as a matter of fact, he did."

"Did he say he was coming with his friend?"

"Actually, if you want to know the truth, he said he was going to split the cost with some nurse he had just met."

Silence.

"Are you still there, Leta?"

"Yes, I'm here, but I'm pretty upset . . . not at you, Jane . . . but at him."

I was asking myself, *How had he been able to call "my" friend and ask to rent the same place where we had spent so much time together?* It was bad enough that he was going to take some girl with him on vacation without letting me in on his secret, but to spend it at the same place was completely heartless of him. I just couldn't believe it.

As any friend would do, Jane made an effort to appease and comfort me.

"If you want, I won't rent it to him. I can call back and cancel out."

"No," I replied, "that won't be necessary. But thanks for telling me the truth."

"Well, quite honestly," she said, "I thought it rather forward of him to do that, but then he apparently wasn't thinking how it would affect you."

"It's fine, Jane, don't worry about it," I assured her. "I'll be in touch later."

I felt like I was suffocating. *How can he do this to me?* I asked myself as I hung up the phone. *He said he would stay with me while I was getting cancer treatments.* But here we were, at the "after that" point in our relationship.

Admittedly, I suggested at some point that I thought it would be a good idea if he got on with his life, since our marriage plans seemed to be unraveling, but I didn't mean for him to be "getting it on" with someone else. That was naïve of me, of course.

If Jon wanted a family of his own, something he vehemently denied whenever the subject would come up, I most certainly could not have contributed to his plan. I had already raised a family, and it was an element in our relationship that didn't appear to be missing, as far as I could tell. But Jon obviously changed his mind and began embarking on a search for someone to help awaken those dormant parental desires. I felt abandoned and deceived.

I could not allow the day to end without confronting Jon about his proposed trip to the beach.

I arrived at his apartment unannounced. As I parked the car in his driveway, I began rehearsing the words I would say, but they were forgotten long before reaching the last step leading to his door.

It was the first time I ever felt it necessary to knock on his door before entering.

He opened the door, dressed in his usual jeans and bare feet. Compassion filled his eyes, and I knew he knew why I had come. He invited me in. Almost as though the scene had been set for some dramatic production, and the actors were now taking their place on the scene, we took our places on the floor, just like we had done so many times before when we wanted to talk about things personal. Tears raced ahead of the words I planned to say.

His arms reached out for me. Then he loosed his arms and distanced us just enough so he could look into my eyes.

"I already know what you're going to say, sweetheart," he began, "and believe me, I didn't want to hurt you, but we did decide to go on with our lives, didn't we? I mean, this isn't the first girl I've been with since that discussion."

His additional disclosure ripped through my carnal body and I thought I was going to die. I thought we had only discussed but hadn't agreed on going our separate ways.

"But I love you, Jon," I cried.

I believed that love could conquer everything. It was for love that I lived, and quite possibly the same reason I felt I was going to die.

"Sweetheart, I haven't stopped loving you," he said with the gentleness of a friend, "but I know now that I should never have encouraged our relationship in the first place. It has taken me years to realize that, but for whatever reason, I fell in love with you and I could never imagine life without you. I came to depend on you so much . . . too much. There will always be a part of me that belongs to you and you to me. We have been through so much together that it would be impossible to forget the years we have spent together. But my love for you is different now."

He didn't have to say any more. As a woman, I knew exactly what that meant. He had fallen in love with someone else.

Our bond had grown so strong over the years that I felt as though he had just reached into my body and hand-dipped my heart right out of my chest.

I experienced a prolonged and indescribable pain as the roots of our love were being ripped from other organs of my body where love was attached. I now fully understood what the Bible meant in 1 Corinthians when it said, "Do you not know that the one who joins himself to another person (through intimacy) is one body with her?" Jon and I had joined together in intimacy, and now our flesh was being torn apart in a torturous procedure.

Marriage was God's plan to eliminate the pain of such separations, but it's a lesson few of us ever learn. I learned too late that God gave guidelines for love and marriage for my protection, not for His, and now I was reaping the consequences of following my own set of rules.

Clearly, I felt as though I was literally torn in two and that half of me was bouncing around like the bodies of chickens whose necks I had chopped off as a youngster.

As I regained my composure, Jon slowly began describing the girl he had met. She was a Christian girl, he said, a nurse and the daughter of very religious parents. She was very intelligent and considerably younger than he was. He said that he had met her at our church and had immediately become infatuated with her. He told me she was very nice, and that he thought I would like her. He said she was very understanding regarding our relationship. At the time, according to him, she understood how so many years with one person would seem like a marriage, and she had sympathy for me; he liked that she considered my feelings as well as her own.

How can Jon's new friend understand the bond of our relationship? I asked myself, seriously doubting that she could.

Then Jon promised me three things: We would continue with our plans to attend a Christian concert together; we would go to Maryland for dinner with our friends as planned; and he would take me to dinner for my birthday. At that moment, none of those things seemed to matter anymore; they were just signs of the "end times." But what it did do was provide me with an opportunity to hopefully salvage our relationship. I just knew I could keep us together somehow; the same assurance I had with regards to my family; only this time, I hoped for better results.

I left Jon's apartment that night more than distraught, but not yet defeated.

*   *   *   *   *

The night we attended the Christian concert was the most difficult of all. Steve Green, the Christian soloist, sang a song called "Friends." Jon looked at me, and our friends sitting around us looked at us. It became apparent that they had already been briefed on the situation and were feeling their own kind of pain for the two of us.

As Steve Green's words "forever friends" ended the song—and the evening—Jon's tear-filled eyes found mine, and I was thinking—*He still loves me, and I know he will not leave me.* And he was thinking, *I do love her, but not like I love Lisa.*

When the crowd dispersed and we finally left the concert hall and walked toward the car, hands that once came together easily now remained awkwardly apart. I wondered why I had sought so hard and long for the right outfit to wear that evening, the perfect perfume, and the particular care I had given to my hair and makeup—none of which appeared to have impressed Jon one bit. My face was covered in tiny ant-like paths, leading down my cheeks and neck; my makeup gathered in the tiny gutters of my face, like mud after the rain.

We drove home in contemplated silence.

Then it was October.

*   *   *   *   *

My birthday came quickly, and so did Jon's call. The interim period between the concert and my birthday was spent in long agonizing phone conversations between us. I began to sense the end of something very special . . . very wrong. All the tricks I had learned and developed over the years, with the help of my creative mind, enabling me to sell products and lengthy advertising contracts to others, were now useless in helping sell myself to Jon. I had nothing left with which to fight. I had lost a lot of weight and had purchased a whole new wardrobe, hoping to impress him. I thought if I dressed irresistibly, I would become irresistible. But that is not where beauty resides. It only got me deeper and deeper into debt.

I had spent a great portion of my divorce settlement on everything that I thought would bind me securely to Jon. Not only was it an unwise and a foolish thing to do, but it had devastating results. I couldn't figure out how to stop living the lifestyle I had grown accustomed to while still married to Mitch—the same one that had made an impression on Jon, but which left me with years of debts and tears of regrets.

*   *   *   *   *

Jon and I drove to a little steak house in Minden, a place he had chosen to celebrate my birthday. We took seats in a corner booth. As we waited for our food, I opened the birthday card Jon had handpicked just for me. Immediately I noticed that the picture and signature appeared at odds with each other. On the front of the card was a picture of two prisoners . . . a male and female prisoner. They were dressed in the traditional black-and-white-striped prison garb, connected by a ball and chain. The card read, "Together forever," and inside the card it read, "Forever Friends." But, as my eyes traveled to the bottom of the inside page of the card in search of the words "I love you," I read instead: "Happy birthday, Leta, Jon." My heart collapsed.

The tears came again, in streams and rivers of sadness. There were no more planned events leading to the next time; no more shared dinners over spontaneous laughter and intermittent kisses—no promises for tomorrow.

The birthday party was over . . . and so much more.

As I slid into the car seat beside him, I felt like I was going to be driven to the end of the world and dropped off.

His car came to a stop in front of my house. The engine was still running, a clear mechanical message, I thought. I leaned toward Jon in an all too theatrical expectation of an endless kiss. Before my hand reached the face that I had long ago memorized and idolized, he said, "No, Leta, it isn't that way between us anymore."

The pain of rejection stirred in my bowels, the dwelling place of my emotions. I wanted Jon to be happy. But I didn't want to be sad. The two soured in my stomach. The moment I stepped inside my house I began to lose my mind. I replayed over and over again the many times we had talked about marriage and how I had been the undecided one. From there I began a slow downward spiral into the depth of despair. I tried to function normally by forcing myself to continue my usual activities, only to find that I had little or no energy to handle even the mundane things a day brings.

*   *   *   *   *

The church choir had been one of my favorite things to participate in, and I enjoyed the fellowship that went along with being involved in that small group. Determined to succeed at overcoming grief, I decided to continue that activity, expecting blessings and strength for the days ahead. Unfortunately, the Sunday morning we were scheduled to sing ended in disaster.

As we entered the choir loft and I had taken my seat, I looked out over the congregation. There in the second row sat Jon and Lisa. His arm was around her shoulder, and in the same way he once looked at me—with love and longing—he was now looking at Lisa. My heart stopped and I was left with short intervals of labored breathing. I felt like the walls were squeezing the life out of me. I reached for the girl beside me as I began to feel myself collapsing. Before my knees completely folded beneath my body, the girl beside me took my arm and held me up. She quickly whispered in my ear, "You are going to be just fine; don't let them get to you. It's a pretty lousy thing to do, but you just sing like you have never sung before."

And so I sang . . . all the words that I no longer believed were true.

... TWENTY-SEVEN ...

Filled with anguish—something felt and never fitly described, except within the pages of C. S. Lewis's book, *A Grief Observed*, where I found the only adequate recounting of inconsolable grief—I limped into the next day. No matter how hard I tried, I couldn't find God in my pain.

I did not remember leaving the church building that Sunday. But I recall standing in the middle of the parking lot bewildered and disoriented. Cars and people passed me like curious onlookers trying to avoid a beggar on the street. Several well-meaning people, including Jon, rushed to my side, but their words rang hollow in the corridor of my despair.

A friend, whom I later referred to as "Sherlock," because of our mutual interest in private investigating, hurried to my side. She remained faithfully by my side, as well as spending vast amounts of time on the telephone with me. Mostly, she listened; mostly, I cried. When I rambled on and on, rehashing the same things over and over again, instead of telling me to "get on with it, or get over it," she endured my ramblings until she would literally fall asleep at the other end of the line. I would occasionally call out her name just to make sure she hadn't hung up on me. She presented no endless words of advice or criticism—just quiet compassion.

My emotional descent continued; I began spending more and more time in bed. During one of those days, when I could no longer find a reason to get out of bed, Jon came to check on me. I heard his footsteps on the kitchen floor as he walked through the living room and up the stairs to my bedroom. The sound of his car, like the sound of his walk, announced his arrival long before he ever came into view. When he walked into my room, I saw through my red puffy eyes someone who was very concerned about me. What he saw was fittingly expressed in his own words. "You look like an eighty-year-old woman!" He sat on my bed and wiped the tears from my cheeks with his handkerchief. I had no energy to respond. I was mentally in the process of dying.

Jon's concern for me quickly changed to disappointment. I could see it in his face . . . the one I knew so well. He had known me as a strong woman, one whom he had come to rely on and love, a person who had made some very important decisions in her life; but that day, he saw quite a different person, and it didn't please him.

Instead of sympathy, he chose to rebuke me for allowing myself the luxury of despair. When he finally left my room, I clung to the thin, worn handkerchief he had left behind. I kept that handkerchief for years, refusing to wash it, for fear of losing the smell of him.

Maureen, my life-long friend, hadn't escaped the tremors of my hopelessness either. She received the appended remains of my gloom. She had somehow always been able to reason me through most of life's tragedies, but even she became frustrated with my repetitious narration of wrongs. But she, too, remained faithfully by my side.

Love was being defined, and proven, by two very close friends, but I was too pain-impaired to recognize it.

*   *   *   *   *

For three very long years, I wallowed in sorrow and self-pity, functioning only enough to survive. Food became a plaything; I kept turning it over and over on my plate, but I never ate it. I no longer prayed, went to church, or read my Bible—and I stopped talking to God. Instead . . . I SCREAMED AT HIM! I felt I had sacrificed my own happiness to please Him, and where had it gotten me? Angry is where it had gotten me, and it caused me to lose the one person who meant the world to me. Without Jon, there didn't seem to be any reason to live.

In a desperate move to eradicate my past, instead of accepting what God had for my life, I deliberately destroyed a complete work of prose and poetry that had been accepted for publication by a New York publishing company. It was as though the destruction of my former thoughts would somehow erase years of unhappiness, pain, and disappointments. I wanted nothing to do with my past; and as far as the future was concerned, I wanted to cancel that altogether. I came to regret that action later.

It was time to get help; even I knew that much.

At a time like that, recommendations come hard. In my opinion, no one could have possibly been qualified to reverse the direction of my hurt. If God worked in mysterious ways, His wonders to perform, as He claimed, then why hadn't He performed that acclaimed magic on me? I complained.

Many years later, I wrote these words on the inside cover of my Bible—a quote from our Pastor of Music at the Evangelical Free Church of Hershey. It serves as a constant reminder that *"if you plant seeds of anger, you will harvest a field of bitterness."* I can attest to the truth of those words of wisdom in my own life.

*   *   *   *   *

I sat for a long time on the wooden bench outside the building that housed the counseling services—the one that had been recommended to me by some well-meaning friends. Ten minutes of my appointed time had already elapsed.

Slowly, I made my way to the main door of the building. Only a set of brick steps stood between the second-floor office and me, where the sign "Christian Counseling Services" invited me to enter. For a few seconds, I entertained the idea of running back to the safety of my car. Personal interrogations frightened me, and I found them to be immensely intimidating. Years earlier, I had revealed everything, down to my skeleton, to a marriage counselor, and now here I was again, about to have my soul "plucked" from my bones. Various thoughts scrambled for position as I put my fingers over the brass handle before letting myself in.

Foreboding, as they may seem, most waiting rooms are, in and of themselves, quite harmless. First of all, they're filled with wrinkled and torn outdated magazines . . . with holes . . . evidence of the presence of coupon-clipping bandits—nothing harmful there; but what bothers me most about waiting rooms is that sometimes you feel like they're going to be your final resting place. Thankfully, that wasn't the case the day I met Mr. Graybill, the counselor unfortunate enough to get me as a patient. Otherwise, I'd have probably been out of there in a hurry!

It wasn't long before I was sitting across the room from a very attentive gentleman. He greeted me as though I was the first patient of the day—which I knew was not the case, primarily because plucking sounds seemed to be pouring out of every room. Obviously, I wasn't the only one having problems.

For the next year or so, I made weekly excursions to the counselor's office. With each visit, I was instructed to take specific steps leading to recovery from a serious bout of debilitating co-dependency and low self-esteem. The significance I once felt when I came to know Jesus had somehow vanished, or at the very least was on a sabbatical.

Instead of praying, which incidentally opened and closed every counseling session, I was required to read a Psalm from the Bible every night, an exercise recommended by the counselor. I hated it. It only reminded me of what I thought God had taken away from me. But quite unexpectedly, by that time, I gained such a tremendous amount of respect for the man with the gentle voice, even though his words sometimes cut like a serrated knife through my attitude of self-imposed punishment, that I found myself following his advice.

As I neared the end of my counseling sessions, and with the approval of my counselor, I decided to meet with Jon and his girlfriend and ask for their forgiveness for my extreme reaction to their relationship. It was to have been the beginning of thinking more highly of others than I thought of myself, as God tells us to do in His Word. I can honestly say that, at the time, I was totally sincere when I fulfilled that assignment. But as the days passed, and I heard that Jon and Lisa were engaged with plans to marry shortly thereafter, hurt and bitterness made their return visit. As I began entertaining those culprits of doom and destruction, I was handed the final exam on my many years of counseling.

Jon called me one day and asked if he could come and retrieve a large kite that he had left behind when he moved out of my cottage. When he arrived at my door, he informed me that he and Lisa wanted to take the kite along on their honeymoon. I struggled to hold back the tears as I made a valiant effort at congratulating him on his engagement and forthcoming marriage. But I failed miserably.

He put his arm around me and, for the last time, wiped away my tears. He told me that he had made the right decision when he decided to marry Lisa, and that he only wished it hadn't caused me so much pain. With that, he walked out of my life.

Not until the following day, as I was leaving for work, did I notice the words "I Love You" written in chalk on a small heart-shaped black-board that hung at the back door of my cottage. The message was in Jon's handwriting. He did love me, but not in the same way he did before. I knew that.

Jon married. And before I could retrieve the blackboard from my back porch to be memorialized along with the worn handkerchief, my friend "Sherlock" took the liberty of erasing those three words from my blackboard.

I was eventually reunited with the dignity that comes from acceptance. But my heart remained an open sore.

*   *   *   *   *

Self-prescribed, I took a job in a busy orthodontic office in Minden, in addition to the seasonal operation of Mixed Blessings. By keeping myself busy and overly committed, I had hoped to cut down on my think-ing time, but that, too, failed.

One of the doctors I worked for, and with whom I became a good friend, was a Christian. He himself had a grand testimony as to how God worked in his life. It was no coincidence that I found myself working in that practice.

During one of our coffee breaks in the "pig-pen" (the name we gave our lunchroom), we were discussing the doctor's love of flying . . . and my loathing of it. He said he owned and had flown his own airplane, but that he had had the plane up for sale for over two years and hadn't had one sound offer. We talked extensively about my recent heartbreak, but I didn't tell him how it had affected me spiritually. But when he asked me to pray that he would sell his airplane, I had to confess to him that I no longer believed that God heard my prayers; and no matter what he said to try and convince me otherwise, I rejected his wisdom.

That was the moment I decided to do something generally frowned upon by most churches I had attended and, I would say, was probably discouraged in Scripture as well; I put out a "fleece"—something associated with Gideon of the Bible. It means specifically challenging God or, as some would say, testing God to answer—or else! Somewhere in the back of my mind I recalled having read a verse in Ezekiel where God said, "Prove Me, to see that I am God."

That same night, after the doctor and I had talked about his airplane situation, I spoke to God for the first time since angrily shouting at Him for taking Jon away from me. I told Him that if He really heard the prayers of individuals—my prayers in particular—He was going to have to prove it to me by helping my employer sell his airplane. Evidencing a miracle was the only way I was ever again going to believe in the power of prayer again, I told Him. I also reminded Him of who He was (as though He had forgotten), and in return, He assured me that He still loved me. Our opinions of one another were quite opposite. I had been utterly disillusioned by how He had worked in Jon's and my situation. He responded with some reminders of His own: He had given His life for me; He had set me free! I had become His adopted child the day I trusted Him for my salvation . . . an inheritance from above . . . surpassing all earthly riches—a daughter of a King!

When I ended my conversation and time of unchained prayer with the supposedly miracle-working God, I felt a little "shame-faithed." But I was still determined to have Him prove Himself to me. He knew that I had reached the end of my spiritual rope. He had promised me that He would never leave or forsake me; had He really meant it, I wondered.

I went to work the next day expecting nothing more than a room full of patients.

Halfway through the day, I picked up one of our three phones that had been ringing. A very business-like voice on the other end of the line asked to speak with my employer. The doctor took the call in the "pig-pen," away from the hustle and bustle of the patients and his staff. After about twenty minutes, he walked by my desk with a broad, upside-down, rainbow smile on his face.

"Guess what, Leta. I just sold my airplane!" he exclaimed.

I couldn't reply. I quickly grabbed his arm and led him back to the lunchroom where I broke down in "belief." I began to explain, with more tears than words, about my conversation with God the night before. He listened intently. He, like myself, was unable to deny God's timing regarding the sale of his airplane. He claimed that he had all but given up on selling it by that time. We both believed that God had thrown out a life vest to save me from spiritually drowning, and that he (my boss) had simply been a beneficiary of that rescue.

Never again would I have to test God's faithfulness, certainly not by "putting out a fleece." He had been faithful in hearing and answering my prayers, and it changed my life. If He never answered another prayer, I would still know that my requests were being considered. Why He chose to answer my prayer at that time, and in that way, I cannot be absolutely certain, but I will definitely make it a point to ask Him when I see Him someday . . . if I am not too distracted by His resplendent face. Until then, I accept the miracle of answered prayer in my life.

I also cannot speculate on why God doesn't respond with the same clarity to the prayers of others when they petition Him with equally urgent requests. But what I do know is of far greater importance: God IS paying attention—it's just that *His answers happen to be as diverse as our requests.*

For the second night in a row, I found myself on my knees. But that night I confessed all my sins—darkly hidden and plainly seen. I bathed in the fresh water of repentance and forgiveness, and I claimed His promise that "if your mother and father forsake you (*or your friends or loved ones do the same*), I will never leave or forsake you!" (Italics mine.)

My past no longer counted against me; it was removed as far "as the East is from the West," remembered no more by a merciful God. I was given another opportunity to live triumphantly . . . victoriously unencumbered by the baggage of my past. I had built my life on the faults of others, which positioned me for an earthquake of disappointments. But now I was free to enjoy an accusatory-free life. I was without excuse. My account had been wiped clean. I wanted no less for those whom I felt had left me down over the years. It was time for exhaustive forgiveness.

Little did I realize that following my mountaintop experience, I would soon be faith-tested again.

*   *   *   *   *

My stillborn desire to rejoice over the happiness of others came suddenly alive! As I shared what God had done in my life in erasing years of bitterness, I prayed that the relationship between my children and their father (and his wife) would heal. Not that things would ever be the same again; not that they wouldn't be remembered (we're not God), but that there would be a new released freedom to love even those who had hurt us deeply. It was difficult to admit, but my name appeared on that list of people to forgive. It was a battlefield of emotions. The war was won, but emotional skirmishes erupted like wildfires in a forest—some forever inextinguishable.

The reality was . . . what Mitch and I had written on the lives of our children couldn't be erased as chalk-words on a blackboard. Only God possessed that power.

*   *   *   *   *

I remained close to Jon's family and his extended family. In retrospect, I can now see that it was probably a way for me to remain attached to Jon. But as time passed, I realized that they meant more to me than just a connecting link to Jon. They had become special people in my life—friends—and now I was ready to accept them for who they were because I now realized and understood who I was.

While I was visiting Jon's father and stepmother in eastern Pennsylvania for a weekend, I received a distressing phone call informing me that Maureen's husband had died unexpectedly. I immediately rushed back to Laurel Lake to be with her.

I found Maureen exceedingly grief-stricken by her husband's unexpected death. My normally strong, independent friend, who had helped sustain me through my most difficult times, appeared devastatingly lost in mourning. As I sat beside her, it became clear that she had been sedated; she was confused and listless. It hurt me terribly to see her suffer that way. We had always been there for each other over the years, but I found myself praying that our friendship would be particularly meaningful during that time. Maureen's husband had really been her best friend (I was her second); his death produced a tremendous amount of grief. Although I hadn't lost Jon to death, nevertheless, I knew a little of what Maureen was going through.

*   *   *   *   *

We spent periods of time together after her husband's death. Never were there ever two closer friends.

Months after Maureen's husband's death, while we were having dinner together one evening, I suggested that she might want to consider joining me in my business. I did so with some apprehension, however, since Mitch, who had a keen business head, had always warned: "Never go into business with a friend unless you hold seventy-five percent interest, and then be prepared to lose them as a friend at some point." Maureen and I had now been best friends for thirty-some years, and I was sure that we would always be able to rise above any differences between us.

Mixed Blessings was growing, demanding more and more of my time . . . and money. Maureen's expertise in antiques, her independent financial situation, and our unique friendship seemed to be a matchless combination for a lasting partnership. Also, I thought it would be a very good diversion for her following the loss of her husband.

Maureen and I had vowed to take care of one another in the wintry years of our lives. In my mind, a business relationship was just another step toward that end and, at the time, I believed she felt the same way. And so we made plans to unite our talents and energy in converting Mixed Blessings from a gift and craft shop to an upscale antique and collectibles business. Before we began our first day of business as partners, we engaged in some very important covenants. We agreed that, no matter what happened during our business tenure, our friendship was more important than any business partnership. We also agreed that, should either one of us decide to leave the business, we would discuss it before any decisions were made to dissolve the partnership. And if we were ever forced out of business, which at that time seemed highly unlikely, neither of us would remain in business. It was just one more way of protecting our friendship from the evils that such a situation might bring about. It was a promise I intended to uphold.

Profitability, and fun, made working together a great experience for us. We grew even closer during the first few years in business together. Maureen and I spent weekends searching the dusty corners of buildings and attending auctions in search of unique antique items to sell. We purchased tables of glassware and boxes of wrapped treasures from elderly folks wanting to reduce their personal inventory before moving on to smaller living quarters. Sometimes, we disappointed ourselves when we paid much too much for an item. Conversely, we'd do a couple high-fives when we felt we had been slipped a golden slipper—paying pennies for something worth a whole lot more! Maureen always warned, "Don't buy anything you wouldn't want to keep yourself, because you just may have to live with it." To this day, I own and display a few of those mistakes.

The balance between us, as partners, began to shift following a regrettable business decision: the introduction of a family member into our business, not as a partner, but for the opportunity to sell her own inventory of merchandise. Maureen asked me if I had any objection to her daughter renting a spot in our shop, explaining that her daughter enjoyed buying and reselling jewelry, and that she could be a great help to us in the shop. Not wanting to disappoint Maureen, or cause any rift between us, I conceded to the change. In the back of my mind were Mitch's words and the proverbial "you could be opening a whole new can of worms" cliché.

Not having spent a great deal of time with Maureen's daughter since she had grown up, I was unacquainted with any personality irregularities, and I hadn't guessed what her feelings might be towards me, her mother's closest friend.

It didn't take long to notice that the contents of the shop were being rearranged; business decisions that Maureen and I had made were conspicuously being revised, and customers began to complain to me about the verbal exchanges taking place between themselves and my best friend's daughter. Since the shop had been solely mine for many years, it was only natural that most of the complaints were being registered with me.

It eventually became necessary for me to sit down with Maureen and talk to her about the situation. Such a confrontation stood a good chance of strengthening our business relationship or, conceivably, destroying it. But it was something that needed to be addressed.

Maureen listened as I shared my concerns. I was very careful not to offend her, cognizant of the truer-than-true saying that "blood is thicker than water." To condemn her daughter in any way would have been a death sentence on our friendship. But at the same time, I recalled the words from the Bible: "Better are the wounds of a friend than the kisses of an enemy."

After meeting with Maureen, she told me that she herself had often been driven to tears by her daughter's verbal attacks, and that it was highly probable that what the customers were reporting was closer to the truth than she cared to admit. Maureen assured me that she would talk to her daughter concerning the things we discussed.

Not long after I considered the matter resolved, another business practice began to manifest itself. Maureen and her daughter began buying merchandise together and selling in our shop, and Maureen and I began buying less and less together. The business was no longer operating as a partnership. When I mentioned the fact to Maureen, she said that her daughter felt that she had been spending too much time antique searching with me and, as a result, she decided to shop with her daughter more frequently in order to "keep her happy." I tried hard to understand Maureen's thinking, but the fact remained, we had certain obligations as business partners, and that should not have, to my way of thinking, been the least bit threatening to her daughter.

In the meantime, there was a couple who had been coming into our shop over the years asking to be put on a list of people wanting to sell their merchandise in our shop when and if space ever became available. At the time we had nothing to offer them, but as time passed and additional space became available, Maureen and I discussed having them join us in the shop with their consignment merchandise. They were so excited and grateful when we gave them the news. They immediately pitched in with many of the daily chores related to the opening and closing of the shop, which had been a major job for the two of us. Unanticipated, however, were the doubly bittersweet changes about to take place in the business and in my life.

Having worked very hard at maintaining Mixed Blessings for the purpose of a comfortable and enjoyable retirement, and in hopes of having it provide the opportunity to move to a warmer climate in the winter months, as Maureen had already done, I had perhaps become a little too future-complacent. My business sense had dulled, and my former submissive nature seemed to reign anew. No longer did Mixed Blessings provide enjoyment. Instead, each week seemed to begin with a different set of problems.

Suddenly, I felt emotionally handicapped and occupationally threatened. I couldn't express my feelings to Maureen for fear of endangering our close and nearly life-long friendship. So I sat back and let things eat at me like buzzards on a bleeding carcass. An atmosphere of distrust began to creep in as slyly as a fox in a chicken coop, and I didn't know what to do about it.

During one of our very heavily attended community art shows that year, the wife of the couple whom we had finally agreed to have in the shop, accused my daughter, who was helping us out during that busy time, of taking money from the business. Maureen came to where I was working a sales booth outside and said that I had better talk to my daughter, that she had been accused of stealing money from us. When I confronted my daughter, whom I knew wouldn't even steal first base in a ballgame, her explanation of what happened was entirely different than her accuser, and my daughter's version proved to be true in the end. What surprised me more was Maureen's willingness to believe the accusation before knowing the complete facts of the matter.

From that moment on, Maureen and I had weekly discussions as to whether or not we should ask the new couple to remove themselves from the shop. But when the woman agreed to apologize for wrongly accusing my daughter of something she hadn't done, we were commanded by obedience to our faith to accept her apology and to forgive her. So we agreed to allow them to continue selling their merchandise in our shop. They appeared to be extremely relieved and surprised by the offer of forgiveness extended to them. I considered it a small test on what God had been teaching me about forgiveness. I really wanted it to be my final exam, but God had other plans.

* * * * *

As the season for Mixed Blessings ended, fall began with more than a change of colors. An undercurrent, much like the hidden danger beneath ocean waves, produced a number of uncertainties on the shore of my plans for Mixed Blessings. I wasn't at all sure I would survive the tide of change that would, in all likelihood, accompany the next season.

Like bad food one tries to avoid, the subject of my unrest was rarely discussed between Maureen and me; and my concerns did not end when the large boards were nailed over the doors and windows of the shop, marking the close of another business year. Quite expectedly, some of the irritating nuances were removed when the shop closed but, at best, it applied only a temporary tourniquet on the already strained relationship between Maureen and me.

Maureen left for a warmer winter climate; I remained behind licking my skeptical wounds.

For the remainder of the year, I agonized over how and why things had managed to get so out of control. I had my own ideas on why the sweet beginnings of Mixed Blessings had turned sour; but by that time, I no longer trusted my own judgement in matters that concerned the shop. By the time our summer season had ended, so much distrust had developed and, without exception, it all seemed to point to jealousy and the love of money.

The personal improprieties that took place had not gone unnoticed by others. During the winter months, numerous people came to me suggesting that I return to sole proprietorship of the business. I did not take those suggestions to heart for various reasons, but particularly those that might have jeopardized Maureen's and my friendship. I somehow fooled myself into thinking that the following year would be different, and I couldn't help wonder what those people knew that I didn't know.

*   *   *   *   *

A group of Christian singles gathered around a television set on New Year's Eve that year to watch the ball drop on Times Square—our way of feeling included in the celebration that traditionally introduced the beginning of a brand new year. The host's table was filled with potluck entrées and mouth-watering desserts. I joined the others in gorging myself on the food and fun of that evening. After the ball dropped and the merry-making and fireworks ended, I said my good-byes and wished everyone a Happy New Year and headed for home.

It was two-thirty a.m., New Year's Day, when I finally crawled into bed. But I couldn't go to sleep—retribution for my unhealthy eating habits, I thought. I was suffering from an acute case of indigestion and heartburn. After downing about a dozen or so Tums, I tossed and turned like a salad as I tried desperately to find just the right position that would grant me some degree of relief. After that failed, I sat up in bed in disgust. By five o'clock a.m., I was sitting with my legs hanging over the side of the bed dripping with perspiration. I tried digesting more of the flavorful candy-like Tums, thinking that perhaps I hadn't taken enough of them to ease my pain. By six o'clock a.m., New Year's Day, I was still sitting on the side of the bed, only by that time my hands were tingling all over and my breathing was labored. Thinking that I had nothing more than an exaggerated case of indigestion and heartburn, I, nevertheless, found myself calling Maureen, who had returned to Mt. Laurel for the holidays. Waking her, I told her about the pain I was experiencing.

"Did you think to call the doctor?" she asked.

"No, Maureen, I called you. It's New Year's Day! Wouldn't my doctor just love it if I got him out of bed on his day off? It's bad enough that I'm calling you and getting you out of bed," I said, in my halfhearted attempt to apologize. "I'm only calling you in the event it really is something more serious, which I know it isn't. I just thought it would be a wise thing to do—to tell someone about what's going on."

"Please call your doctor, Leta, because if you don't, I will," she replied.

I knew Maureen well and I had no doubt that that is exactly what she would have done, so I relented and promised her that I would call him. That was her way of checking up on me to see if I had done what I promised.

I dialed the long-distance number. On the other end, I heard the voice of my family doctor. I began by apologizing for arousing him from his sleep. He assured me that he was not the least bit offended by my early-morning call. He was a conscientious physician and obviously considered those kinds of disturbances part of his dedication to the profession. I reluctantly began to describe my symptoms. Before I finished, he said, "Get yourself to the closest hospital. Either call an ambulance or, if you have a neighbor close by, have them drive you. I am fairly certain you are having symptoms of a potential heart attack."

First, I thought to myself, *Me—heart attack? No way! I'm a tennis player, a skier, and a jogger. I can't be having a heart attack.* Secondly, I picked up the phone and called Maureen.

"It's me, Maureen," I said, thinking she may have gone back to sleep and forgotten that she had told me to call her back. "The doctor says I am supposed to get to the closest hospital. Can you drive me there?"

"I'll be there just as soon as I slip on some clothes. Hang in there; I'll be there in a few minutes."

I thought to myself, *She didn't even ask me what was wrong.* I immediately called the local hospital, as the doctor had instructed, and told them that I was on my way and that, according to a conversation with my family physician, I may be on the verge of having a heart attack. They told me that they would be awaiting my arrival.

As Maureen drove cautiously into town, I kept urging her to drive faster on the deserted highway. The pain continued to worsen.

We arrived at Minden Hospital in less than fifteen minutes, but it seemed more like an hour. As I walked through the automatic emergency doors, I was asked to have a seat on a wheelchair, one that had obviously been waiting for me. From there I was wheeled to the admissions window. By that time I was bent over in sheer agony. In order to avoid a death scene in the waiting room, they decided to forego the questioning and have Maureen provide the information they needed.

It was New Year's Day. All of the heart specialists were either out of the hospital, out of town, or "out on the town." Their absence led to the administration of a tiny pill that I was instructed to place beneath my tongue, which immediately eased my pain. The doctor on duty ordered some routine tests while an intern from a nearby teaching hospital, who happened to be on duty at the time, was called to my side to access my condition.

Thanks to that very prudent intern who, not wanting to take any chances in making an incorrect diagnosis, admitted me to the hospital under constant observation and medication until the heart specialists returned from the New Year weekend.

Maureen was by my side during that time and had the responsibility of contacting members of my family. If ever my children looked like angels, it was during that ordeal. Their presence was very comforting.

Prayers—and lots of them—began their journey to God's ears.

Several days before I was driven to the hospital with chest pains, I had a cast removed from my left foot. I had broken my foot in six places when I slipped off a rock I had been standing on while raking leaves at my cottage. I was in the early stages of therapy with an orthopedic group as part of my rehabilitation when I suddenly found myself in the hospital. This bit of information is significant to the rest of the story.

When the specialists reviewed my case, I was transferred by ambulance to a nearby, fully equipped hospital for further tests. Dr. Glick, a cardiologist I have come to respect greatly, was the specialist selected to perform my angioplasty. Unfortunately, after a great number of attempts to coax the artery open, he poked his head from beneath the tent-like sheet that covered my lower extremity—making something serious appear comical to me—and apologized that the procedure had not been successful.

"What next?" I asked.

"The only recommended alternative," he replied, "is bypass surgery. But I want you to talk with one of the heart surgeons first. They're the experts."

... TWENTY-EIGHT ...

A sports medicine doctor and a friend of my son Thomas, who happened to be an orthopedic surgeon for the United States Olympic Team at the time, recommended a friend of his to us who happened to be a well-known heart surgeon in the hospital where I was admitted.

A few phone calls later I had a visit from Dr. Hart (yes, that really was his name). He came to see me at the request of his orthopedic surgeon friend. *God was working in mysterious ways, His wonders to perform.* I felt entirely blessed by how things had come together so quickly. I had no doubt that someone's prayers were being answered.

After sharing his medical opinion with me, Dr. Hart assured me that, if I had been his wife or his daughter, I would not leave that hospital without a bypass operation. That was good enough for me. I only hoped that he and his wife had a great relationship, and that he hadn't just had an argument with his daughter over her choice of boyfriends.

I was scheduled for surgery several days later.

*   *   *   *   *

A number of things took place the day before my surgery. It was suggested that I watch a video meant to inform me of heart bypass surgery procedures; after hearing about my impending heart surgery from a family member, Jon called to ask whether or not he would be permitted to visit me; and, I was inundated with visits from supportive friends and family.

As far as the video was concerned, I had no desire to acquire any amount of visual enlightenment about what was going to happen to me in that operating room. As a matter of fact, I recall the moment the nurse walked in the room with the video in her hand.

"If you don't mind," I said to her, "I would rather not know what they're going to do to me, or where, for that matter. I like surprises. When they crack open my chest and reach in to rearrange my belongings, I really want to be 'out of town.'"

The nurse chuckled.

Then there was the call from Jon. The surgery I was about to undergo, although unlikely, had the possibility of unexpected complications that could be fatal, so I was touched when he asked to visit me. I asked him if his wife would be coming along with him. He said that she had decided to remain behind, and that his visit would be brief.

Time had been a great healer, as well as the counseling I received, but God was the Great Physician. And now my life was in His hands—in more ways than one.

* * * * *

The room was overflowing with people by the time Jon arrived. My friends and family greeted Jon with genuine warmth. Shortly thereafter, the nurse came in and, quite sternly, directed all but two or three people to exit the room, asking them to take turns visiting so as not to over-excite me. How could she have known that the tall, dark, handsome visitor standing by my bed produced enough excitement to send the entire patient-load of that hospital into cardiac arrest!

As Jon bent over my bed to give me a hug, I tried very hard not to cry. I didn't want it to be a somber reunion. I prayed silently for God to calm my heart, and He did. Jon wished me the best and said that he would pray for me. After several awkward minutes, I engaged him in conversation about his children. As we talked about them, I could see the pride of fatherhood in his face. I discovered, much to my own surprise, that I was actually happy for him. The old "hang-me-on emotions" were gone, replaced by a different kind of love—agape love. I only wished that his wife had been there to see the results of what God had done in my life with regards to Jon. She would have been pleased. He kissed me on the cheek, squeezed my hand, and then before leaving the room, he smiled as if to say, "You are in God's hands." He then walked out the door. Sarah, my daughter, came to my side and a few tears rolled down my cheeks. Somehow she knew I had released all the contents of my heart into the hands of the Lord at that moment, including the feelings I had for Jon.

As the rest of my family prepared to leave their homes in varying states to be by my side, I was being rolled into the operating room.

* * * * *

The surgery was successful. There was only one exception to the flawless events that took place during my stay in the hospital. While the mass of tubes inserted into nearly every possible part of my body were still intact, and I was still incoherent, the attending nurse persisted in bend-ing my feet back and forth in an effort to awaken me. Her efforts brought me back to life very quickly since the pain she caused was far worse than heart surgery . . . at least up until that point. With each bend of my left foot (the foot that had just been removed from a cast), I tried to cry out. I had already mentally shot her right through the heart! *She's breaking my foot all over again,* I remember thinking; one rarely holds a conversation while tubes are stuck in one's throat. I was sure she thought the tears running down my cheeks were just a sign that life had returned to my body. Not until I was out of intensive care and in my semi-private room was I able to reveal the suffering that nurse put me through. She was very apologetic when I told her about my foot. I told her how close she came to being murdered but that, fortunately for her, my hands were tied—and they were.

Open-heart surgery, like my experience with cancer, was another special time for me; it was another faith test, one that God used to draw me even closer to Himself.

Benjamin, who at the time was training to be an RN, remained by my bedside for almost the entire time of my hospitalization. All of my children were immensely helpful and supportive during that time. I felt undeservingly blessed!

Today, I consider each life-threatening experience a sort of "staff meeting" with the Creator. That same God continues to make the purpose of His goodness known to me by allowing me to share with others going through similar challenges what He has done for me and what He is capable of doing for them. It is a privilege I do not take lightly.

Not long after I was discharged from the hospital and had resumed normal activities, I was told that Mitch had also experienced some heart problems—another one of God's staff meetings, I supposed.

*   *   *   *   *

Before long, Maureen and I began preparing for another busy summer season at Mixed Blessings. It was 1995 and I was feeling great, better than I had felt in some time. It truly was a new year for me.

*   *   *   *   *

If faith moves mountains, enabling us to withstand the seemingly unconquerable circumstances of our lives, then I had spent the majority of mine in an exercise gym where God, my personal trainer, was helping me build muscles of faith for events yet to come.

*   *   *   *   *

A burst of new life that consistently accompanies the beginning of spring was evident everywhere, and the winter that brought more pain than snow was now history.

Maureen and I worked diligently to stock Mixed Blessings with new and exciting items; and each year, we would strive to be more creative in our presentation of the items we hoped to sell. We opened our doors for business the weekend before Memorial Day, just as we had done in previous years.

Typically, opening the shop each season was fun and exciting; but not so typical was the lack of harmony between Maureen, her daughter Karen, and me. No matter how hard I tried to get along with Karen, it clearly became a battle I was not confident I could win. But there was something else that bothered me very much.

On numerous occasions, Maureen and I talked about disagreements we both had with our respective children; but it hurt me terribly when she would tell me how the daughter she idolized had verbally abused her. But, as always, she would revert to her safety net—the "I just turn it off" response, and I would end up being the only one upset over it. I had such a burden for Maureen's daughter that I could not rest until I wrote her a letter telling her how God had worked in my life and how much I knew He loved her, too. I wanted to share my faith with everyone, but I especially wanted to share the good news of Jesus with my best friend's daughter. Sadly, my message was rejected. If there had ever been a flicker of affection for me before, my letter clearly snuffed that out—and the distance between us widened.

It was to be another difficult year at Mixed Blessings. There didn't seem to be any way of resolving the differences between the three of us, short of getting rid of the business. I grew more intimidated each day by Karen's assertive presence. It was like tournament chess; I'd walk away from the problem, knowing that eventually I would have to come back and make a move. But unlike a chess game, at season's end, nothing changed.

Maureen left for her winter home in the southwest, and I continued working at the orthodontic office.

I was extremely fortunate to be blessed with an abundant number of friends and, over the winter months, I found myself too busy to think about the unresolved issues concerning Mixed Blessings. I had also gotten involved in numerous church activities. Worshiping God every Sunday with other believers was a soothing ointment on my life, and I longed to know God better.

January 1996—still very cold, and four months away from spring—I began thinking about Mixed Blessings. But the anticipation I usually felt about that time was absent. I wasn't looking forward to buying antiques . . . and the closer we got to opening day, the more my stress level increased.

It took less than a month after opening day to realize that something was terribly amiss. I found myself treading on thin ice every day, carefully skirting anything that had to do with Maureen's daughter. As well, I was more reluctant than ever to talk to Maureen about the things that concerned me—something we had always been able to do with considerable ease in the past. There was no denying the evidence of a strained friendship, and the relationship (what little there had been) between her daughter and myself was thoroughly defunct. Additionally, and to make matters worse, I heard from several reliable sources that there was talk about my being forced out of business, implicating several people currently selling merchandise in our shop. Since rumors never held much credence with me, I ignored them. The atmosphere, nevertheless, became unsettling and, before long, the time Maureen and I spent working together at the shop was all but eliminated. At her suggestion, we began working alternate shifts. My heart was heavy, knowing that the friendship Maureen and I had so carefully guarded over the years was somehow being sabotaged. In spite of all the evidence pointing to an eventual crisis, I chose to believe the best—that no one would underhandedly work evil behind my back.

Another season came and went and, once again, Maureen headed for her winter retreat. The fact that she was not available during the winter months provided us with an excuse for avoiding a confrontation regarding the rumors I had heard and the gloom that had settled over the business . . . and our friendship.

With the introduction of computers to "our" manual world, I was the first, between Maureen and me, to take advantage of this modern method of communication. After becoming more proficient at operating my computer, I encouraged Maureen to get one as well, enabling us to e-mail back and forth from Pennsylvania to her home in the southwest at a relatively low cost—something that literally boggled our ancient minds. But it was a great way to communicate, and we took advantage of it.

One evening, after I had been on the computer for an extended period of time, I finally gave the phone a chance to ring. It had been much too expensive to put in a separate line, so the computer and the telephone always had to compete for "first dibs" at my house. It was Michael Banks' sister-in-law.

"Leta, this is Janet, Michael's sister-in-law," she announced. "I know it has been a long time, but I have some bad news. Michael passed away yesterday."

I didn't know what to say or how to reply. I never thought of Michael dying. All I could think about then was that the handsome State

Policeman—the one I had known and loved—was gone and forever re-moved from this world. Once again, I was driven into the safety of God's arms. As I wiped the tears from my eyes, I wished that Michael and I would have had an opportunity to talk just one more time, but it wasn't meant to be. I had asked him never to call me or even to try and see me, and he had honored that request for many years. I grieved his passing.

Even though Michael and I hadn't seen each other for a long time, Michael's death resulted in my making some very astute observations. For some reason, God seemed to be eliminating the men in my life, and the only explanation I could come up with was that He wanted to become my All in All!

Unlike the people who had worked hard to gain entrance into the best life had to offer in 1935, when Jean Marlow frequented Blairsouth Estate, I had been given a position of royalty as a free gift the day I put my trust in Christ. I fully expected to reign with Him one day. But the process I had to go through to learn that valuable truth was excruciatingly painful.

When I realized how much I had grieved God over the years—and then experienced absolute comfort and forgiveness through repentance—I penned several letters to people whose names God had put on my heart. I told them about God's unconditional love; I wanted them to know how much I cared for them, but more than that, I wanted them to know how much God loved them—the same message I had shared with Maureen's daughter Karen. Michael had been a recipient of one of those letters. He responded by accusing me of being melodramatic and fanatical regarding my beliefs. The others said it was fine for me to feel that way, but I wasn't to try and convert them! I was greatly saddened by their indifference. Whether or not Michael accepted Christ, by faith, before he died, I would never know, but I prayed that he had. As far as I could tell, according to the Bible, it was a choice for the living to make—and too late for the already dead. I was so thankful that I had made that decision when I was sixteen years old, only a short time before that fatal automobile accident—the same night I met Michael Banks.

Michael's death, and Jon's marriage, posted the end of an era for me, the era of relying on people for my security. In the end, none had really been able to save me.

* * * * *

The fall of 1997 proved monumentally significant in the lives of my children and myself.

It was Saturday afternoon. I had been out shopping for several hours when my growling stomach reminded me that I hadn't eaten breakfast that morning. I decided to stop at a local tavern known for their delicious luncheon salads. As I pulled on the emergency brake and prepared to exit my car, my cellular phone began to ring. Rarely would I receive calls in my automobile, mostly because I would forget to plug it into the cigarette lighter, not to mention the fact that the battery remained uncharged since the day I bought it. But, for some unexplainable reason, that day my cell phone was not only on, but the battery was charged. After debating between my appetite and my curiosity, I finally decided to answer the phone. I immediately recognized Thomas's voice; I knew right away that something was terribly wrong.

"Mom, this is Tom," he said, his voice sounding as though he had been crying. "I have some bad news; Dad passed away this morning."

Suddenly, my appetite was gone and there was another kind of feeling in the pit of my stomach.

I was aware that Mitch's health had been slowly deteriorating over the last several months; nevertheless, I was shocked when Thomas told me he had died. Mitch had always boasted of being able to conquer just about everything and everyone; but cancer, dementia, and heart disease had finally conquered him. Mitch was gone. I thanked Thomas for letting me know, and I asked him if there was anything I could do. He said, "No." I knew that he wanted to grieve alone. I sat in the parking lot for some time. Of all the thoughts I had at that moment, not one prepared me for the events that followed Mitch's death.

It was very clear that, during Mitch's illness, Mitch's wife preferred not having his children visit him; the exceptions to that rule were infrequent. Sarah and her children were specifically dissuaded from visiting. Sarah's spiritual convictions and openness in talking about God were met with disdain, so her attempts to visit with her father grew less and less. She grieved over the growing distance between them. She, like her brothers, had longed for a close relationship with their dad; but it remained an elusive dream. Sarah later admitted that she felt the distance between her and her father began when she was born. She believed that her father had never loved her. Ironically, Sarah was the one who had baked and decorated the wedding cake for her father's wedding reception when he remarried, leaving her completely and understandably perplexed by the standoff between the two of them. That is when I became preoccupied with developing a closer relationship with my daughter; I knew she had some of the same feelings I had had when I was growing up, and I wanted something different for her. I wanted her to feel loved.

Uninvited by Mitch's wife and her children to have Sarah and her family join them in the front row at the funeral home during Mitch's funeral, Sarah, her family, and I sat in the last row of seats provided for friends and acquaintances. Unlike Sarah, her brothers refused to be estranged from the situation, and they chose to sit in the front row with Mitch's wife.

Completely disregarded as family members following Mitch's funeral, all but one of our children were discouraged from visiting their deceased father's home and, for some, communication was suspended altogether. Strangulation of family ties on their father's side affected some of the children more negatively than it did the others, and the alienation was never fully understood. Other than myself, there were no other relatives to provide a family connection; extended family is something a foster child rarely has to offer. I was fortunate, however, to have had special families in my life, like the Witman and Weidman families while I was growing up, which afforded me some notion of kinship. Certainly, it was not the same as having blood relatives, but it was not much different either, as I discovered. But I sensed that my children weren't even going to have that much.

Another piece of my heart fell away as I watched the responses of my grieving children. Death interrupted their life-long desire to win their father's affection. But I believe the grieving process of not having a loving and affectionate father began long before their father's death.

As is customarily done, the will was read and the unraveling truth pushed death's painful knife further into the hearts of the children.

During the last days of Mitch's life, I was told he had spoken with several of the children. He said that he wanted them to know that the money from his life insurance policy was the only inheritance they would receive. He indicated to Luke, the only one remotely interested in the automobile business, that he would naturally take over the business. Even as he shared those things with them, their expectations remained guarded. I know they wanted very much to believe that, in the end, it was his way of saying he cared about them, but their concern was mostly for their dad and what he was going through at the time.

Crushed beyond words or explanation was the day the children leaned that they had been completely excluded from their father's will, contrary to what they had been told. Not only had Mitch excluded them financially, but also, he hadn't so much as left them one of his favorite watches, articles of clothing, photographs, or Airborne memorabilia. As they have said many times, "It wasn't the money . . . it was the love principle."

I have come to believe one of three things. Using the children, Mitch was able to administer one final attack on me; while under heavy medication, he changed his will (by consensual means, or otherwise); or he was totally incoherent when he made his wishes known to the children during the weeks preceding his death.

The reality of how he felt about his own children, confirmed by the disinheritance, utterly tore them, and me, to pieces. Now Mitch's step-children stood to receive what I thought our children deserved, if for no other reason than to compensate them for the way he had treated them.

Because of how God worked in my life, and in the lives of my children, to one extent or another, forgiveness was the only hope for closure—the only direction any of us could go. Unfortunately, forgive-ness doesn't guarantee forgetting. I believe what took place will live long in the memory of my children. But, unlike their father, they willingly extended the grace of forgiveness and, in turn, have been able to live their lives unencumbered by bitterness.

I prayed that the events surrounding Mitch's death would draw us, as a family, closer together.

*   *   *   *   *

What seems like "forever ago," the residual effects from the decision I made to leave Mitch still has "ever present" consequences. The actions we take, and the decisions we make, communicate our love for others, or they brand them with disturbing memories, and in my case, memories of a broken home, and that has always disturbed me.

By the time winter ended, the conversation still centered on the "why" of what took place after Mitch's death, but soon the weariness of the search for answers gave way to resolve and remains a subject rarely discussed between us to this day. But I do not kid myself; even though they do not show it and do not speak about it, the pain of that moment continues to fester deep inside the minds and hearts of my children— of that I have no doubt.

If ever there was a time when I needed to experience the power of faith, it was during the months following Mitch's death . . . before the next devastating event that threatened to capsize my world.

*   *   *   *   *

My hunger for truth, found only in God's Word, increased during those months, and I came to the realization that if I was going to experi-ence the victory that faith provides in failing circumstances, I would have to make that faith alive and practical. That meant I had to ask myself a very poignant question. "Am I thoroughly convinced concerning the life, death, and resurrection of Jesus Christ?" If my answer was "yes," then there was no alternative for me but to trust that same God for everything . . . for all the things that would come into my life, present and future.

I could not change the events of the past, but I could allow the lessons learned from my past to make a difference for my future. That meant relinquishing control over my life and putting it into the capable hands of the One Who created me, knew me, and loved me even before I appeared in fetal form in the womb of Jean Marlow. I was going to have to rely on the One person in my life Who came to stay and Who promised never to leave or forsake me. Why it had taken me so long to discard the life-long baggage I had been carrying for the better part of my life, I don't know, except for God's perfect timing.

At the first sign of victory in my life, another devastating event was about to take place. I never imagined myself a "Job," but I was beginning to understand him a whole lot better. Compared to Job, I had suffered very little, but we did have one thing in common—the same God loved and attended us both.

*   *   *   *   *

The winter of 1997 refused to let go until it had exacted an onslaught of personal damage. The only difference between that battle and all the others was that I was now armed; I had taken up the shield of faith.

What could have proven every bit as personally destructive as any one circumstance in my life provided an opportunity for me instead—one I had often hoped for, but had never been given. What the evil one meant for harm, God meant for good. Was it God's way of saying, "I was here for you all the time, Leta, but this is the first time you really allowed Me to have an active part in your life." I don't know, but it certainly seemed that way. I only know that my response to the next traumatic event in my life involved supernatural power; and it didn't come from me.

*   *   *   *   *

The opportunity God gave me was the time to write this memoir about growing up as a foster child . . . the influence it had on my life and how it affected others. And it came out of unexpected heartbreak. It made me think of watching chickens hatch on the farm when I was a little girl; the egg that housed the beautiful little chick had to crack before it was able to produce new life.

There is hope for those of us who feel "less significant" as a result of the circumstances into which we are born: for the orphans, adopted and foster children, and children from dysfunctional homes. When we see who we really are in God's eyes—we are royal property, loved and cherished by an awesome Father—He meets us right in the fire of our circumstances.

As certain as I am of God's love, I am equally convinced that parents are correspondingly significant in the lives of their children. He has given us a role to play, and if we insist on playing by our own rules (as I have done many times) or by someone else's for that matter, we can expect to lose. Victory is in Jesus!

I don't want to live one more precious moment being a contrary Christian. The lessons are too hard; and even though my God is a God of second chances, I have come to respect His guidelines. I am convinced that mere man would never have written such stringent guidelines for living as we find in the Bible, apart from the inspiration of God; he is much too liberated for that, which gives tremendous credibility to the authorship of the Scriptures. "*So*, for me and my house, we will serve the Lord."

* * * * *

As I gathered the mail in my hand on a blustery winter day in December of that year, returning to the warmth of my cozy cottage, I began opening the numerous envelopes piled on my lap.

... TWENTY-NINE ...

Unlike most mail that sits on the kitchen table unopened for days on end, I have always been one to give my immediate attention to each and every piece.

One after another, I began to sort through the heap of envelopes, advertisements, and catalogs. One envelope in particular caught my eye. In the upper left-hand corner of a business-sized envelope was a logo bearing the name: Laurel Lake, Board of Directors. The letter was addressed to Mixed Blessings.

Expecting nothing more than a copy of the new contract for the upcoming summer season, I wound up utterly confounded by the contents of the opened envelope.

After nearly seventeen years of operating Mixed Blessings, the Laurel Lake Board of Directors chose to inform us via U.S. mail that they had received a considerable monetary offer from another party for the lease of the building that housed Mixed Blessings. The letter also stated that the Board was accepting sealed bids from all interested parties.

I became physically ill as I read and re-read the letter, but each time the words remained exactly the same.

Having diligently maintained the integrity of Mixed Blessings, and having always had Laurel Lake's best interest at heart, I was traumatized by the news. The possibility of losing the business . . . my projected source of retirement income . . . was very upsetting to me. I searched every corner of my mind to come up with any personal or business transgressions by us that would have caused the Board to make such an unanticipated change; I found none.

The legal components of our contract with the Laurel Lake Board of Directors stated that, unless the terms of our contract were deliberately broken, and if we accepted the cost of leasing the building, we were entitled to a continuation of our lease each consecutive year. Strangely, there was no reference to our contractual rights in the letter.

The amount the Board was offered, as I discovered later, was far more than we had been paying, and a lot more than we would be willing to pay for so short a business season. Most certainly, it was an incredible business opportunity for the Board of Directors of Laurel Lake, but to us, it seemed like a downright unconscionable and unethical maneuver.

Before contacting Maureen or our attorney regarding the matter, I decided to call the secretary of the Board and question the legal aspect of their actions and to ask exactly why they had broken ranks with the normal procedure for lease renewal. I was also interested in knowing whether or not they had done the same thing with regards to the other businesses managed by the Board of Directors as well. When contacted, the secretary, in an almost belligerent tone of voice, replied, "Well, you have had the business long enough and we thought it was about time that someone new had a chance at that business." When I reminded her of the wording in the contract, she said, "No, those words don't exist in your contract."

As a result of the surprising hostility of the Board's secretary, I decided to get in touch with the Laurel Lake Board president and repeat verbatim the conversation between their secretary and me on the telephone, which I had inadvertently recorded when I forgot to disengage my message machine.

When I reached the president, I not only relayed the exchange that had taken place between the Board's secretary and myself, but I also pointed out number fifteen in the contract which guaranteed us the building for the following season. Firstly, he expressed astonishment regarding the secretary's attitude. Secondly, he completely disagreed with the secretary's explanation that "it was time for Mixed Blessings to have a new owner." He assured me that we would indeed have the opportunity to renew our contract for another year if we met the asking price of the lease.

My phone call to the Board president was quickly followed by a call from the Board secretary apologizing for her incorrect and misleading explanation of why the Board decided to open the lease to the highest bidder. She admitted that the contract had guaranteed us renewal of the lease for another year.

The building that housed Mixed Blessings remained unheated and without insulation, allowing a maximum of three months in which to comfortably operate a business. The price the Board was suggesting, based, of course, on the offer they had already received, was disappointingly prohibitive and unfairly determined. At least that is how I saw it.

It was time to meet with our attorney. But, before doing so, I had to contact Maureen at her southwest residence to inform her about what had taken place.

Because of the urgent nature of the news, I decided to bypass the computer and telephone her instead.

Word for word, I read the entire letter to Maureen . . . not exactly the ideal way to communicate such an important matter; nevertheless, the intent of the letter was reasonably clear. When I had finished, I expected some verbal display of outrage, or at the very least, some degree of shock. Instead, I sensed that my phone call had not come as a total surprise.

I was flabbergasted when she suggested that several couples may have been responsible for orchestrating an underhanded scheme to obtain our business, and that one of the couples happened to be very good friends of mine and had managed the shop for me when I first opened the business. I found the accusations incredulous.

I don't know why, but her exclusive knowledge regarding the suspected, behind-the-scenes activities to take over the business did not register with me at the time. I did question in my mind, however, how my friend and business partner, who was living in the southwest at the time, seemed to know more about what was happening in Laurel Lake than I did. I could only surmise that she was getting information from her daughter, who, coincidentally, was dating one of the couple's sons whom she had implicated in the suggested takeover scheme. It was not conceivable to me that either couple would ever operate behind my back. Instead, I was more inclined to believe that the large bid had come from an outside source, and not from residents of Laurel Lake.

Maureen went along with my idea to contact our attorney to see exactly where we stood on the issue, but she appeared convinced, along with me, that we shouldn't renew the contract at such an exorbitant price, even if we had been able to afford it. "It is a principle thing," she said.

I met with several attorneys regarding the contract issue, and they assured me that, according to our contract, we indeed held the option to lease the building for another year, as long as we were willing to meet their price. While the Board's actions were not deemed illegal, according to the attorneys, what they did and how they did it was determined to be highly unethical. They couldn't imagine why either one of us would even want to retain the shop under the prevailing circumstances. They suggested that we might be in for a year of unnecessary badgering and, in the end, lose the shop anyway. The decision was entirely up to us. They would have been more than happy to represent us, they said, having absolutely no doubt that we had the right to retain the shop; but their professional and personal recommendation was that Maureen and I terminate our relationship with the unprincipled Laurel Lake Board of Directors.

I called Maureen and told her what the attorneys had said. After much long distance deliberation, we decided to withdraw our interest in leasing Mixed Blessings.

Thankfully, I still had another job that would help sustain me through the months when my income would begin to reflect the effects of losing Mixed Blessings.

The decision was made, and there was nothing left but to inventory the contents of the shop and send the contents to a local auction house for sale. Maureen assured me that she would fly home to help me tie up all the loose ends.

When the decision was finally made to give up the shop, I sat down and cried. I had spent so much time, love, and money turning Mixed Blessings into a prosperous summer business, and now I was going to lose it. It did not seem to affect Maureen the same way it did me; after all, she was a very wealthy woman and she didn't need the money that the business generated. For her, it had been a diversion—a nice diversion—but the lost income was not going to affect her like it was going to affect me.

A week before Christmas, I found myself completely alone in my search for an auction house willing to pick up the remaining merchandise from the shop. Maureen had called and said that her daughter did not want her to fly home, and that her daughter was going to pack and remove their combined merchandise from the shop. I would then simply be left with packing and selling the merchandise jointly owned by Maureen and myself. The job of itemizing, costing, and packing the contents of the shop, in a building without heat and in near-freezing temperatures, remained exclusively mine. I felt terribly let down.

A number of Christian friends who had been aware of my circumstances offered to help with the dismal cold chore of closing the shop for good. Maureen said she would help with the expenses of taking my friends out to dinner for the work they had done and for taking her place, which she did. After sixteen years of business, with cold hands and an even colder heart, I said a sad farewell to Mixed Blessings. My friends surrounded me with love, support, and sympathy. It really felt as though I had lost a member of my family.

A few weeks later, before relinquishing the keys to Mixed Blessings (with mixed feelings), I decided to check the building to make sure it was emptied of everyone's merchandise, as the Board requested.

I entered the ice cold building, but I didn't begin to shiver until I saw all the merchandise owned by my partner and her daughter, and a room full of merchandise owned by one of the couples Maureen had implicated in the takeover, still sitting in the shop. Since the Board demanded that the building be entirely vacated by the first day of January, I became concerned. I e-mailed Maureen as soon as I returned home.

I began by asking her to inform her daughter, who just happened to be visiting with her at the time, that all the remaining merchandise had to be removed from the shop in a matter of days. The reply I received conjured up numerous questions in my already jumbled mind.

Her first e-mail response spoke of her daughter wanting to remain in business with the new owners. I thought that rather peculiar, in light of the Board's request to have *all* merchandise removed by a particular date. When I questioned her explanation in a return e-mail note, she said that her daughter had talked to the Board's secretary and that she had been given permission to keep their inventory in the shop. What exactly had been going on that I hadn't been privy to, I wondered. I was in a state of disbelief.

There were numerous e-mails after that, but none of them from Maureen. I was told to address any questions I had to her daughter Karen. According to her daughter, her mother had no intentions of getting into any more discussions with me on the subject of the shop. I was totally mystified.

Before e-mailing Maureen again, I received information that "Maureen and her daughter" had planned all along to remain in the shop with the new proprietors, and that they both had been aware of the behind-the-scenes activities to take over the shop. It just so happened that the couple whose son Maureen's daughter was dating—the same couple we welcomed into the shop to sell their merchandise and the same couple who had falsely accused my daughter of stealing money from our business—had now become the new proprietors of Mixed Blessings.

The pain of deception was indescribable.

*   *   *   *   *

As I soon discovered, the fact that I allowed God to take control of my life hadn't necessarily guaranteed me protection from future disappointments and pain. But what it was able to do was provide me with a different heart attitude when those occurrences revisited my life.

When I first received the letter informing us that the shop lease was going to be opened to the highest bidder, I became outraged. My first thought was to compose and send a biting letter to all the local newspapers revealing the injustices and business practices of the Laurel Lake Board of Directors. Instead, God spoke clearly and succinctly to me about what He expected from me, since I was now under His tutelage.

Shortly thereafter, I found myself, pen in hand, writing words that did not originate with me. God guided my pen as I wrote and thanked the Board for the many years of business that I was privileged to have at Mixed Blessings, and that I also wanted to wish the new owners much success. God kept on dictating His message to my heart, asking me to tell the Board that I wanted to treat them the way I would have wanted to be treated, and to think more highly of them than I thought of myself. What a turnaround for me! But I obeyed. And with that obedience, I was rewarded with a peace that truly passes all understanding. It was as though God had posted a sign at the door of my heart that read: "Keep out," preventing the customary bitterness from leaping over the hedge of God's protection and back into my life.

The deepest injury, however, was still on the loose waiting to eradicate the victory I had experienced as a result of doing God's will.

*   *   *   *   *

There was one final e-mail between Maureen and me.

I wrote questioning why she had refused to write to me, telling her that I had wanted to hear from her, and not from her daughter. I told her how I would miss our time together in the shop, and that I was so grateful that our commitment not to allow anything that happened in the business to affect our friendship still appeared to be intact, safeguarding our forty-five-year friendship. I even suggested that when she returned we should discuss opening another shop elsewhere.

With one click of the mouse, her reply read apologetically across my monitor screen.

"Leta, Karen wants me to remain in business with her at Mixed Blessings. I enjoy people, I love antiques, and I can well afford it. I wasn't going to do it at first, but she talked me into it."

Heavy-hearted and feeling betrayed, I replied, "What about our agreement?"

Her last words cut like a razor blade across my soul.

"I'm a businesswoman first," was her simple terse reply.

When I tried contacting her again, her daughter e-mailed back stating that she was going to take the computer out of her mother's house and that I should not try and e-mail her again.

The words, "I'm a businesswoman first," kept reverberating in my head.

What happened to the friendship we had guarded so carefully? I kept repeating to myself.

I felt so betrayed.

Then Jesus gently reminded me that a friend, too, had betrayed Him, and yet He loved and asked His Father in Heaven to forgive His betrayers. Suddenly, I identified with Jesus; and although I was downcast and sorrowful, I was not stranded in my remorse . . . without resource. As quickly as I had once turned away from God, I now ran to curl up beneath His wings. And His love took me in.

But the end was not yet.

*   *   *   *   *

The following days were filled with sadness, but not with bitterness. I knew that if I remained in Laurel Lake, it would be a constant reminder of all the things that happened leading up to that moment; and, although I felt no animosity toward Maureen, I knew that our relationship would never be the same again. It was time to move on.

I found myself crying and literally getting sick in the stomach every time I passed the boarded-up building that I had affectionately named Mixed Blessings, but nothing compared with the sadness of losing the life-long friendship I had with Maureen.

Something I had heard from a Bible teacher some years earlier came back to me like a flower planted in a garden of memory, waiting to be picked at just the right time:

God sees the potential of His children and appoints
the experiences necessary for them to fulfill their destinies.

Within five months' time, I had sold my cottage and had moved out of town and into a lovely townhouse that I was sure God had prepared just for me. I moved with peace in my heart, knowing that God was in the move. And He has had me "on the move" ever since . . . in service and obedience to Him. It was one of the few times I did not intervene in God's plan for my life.

I could no longer allow myself the selfish luxury of holding bad memories hostage in my mind, nor could I withhold forgiveness from those who had deeply hurt me. I had to forgive myself; it was the only way to break free from the bondage of my past.

The devastating events in my life—abandonment, physical abuse, a broken home, divorce, failed love relationships, illness, and the loss of my best friend—were only pebbles beneath my feet, stepping stones leading me to the solid ROCK. And that Rock is Jesus.

Nothing compares with the peace that comes from getting right with God. My cup runneth over with JOY!

For so many years, I counted on peers, people, performance, and things as agencies of self-worth, but now I know that that is not where significance is realized. It can only be found in the person of Jesus.

I have been on a long journey in search of love, and I have needlessly carried the baggage of my past with me. But the moment I put that baggage down at the feet of Jesus was the day I could honestly say, "I have been . . . I am now . . . and I will always be loved with an everlasting love!"

I have experienced the purest form of adoption. I am the daughter of a King! "The lines have fallen to me in pleasant places; indeed, my heritage is beautiful to me. In His presence is fullness of joy, and in His hand there are pleasures forever." ABBA Father!

Daily, I am challenged to remember these words: whether traveling on a dry, parched path lined with disappointment and sorrow or the rich, vibrant-colored flower garden of victory, as a child of God, I never travel alone.

And you shall remember all the ways which the Lord your God has led
you in the wilderness these (many years), that He might humble you,
testing you, to know what was in your heart, whether you would keep His
commandments or not. **Deuteronomy 8:2**

To God Be the Glory . . . For the Things He Has Done!